ISLAM UNDER THE ARABS

ISLAM UNDER THE ARABS

By

ROBERT DURIE OSBORN

MAJOR IN THE BENGAL STAFF CORPS

GYAN

Published by

Gyan Publishing House
5, Ansari Road
Daryaganj, New Delhi-110002
Phone: 011-47034999, 9811692060
E-mail: books@gyanbooks.com

Distribution Network
gyanbooks.com
India, USA, Canada, UK, Australia, France

ISBN : 978-81-212-6344-3 (PB)
First Published, 1876

2nd Impression 2022

Printed at: Gyan Press, Delhi.

ISLAM UNDER THE ARABS
Author: ROBERT DURIE OSBORN

ISLAM UNDER THE ARABS

BY

ROBERT DURIE OSBORN

MAJOR IN THE BENGAL STAFF CORPS

1876

PREFACE.

I THINK the purpose of this book will be explained most easily by stating how it came to be written.

Any officer who has served in India with native troops must have perceived how genial and cordial are the relations among all ranks, from the commanding officer down to the private, so long as a regiment is on active service. The dangers and hardships which have to be endured by all, keep alive and strengthen the feeling of comradeship. But when the regiment returns into quarters this feeling dies away. It is not that the English officer is, at heart, less interested in the well-being of his men, but that there is no longer any object of interest common to both, outside of the mere routine of their profession. They have nothing to talk about. The native soldier knows nothing of English history or of anything that interests Englishmen; and very few English officers know more of the men they command than that they are *called* Sikhs, Afghans, Ghoorkhas, or Mahrattas. What these names signify—what was the history of those who bear them, in the past: what are the memories which still thrill them with pleasure or pride—these are matters of which the officers in our native army have small knowledge. And what a potent magnet for winning the hearts of our native soldiers is, from this ignorance, permitted to rust unused, is known only to those who do possess this knowledge, and have watched its effects.

Eight or nine years ago, being in England upon medical certificate, it occurred to me that I might usefully employ my leisure in drawing up brief historical sketches of the races from which our native army is chiefly recruited. A work of this kind, it seemed to me, was just what young officers needed to put them in the way of understanding the men they had to command in the field and in quarters. I had collected a large quantity of matter concerning the Mahrattas, the Sikhs, and the Afghans; but when I commenced to deal with Muhammadanism in India, I found myself at fault. The (so called) Mogul empire was a mystery for which I could find no satisfactory explanation. Under the stress of what impulse had these invaders abandoned the uplands of Central Asia to erect an empire at Delhi and Agra? They styled themselves Muhammadans, but it was clear that the religion they professed, and which they affirmed to be identical with that in the Koran, had passed through a number of transforming influences before it assumed the form it exhibited in India. What was the history of these transformations? Elphinstone told me nothing of them. I found no light in the Persian historians of the Muhammadan empire.

I resolved to follow Baber and his hardy adventurers over the summits of the Hindoo Khosh. In his paternal kingdom of Ferghana, I should surely discover the clue to guide me through the labyrinth. But there was only confusion worse confounded. Over the whole extent of Central Asia there was nothing to be heard or seen but a confused noise of battle and garments rolled in blood. The dim outlines of fleeting dynasties rose and disappeared in the confusion; conquerors emerging apparently from the Inane 'hasted stormfully across the astonished earth, then plunged again into the Inane.' And what was strangest of all, the Muhammadan historians who recorded this anarchy seemed to find nothing strange or anomalous in it. The Faithful had always managed their affairs in this way, and no one appeared to entertain a thought that the work of existence could be carried on in a less bloody and riotous fashion. All that was done was being done strictly according to the Book and the Traditions, and the interpretations of orthodox doctors—and what more would you have? God was great and Muhammad was His Prophet; of what use was it to strive against destiny?

I perceived, then, that to understand the events of Muhammadan history I must trace them upwards from their source, in the teaching of Muhammad at Mekka and Medina. I was encouraged to undertake this enquiry by the fact that there does not exist any English book which treats of the growth of the Muhammadan religion. The present volume is the first fruits of this enquiry, which has occupied me during the past seven years. It constitutes a whole in itself, and is the first of a series of works which will trace the progress of Islam from Mekka to Delhi. The second work will be entitled 'The Khalifs of Baghdad,' and the third, 'Islam in India.'

The period of Muhammadan history which extends from the first preaching of Muhammad to the destruction of Baghdad by the Mongols, falls naturally into three divisions:

The rule of the Arabs;
The rule of the Persians;
The rule of the Turks.

The present volume deals with the first of these. This period terminated in A.H. 132 with the overthrow of the House of Ommaya and the accession to power of the khalifs of the House of Abbas. As the arrangement of my subject is somewhat novel and peculiar, a few words in explanation of it are necessary. First, then, I would ask my readers to keep in mind that I am not writing a history of Muhammad or of the khalifs of the House of Ommaya, but of the Muhammadan religion. In dealing, therefore, with the life of Muhammad, I have touched upon those incidents only which had an influence in the building up of the religion he taught. And so also with the events in the after-history. I have passed over in silence, or with only passing mention, the conquests of the Arabs and their interminable wars with the Byzantine empire, because, important as these are historically, they had no influence on Muhammadan theology. Muhammadan theology was the product of internal discords; it was the result of jarring political ambitions investing themselves with a religious sanction, in order to harden the hearts and inflame the fanaticism of the partisans on either side. These civil wars, consequently, I have treated in detail.

The first part, entitled 'Islam,' follows the history of the Muhammadan religion from its origin at Mekka, until the body of the Faithful was rent into two irreconcileable factions, the *Sunnis* and the *Shias*.

The second part, entitled 'The Fatimides,' traces the growth of the *Shia* heresy. It endeavours to show that the central tenets of this sect grew directly out of the circumstances in which it was placed. It gives an account, first, of its unsuccessful contest with orthodoxy, under the designation of 'the Karmathians;' then of the empire it founded in Northern Africa; and lastly, it relates how, using this empire as a base for further operations, it obtained possession of the rich province of Egypt, whence it planted, like a wasting cancer, in the very centre of the dominions of the Bagdad khalifate, that terrible organisation known in history as 'The Assassins.'

The third part, entitled 'The Khalifs of the House

of Ommaya,' resumes the history of the orthodox party at the point where the close of the first part left it. The object of this section is to exhibit the events which enabled the vanquished Persians to rise against their Arab conquerors, and place a khalif of their choice at the head of Islam. These events were due to the want of fusing and uniting power in the religion of Muhammad. Accordingly in the first chapter I have given a sketch of what the Arabs were previous to their conversion; and in those which follow I show how, when they became masters of Asia, the old feuds and the old passions continued to occupy them, to the complete exclusion of other and higher interests, until the weakness engendered by these discords enabled the subject populations to unite and drive them from power.

In the 'Khalifs of Baghdad' (which I hope to have ready for publication in about a year from this time), I carry on the history to the destruction of Baghdad. This volume is chiefly taken up with an account of the expansion of Islam into a theological and political system, and the unsuccessful attempt of the khalif Mamun to subject the Koran itself to critical tests sanctioned by the reason and the conscience.

The third volume will, as I have already said, bear the title of 'Islam in India.' The political fortunes of Muhammadanism in India have been followed, down almost to the present day, in the writings of Elphinstone, Erskine, Grant Duff, Briggs, and other less known authors, but no endeavour has as yet been made to depict 'Islam in India' as a spiritual force acting upon and being influenced by the indigenous religions. This is what I purpose to attempt in this part of my work, obtaining my materials from the abundant Persian literature of the past Muhammadan period, and from the Oordoo which has sprung up so luxuriantly since the advent of British rule, and the introduction of the printing press.

In the present volume I have given no references at the foot of the page, but at the end of the volume the reader will find a list of the authorities which have been used in the composition of each chapter. Among these, however, there do not occur the names of two writers to whose works I am, nevertheless, greatly indebted, though not exactly in such a way as admits of particular specification. They are Weil, the author of the 'Geschichte der Chalifen,' and R. Dozy, the author of 'Histoire des Musulmans d'Espagne.' It was my misfortune—one inseparable from writing history in a remote country like India—not to read this last work until the greater part of this volume had been written, and when time was lacking to me to make all the use of it I should liked to have done. It is in my judgment the ablest and most brilliant work on Muhammadan history with which I am acquainted, and those who desire to find a truthful and vivid picture of Arab character and Arab rule cannot do better than read this learned and delightful book.

Muhammadan names are, I know from experience, a constant puzzle and difficulty to English readers. I think a few words of explanation will, to a great extent, render them at once intelligible. A Muhammadan may be designated by any one of three titles. Thus, for example, the Prophet may be called 'Muhammad,' which is his own name; or 'Abou Kasim,' which signifies 'the father of Kasim,' a son of his who died when young; or he may be called after his father, 'Ibn Abdallah,' which means 'the son of Abdallah.' The word 'Abd,' which appears continually in Muhammadan names, signifies 'servant' or 'slave;' thus Abdallah' means 'the servant of God;' 'Abd al Rahman,' 'the servant of the Compassionate.'

11 Marlboro' Road, St. John's Wood:

March 1876.

CONTENTS.

PART I.

ISLAM.

PART II.

THE FATIMIDES.

PART III.

THE KHALIFS OF THE HOUSE OF OMMAYA.

PART I.

ISLAM.

CHAPTER I.

MUHAMMAD AT MEKKA.

A.D. 612–622.

THERE is one remarkable assumption that runs through all the warnings, denunciations, and appeals of the Koran. The God of whom the Prophet speaks is not an unknown God. The guilt of his fellow-tribesmen, the justification of their impending doom, are deduced from the fact that they did know this God, while they honoured dumb idols. 'Whose is the earth and all that is therein, if ye know?' asks Muhammad; and he anticipates their reply: 'They will answer, "God's."' 'Who is the Lord of the Seven Heavens and the Lord of the Glorious Throne?' 'They will say, "They are God's."' 'In whose hand is the empire of all things, who protecteth, but is not protected?' 'They will answer, "In God's."' 'How, then,' he asks, 'can ye be so spellbound?' Sprung from the seed of Abraham, the memory of their august parentage was fondly cherished by the tribes dwelling in and around Mekka, to whom specially these words were addressed. A persistent, though confused, apprehension of a Divine unity underlying the multiplicity of idol gods had remained of that spiritual heritage which the Father of the Jewish nation had bequeathed to them. And, since the ruin of

Jerusalem and the spread of Christianity, that apprehension had been quickened into a comparative clearness by intercourse with Jews and Christians. Jewish tribes were intermingled with Arab at Medina. In Syria more than one tribe of kindred origin with themselves professed Christianity. In Yemen a Christian dynasty had existed for nearly a century. The Arabs who dwelt in Mekka were the great traders among their countrymen. Their karavans were continually passing to and fro between Yemen and Syria; and it was due, doubtless, to the play of these various religious influences that we find towards the end of the sixth century of our era, scattered through Arabic poetry, numerous traces of a deep sense of the unity of God, His unapproachable supremacy, and a lively consciousness of the moral responsibility of man. 'All things,' says one poet, 'without God are vanity.' 'God,' says another, 'is alone the True and the Righteous, and sin is the attribute of man alone.'

The people who professed this Theism were termed Hanyfs. The Arabic writers give the names of several men contemporary with the Prophet who were thus designated. Muhammad considered himself in his early days to be one among them. The chief of their tenets appears to have been that the pure worship of God had been revealed to Abraham in a book sent down from Heaven; this book had either been lost or subjected to so many interpolations, that its primary significance was forgotten; and the spiritual well-being of mankind depended upon its re-discovery.

In the pre-Islamite times of Arabia the chief man among these wistful and anxious spirits is undoubtedly

Zaid, the Inquirer. He rejected the worship of idols, protested vehemently against the murder of female infants, and refused to eat meat offered in sacrifice to idols. 'I seek,' he said, 'for the God of Abraham alone.' Day after day he would repair to the Kaaba and pray for enlightenment. He used to be seen leaning his back against the wall of the temple, absorbed in meditation, his silence broken at intervals by passionate appeals to Heaven. 'Lord,' he would cry, 'if I knew in what manner Thou oughtest to be worshipped, I would obey Thy will, but I am in darkness.' Then he would throw himself down with his face to the earth. His soul could find no rest so long as he dwelt at Mekka amid a people wholly given up to superstition. He determined to travel through the world, searching after the knowledge of God; but for many years his wishes were successfully opposed by his family. At last he effected his escape. He traversed Mesopotamia and Syria; he conversed with Christian monks and Jewish Rabbis; but the satisfaction his soul craved after he could nowhere find, and he returned to die in his native land.

Another of the heralds of the Prophet, and the one who stands in closest connection with him, is Waraka, the cousin of Muhammad's first wife, Kadija. He was the most learned Arab of his time; had all his life maintained intimate relations with Jews and Christians; had studied Hebrew, and read the books of the Old Testament in the original. Like Zaid, he was utterly dissatisfied with the gross and incredible idolatry of his compatriots. 'Our countrymen,' he said, 'walk in a wrong way; they have departed from the religion of

Abraham. What is this pretended divinity to which they sacrifice victims and round which they make solemn processions? A block of stone, dumb and insensible, powerless either for good or evil. All this is wholly wrong. We ought to seek the pure religion of Abraham.' When the Prophet commenced his preaching, Waraka was at first inclined to concede his claims; but when Muhammad strove to strengthen his position by means of wild legends, which he affirmed to exist in the Books of Moses and elsewhere, Waraka's knowledge of the Hebrew Scriptures convinced him of the hollowness of Muhammad's pretensions. Waraka denounced him as an impostor, and withdrew to Abyssinia, where he became a Christian. It is even said that he translated a part of the Four Gospels into Arabic.

The influence of this Theism necessarily extended beyond the immediate circle of the few who explicitly professed it. It awakened a spirit of inquiry, and broke through the callous crust of conventionalism in many minds. Muhammad entered upon a field the soil of which had been broken up to receive the seed he cast upon it. Wherein he differed from his predecessors was the voice of authority with which he spoke. He transformed the Hanyfite Theism from a tenet of speculative minds into a Divine revelation. There was no god but God, and Muhammad was His prophet. It was this second dogma, 'forced as a Divine revelation into the belief of so large a part of mankind, which was the power, the influence, the all-subduing energy of Islam; the principle of its unity, of its irresistible fanaticism, its propagation, its victories, its empires, its duration.'[1]

[1] Milman's *Latin Christianity*, vol. i. p. 455.

Muhammad was approaching his fortieth year before that inward change became apparent which converted him into the Prophet of Arabia. What had first inspired him with his contempt and hatred of idolatry is a matter of speculation. Doubtless his karavan journeys to Syria, by bringing him into intercourse with Jews and Christians, did much to reveal to him that there were worthier objects for man's adoration than the trees and shapeless stones worshipped by his countrymen. But, judging from the Koran, I should be inclined to think that the beauty, the order, the all-pervading life in Nature, first carried him above idolatry to the apprehension of a one God. Like all men of poetic temperament, he was deeply moved by this spectacle. And the noblest passages in the Koran are those where he makes appeal to this testimony to establish the wisdom and beneficence of the Creator:

> The dead earth is a sign to men; we quicken it and bring forth grain from it, and they eat thereof:
>
> And we make in it gardens of the date and vine: and we cause springs to gush forth in it;
>
> . . . .
>
> A sign to them also is the night. We withdraw the day from it, and lo! they are plunged in darkness;
>
> And the sun hasteneth to her place of rest. This is the ordinance of the Mighty, the Knowing!
>
> And as for the moon, we have decreed stations for it, till it change like an old and crooked palm branch.
>
> To the sun it is not given to overtake the moon; nor doth the night outstrip the day; but each in its own sphere doth journey on.
>
> Sura xxxvi. v. 34–40.

That the Being who created all these marvels could reside in idols of wood and stone was to him altogether incredible; but not less so was the notion that these idols symbolised a plurality of gods in the regions beyond the sky. A number of gods involved a number of wills, a variety of characters and conflicting purposes. Such a belief introduced into the invisible world all the strife and disorder which prevailed in this, and which could not co-exist with that calm and majestic harmony whereby the earth renewed her life with each returning Spring, and day and night followed in ever recurring succession. The hatred of idolatry naturally increased, as a life of meditative solitude nourished this belief in a Divine unity, to greater strength and clearness. Men seemed to be wantonly rushing down into abysses of falsehood with the light of truth shining all around them. There are a few fragments of verse preserved in the Koran which are supposed to belong to this period. They are full of a profound emotion—broken, almost inarticulate utterances—the heart bowed down beneath the weight of its own thoughts and unable to give them fitting expression.

The scene of these musings was in keeping with their tenor. The spot whither Muhammad repaired during these trances of thought was a cave at the foot of Mount Hira, about two or three miles north of Mekka. The country round is bleak and rugged—bare, desolate hills and sandy valleys destitute of vegetation, and near at hand the last resting place of the 'Inquirer' Zaid—a silent warning to the future prophet of the vanity of his thoughts and the futility of his hopes. For he, too, had expended his life in the search after God, and died here broken in heart from hope too long deferred. One day, amid the silent rocks, Muhammad had a dream. An angel appeared before him and said, 'Read!' 'I cannot read' was the response. The angel repeated the command and received the same reply. Then the heavenly messenger spoke as follows:

> Recite thou in the name of the Lord who created—
> Created man from clots of blood—
> Recite thou! for thy Lord is the most beneficent
> Who hath taught thee the use of the pen;
> Hath taught man that which he knoweth not.
>
> Sura xcvi.

A flash of joy shot through Muhammad's heart. But the darkness of doubt gathered more heavily after this momentary break. There was no return of the celestial visitant. He wandered among the bleak rocks as before, but no angel forms rose against the sky, no angel voices broke the terrible silence. The Prophet thought himself the sport of evil spirits; he is said even to have meditated suicide, when again the angel appeared, though he heard no voice. Later he enjoyed a third visitation, which he has described in the fifty-third Sura. He saw the angel, and heard him speak, and received the joyful assurance that he (Muhammad) was the chosen of God. The angel then vanished. Muhammad fell senseless to the earth. On recovering his senses he hurried back to his family. 'Enshroud me, enshroud me!' were the first words he uttered. They wrapped a cloak round him and sprinkled water on his face; and again the voice of the angel came to him, saying:

> O! thou enwrapped in thy mantle!
> Arise and warn!
> Thy Lord—magnify him!
> Thy raiment—purify it!
> The Abomination—flee it!
> And bestow not favours that thou mayest receive again with increase,
> And for thy Lord wait thou patiently!

It was, then, no dream of his imagination that beyond the blue vault above, there was a Being who had regard to the children of men, and that He had chosen Muhammad as His messenger to an unbelieving generation. The heart of the Prophet was now at rest, and his joy and gratitude flowed forth in what appears to me as the most touching passage in the Koran :

> By the noonday brightness
> And by the night when it darkeneth !
> Thy Lord hath not forsaken thee, neither hath He been displeased,
> And surely the Future shall be better for thee than the Past,
> And in the end shall thy Lord be bounteous to thee, and thou be satisfied.
> Did He not find thee an orphan, and gave thee a home ?
> And found thee erring and guided thee ?
> And found thee needy and enriched thee ?
> As to the orphan, therefore, wrong him not ;
> And as for him that asketh of thee chide him not away ;
> And as for the favours of thy Lord tell them abroad.
>
> Sura xciii.

The assumption of the prophetic character raised at first no ill-will against Muhammad. The people thought him mad ; and in the East, as everyone knows, madness is generally supposed to be accompanied by a measure more or less of Divine inspiration. There was, too, nothing in his earliest utterances which threatened a root-and-branch destruction of the old tribal modes of worship. They consisted of brief, vehement exhortations to lead right lives, together with allusions to 'the Last Day,' the terrors of which weighed upon the Prophet's soul with all the awfulness of a close-impending reality. The tenacious memory of the Arab seized readily upon these rhymed utterances, instinct as they were with the life and fervour of deep conviction. They circulated rapidly from tribe to tribe till they became known in localities remote from

Mekka. The common people commenced to regard Muhammad as a man inspired. It was for the Prophet a spring time full of hope and on-looking thoughts; and he gives expression to his thankfulness in the ninety-fourth Sura:

> Have we not opened thine heart for thee?
> And taken off from thee thy burden
> Which galled thy back?
> And have we not raised thy name for thee?
> Then verily along with trouble cometh ease,
> Verily along with trouble cometh ease—
> But when thou art set at liberty, then prosecute thy toil,
> And seek thy Lord with fervour.

But the opposition only slumbered. As soon as Muhammad abandoned generalities to denounce idolatry, it awoke to life. Mekka, planted in the midst of an arid desert, owed its existence to the possession of water and to its situation as a convenient resting-place for the karavans passing between Yemen and Syria. The worship of the black stone had elevated this halting-place into a spot of peculiar sanctity. From time immemorial the tribes had gone up thither to worship. The tradition was that the Kaaba had been built and the ceremonies of the pilgrimage instituted by the patriarch Abraham and his son Ishmael. Mekka itself and the holy places were occupied by the Kuraish, the tribe to which Muhammad belonged. This position invested them with a peculiar dignity and sacredness above the other tribes of Arabia; nevertheless, the Temple and the sacred places were in no way their property, with which they could do as they pleased. They held them, one might say, in trust for the tribes of Arabia generally; and it is necessary to note this fact as explaining the motive of their opposition to Muhammad.

Mekka was the centre of a system of idolatry, the branches of which extended through other tribes. Westward from Mekka, as far as the sea, wandered the wild tribe of Kinana, closely allied with the Kuraish, both politically and by blood. They served the goddess Ozza. She was represented by a tree at a place called Nakhla, a day and a half's journey from Mekka. South-east from Mekka dwelt the tribe of Hawazun. Their central point was the pleasantly-situated Tayif, and their favourite idol was the goddess Lât. A third divinity of remarkable sacredness was the goddess Manah. She was represented by a rock on the karavan road between Mekka and Syria. In addition to these, more than two hundred images were arranged round the Kaaba, which represented the tutelary deities of the more distant tribes who came up yearly to the pilgrimage. The heathen Arabs believed in all these gods indifferently.

A reformer like Muhammad appearing at Mekka became in consequence a very serious danger to the Kuraish. If at his calling they repudiated the established religion—nay, if they were even suspected of thinking or speaking with irreverence of the various tribal deities committed to their safe keeping—they would become an object for the vengeance of all the tribes of Arabia. Such a war could have but one of two issues. Either the Kuraish would be completely exterminated, or they would be expelled from the sacred territory and their ancestral homes as apostates who had betrayed their trust. Any half measures were equally impossible. To have repudiated Lât and Manah and Ozza would have been tantamount to a declaration of war against the tribes who honoured those divinities, and would have closed against them the traffic routes leading out of Mekka, so destroying the karavan trade by which they lived. To have thrown down the idols in Mekka would have convicted them of being unfit guardians of the sacred territory, and would indubitably have created an Arabian confederation for their destruction. It was, in fact, the instinct of self-preservation which united the leaders of the Kuraish against Muhammad. This is apparent from the language attributed to them in the Koran: 'If we follow the way in which thou art guided, we shall be driven from our homes.'

The battle against the new faith was carried on in two ways—by persecution and by argument. It is with the last only that I am concerned in this book.

In the beginning of his career Muhammad strove to terrify his tribe into belief by terrific pictures of the Last Day. He piles up epithet upon epithet in the endeavour to paint it. It is called 'the terrible fire;' it is 'the day when men shall be like scattered moths, and the mountains shall be like flocks of carded wool;' it is the hour when 'earth shall cast forth her burdens,' 'when the sun shall be folded up, and when the stars shall fall;' 'when the female child that hath been buried alive shall be asked for what crime she was put to death':

And when the leaves of the Book shall be unrolled,
And when the Heaven shall be stripped away,
And when Hell shall be made to blaze,
And when Paradise shall be brought near,
Every soul shall know what it hath produced. . . . .

. . . .

And whosoever shall have wrought an atom's weight of good shall behold it;
And whosoever shall have wrought an atom's weight of evil shall behold it.

But these warnings fell upon deaf ears. The Kuraish were utter materialists. A resurrection after death was a subject of scorn and incredulity; and Muhammad strove in vain to shake their scepticism. 'What,' said they, 'after we shall have become bones and dust, shall we in sooth be raised a new creation?' 'Yes,' thundered the Prophet, 'though ye were stones or iron, or any other creature to you seeming yet harder to be raised.' 'Who shall bring us back?' 'He who created you at first.' And then he points out again and again that there is a continual bringing of life out of death going on in the world about them. God banks up great masses of rain-cloud, and drives them over a land barren, parched and dead, and it breaks into life and freshness, and 'brings forth corn of which your cattle and yourselves do eat.' He reminds them of the mystery of man's birth, his secret growth in the womb; and demands if a new birth after death be a whit more marvellous than this primary birth into the world. But his arguments were unavailing. The Kuraish sneered at his threats as 'fables of the ancients;' they taunted his disciples as 'the followers of a man that is enchanted.'

Defeated here, Muhammad took up a new line of attack. For the terrors of the Last Day he substituted a temporal calamity shortly to fall on Mekka. His theory was this: To every land that had been visited by some Divine calamity, a prophet had first been sent as 'a warner.' Only when the land had rejected his summons to repent, had the measure of their iniquity been filled, and God's wrath fallen upon them. Muhammad carried on the succession of these messengers; he was charged with a commission precisely the same as theirs. The earliest prophet was Noah; then Lot; then Moses and Aaron; then Houd, who was sent to the tribe of Ad; then Saleh, who was sent to the tribe of Themoud. They had, one and all, been met with derision and unbelief; but where now were those who had disregarded their words? The Deluge had swept away the enemies of Noah; a fiery rain from Heaven had destroyed the cities of the plain; Pharoah and his army had perished in the sea; a miraculous visitation had extirpated the tribes of Ad and Themoud. Let the Mekkans, therefore, be wise in time.

There can be no doubt that Muhammad believed with a complete assurance in the soundness of this induction. His isolated position, his confident tone, gave force and terror to these predictions. The people of Mekka were for a while startled from their indifference. Upon his few followers the impression was so profound that even after his death they awaited fearfully the accomplishment of these threats. But when day after day, month after month, and even years passed away and nothing came of them, the sentiment of terror softened by degrees into the milder one of curiosity, and from thence passed into that of derisive incredulity. Muhammad strove vehemently to preserve the earlier state of mind. He repeated his typical instances again and again. The Suras of this period contain little else than a wearisome reiteration of them. But after the first feeling of alarm had worn away, it was wasted labour to attempt to renovate it. The very plurality of the threats had the effect, curiously enough, of depriving them in part of their significance. These astute infidels appear to have argued thus: If we are to be drowned in a deluge, the shower of stones must be a superfluity; if we are swallowed up by an earthquake, we cannot then be transformed into dogs and swine. Gradually they took up a bolder attitude. They said they were wearied of hearing these threats and awaiting their fulfilment. They did not intend to believe in the mission of Muhammad or to change their religion, and demanded that the punishment, whatever it was, should descend upon them without delay. This was an unforeseen difficulty for Muhammad. He replied that the purposes of God were not to be hastened in order to gratify the impatience of the Mekkans. But when pressed for a date, he shifted his ground, and said that the presence of the Faithful in Mekka alone averted the doom from the unbelieving city. The retort was ready. There was nothing the Kuraish desired more earnestly than to be rid of the Faithful altogether. They were the cause of trouble and dissension. Let them depart without further delay, and Mekka would gladly run the risk of incurring the threatened doom. Muhammad, in this way, was, one might say, driven into a corner, and compelled to surrender at discretion. He had to confess that he had overstepped his commission; he was only 'a warner;' the times and seasons of God's purposes were known to God alone.

But this confession was only the beginning of sorrows. Muhammad's appeal to the earlier prophets raised around him a swarm of difficulties which stung like hornets. He had appealed to the testimony of these prophets as evidence of his own mission. His message, he had said, was essentially the same as theirs—a transcript of the eternal decrees of God written on the Everlasting Table. Granted. But if Muhammad was in truth a prophet like to those who had preceded him, he must be armed with similar credentials. Their message was attested and enforced by acts of supernatural power apparent to anyone who had eyes to see. Angels visited them; they could work miracles; a staff in their hands could be transformed into a serpent, and living camels at their bidding sprang forth from the heart of a rock. The sinfulness of those who rejected these messengers consisted in this—that they discredited a warning accompanied by such manifest tokens that it came from God. Muhammad should not find the Mekkans so obdurate. Let him work a miracle and they would believe forthwith. He might in this way do his countrymen signal service materially not less than spiritually. Let him turn the barren soil round Mekka into 'a garden of palm trees and grapes, and cause forth gushing rivers to gush forth in the midst;' or 'create a house of gold;' or 'mount up into heaven,' and from thence 'send down to them a book that they might read.'

Muhammad was obliged to confess that he possessed no such power; but this impotence, he asserted, was occasioned by their unbelief. God withheld this gift, because, had it been conceded, their scepticism would have remained unshaken:

> We will not send down the angels without due cause; the infidels would not in that case have been respited.
>
> . . . .
>
> Even were we to open above them a gate in Heaven, yet all the while they were mounting up to it
> They would surely say: 'It is only our eyes are drunken—nay, we are a people enchanted.'

The Mekkans were acute enough to see that this assumption of their scepticism was merely an evasion of the difficulty. At the worst they could not be more unbelieving than the nations before them, who had been destroyed for their persistent incredulity. These had not been punished until they had closed their hearts against the testimony of the miraculous; why then should the Mekkans be treated otherwise? They pressed this point hard; and there can be little doubt that the perplexity of the situation drove Muhammad to the first of those deviations from truth which multiplied as he grew older, and which had such a woeful influence on the subsequent destinies of Islam.

He was brought face to face with the question which every spiritual reformer has to meet and consider, against which so many noble spirits have gone to ruin. Will not the *end* justify the *means?* 'Here am I, a faithful servant of God, eager only to enthrone Him in the hearts of men, and at the very goal and termination of my labours I am thwarted by this incapacity to work a miracle. It is true, as these infidels allege, that the older prophets did possess this power; and I, unless the very reason and purpose of my existence is to be made a blank, must also do something wonderful. But what kind of miracle?' In his despair Muhammad declared that the Koran itself was that constantly-recurring miracle they were seeking after. Had they ever heard these stories of Noah, Lot, Abraham, Joseph, Zacharias, Jesus, and others? No; neither had he. They were transcripts made from the 'preserved Table,' that stood before the throne of God. The archangel Gabriel had revealed them to Muhammad, written in pure Arabic for the spiritual edification of the Kuraish. Thus, in the 12th Sura, where he details at great length an exceedingly ridiculous history of Joseph, he commences the narrative with these words as spoken by God:

> These are the signs of the clear book. An Arabic Koran have we sent it down that ye might understand it.
>
> In revealing to thee this Koran (i.e., *this sura or chapter*) one of the most beautiful of narratives will we narrate to thee, of which thou hast hitherto been regardless.

And at the close we are told:

> This is one of the secret histories which we reveal unto thee. Thou wast not present with Joseph's brethren when they conceived their design and laid their plot; but the greater part of men, though thou long for it, will not believe. Thou shalt not ask of them any recompense for this message. It is simply an instruction for all mankind.

And again, in the 69th Sura, he declares respecting the Koran:

> It is a missive from the Lord of the worlds;
> But if Muhammad had fabricated
> Concerning us any sayings,
> We had surely seized him by the right hand,
> And had cut through the vein of his neck.

It would be easy to multiply extracts of similar purport, but the above will suffice by way of illustration. There are modern biographers of the Prophet who would have us believe that he was not conscious of falsehood when making these assertions. He was under a hallucination, of course, but he believed what he said. This, to me, is incredible. The legends in the Koran are derived chiefly from Talmudic sources. Muhammad must have learned them from some Jew resident in or near Mekka. To work them up into the form of rhymed suras, to put his own peculiar doctrines in the mouth of Jewish patriarchs, the Virgin Mary, and the infant Jesus (who talks like a good Moslem the moment after his birth), must have required time, thought, and labour. It is not possible that the man who had done this could have forgotten all about it, and believed that these legends had been brought to him ready prepared by an angelic visitor. Muhammad was guilty of falsehood under circumstances where he deemed the end justified the means.

The falsehood failed, however, to produce conviction in the minds of those for whose benefit it had been devised. 'They turned their backs on him,' so the Koran tells us, 'and said: "Taught by others, possessed."' They even seem to have indicated the man who instructed him; for Muhammad repeatedly refers to some such assertion, affirming that he whom they pointed at did not know Arabic, and could not therefore have composed an Arabic Koran. He says in one place (Sura xxvi. v. 103, *et seq.*):

> And when we change one verse for another, and God knoweth best what He revealeth, they say, 'Thou art only a fabricator.' Nay! but most of them have no knowledge.
>
> Say; the Holy Spirit hath brought it down with truth from thy Lord, that He may stablish those who have believed, and as guidance and glad tidings to the Moslems.
>
> We also know that they say, 'Surely a certain person teacheth him.' But the tongue of him at whom they hint is foreign, while this Koran is in the plain Arabic.

To this the Mekkans retorted that he had supplied the materials, and Muhammad had worked them up into their present shape. There was no reply from the

Prophet, and there can be little doubt that the Mekkans were right both as to the man and his participation in the composition of the Koran. Whoever he was, he must have been in constant and intimate communion with Muhammad, to have incurred suspicion. In truth, Muhammad confesses so much by his eagerness to clear himself of the charge. Had, then, these suspicions been groundless, nothing would have been easier than to demonstrate the fact by the man's own confession. Such a confession, moreover, would have greatly strengthened Muhammad's position; but the Prophet attempts nothing of the kind. He evidently felt that his enemies had struck him hard in this matter. He returns to the accusation again and again, but only to repeat the same statement, that a man unlearned in the Arabic language could not write a pure Arabic Koran. As the Mekkans had never said he could, the irrelevancy of the argument only confirmed them in their suspicions.

In argument, therefore, Muhammad may be said to have been beaten along his whole line. The sceptics attacked all his positions and carried them. He could furnish no proof that he was a prophet. The power to work miracles was denied to him; his predictions were falsified by the event; his (so-called) revelations were rightly believed to have been obtained through human agency. In abandoning Mekka he acknowledged his defeat. Still, the germs of future success had been planted in the midst of seeming discomfiture. He departed, carrying away with him the flower of the Kuraish. Abou Bakr, Omar, Ali, Talha, Zobair, and the other 'companions of Muhammad,' left none equal to themselves when they shook the dust of their ancestral city from off the soles of their feet.

The sceptical arguments of the Mekkans are directed, it must be observed, not against the creed of Muhammad, but against his authority as a prophet. All the conservative interests natural to man had been ranged against him. The political dangers consequent on a change of religion were very great. The great majority of men, too, are always the obedient 'children of the established fact.' Just because they do not believe in any religion with much fervour, they are loth to change that in which they have been brought up. They are conscious of no urgent spiritual needs which crave if they be not satisfied. The religion which is everybody's religion furnishes what they want much better than a new one could. It stamps them with the image and superscription of respectability, and gives them an honourable position in society. Such easy-going spirits there were among the Kuraish as everywhere else. Our fathers, they said, worshipped Hobal and Manah, Lât, and Ozza, and 'shall we abandon them for a crazed poet?' When, therefore, the polemical discussion made it clear that Muhammad had nothing but his own inner conviction to urge in favour of his creed, they ceased to pay heed to him. These worthy souls—at least the most of them—had no desire to persecute the votaries of the new faith. All they wanted was a quiet life; and, as that seemed unattainable so long as Muhammad remained at Mekka, they heartily wished he would take himself off and trouble them no more.

But there is in every community not doomed to stagnation an inner circle which, like salt, preserves the mass from corruption. This is formed of the speculative and critical spirits discontented with the established facts which confront them—the minds that have caught glimpses of unknown worlds beyond the circuit of the conventional horizon. Individually their labours may seem to have but small results, but collectively theirs is the power which makes 'the great world spin for ever down the ringing grooves of change.' Such were the men whom Muhammad drew away after him from Mekka. The forerunners of the Prophet had sapped in their minds the belief in idolatry. The Theism taught, though in crude form, by Zaid, Waraka, and others, had stirred the reason and the conscience of these nobler intellects. Muhammad gave expression to their inarticulate convictions. He was, one might say, the Martin Luther of the Arabs—not so much the creator of a new religion as the interpreter of thoughts 'in the air.' The negative arguments of the Mekkans had no effect on them; they needed no miracles to attract them to the person of Muhammad. They believed the creed he taught because it seemed to supply what they had been seeking after; and they believed in him because he had promulgated the creed. That there is no god but God was a tenet which their moral and intellectual being emphatically affirmed; that Muhammad is His prophet was a fact demonstrated by the light he had poured into the dark chambers of their minds. The one proposition was inseparably linked to the other. At the moment, then, of seeming defeat we can see now that the success of Islam was assured. The seventy men who followed the Prophet to Medina not merely drew away the heart's blood from the Kuraish—they planted in the city which gave them shelter an *imperium in imperio*, bound together by the strongest of all ties, the sense of a Divine calling. Muhammad was the wielder of this mighty force. It remained with him to make it an instrument of evil or of good. How he used it will be related in the next chapter.

The Suras delivered at Mekka contain all the theology (properly so called) of Islam. Those delivered at Medina are devoted almost entirely to the organisation of the new Faith as a polity; the regulation of marriage, divorce, concubinage, slavery, &c.; the definition of the relations that are to exist between it and other faiths; and the settlement of a number of small matters connected with the private concerns of the Prophet and his wives. This chapter, then, may be fitly concluded by setting forth the distinctive doctrines of this theology.

Muhammad was neither philosopher nor metaphysician. No speculative difficulties troubled him as to the sources of creative power, or the relations between man and God. An omnipotent self-conscious Being was the first cause. He had said 'Be!' and the universe had started into existence. That was the whole account of the matter. Muhammad deemed it a monstrous absurdity to suppose that the attributes of man gave him any peculiar claims on the consideration of God. But it was worse than an absurdity; it was blasphemy to suppose that man could claim any spiritual kinship with his Creator—that any particle of the Divine essence had been breathed into him. 'Almost,' he cries in horror, 'might the very heavens be rent thereat, and the earth cleave asunder and the mountains fall down in fragments. Verily, there is none in the heavens and the earth but shall approach the God of Mercy *as a slave.*' God sits in awful and unapproachable majesty. He has fashioned man as an artificer fashions an image out of clay. There is no living bond between them. God is called the Merciful and Compassionate; not because love is of the essence of His nature, but because, though all powerful, He forbears to use His might for man's destruction. He might smite man with plagues; He might cause him to perish of famine or the lingering agonies of thirst; He might envelope the earth in perpetual darkness; but out of His mercy and compassion He does none of these things; He gives men rain and fruitful seasons, and genial sunshine. But He is not less the inscrutable despot, acting upon no principle but the caprices of His will. He creates the soul, and 'breathes into it its wickedness and piety.' He 'misleadeth whom He will, and guideth whom He will.' 'Whomsoever God shall please to direct He will open his breast to receive the faith of Islam; but whomsoever He shall please to lead into error, He will render His breast straight and narrow as though he were climbing up into Heaven. Thus doth God inflict a terrible punishment on those who believe not.'

Hope perishes under the weight of this iron bondage. There are in the Koran no forward glances to a coming golden age when the earth shall be filled with the knowledge of the Lord as the waters cover the sea, such as irradiate the hymns and prophecies of the Old Testament. There is no communion of man's spirit with the Spirit of God; none of that loving trust which casteth out fear. There are not even any aspirations after spiritual perfection as bringing a man nearer to God. 'God,' to quote the words of Dean Milman, 'stands alone in His nature, remote, unapproachable; in His power dominant throughout all space, and in all time, but divided by a deep and impassable gulf from created things. The absorption into or even the approximation towards the Deity by contemplation in this life or perfection in the life to come, are equally foreign to the Koran.' Muhammad took the world as it was; war, concubinage, slavery, were all divinely-constituted elements of society. What we understand by a social reformer would have appeared to Muhammad an impious man who presumed to interfere with the arrangements laid down by the Creator. The business of a wise man is not to question but submit, and by confession of the Unity escape the torments of Hell.

Fatalism is thus the central tenet of Islam. It suffices to explain the degraded condition of Muhammadan countries. So long as Muhammad lived and God did stoop to hold communication with men, the effects flowing from it were in a measure obscured. But when he died, the Deity seemed to withdraw altogether from the world he had created. The sufferings, sorrows, crimes, hopes, and struggles of men became a wild and ghastly orgy without meaning or ulterior purpose. The one rational object which a sober-minded, practical man could set before him was, in this life, to keep aloof from all this senseless turmoil, and, by a diligent performance of the proper rites and ceremonies, to cheat the Devil in the next. And so it has been always. History repeats itself in Muhammadan countries with a truly doleful exactness. The great bulk of the people are passive; wars and revolutions rage around them; they accept them as the decrees of a fate it is useless to strive against. All power passes accordingly into the hands of a few ambitious and turbulent spirits unencumbered with scruples of any kind; animated by no desires except those of being rich and strong. There is never a sufficient space of rest to allow institutions to grow up. Each adventurer as he rises to the summit of his ambition can keep his unsteady footing only by smiting down those who are climbing after him. Sooner or later, of course, he sinks to give way to another; and so the scene shifts and changes, until utter exhaustion and swift corruption (the state of the Muhammadan world at the present day) supervene on this insane and convulsive activity. The purer and nobler natures which exist in all communities are compelled to have recourse to mysticism to find the food they need. By abstraction from all worldly concerns, and lonely meditation, they strive to conform their lives to that idea of goodness of which their conscience testifies; and thus the salt of society—the moral purifiers—are gradually withdrawn from it. The Koran pulverises humanity into an infinite number of separate atoms. The one common duty laid upon the Faithful is to be the agents of God's vengeance on those who believe not. These are to be slaughtered until they pay tribute, when they are to be allowed to go to Hell in their own way without further molestation. But the subject of religious war or *jehad* cannot be properly treated until the Medina suras are taken into consideration.

The earth, according to Muhammad, is flat—stretched out as a carpet, with the hills planted on it in order to keep it steady. 'He (*i.e.* God) hath thrown firm mountains on the earth lest it move with you.' The world is not tenanted by men and animals only. It is the dwelling-place of innumerable djinns. They are 'created of subtle fire.' Hell will be filled hereafter with djinns and men. Not all, however, of the djinns are evil. In the 72nd Sura (entitled djinns) Muhammad relates how one night as he journeyed between Mekka and Tayif, he recited passages from the Koran which were overheard by a company of djinns, who, exclaiming, 'Verily, we have heard a marvellous discourse,' proclaimed themselves of the number of the Faithful. The evil djinns are the tempters who lead men into sin and unbelief. They steal up to the gates of Heaven to overhear the secrets of God. The stars are a vast magazine of fiery darts to hurl at these inquisitive demons. The shooting stars seen on a clear night are these celestial arrows flung by angelic hands:

> We have adorned the lower heaven with the adornment of the stars.
> They serve also as a guard against every rebellious satan.
> That they overhear not what passeth in the assembly on high, for they are darted at from every side,
> Driven off and consigned to a lasting torment;
> While if one steal a word by stealth, a glistening flame pursueth him.

Nevertheless, by these perilous excursions the djinns do gather fragments of the truth, and thereby decoy men to destruction. They descend on every lying, wicked person, and impart to him what they have heard. They cause men to be puffed up by these partial glimpses of the truth, and so lead them blindfold into Hell.

Eblis, the principle of Evil, is the lord of the djinns. He was originally among the chief of God's angels. The story of his expulsion from Heaven is given several times in the Koran. It is as follows: When God created Adam he said to the angels, 'Prostrate yourselves unto Adam,' and all prostrated themselves in worship save Eblis. 'What,' demanded God, 'has hindered thee from prostrating thyself in worship at my bidding?' 'Nobler,' retorted Eblis, 'am I than he; me hast Thou created of fire; of clay hast Thou created him.' God said, 'Get thee down hence; Paradise is no place for thy pride; get thee gone hence; one of the despised shalt thou be.' He replied, 'Respite me till the day when mankind shall be raised from the dead.' This God concedes to him, and ever since Eblis has been at large, directing and superintending the machinations of the evil djinns. He beguiled Adam and Eve, and brought about their expulsion from Eden; and he is 'the tutelar' of every unbelieving sinful person.

Another order of spiritual beings who mingle among men are the angels of God. The hosts of these are innumerable. Their functions are many. They succour the faithful in the day of battle. Five thousand of these invisible auxiliaries fought on the side of the Moslems at the victory of Bedr. At Ohod, a similar number were present, but the Faithful having been worsted on that day, it is conjectured that they did not take an active part in the fray. The angels are likewise spies over the lives of men. Every man is accompanied through life by 'a succession of angels before him and behind him, who watch over him by God's behest.' They relieve each other at their post, and thus it is that the most secret thoughts of a man's heart are communicated to God, and 'noted in a distinct writing.' This becomes, what we may call, his character roll at the Day of Judgment. It is abominable to suppose, as the heathen Arabs did, that the angels are women. 'What!' demands the Prophet, 'hath your Lord prepared sons for you, and taken for himself daughters from among the angels? Indeed, ye say a dreadful saying.' Nineteen angels guard the gates of Hell. On the Day of Judgment, eight angels will bear up the throne of God, and a vast multitude of them will encircle the Deity, hymning his praises, and interceding for the believers, saying,—

> O, our Lord! thou embracest all things in mercy and knowledge; forgive, therefore, those who turn to Thee and follow Thy path; keep them from the pains of Hell!

The terrors of the Last Day are depicted with great minuteness. It will be heralded in by a shattering to pieces of the whole visible world. The sun will be folded up. The stars will fall. The mountains will be set in motion. The she-camels will be abandoned; and the heavens will be stripped away like the skin of an animal when flayed. Then the earth will cast forth what was in her and become empty. Then those whose character roll is placed in their right hands will enter Heaven with joy; but those who receive it in their left hands[1] in the fire shall they burn. But perhaps the most vivid passage is this:

> There shall be a blast on the trumpet, and all who are in the heavens and all who are in the earth shall expire, save those whom God shall vouchsafe to live. Then shall there be another blast on it, and lo! arising they shall gaze around them.

---

[1] The actual words are, 'He whose book shall be given him be-

And the earth shall shine with the light of her Lord, and the books shall be set, and the prophets shall be brought up and the witnesses; and the judgment shall be given between them with equity; and none shall be wronged.

And every soul shall receive as it shall have wrought, for well knoweth He men's actions.

And by troops shall the unbelievers be driven towards Hell, until, when they reach it, its gates shall be opened, and its keepers shall say to them, 'Came not apostles from among yourselves to you, reciting to you the signs of your Lord, and warning you of the meeting with Him on this your day?' They shall say, 'Yes.' But just is the sentence of punishment on the unbelievers.

It shall be said to them, 'Enter ye the gates of Hell, therein to dwell for ever!' and wretched the abode of the arrogant!

But those who feared their Lord shall be driven on by troops to Paradise, until, when they reach it, its gates shall be opened, and its keepers shall say to them, 'All hail! virtuous have ye been: enter then in to abide herein for ever.'

And they shall say, 'Praise be to God who hath made good to us His promise, and hath given to us the earth as our heritage, that we may dwell in Paradise wherever we please!' And goodly is the reward of those who travailed virtuously. And thou shalt see the angels circling around the throne with praises of their Lord! and judgment shall be pronounced between them with equity: and it shall be said, 'Glory be to God, the Lord of the worlds.'

Sura xxxix. *The Troops.*

Hell and Heaven are painted with an abundance of detail. The denizens of Hell will dwell 'amid pestilential winds and in scalding water, and in the shadow of a black smoke, not cool, and horrid to behold.' Draughts of boiling water will be forced down their throats. They will be dragged by the scalp and flung into the fire. Garments of fire will be fitted on to them. They will also be beaten with iron maces. So often as they

hind his back.' The Muhammadans believe that the right hand of the damned will be chained to the neck; the left chained behind the back.

endeavour to escape out of Hell because of the anguish of their torments, they will be dragged back, their tormentors exclaiming, 'Taste ye the pain of burning.' So often as their skins are well burned, other skins will be given them in exchange, in order that they may taste the sharper torment, for 'God,' says the Prophet, with great gusto, 'is mighty and wise'—a curious illustration this of the Divine sagacity.

The Faithful, on the other hand, will be led into 'gardens of delight' and repose on 'inwrought couches.' Youths endowed with immortal beauty will go round about to them 'with goblets and ewers and a cup of flowing wine.' Their brows will not ache from it, nor their senses fail. The wives, too, of the Faithful, 'on soft green cushions and beautiful carpets shall recline.' The fruits of the gardens will hang within easy reach—the pomegranate, the date, and all that is pleasant to the sight and the taste. And there will be the houris, with 'large dark eyes' and 'swelling bosoms,' endowed with immortal loveliness, and 'kept close in their pavilions, whom man hath never touched nor any djinn,' but who are now freely lavished upon the fortunate believer.

How far Muhammad intended this last description to be taken literally is a vexed question, but one which cannot be passed over as of little importance. There is no doubt that in the palmy days of Baghdad, the contact with Greek philosophy, and the infiltration of Christian thought, operated as very potent solvents on the coarse materialism of the early Arab faith. Philosophic minds —the 'wise' as they were called—dealt with the legends and the language of the Koran just as the Neo-Platonists treated the mythology of Greece. Muhammad's Paradise as well as much else were refined away into allegory. The streams that flow through Heaven and Hell became the pleasures and pains endured during the processes of the soul's progress and regress. The rivers of milk were held to signify rivers of knowledge for noble persons. The celestial wine served out to the Faithful was the removal of terror, fear, and sadness. And the dark-eyed houris 'concealed in the pavilions' were scientific secrets hidden from the eyes of the profane by a veil. It seems to me only necessary to state these allegorical interpretations to feel assured that nothing so feeble and colourless as this was in Muhammad's mind when he set forth the delights in store for the true believer. Certainly, the Faithful in Islam rejected such notions with scorn and indignation. They held to the literal interpretation, and the orthodox doctors have drawn out the joys of Paradise in great detail, down even to the most curious particulars,—such, for example, as that seven thousand virgins will be allotted to each believer, 'the marrow of whose ankles will shine through their seventy dresses.' The sensualising effect of this conception of the heavenly 'crown of righteousness' has worked dire evil in all Muhammadan countries—poisoning the springs of domestic happiness, and irretrievably checking the spiritual growth of humanity; and for these evils Muhammad must under any circumstances be held responsible. A religious teacher is at best profoundly culpable who sets forth the spiritual blessings of Heaven under the images of animal sensuality. But in estimating the character of the Arabian prophet we are bound to inquire what probability there is that he intended to be understood allegorically at all. No correct judgment can be given on the spiritual significance of the Koran, so long as this point is undecided. My conviction is, that Muhammad intended his words to be taken literally. I will briefly give the reasons which have led me to this conclusion.

The mind of Muhammad was one but lightly burdened with the sense of mystery. It was thoroughly materialistic in all its conceptions. The first crude conception of an explanation seemed to him always a perfectly satisfactory one. He saw no difficulties. The earth was flat and kept steady by the mountains; that appeared to him a cosmogony as satisfactory as it was simple. There were seven heavens—good solid substantial firmaments—and the lowest, a magazine of fiery darts for hurling at the djinns. That seemed to him a sound and reasonable explanation of the blue sky and the stars. The djinns and the angels, though created of subtle fire, are in all other respects the same as men. Even God's omnipresence is not an attribute of the Divine nature, but an effect brought about mechanically by a system of organisation—troops of angels on constant duty over the hearts of men. In Hell, again, the punishments are all of a thoroughly material description; and no one supposes that these are to be understood symbolically. Why, then, are the pictures of Paradise to be accounted an exception to this general rule? Assuredly, there is nothing either in the character of the Prophet, his conception of humanity, or his relations with women, to give probability to such a supposition.

The argument commonly urged in favour of the allegorical interpretation is that these descriptions do not occur in the later suras of the Koran; and that when written Muhammad was content with a single wife. From this it is inferred that, from whatsoever motive prompted, these descriptions could not have been the result of an excess of animal passion. It is easy to show that the inference is a fallacious one.

Among the Arabs a man could not get a wife unless he had sufficient property to grant her a marriage dowry. And so extreme was Muhammad's poverty as a young man, that until Kadija offered herself to him, he had not dared to ask the hand of anyone in marriage. His marriage to Kadija placed him in comfortable circumstances, but not in a position to contract other alliances. Kadija kept all her fortune in her own hands; and Muhammad was, in consequence, as poor as before so far as other women were concerned. His moderation was compulsory, and therefore does not admit of being made the basis of such a theory as I am arguing against. What, however, we do know, is that no sooner was the restriction of poverty removed, then Muhammad gave the rein to his passions. He showed himself ready to gratify them at all costs. His love for Ayesha offered no obstacle to constant additions to his harem—nay, he had recourse to special revelations to sanction his amours. At almost every large capture of women the fairest was set aside by the Prophet as his private property. Distant kings and chiefs who desired to win his favours, mined their way into his heart by presentations of beautiful slaves. At the time even of his death, a fresh wife was on her way to Medina. Simultaneously with all this (as I shall have to show in the following chapter), there is a general decadence in the character of Muhammad. The lofty and impassioned teacher is transformed into the Oriental despot, reaching his ends through assassination, massacre, and war. If, then, these sensuous descriptions of Paradise are omitted from the later suras, whatever the cause, the omission could not have been due to a purification of the 'eye of the mind' revealing a higher ideal of spiritual blessedness. The more probable cause, assuredly, is satiety. The pleasures which appeared so intense when out of reach, that Muhammad could think of no reward so fitted for the believer in Paradise, palled as soon as they were enjoyed without restriction. Such has always been the fate of loveless sensuality.

Muhammad, beyond doubt, was warmly attached to Kadija; he asserts repeatedly that he was so; and he would have been destitute of all gratitude had he been indifferent to the woman who emancipated him from poverty and was the first to believe in the reality of his prophetic mission. But the marriage had not been one of Muhammad's seeking. He had, as we should say, married for money, not for love. And even had love existed from the first, love, as understood by Muhammad, was a very different thing from love as understood in England in the nineteenth century. A man must needs prefer one woman to another—so much Muhammad would have allowed. He preferred Ayesha to his other wives, but that the sequence of this preference should be a repudiation of and complete abstinence from all other women would have seemed to the Prophet monstrous and unreasonable. Four wives were compatible with the most rigid asceticism; and to these might be added, with the approval of a beneficent Creator, as many female slaves as 'your right hand possessed.' With such a conception of the divinely-ordained relation between the sexes, and with his violent passions, it must have been to Muhammad a positive torment to be tethered to one wife, and that an aged one. His thoughts turned longingly to the felicitous state of the Persian king—the greatest monarch known to the Arabs—with all the beauties of the East at his disposal, enshrined in bowers of appropriate loveliness and luxury. This, surely, was the intensest happiness on earth. This, then, must be reserved in Heaven for the true believer.

For the good Muhammadan, it must be remembered, undergoes no change by reason of his admission into Heaven. Muhammad's doctrine is the exact opposite of St. Paul's; it is flesh and blood which inherit *his* Paradise; and such being the case, the delights of Paradise must be most consonant to human flesh and blood as it existed in Mekka. Hence, as has been often pointed out, the descriptions of Paradise answer exactly to the accounts of the harems kept by those magnificent Persian despots. Ahasuerus, in the Book of Esther, leads the life of the Faithful in Paradise. He 'appoints officers in all the provinces of his kingdom, that they may gather together all the fair virgins unto Shushan, the palace.' It takes an entire year to fit these young ladies for presentation to the king—six months with oil of myrrh, and six months with sweet odours.' Such was the life which fired the imagination of the Prophet at Mekka, and he constructed his Paradise accordingly. He could have imagined none which appealed with a more potent attraction to those whom he addressed.

CHAPTER II.

MUHAMMAD AT MEDINA.

A.D. 622—630.

ACCORDING to Arab traditions, the territory round Yathrib (as Medina was called before the flight of the Prophet converted its title into 'the City') was peopled in a remote period by Amalekites. Yathrib, a chief of this tribe, settled, it is said, on the spot which still bears his name; and, by degrees, a town rose up, the foundation of which is attributed to him. The valley was well watered, and rich in palm trees; and the Amalekites prospered until they were assailed by the Jews. In what manner these early settlers were driven out by the Jews there is no certain account. The traditions differ. Some of the accounts are evidently derived from a confused and fragmentary account of the destruction of the Amalekites by Samuel and Saul. Others, again, affirm that the first Jewish settlers that arrived in the Hejaz were fugitives from Jerusalem when that city was taken and destroyed by Nebuchadnezzar. It appears most probable that the number of the Jews settled in and about Yathrib was swelled by successive emigrations. The author of the 'Kitab al Aghani' mentions one about the time when Pompey reduced Judea to the condition of a Roman province. A further emigration probably took place when the city was destroyed by Titus (A.D. 70), and a third to escape the bloody vengeance inflicted by Hadrian upon the chosen people, in retaliation of their last desperate effort to throw off the Roman yoke (A.D. 136). Some Arab hordes were at that time spread about the country, but not in sufficient numbers to dispute the possession of the country with the Jews. Yathrib became the residence of the noblest and wealthiest families among the Jews. Castles, or fortified houses, quadrangular in shape, studded the town and the suburbs. Fresh bands of emigrants, as they arrived, constructed similar habitations for themselves. The largest and most powerful of these Jewish tribes were the Bani Koraizha, the Bani Nadhir, and the Bani Khaynokha.

Such was the state of the country when the two Azdite families of Aus and Khazraj—a part of the great emigration from Yemen on the breaking up of the Dike of Mareb—arrived in the neighbourhood of Yathrib. The date of their appearance is conjectured to have been about A.D. 360. Aus and Khazraj were brothers. The emigrants consisted of the third or fourth generation in descent from them. A treaty of alliance was concluded between the new comers and the Jews. They lived amicably together, until in the course of the next two centuries the Arabs had become the equal of the Jews in numbers and prosperity. They were idolaters, and the names of the idols, Lât and Manah, appear in the composition of their family names. It was inevitable, as soon as the two races approached to equality, that hostilities should break out between them. The struggle terminated in favour of the Arabs, who succeeded in massacreing the chief men of the Jews at a banquet to which the latter had been invited under the pretence of arranging a peace. But the Jews, though weakened, were still formidable, and the Arabs deemed it expedient to subject them to a second massacre. The Arabs appear to have suffered from a poverty of invention, which is only less surprising than the credulity of the Jews. The former had recourse to their old device of a banquet; the latter fell innocently into the snare, and were once more massacred. The Arabs thenceforth became the undisputed sovereigns of the Yathribs, the Jews being reduced to the condition of their clients or *mawlas.* These events took place about A.D. 492-95.

But the tribes of Aus and Khazraj, true to the Arab instinct, had no sooner vanquished the common enemy than they turned their weapons against each other. Blood feuds, pursued with unrelenting pertinacity, were the occasions of wars, which raged almost without intermission until within six or seven years of the flight of Muhammad to Medina (about A.D. 615), when the power of the Khazraj was temporarily crushed on the field of Boath. Had the Jews been at unity among themselves, these discords might have been made the stepping-stones to recover their old ascendancy. They had but to fling their undivided weight on the side of one party in the quarrel, and the other must have been exterminated. But there was the old insurmountable obstacle to united action. The Jews were troubled with family dissensions, and these dissensions, like 'the wrath with those we love,' worked like madness in the brain. They were more eager to prosecute personal revenges to the bitter end, than to destroy the common oppressor and enemy. It was sufficient that one Jewish tribe had espoused one side of the quarrel between the Arab tribes to make the others espouse the opposite. And so it came to pass that while the Kuraizha and the Nadhir fought under the banners of the Aus, the Khaynokha were numbered in the ranks of the Khazraj. Fatigued by these dissensions, and feeling that the only way to put a stop to them was by submission to a common authority, the two rival tribes determined to elect a king. They were disposed to crown Abdallah, son of Obay, a leading man among them, and one who throughout their long wars had more than once shown a rare spirit of wisdom, moderation, and peacefulness. But at this time occurred the 'Flight to Medina,' and the introduction of Islam gave an entirely new direction to the thoughts and actions of the people.

From the short sketch of the state of society at Medina, the reader will perceive that Muhammad, as the founder of a new faith, had to work under conditions widely different from those which surrounded him in Mekka. In some respects his task was easier; in others, his difficulties were increased. At Mekka, his arguments, threats, entreaties, and exhortations had striven in vain to penetrate the materialism of Mekkan idolatry. The Mekkans could not believe, from sheer incapacity to rise to the spiritual level of the new creed. In Medina this difficulty was in great part removed. Association with the Jews had familiarised the Arabs of Medina with the leading ideas of Islam—the unity of God, the succession of the prophets, and a future state of rewards and punishments; and their national pride persuaded them to give a willing credence to the notion that the last and greatest of the prophets had been selected from among the Arabs. To this state of preparedness we may, without doubt, attribute the rapid spread of the Prophet's creed at Yathrib.

On the other hand, Muhammad had to encounter difficulties which at Mekka he had never experienced. The ignorance of the Kuraish had enabled him to give what account he pleased of the suras he recited to them. When he asserted that his foolish and extravagant legends about Noah, Abraham, Joseph, Solomon, and others had been made known to him by the archangel Gabriel, and that they were identical with similar stories in the sacred books of the Jews, the Mekkans might and did discredit both the one assertion and the other. But they lacked the knowledge requisite to demonstrate their falseness. At Medina it was different. Here Muhammad was confronted by the very people, and the very books, to whom he had made appeal in order to confirm the veracity of his mission. He had placed the Jews on a level with the Faithful in the sight of God. The doctrine laid down at Mekka was that 'to every people God had sent a messenger.' Moses was the prophet of the Jews as Muhammad was the prophet of the Arabs. The Pentateuch and the Koran were copies of one and the same book existing throughout all eternity on the Everlasting Table that stands in front of the Throne of God. Muhammad's ignorance of the Jewish Scriptures had caused him to commit himself to these positions. As soon, then, as he was confronted by the veritable Jewish Scriptures, it became a life and death struggle between him and them.

Either he must confess himself an impostor, or denounce the Jews as 'infidels,' who had tampered with the sacred writings committed to their charge, and, as such, deserving of extermination in this world, and reserved for hell fire in the next. Muhammad chose the latter alternative; and no better proof can be given of the extraordinary ascendancy he had acquired over the minds of his followers, than the fact that he executed this sudden and complete change of front without shaking their faith one jot.

These followers formed a body more numerous, more compact, and better organised than was possible at Mekka. The fugitives of his own tribe, in accompanying him to Medina, had cut themselves asunder from the family and tribal ties which held the first place in the thoughts and affections of the ordinary Arab. They were men without a home; without an occupation. Religion had become their profession; devotion to the Prophet was the spiritual tie which bound them together. Not less fanatical was the feeling of those Arabs of Medina who had invited the Prophet to their city—the *Ansars*, or 'Helpers,' as they are called in Muhammadan history. At a feast of brotherhood, given by Muhammad for that purpose, the fugitives of Mekka and the helpers of Medina pledged themselves by pairs to an union so close that each regarded the other as his heir, to the exclusion of his blood relations. In the fragmentary condition of Arab society, it is impossible to over-estimate this element of strength. Muhammad became a king whose power extended to the world beyond the grave. Death, at his bidding, was merely a momentary agony which bore the sufferers to an eternity of bliss. He was the absolute lord of the consciences of his subjects; the thing that was right was the thing that he decreed; there was no other standard by which to measure the thoughts and acts of men.

In this, as in the preceding chapter, I do not purpose to give a narrative of the events in Muhammad's life at Medina, but to refer to them only so far as is necessary to explain the development of his creed. From the time of his arrival at his new home, Muhammad the Prophet may be said to disappear, and a very inferior personage to have taken his place—Muhammad, the party leader and ambitious politician. He has a double task before him—the one, to fit his creed with a new and independent foundation, that on which it had been built at Mekka having broken down under the criticism of the Jews at Yathrib; the other, to mould his followers into a mighty and aggressive force fit for an aspirant after universal dominion. The character of the Koran becomes sadly altered under the pressure of these new necessities. Its dreary and monotonous pages are no longer relieved by those flashes of inspiration which occasionally cheer us in the suras delivered at Mekka. The endeavour now is to found a Polity, not to communicate a message from God. In effecting this, the crimes and the blunders of the Prophet were many, but the worst sin of all was the attributing of a Divine sanction to his crimes and blunders. Islam, as a Polity, was adapted to the rude and simple wants of the only social system with which Muhammad was acquainted; its ethical spirit was in harmony with the imperfect code of morality which commended itself to the barbarous Arab conscience. But to the Polity erected on these rude lines was given the attribute of

Finality. In order to enforce obedience, and eliminate the spirit of opposition, Muhammad asserted that it was, down to the minutest details, the work of a Divine legislator. After him, no further communications from Heaven were to be asked or expected. He was the seal of the prophets. He had been commissioned to lay the foundation of a system which was to endure unchanged until the end of all things. It was thus that Muhammad perverted the consciences of his followers, and consigned the whole Muhammadan world to a state of immobility. He walled up with his own hands at Medina the passages to that higher life of which he had given the Arabs a glimpse at Mekka.

Although the fugitives from Mekka had been received with the utmost kindness and hospitality by the Faithful at Medina, still much distress was experienced by those among them who had no property of their own and were unacquainted with any handicraft. Thirty, or, according to some writers, seventy men were houseless and almost naked. They slept under the covered part of the Mosque, and depended for their food upon the charity of the Prophet. It was their wretched condition which evoked the urgent appeals that appear in the Medina suras to the rich Faithful to support their indigent brethren. Charity is likened to a grain of wheat planted in the soil which returns sevenfold to the sower. The fear lest too great a liberality should impoverish the donor is rejected as a suggestion of the Devil. Still, the most liberal almsgiving could not permanently provide a living for the destitute; but there was another means of livelihood, congenial to the Arab mind, and carrying with it no stain of disgrace or immorality. This was robbery. Why should not the Faithful eke out their scanty means by adopting this lucrative and honourable profession, which was open to everyone who had a sword and knew how to use it? The infidels of Mekka who had driven them from their ancestral homes were merchants. Their karavans, laden with wealth of all kinds, were continually passing between Arabia and Syria. Surely, to despoil these infidels and employ their property to feed the hungry and clothe the naked among the people of God, would be a work well pleasing in His sight. Muhammad was not long in obtaining a revelation to the effect that 'a sanction is given to those who, because they have suffered outrages, have taken up arms'—that God is well able to 'succour those who have been driven forth from their homes wrongfully, only because they say, "Our Lord is the God."' Parties were accordingly organised and despatched in different directions to intercept the Mekkan karavans. To fight on the path of God, to give freely for the cause of God, were represented as among the highest virtues of the Faithful. And thus was the first advance made in the conversion of the religion of Islam into the religion of the sword.

For some time these expeditions were unsuccessful. But in the year 624 was fought the battle of Bedr, a battle in its effects on the destinies of the world hardly less memorable than that of Marathon. The story has been so often told that there is no need to repeat it here. Suffice it to say that a few hundreds of the Faithful overthrew a greatly superior force of the Kuraish. Several of the Prophet's bitterest persecutors perished in this engagement. Muhammad was exultant. He taunted the corpses of his enemies as they were flung, naked and without ceremony, into a well on the field of battle. 'Woe to you,' he said, 'ye fellow-tribesmen of the Prophet! You have held me to be a liar while strangers have believed me. You have exiled me, and others have given me a home. You have been bitter against me when strangers have protected me. My God has done that which He said he would do!' The companions of the Prophet said to him, 'O, Apostle of God! speak you thus to the dead?' 'Verily,' replied the Prophet, 'they hear and understand as well as you do; only they are not able to respond.'

To his own followers he declared that it was not they, but God, who had won the battle. The overwhelming numbers they had overthrown were a clear proof that a supernatural power had given strength to their arms and sharpness to their swords. Thousands of angels, rank on rank, had fought beside the Faithful, though unseen of mortal eyes. Therefore, they need never fear whatever odds confronted them. But should any be faint-hearted and turn his back in the day of battle, he would incur the anger of God. Hell shall be his abode, and wretched the journey thither. Fair seeming to men is the love of pleasures from women and children, and treasures of gold and silver. Such are the enjoyments of this world's life. But there is a better home with God. There, there are gardens beneath whose pavilions the rivers flow, and wives of stainless purity and acceptance with God. There the Faithful will abide for ever, for God forgetteth not those who serve Him.

The battle of Ohod in the succeeding year, when the

Faithful sustained a sanguinary defeat, failed to destroy the enthusiasm kindled by Bedr. The disaster of that day was so plainly due to a breach of the Prophet's orders by a part of the Moslem army that it rather deepened the sense of Muhammad's prescience and sagacity. He represented the defeat as a trial of faith. The Faithful had been confident overmuch. They had thought it an easy thing to look death in the face, with Paradise before them on the other side of the grave. But when death actually confronted them they had fled. They had been weighed in the balance and found wanting. Did they think that they could enter Paradise ere God had taken knowledge of those who did valiantly? They were not to be cast down by this reverse. No one could die except by God's permission when the term of his life was reached. It was Satan who had caused them to turn the back on the day the hosts met. Neither were they to mourn over the slain. Alive with their Lord, these were richly sustained; rejoicing in what God of His bounty had vouchsafed them, and looking forward with joy to those who were to follow after them. For God suffereth not the reward of the Faithful to perish.

The fearless and devoted spirit excited by these exhortations reached its culminating point after the failure of the grand attempt made by the Kuraish to capture Medina two years after the battle of Ohod. Abou Sofyan, the bitterest and ablest enemy of the Moslems at Mekka, organised and headed this expedition. From the number of tribes engaged in this enterprise the war is spoken of in the Koran as 'the War of the Confederates.' Ten thousand men were marching upon the city of refuge.

In Medina there was general consternation. The Prophet promised victory, but his words fell upon unheeding ears. The people beheld in anticipation a more fearful slaughter than that of Ohod, making the streets of the city run red with blood. At this conjuncture a Persian who chanced to be resident in Medina suggested that they should fortify the place with a ditch and a rampart, as the Persians under similar circumstances were in the habit of doing. This simple device sufficed to disconcert the besieging army. They gave loud expression to their disgust. 'Never before,' they complained, 'had the Arabs made war in this fashion.' For two weeks they gazed at the ditch, incapable of devising a means to pass it. Still, by a succession of feint attacks they wearied the defenders, and Muhammad prayed aloud for a miracle to destroy the host of the Infidel. There was no response. He then had recourse to bribery, which succeeded immediately. He made secret proposals to certain tribes of the Confederation, undertaking to make over to them a third of the Medina date crop if they would abandon the Kuraish. This bait was too attractive to be resisted, and they withdrew. Their desertion greatly discouraged the remainder of the host, and a fortnight after the commencement of the siege a storm of wind which overthrew their encampment completed their discomfiture. Abou Sofyan was the first man to mount his dromedary and ride off in the direction of Mekka. The army followed, retreating unmolested, but with the utmost haste and confusion. Here was a clear proof that God and His angels fought on the side of the Faithful. 'O, believers!' says the Prophet, 'remember the goodness of God towards you when the armies came against you, and we sent against them a blast and hosts that ye saw not; for the eye of God was upon your doings. When they assailed you from above you and from below you, and when your eyes became distracted, and your hearts came up into your throats, and ye thought divers thoughts of God, then were the Faithful tried, and with strong quaking did they quake.'

From this time, if we except the battle of Mouta, when the Faithful were defeated by the troops of the Byzantine emperor, the career of Muhammad was one of almost unbroken triumph. The condition of Arabia chanced to be at that time exceedingly propitious to the building up of a new power. The tribes of Bedouin Arabs, despite their wandering habits and love of lawless independence, had been accustomed to yield a kind of feudal allegiance either to the Himaryite Tobbas of Yemen, or the monarchs of Persia. And when tormented beyond endurance by their own blood feuds, they had been used to solicit from one or other of these sovereigns the nomination of some chief of distinction to be king over them until their bitter feelings had been coerced into quiescence. But at this time the dynasty of the Himaryite Tobbas had been subverted, and Persia, torn by internal dissensions, was not in a position to take cognisance of the disorders in Arabia. All eyes, therefore, turned eagerly towards the new power that was being founded in Medina. Deputations from the different tribes were continually arriving in Medina soliciting the protection and friendship of the Prophet, and the despatch of missionaries to instruct them in the principles of the new faith. Many were eager, by a nominal adherence to Islam, to purchase immunity from the predatory raids of the Faithful, which year after year were carried on in every direction on a scale of increasing magnitude. The Prophet was no longer a homeless fugitive, dependent for his life upon the hospitality of strangers. He was a powerful prince, who with a word could collect twenty thousand soldiers. He was rich in arms and horses and all the munitions of war. His glory reached its height in the month of June A.D. 630, a little less than eight years after his flight from Mekka, when he re-entered that city in triumph at the head of ten thousand men.

It was then that the vision of a world far beyond the confines of his native land, subject to Allah and His Prophet, rose before the imagination of Muhammad. The sword which had achieved so much already, had yet a grander task to accomplish. It was to become the instrument whereby he should ascend to universal dominion. The ninth sura is that which contains the Prophet's proclamation of war against the votaries of all creeds other than that of Islam. Those, he says, who strive with their substance and their persons on the path of God shall be of the highest grade with God. Tidings from Himself shall God send them, and of gardens in which lasting pleasure shall be theirs. But those who treasure up gold and silver, and expend it not in the way of God, shall suffer a grievous torment. Their treasures shall be heated in hell fire, and their foreheads and their sides and their backs shall be branded with them. Some there are who delight to stay behind God's Apostle, and allege the heat of summer as a pretext for not contending with their persons and their riches in the cause of God. A fiercer heat will such backsliders experience in the fire of Hell.

Neither thirst nor labour nor hunger can come upon those who are fighting in the path of God; for all that they do or suffer is written down in the Book of Life as a good work. A hundred of the Faithful, if they fight with constancy, shall overcome two hundred of the Infidel; a thousand shall cause two thousand to fly. There are twelve months in the year, four of which are sacred; but those who join gods with God are to be attacked in all indifferently. The Faithful are to seize them, besiege them, and lay in wait for them with every kind of ambush. The Jews and the Christians are specified as objects of the special vengeance of the Faithful. The Jews say that Ezra is the son of God; and the Christians take their teachers and their monks and the Messiah for lords beside God, though bidden to worship God only. Therefore they must be fought with until they pay tribute out of hand. Do the Faithful imagine that the giving of drink to the pilgrims and the visiting of the holy places are actions as meritorious as those performed by him who fighteth for the cause of God? They shall not be held equal with God. Verily, if God had pleased, He might have taken vengeance on the Polytheists without the assistance of the Faithful; but He hath commanded the Moslems to fight His battles in order to prove them. Therefore, wherever they encounter the unbelievers let them strike off their heads, until they have made a great slaughter of them. But if they shall convert, and observe prayer, and pay the obligatory alms, then let them go their way, for God is gracious and merciful. A fifth part of the spoils taken in war is to be set aside for God and His Prophet and the poor; the rest is to be divided equally among the host.

Such was the character of the Sacred War enjoined upon the Faithful. It is Muhammad's greatest achievement and his worst. When subjected himself to the pains of persecution he had learned to perceive how powerless were torments applied to the body to work a change of conviction in the mind. 'Let there be no violence in religion,' had then been one of the maxims he had laid down. 'Unto every one of you,' he had said in former days, speaking of Jews and Christians, 'have we given a law and an open path; and if God had pleased He had surely made you one people; but He hath thought fit to give you different laws, that He might try you in that which He hath given you respectively. Therefore, strive to excel each other in good works; unto God shall ye all return, and then will He declare unto you that concerning which ye have disagreed.' But the intoxication of success had long ago stilled the voice of his better self. The aged Prophet standing on the brink of the grave, and leaving as his last legacy a mandate of universal war, irresistibly recals, by force of contrast, the parting words to his disciples of another religious teacher, that they should go forth and preach a gospel of peace to all nations. Nor less striking in their contrast is the response to either mandate;—the Arab, with the Koran in one hand and the sword in the other, spreading his creed amid the glare of burning cities, and the shrieks of violated homes, and the Apostles of Christ working in the moral darkness of the Roman world with the gentle but irresistible power of light, laying anew the foundations of society, and cleansing at their source the polluted springs of domestic and national life.

For the sake of clearness I have brought together in a consecutive form all that I wished to say on the subject of *jehad*. But coincidently with the development of this teaching there was the long struggle with the Jews of Medina, which gave to Islam its ritual, and a knowledge of which is indespensable to a proper estimate of the Prophet's character. The story of this I have still to tell. There were from the outset two parties in Medina strongly opposed to the Prophet. The one consisted of Arabs headed by that Abdallah, son of Obay, who but for the appearance of Muhammad would have been elected King of Medina. Abdallah naturally enough bitterly resented the advent of the Prophet, which deprived him of the leadership of his native city; and though awed into an outward conformity to Islam, both he and his friends were at heart the enemies of the Prophet. This party is spoken of in the Koran as 'the Hypocrites.' The other party was made up of the three Jewish tribes. Had these parties been able to act with the unanimity of the Moslems, the probability is that Islam would never have inundated the world. But the Jews were divided among themselves; 'the Hypocrites,' though cordially detesting the Prophet, could not induce themselves to combine with the Jews against men of their own race; and so it happened that both parties were destroyed in detail—the Jews by expulsion and extermination; the Arabs by gradual absorption into the body of the Faithful, partly from conviction, but more so from a sense of expediency.

At Mekka the new faith had had neither sacred building nor ritual. Almost the first act of the Prophet, on arriving at Medina, was to supply these wants. A plot of ground was selected, and the first rude Muhammadan Mosque erected. It was a very simple building, supported on the trunks of palm trees, and the roof covered in with palm branches; but in its shape and general arrangements, the pattern after which all the mosques throughout Islam have been built ever since. At first the *kibla*, or point towards which the Faithful turned their faces when praying, was Jerusalem. Muhammad intended thereby to signify that his creed was one and the same as that which had been taught by Moses and Jesus. There can be no doubt that at Mekka he had built upon this assumption of identity with the most perfect assurance. And on his arrival at Medina he entered into a league of amity with the Jews, in which the latter were stated to be on a footing of religious equality with the Faithful. But these amicable relations were of very brief duration. Muhammad demanded that the Jews should recognise him, not merely as a prophet sent to the Arabs, but also as the prophet like unto himself whom Moses had promised to the Jews. He grounded this pretension on the fact (as he supposed it) that the revelations contained in the Koran were the same as those in the Pentateuch. The Jews rejected the demand for allegiance, and denied the truth of the proposition on which it was grounded; they produced their sacred books, and by demonstrating the utter absence of resemblance between them and the Koran, turned the argument of the Prophet against himself. It became then a matter of necessity either to give up Islam altogether, or to sever its connection with Judaism. Muhammad was not long in making his choice.

On January 16, A.D. 624, after sundown, a man entered

the Mosque and cried to the Faithful assembled there: 'I come from the Prophet, and bring you the intelligence that God has changed the *kibla*; turn your faces towards the *kaaba* of Mekka, for this is now your *kibla*.' This sudden change from Jerusalem to Mekka is represented in the Koran as a trial of faith. Mekka, in the counsels of God, had always been the true *kibla*; Jerusalem had been named for a time only, that God 'might know him who followeth the Apostle from him who turneth on his heels; the change is a difficulty, but not to those whom God hath guided.' The morality of this act is, doubtless, as bad as it can be; it is impossible to suppose that in giving a Divine sanction to this change Muhammad was not guilty of conscious mendacity; but its worldly wisdom cannot be questioned. Those who 'turned the heels' were, of course, the Jews. They had been tried by this test and failed. They clung to Jerusalem as the true seat of holiness in opposition to a Divine command which had transferred that privilege to Mekka. They were henceforth infidels; the Faithful must cease from all commerce with them, and especially must they be careful not to read their (so called) sacred books; for these, under the guidance of the Evil One, had been tampered with in order to cast discredit on the veracity of the Prophet. By the change, too, of the *kibla* to the *kaaba* of Mekka, Muhammad not merely removed a great danger to the constancy of his followers, but at one stroke he brought his teaching into harmony with the old traditional belief and veneration of the Arabs. There was no longer any violent rupture with the past involved in the reception of Islam; it became merely a purification of the national creed;

and thus it was enabled to strike its root in the Arab mind with a binding force which it could not have possessed had it retained its cosmopolitan character.

Hitherto when the time of prayer came round, a crier had gone through the streets of Medina to summon the Faithful. But with the change of the *kibla* it was thought expedient to adopt some less rude method of summons. No revelation on the subject having been made to the Prophet, various plans were proposed by members of the congregation. The Prophet suggested that a gong should be beaten. But this did not please the Faithful, because the gong was already used by the Christians. At last one of the Medina converts had a dream; he saw a man, clothed in green, stand on the roof of the Mosque, and heard him shout: 'God is great! God is great! There is no God but Allah!' By Omar's advice this was adopted as the signal to summon believers to prayer, and it has remained so to this day.

The next regulation prescribed to the Faithful was the fast during the month Ramadhan. The idea has evidently been borrowed from the Christian's Lent in memory of Christ's death and passion, and the Jewish Passover in commemoration of the deliverance from Egypt. In like manner Muhammad decreed that this month Ramadhan should be held peculiarly sacred, as that 'in which the Koran was sent down to be man's guidance, and an explanation of that guidance.' 'As soon as any one of you observeth the moon let him set about the fast; but he who is sick or upon a journey shalt fast a like number of other days.' To demonstrate, however, that the Muhammadan practice was not a servile imitation from the Jewish or Christian ceremonial, the period for fasting was reduced from forty days to a lunar month. All night the Faithful were permitted to 'eat and drink until ye can discern a white thread from a black thread by the day-break'; after that they were to 'fast strictly till night.'

Finally, scattered through the Medina suras, are a number of directions on the subject of prayer. The true believers, before they pray, are to wash their faces and heads, their hands up to the elbows, and their feet and ankles; or should they be in a state of impurity, they are to wash all over. Should there be no water at hand they are permitted to take fine clean sand and rub their hands and faces therewith. There were five stated periods during the day wherein a believer was to offer prayer: (1) At daybreak, 'for the prayer of daybreak is borne witness unto by the angels'; (2) when noon is past and the sun begins to decline from the meridian; (3) in the afternoon before sunset; (4) in the evening after sunset and before the day be shut in; (5) the Faithful were to 'watch some part of the night in the same exercise, as a work of supererogation for them; peradventure their Lord would raise them to an honourable station.' Prayer according to the Prophet was 'the pillar of religion' and 'the key of Paradise.' 'There could,' he once said, 'be no good in that religion where there was no prayer.' Almsgiving is also a practice to which the Faithful are repeatedly exhorted in the Koran. It is classified under two heads, *legal* and *voluntary*. The legal alms are those which are obligatory on all Moslems; and Muhammad, so long as he lived, collected them himself for distribution among the poor and needy. Voluntary almsgivings are among the most meritorious actions which a believer can perform; and Muhammad is said to have declared that those who do not pay their legal contributions duly, will at the resurrection be tormented by serpents twisted round their necks.

These regulations had the effect of placing Islam on a basis of its own. But this was not sufficient. So long as the Jewish tribes resided in Medina the Prophet could never feel secure of the allegiance of his followers. The Jews were a perpetual testimony of the falseness of his pretensions. Until they were destroyed or expelled, he stood upon a mine which might at any moment be fired, to the utter destruction of himself and his plans. But only after the victory of Bedr did he consider himself strong enough to take active measures against them. These at first took the form of assassination. The first victim was a woman, Asma, daughter of Marwan; she had composed some satirical verses on the Prophet and his followers; and Muhammad, moved to anger, said publicly: 'Who will rid me of this woman?' Omeir, a blind man, but an ardent Moslem, heard the speech, and at dead of night crept into the apartment where Asma lay asleep surrounded by her little ones; he felt about in the darkness till his hand rested on the sleeping woman, and then, the next instant, his sword was plunged into her breast. The next morning, at the Mosque, Muhammad asked him: 'Hast thou slain the daughter of Marwan?' 'Yes,' answered Omeir; 'is there any cause of fear for what I have done?' 'None whatever,' replied the Prophet; 'two goats will not knock their heads together for it.' Then turning to the people assembled in the Mosque, he added: 'If you desire to see a man who hath assisted the Lord and His Prophet, look you here!' A few weeks later another Jew, also an old man—the aged Abou Afak—shared the same fate. He was hateful to Muhammad by reason of his abilities and liberal spirit; and, like Asma, he had been guilty of writing poetical satires on the followers of the new creed. By the order of the Prophet a Moslem entered the old man's house at night, and slew him while he slept.

These dastardly crimes spread terror through Medina. The Jews and those Arabs in Medina who had not embraced Islam understood for the first time the kind of guests they had received into their city. Islam, they discovered, was not merely a bond of union to those who accepted it, which obliterated the influence of all other ties, but also a spirit of hostility towards all who stood without the pale, which shrank from no treachery to gratify its hatred. Muhammad perceived the impression he had made, and determined to strike more heavily.

The Jewish tribe of Khaynoka numbered seven hundred men capable of bearing arms. They were jewellers and workers in gold. This tribe the Prophet resolved to attack and exterminate. There was a slight difficulty in the way. Muhammad had entered into a solemn league of amity with the Jews of Medina, and the Khaynoka had in no particular infringed the conditions of the treaty. A revelation was the convenient method employed for smoothing over this obstacle. The Archangel Gabriel informed the Prophet that 'the worst beasts truly in the sight of God' were those with whom he had 'leagued' himself, and that if he feared treachery from them he might 'fairly' throw back their treaty to them, for 'God loveth not the treacherous.' Encouraged by this communication, Muhammad demanded of the tribe that they should embrace Islam, and receiving a response in the negative proceeded to besiege their quarter. Abdallah ibn Obay, after having pledged himself to march to their assistance, did nothing. The two other Jewish tribes remained trembling in their quarters, short-sightedly supposing their best hope of safety lay in holding themselves aloof from their brethren in danger; and thus the Khaynoka were allowed to perish unassisted. All communication with them was cut off; their provisions were soon exhausted; and at the close of fifteen days they surrendered at discretion. Muhammad gave orders to massacre the whole tribe. But Abdallah, aroused from his inaction by this savage vindictiveness, made such threatening remonstrances that the Prophet, sorely against his will, was compelled to adopt a more merciful policy. The Khaynoka were expelled from Medina; their property passed into the possession of the victors.

The expulsion of the Khaynoka was followed at a brief interval by a third murder. Kab, the son of Ashraf, was one of the chief men of the Jewish tribe of Nadhir. Connected on his father's side with one of the branches of the Kuraish, several of his relatives had been slain in the battle of Bedr. He was guilty of composing elegies on their deaths, and, like the two victims who had preceded him, satires on the Prophet. This was sufficient to determine his death. The Prophet, turning to his companions one day as they conversed about Kab ibn Ashraf, said: 'Who will give his life to God, and slay this man?'

One of the *Ansars*, Muhammad, son of Maslama, replied: 'I—I will go and kill this man.' Among the *Ansars* was a man named Silkan, son of Salama, who was foster-brother of Kab; and Kab, who was a man of much wealth, had always treated his foster-brother with the greatest kindness and liberality. Muhammad ibn Maslama went to this Silkan, communicated to him the wishes of the Prophet, and added: 'If you assist me in this matter I shall succeed, and the work will be pleasing to the Prophet.' Silkan consented; seven others of the *Ansars* proffered their assistance; and at the time of evening prayer they took their leave of the Prophet, and set out upon their expedition.

Kab dwelt in a fortified house at some little distance from Medina. The conspirators arrived at the door late at night. Kab, who had recently married, was sleeping with his bride on the roof of the house. Silkan, leaving his companions in the road, approached, all armed, close under the walls of the fort, and called Kab by name. 'What do you want at this hour of the night?' asked the young Jewish chief. 'I have come to consult you on some business. If you can descend, come at once; if not, I will return.' Kab rose up to go and meet his foster-brother. His bride, with some secret presentiment of calamity, seized the end of his garment, and entreated him not to leave her. 'It is night,' she said, 'and you know not what may happen.' 'It is my foster-brother,' replied the young Jew. 'I am as sure of him as of myself.' Then, disengaging his dress, he said: 'The noble man responds to an appeal, even should the appeal summon him to death.' With these words he left the castle. His foster-brother, under pretence of speaking to him regarding some money he urgently needed, and which he wished Kab to lend to him, decoyed the young Jew away into an orchard. He was no sooner there than the conspirators sprang upon him; three held him, to prevent the possibility either of his attempting to escape or to defend himself, while the remainder deliberately hacked him in pieces with their swords. They then hastened away to Medina, and entering the presence of the Prophet as he was about to perform the morning prayer, recounted the success of their expedition. Muhammad was exceedingly pleased, and, the chroniclers are careful to inform us, 'returned thanks to God.' He then gave a general permission to his followers to slay any Jews they might chance to meet; and this permission was immediately followed by the murder of a Jewish merchant, apparently for his wealth, by a Moslem, who united a zeal for religion with a proper appreciation of the good things of this world.

After another brief interval the vengeance of the Prophet fell upon the entire tribe of Nadhir. They were accused of having intended to murder the Prophet—a charge grounded upon no evidence except one of Muhammad's 'revelations,' but probable in itself and abundantly justified by the example set by the Prophet. They were blockaded in their quarter. Like the Khaynoka, they were first deluded by a promise of assistance from Abdallah and his party, and then abandoned to their fate. They surrendered; and the same doom fell upon them which had been inflicted upon the Khaynoka. A single Jewish tribe—the Bani Kuraizha—now remained in Medina. A more terrible fate awaited them.

The army of the Confederates had broken up and retired from Medina. The sun of that day which shone upon the deliverance of the Faithful was still high in the heavens, when the heralds proclaimed: 'The Believers are to perform the afternoon prayer in no other place than in the quarter of the Bani Kuraizha, for the Prophet has determined to fight against the Jews.' The Moslems seized the weapons they had laid aside and hastened to obey the summons. It was Muhammad's hope to have taken the Jews by surprise, and slaughtered them at his ease. In this he was disappointed. The Jews were prepared. Their quarter was strongly barricaded; and he was compelled to have recourse to the slower method of reduction by blockade. The Jews made proposals of surrender. They offered to emigrate under the same conditions as their brethren who had been previously expelled. They pleaded piteously that their lives only might be granted to them. The Prophet was inexorable. He was now supreme in Medina. There was no one strong enough to step between him and his victims, and he was resolved to quench the long-protracted thirst of his hate in the blood of his enemies. The Jews must surrender at discretion. They knew what this foreboded. The quarter was filled with the wailing of women and children. One of their chief men said to them: 'Either acknowledge the Prophet, or let us kill our wives and children, and then sally forth and die like men; those are the only alternatives possible.' But the Jews, though they could passively endure martyrdom for their faith, could not find in their hearts the heroic despair needed to follow out this last counsel. Abou Lahaba, an ally and kinsman of theirs, was in the camp of the Moslems. They entreated him to come and advise them. The stern heart of the Moslem was touched by the misery he witnessed. But he could give them no hope. He drew his hand across his throat, to signify the doom that awaited them. They at last surrendered. The men were condemned to death; the women and children to slavery. In vain their old allies, the Bani Aus, pleaded passionately for some mitigation of this pitiless sentence. The savage Prophet asserted the judgment to be that of God, pronounced on high from beyond the seven heavens. Under the personal direction of Muhammad, deep trenches were dug in the market place. Party after party of the wretched Jews, their hands tied behind their backs, were led up to these trenches, forced to kneel down, and beheaded. Their bodies were then flung in and covered over. All that day, and for some time after the sun had set, by the glare of torches, the bloody work continued. Some six hundred men are said to have been slaughtered. The women and children numbered a thousand. Two hundred of these fell to the share of the Prophet. He sold them in Najd and Syria in exchange for weapons and horses. One Jewess, on account of her beauty, he retained as his concubine.

The expedition against the Jews at Khaibar, which took place a few months after, and their reduction to the state of tributaries, completed the suppression of the Jewish power throughout the Hejaz.

These events acted with immense force on the minds of the Faithful. The swift punishment which had fallen upon the Jews seemed to them a marvellous and awful confirmation of all that the Prophet had affirmed regarding their apostasy from the God of Abraham and Moses. The change of the *Kibla* from Jerusalem to Mekka, interpreted by the light of after events, indicated a miraculous foreknowledge, not merely of the obstinate incredulity of the Jews, but of the triumph of the new faith, the purging of the holy places from the abominations of idolatry, and the restoration in Mekka of the true religion of Abraham. For continuously with these events, the sway of Muhammad had extended upon every side. Mekka, it is true, had not yet received back the Prophet she had expelled from her soil. But the Faithful knew that this was merely a question of time and opportunity. She was powerless to resist the warriors that crowded under the banner of Islam. The Prophet had only to demand an entrance, and it would be conceded to him. Nor was this consummation long delayed.

At the commencement of the year 630, Muhammad, at the head of 10,000 men, marched upon Mekka. The inhabitants of Mekka bowed before the storm. The Prophet treated them with politic clemency. Six men and four women were all who were excluded from the amnesty proclaimed to the people; and the only resistance to the entry of the Moslem army was made by a party of horse, commanded by a Kuraishite chief, who was one of those sentenced to death.

Muhammad made his entry into the sacred city mounted on a camel, and covered with a black turban. He was preceded by Ali, carrying his standard, and surrounded by his 'companions.' He advanced as far as the Kaaba, where he was met by the leading men of the

Kuraish. It was on the 20th of the month of Ramadhan that the Prophet made this solemn entry. He dismounted from his camel at the door of the sacred building, and made the customary seven circuits. The inhabitants, meanwhile, having learned that there was to be no massacre, came crowding to the temple. The Prophet, having completed his circuits, ordered the gate of the temple to be flung open. Then all the idols which were placed in or around the Kaaba were taken down and broken to pieces. As soon as the temple had been purged from these abominations, Muhammad entered. Standing erect on the threshold, he uttered these words: 'There is no God, but God alone. He has no companion. He has kept His promise, given victory to His servant, and has smitten the heathen into flight.' Then turning to the crowd of eager lookers on, he said: 'Inhabitants of Mekka, how think you that I shall deal with you?' 'I think,' said a voice from the crowd, 'that thou, who art a noble Kuraishite, returning in triumph to his native land, will treat with pity the old men, pardon the young, and be merciful to the women and their little ones.' At these words the Prophet, we are told, lifted up his voice and wept, and all the people wept with him. Then he spoke: 'I will say to you that which my brother Joseph said to his brothers. I will not reproach you this day; God will pardon you, for He is the most merciful of those who show mercy' (Sura xii. v. 92.) Then he shut the door of the temple, remounted his camel, and rode to the spot where his tent was pitched. The people of Mekka poured thither in crowds to pronounce the confession of faith, fulfilling thus, the words of the Koran, where it is written :

> When the help of God and the victory arrive,
> And thou seest men entering the religion of God by troops,
> Then utter the praise of thy Lord, and implore His pardon ; for He loveth to turn in mercy.

When the inhabitants of Mekka—men and women—had all entered the new faith, detachments were sent out, and the shrines and idols of Lât Manah and Ozza were destroyed. The boundaries of the Holy Territory were laid down anew ; and not a graven image was permitted to remain in Mekka. The triumph of the Prophet was now complete. He did not, however, abandon the city which had given him shelter when a homeless fugitive. Medina continued to be his abiding place as before, and he remained in Mekka for only ten days or a fortnight.

CHAPTER III.

THE PILGRIMAGE OF FAREWELL.

A.D. 632.

The religion of Islam is sustained on 'five pillars.' These are (1) belief in Allah and the mission of Muhammad; (2) prayer; (3) almsgiving; (4) the fast in the month Ramadhan; and (5) the pilgrimage to Mekka. Two years after his conquest of Mekka the Prophet made the pilgrimage to the Holy Places. This act is known as 'the Pilgrimage of Farewell,' because Muhammad died a few months after; and it has ever since been the type after which succeeding pilgrimages have been conducted. This last public act, then, of Muhammad's life ought to be related in detail.

The tradition regarding the origin of Mekka is this: Abraham had become exceedingly rich and powerful, but he was sore troubled in heart because he had no child. When he married Sara he had solemnly pledged himself to give her no rival in his love. But Sara, despairing of becoming a mother herself, presented to Abraham her Egyptian slave, and Hagar became the mother of Ishmael. The extreme joy of Abraham at the birth of this child, and the proud airs assumed by Hagar, had the effect of awakening a bitter feeling of jealousy in the heart of Sara. Abraham perceived that it was necessary to remove out of her sight the objects of her hatred. God, by a special communication, directed him to render this satisfaction to Sara. He brought Hagar and her son to Arabia, and, guided by Divine instructions, conducted them to the spot on which Mekka was afterwards built. It was a desert, without water or vegetation. Abraham was affrighted at the awful solitude. But placing his trust in God, he said to Hagar: 'I leave you here, and remit you to the care of God.' 'What!' cried Hagar, clinging to him; 'will you abandon a woman and a child to perish in the desert?' 'I obey the command of God, replied Abraham, and he left them, returning to Syria. Hagar's scanty stock of provisions was soon consumed. She searched in vain for water to quench her thirst and that of her child. In her despair she traversed with hasty paces the space which extends between the two eminences known at present as Safa and Marwa. The young Ishmael, supposing that his mother was about to abandon him, flung himself on the ground in an agony of grief, and beat the earth with his feet. Instantly a spring bubbled up to the surface. Hagar perceived it, and was filled with joy. But, fearing lest the water should be wasted and sucked up by the sand, she banked up the earth round it, making a small basin. Muhammadans declare that this is the same spring that feeds the well of Zem Zem to this day.

Ishmael grew up amid a tribe of Arabs who dwelt near to the miraculous well. When he was seven years old, Abraham, under Divine direction, led him to the valley of Mina to offer him as a sacrifice to God. Three times Satan interposed in a human form, and attempted to divert the patriarch from his purpose. His endeavours were unavailing. Abraham drove him off with stones. But, as he was on the point of plunging a knife into the bosom of his son, an angel appeared, and ordered him, in the name of God, to sacrifice a ram in the place of Ishmael.

The model of the Kaaba, according to Muhammadan theologians, was constructed in Heaven before the creation of Adam. It was an object of veneration to the angels, and by God's command they made the seven circuits round it precisely in the same manner as the pilgrims do round the Kaaba at Mekka. Adam was the first Moslem. He erected the Kaaba on earth, a perfect facsimile of that which existed in Heaven. When the Deluge overwhelmed the earth, this building, all but the foundations, was carried up into Heaven. These remained hidden in the soil. When Ishmael became a man, he and his father, as usual under Divine guidance, dug and re-discovered these primitive foundations. The Kaaba was re-built upon the foundations laid down by Adam. The angel Gabriel appeared to Ishmael and presented him with the celebrated black stone, directing him at the same time how to fix it in the walls of the temple. When the temple was finished, Abraham and Ishmael consecrated it to God, and the angel Gabriel taught them the prayers and ceremonies of the pilgrimage. Finally, by the order of God, Abraham ascended the hill of Abou Kubais, in the vicinity of Mekka, and in a voice of thunder addressed this invitation to the human race: 'O people! hasten to the house of God!' The voice of the patriarch was heard through all the dwellings of men, and millions of souls, fated to accomplish the pilgrimage, returned answer: 'We are here, O Lord!' All being now complete, Abraham prepared to return to Syria. His last words to his son were: 'My task is finished. I depart, leaving to you this country, and this temple, of which God has constituted you the guardian.'

Between this legendary building of the Kaaba and the first faint dawn of authentic history there is a long interval extending over many centuries. According to the Arabic traditions, during all this extended period the guardianship of the temple remained in the possession of the Djorhomites, a tribe of Yemenite extraction. The Djorhomite chiefs were dignified with the title of *Malek*, or king, and exercised a sort of general supremacy over the Hejaz. Eventually, however, the Djorhomites forgot the respect due to the house of God and profaned it with impious acts. Five men of the tribe formed a plan to rob the treasures in the Kaaba, which were deposited in a cellar within the building, having no lock or fastening of any kind. But the boldest of these robbers, and the only one who dared to enter the temple on this sacrilegious business, was struck dead. The remainder fled affrighted. Subsequently a man and a woman of the tribe committed adultery within the sacred precincts. God instantly turned them into stones. Notwithstanding these warnings the Djorhomites desisted not from their evil ways. They applied to their own profit the gifts brought to the sanctuary, and evilly entreated the strangers who came to Mekka to perform the pilgrimage or visit the holy places.

In the meanwhile the reputed descendants of Ishmael had multiplied in the valley. These were sprung from the four sons of Nizar, the son of Maad, the son of Adnan.

Their names were Rabia, Iyad, Modhar, and Anmar. It is from Modhar that the Prophet descends. Another Yemenite tribe, besides the Djorhomites, was also settled in the neighbourhood of Mekka. When the Azdite tribe had abandoned Yemen, in consequence of the rupture of the dike of Mareb, two families, as I mentioned in the preceding chapter, wandered to Yathrib, the Aus and Khazraj. Others emigrated to Irak, where they founded the kingdom of Hira; others to Syria, where they became known subsequently as the Ghassanides; a single family separated itself from the rest of the community, and established itself at Batn Marr, near Mekka. It acquired the name of *Khozaa* (separation). United by a common feeling of indignation, the Khozaites, the Modharites, and the descendants of Iyad, declared war against the Djorhomites. The latter were defeated and expelled from the Tihama (about A.D. 206). The guardianship of the Kaaba thus became vacant. To this religious function was attached, by prescriptive right, the sovereign authority over the territory of Mekka. As a matter of course, the descendants of Modhar and Iyad fell out, as soon as the Djorhomites were expelled, on the question of succession. The Khozaites held aloof from this struggle, making, apparently, no claim at all to the guardianship of the Kaaba. The contest terminated in the defeat of the descendants of Iyad, and they emigrated in a body to the plains in the west of Irak (about A.D. 206). Their last act was to force out the black stone from its setting in the wall of the Kaaba, and bury it in a secret place. This act of ingenious malignity had the effect desired, and robbed the victors of all joy in their triumph. The disappearance of the black stone spread a gloom over the land.

It so chanced that a Khozaite woman had witnessed (herself unseen) the interment of the stone. She made known the circumstance to the chiefs of her tribe. These made proposals to the descendants of Modhar to the effect that they would undertake to re-discover the black stone if the guardianship of the temple was entrusted to them. The offer was agreed to, the stone disinterred, and restored to its accustomed place; and the guardianship of the Kaaba, with the government of the country, passed into the possession of the Khozaa. Their supremacy lasted about two centuries (from A.D. 207 to A.D. 440).

According to the Arabs, it was during this period that their countrymen turned aside from the pure religion of Abraham and defiled the Kaaba with the abominations of idolatry. Amr, the *Malek*, or king of the Khozaa, made a journey to Balka, a town of the province of Damascus in Syria, and beheld there people worshipping idols. Asking the meaning of this practice, they replied: 'These are our gods. When we ask of them victory, they give it us; rain, they send it; in short, all the prayers we address to them are heard and granted.' Amr, much rejoiced by this intelligence, asked for one of these idols. They gave him Hobal, and he carried it away to Mekka and placed it in the Kaaba. From that time idolatry made rapid progress among the Arabs; the Kaaba was crowded with images, and the religion of Abraham passed out of the memory of men. The last prince of the race of Khozaa was Holayl, son of Hobachiya.

The daughter of Holayl, named Hobba, was married to Kossay, the most eminent man among the tribes of Modhar in and around Mekka. For some time previous to his death Holayl, from extreme old age, had been unable to proceed every morning and unlock the gates of the temple. He had therefore entrusted the keys to his daughter Hobba, and she, in her turn, had delegated this function to her husband Kossay. Kossay was an able and ambitious man, and the office thus accidentally imposed upon him kindled in his mind a determination to assert the rights of his tribe to the guardianship of the Kaaba. As the direct descendants of Ishmael, they were, in the estimation of the Arabs, the legitimate protectors of the sacred soil; but the Khozaa were strong and in possession, and the Modharites had voluntarily conceded their privileges. He hoped at first to have persuaded his father-in-law to allow him to retain in perpetuity the keys of the Kaaba; but Holayl, suspecting most probably the designs of Kossay, made them over, on his death, to a member of his own tribe.

Kossay then resolved to have recourse to force. He communicated his designs secretly to the various tribes descended from the four sons of Nizar, and engaged them to draw together to Mekka during the season of the pilgrimage, when their assemblage would excite no suspicion. Thus reinforced, he declared during the ceremonies of the pilgrimage his intention of re-asserting the rights of his family. The Khozaa were not willing to make a tame surrender of their privileges. Some fierce, but indecisive, battles were fought, when, to stay the further effusion of blood, both parties agreed to submit their claims to arbitration. The arbitrator pronounced judgment in favour of the descendants of Modhar; and the Khozaa, loyally accepting his decision, retired from Mekka, leaving Kossay undisputed master of the temple and all the sacred places.

Hitherto, the veneration of the Arabs for the Kaaba and even the soil that surrounded it was so great that they neither constructed houses there nor even pitched their tents in the vicinity for any length of time. They were in the habit of resorting thither during the day, returning at nightfall to their camps in the hills. Kossay persuaded the Kuraish to erect houses round the temple, as then no hostile tribe would dare to attack them in the sacred territory itself. He divided the ground on which Mekka was afterwards built into quarters which he assigned to each family. Around the Kaaba, an empty space was left, to allow of the seven circuits being made. This space was paved with polished stones, and the Kuraish built their houses beyond the limit of the paving. The same families to whom Kossay assigned residences were dwelling there when the preaching of Islam commenced. Farther to increase the authority of his tribe among the Arabs, he declared that it was their duty as guardians of the sacred territory to entertain free of cost the pilgrims who resorted thither, and he created an office—*Rifada*—the holder of which had the exclusive right of dispensing this lavish hospitality. This office, Kossay retained in his own possession, as among the ancient Arabs no acts won so much applause and admiration as the practice of a lavish hospitality. He also decreed that the ceremony of making seven circuits round the Kaaba, being a sacred one, demanding in him who performs it a state of purity, could not be made in the garments, soiled with all kinds of impurities, which the pilgrims had worn on their journey to Mekka. Garments possessing the requisite purity must be obtained by purchase or otherwise from the Kuraish. The Arabs were not, however, inclined to fill the purses of the Kuraish by acting in the spirit of this ingenious order. They admitted the impurity of their own garments, but they were not prepared to purchase others. They preferred to make the circuits without clothes at all. Consequently, at the season of the pilgrimage, the men encircled the Kaaba in a state of nudity; the women attired in a single chemise, which they had to fling away immediately after. This indecent practice was put an end to by the Prophet. All the tribes were allowed to make the circuits in the clothes they brought with them to Mekka.

But that which augmented the sanctity of the Kaaba, and established the pre-eminence of the Kuraish among the Arab tribes more than all the innovations of Kossay, was the expedition against Mekka by the Abyssinian ruler of Yemen, and its signal failure. Kossay had long since been gathered to his fathers, and the grandfather of the Prophet Abd-al-Mottalib was the chief man in Mekka when this event took place.

Yemen was at this time a dependency of the Christian kingdom of Abyssinia, and ruled by a viceroy. This official had erected at the capital, Sana, a church esteemed to be the most beautiful in the world. According to the tradition of the Arabs, the fame of this edifice spread through all the world, and from all parts of Asia, even from Constantinople, Christians thronged thither in crowds, bringing with them rich gifts. The Abyssinian governor conceived the project of supplanting the Kaaba at Mekka by means of this new building; and thus making Sana the great gathering point of all the Arab tribes. An Arab of the tribe of Kuraish became acquainted with this design. He journeyed to Sana, gained access to the Christian temple under a pretence of desiring to make his devotions, and polluted the high altar. The Abyssinian ruler when he heard of this insult swore to march instantly and utterly destroy the Kaaba. The King of Abyssinia had an elephant named Mahmoud, which had never been present at a battle where the victory had not fallen to the Abyssinian army. He was of immense size, larger than any other elephant in Abyssinia. The Viceroy of Abyssinia wrote to his master, informing him of the pollution practised upon the church of Sana, and his purpose of retaliation, and at the same time solicited that the elephant Mahmoud should accompany the expedition. The king sent him; and the viceroy, at the head of a numerous army, invaded the Hejaz. The Arabs could not draw together forces sufficient to cope with this vast host. Twice, indeed, the tribes on the line of march ventured an attack on the invading army. But they were cut to pieces, and the Abyssinian viceroy drew nigh to Mekka. The Kuraish were in consternation. They assembled round Abd-al-Mottalib demanding what they should do. 'We are not,' said the chief, 'in force sufficient to resist the enemy; when, therefore, the Abyssinians approach we will retire to the mountains and abandon the city. The Lord of the temple is more powerful than we; He will either protect it from its enemies or abandon it to them.' This suggestion was adopted, and the city of Mekka was left without inhabitants. The Kuraish concealed themselves, their wives, their children and their cattle in the neighbouring mountains.

On the morrow of their flight the Viceroy of Yemen approached the gate of Mekka. He was informed that not a soul remained within the town. He then ordered the elephants to be brought forward, that the Kaaba might be destroyed, and the march homewards commenced at once. The great elephant Mahmoud was led into the sacred enclosure. Arrived there, he refused to stir a single step. They beat him with sticks and rods of iron. It was all in vain. All the other elephants were in like manner rooted to the spot on which they stood. While matters were in this position, on a sudden large flocks of birds, like swallows, came flying from the sea-coast, every one of which carried three stones, one in each foot, and one in its bill. These stones they threw down upon the Abyssinian army, and all whom they struck fell dead upon the spot. Then God sent a flood, which swept the dead bodies into the sea, with many of those who had not been struck with the stones. The rest fled towards Yemen, but perished in multitudes all along the road. Their bodies broke out into a kind of spotted eruption, detaching the skin from the flesh. The viceroy alone succeeded in reaching Sana, and he did so only to die from the same spotted eruption which had destroyed his army. One soldier of the Abyssinian army succeeded in escaping across the Red Sea into Abyssinia, and going directly to the king told him the tragical story; and upon that prince asking him what sort of birds they were, that had occasioned this destruction, the man pointed to one of them which had followed him all the way, and was at that time hovering directly over his head. Immediately, the bird let fall a stone and struck him dead at the king's feet. These memorable events occurred in the very year during which Muhammad was born.

The probability seems to be that the Abyssinian army was destroyed by a sudden epidemic of small-pox which raged that year with great violence in Arabia. To the Kuraish, however, and to all the Arab tribes, the deliverance of the Holy City was plainly miraculous. The Kuraish were deemed to be the specially chosen inhabitants of the Holy City and the guardians of the sanctuary. Thenceforth whenever, so we are told, a karavan went forth from Mekka, they tied to the neck of each camel the branch of a tree with a woollen cord. Whenever a karavan passed with these insignia in the desert, in Syria or in Yemen, it was considered sacred from the attacks of robbers and marauders.

During the first fervour of his religious enthusiasm, it had evidently been Muhammad's intention to alienate his countrymen altogether from their reverence for the Kaaba. The degrading worship paid to the black stone had been the main cause why his great predecessors, Zaid and Waraka, had severed themselves from the religion of their compatriots; and Muhammad, in the earlier years of his mission, trod sedulously in their steps. He built up his faith on the foundation of Jewish prophets, Jesus Christ (though not exactly in a Christian sense) being Himself the chief corner-stone, and made Jerusalem the centre of holiness, the *kibla* of prayer. Only after his arrival at Medina, and his disputes with the Jews, does he lay any special stress upon the sanctity of Mekka. But with the change of the *kibla* from Jerusalem to Mekka, the references to the Kaaba become frequent, and the obligation to perform the pilgrimage is repeatedly insisted upon. The first temple, we are then told, founded for mankind is that in Mekka; it is blessed, and a guidance to human beings. To accomplish the pilgrimage is a duty which the Moslem is bound to perform once in his life; or should he be 'hemmed in with foes,' he must send 'whatever offering will be easiest.' Those only are to be permitted to visit the temple of God who believe in God and the last day, and observe prayer and pay the legal alms, and dread none but God. It is not a thing to be permitted for an instant by the true believer that those who join gods with God, and thus become witnesses against themselves, should be permitted to enter the sacred precincts. Vain are their works, and in the fire of Hell shall they abide for ever. The pilgrimage is to be made in the months already appointed for that purpose —viz., Shawal, Dhúlkada, and Dhúlhajja. Whoever undertakes the pilgrimage must keep himself pure from all sin or impurity during the performance of the ceremonies. The pilgrims may, however, take advantage of the pilgrimage for trading purposes, and 'it shall be no crime in them.' The ceremonies were in nearly all particulars retained by Muhammad as they had been in the days of darkness.

There have been few incidents more disastrous in their consequences to the human race than this decree of Muhammad changing the *kibla* from Jerusalem to Mekka.

Had he remained true to his earlier and better faith, the Arabs would have entered the religious comity of the nations as peace-makers, not as enemies and destroyers. To all alike—Jews, Christians, and Muhammadans—there would have been a single centre of holiness and devotion; but the Arab would have brought with him just that element of conviction which was needed to enlarge and vivify the preceding religions. To the Jew he would have been a living witness that the God who spake in times past to his fathers by the prophets, still sent messengers to men, though not taken from the chosen seed—the very testimony which they needed to rise out of the conception of a national deity to that of a God of all men. To the Christians his deep and ardent conviction of God as a present living and working Power, would have been a voice recalling them from their petty sectarian squabbles and virtual idolatry, to the presence of the living Christ. By the change of the *kibla* Islam was placed in direct antagonism to Judaism and Christianity. It became a rival faith, possessing an independent centre of existence. It ceased to draw its authenticity from the same wells of inspiration. Jew and Christian could learn nothing from a creed which they knew only as an exterminator; and the Muhammadan was condemned to a moral and intellectual isolation. And so long as he remains true to his creed, he cannot participate in the onward march of men. The keystone of that creed is a black pebble in a heathen temple. All the ordinances of his faith, all the history of it, are so grouped round and connected with this stone, that were the odour of sanctity dispelled which surrounds it, the whole religion would inevitably perish.

The farther and the faster men progress elsewhere, the more hopeless becomes the position of the Moslem. He can only hate the knowledge which would gently lead him to the light. Chained to a black stone in a barren wilderness, the heart and reason of the Muhammadan world would seem to have taken the similitude of the objects they reverence; and the refreshing dews and genial sunshine which fertilise all else, seek in vain for anything to quicken there.

On Saturday, February 22, A.D. 632, at midday, the Prophet set out from Medina, attended by all his wives and an immense multitude of the Faithful. He had bathed and perfumed himself, and rode at the head of the host mounted on a camel. Wherever the karavan halted, a place of prayer was erected, and the Prophet, dismounting, made his devotions. On March 2, the host halted at the distance of one day's march from Mekka. The next morning (being the sixth day of Dhúlhajja, or month of the pilgrimage) the Prophet entered Mekka. He circled the Kaaba seven times mounted on his camel—for he was too weak to undergo the fatigue on foot—three times rapidly, and four times slowly. Then he kissed the black stone. Then, standing on what is called 'the stone of Abraham,' he offered up a brief prayer to Allah. After which he caused some water to be brought from the well Zem Zem, and drank thereof. Then he performed the seven customary perambulations between Safa and Marwa, repeating the passage in the Koran in which they are mentioned:—

Verily Safa and Marwa are among the monuments of God; whoever then maketh a pilgrimage to the temple or visiteth it, shall not be to blame if he go round about them both. And as for him who of his own accord doeth what is good—God is grateful and knowing.

The seven perambulations completed, he retired to his quarters.

On the eighth of Dhúlhajja (March 5) Muhammad repaired to the valley of Mina, three miles distant from Mekka. Here there were no ceremonies, and here many of the pilgrims assumed the *ihram*, or religious garment.

On the ninth, after morning prayer, the multitude, headed by the Prophet, marched to Arafat, a broad plain at the foot of a hill, on the road to Tayif, and known as 'the Halting Place.' Arafat lies beyond the sacred territory. The tradition attaching to this place is that when Adam and Eve were cast out of Paradise, Adam fell on the island of Ceylon, and Eve near Jeddo, the port of Mekka. After a separation of two hundred years, Adam, having repented, was conducted by the angel Gabriel to a mountain near Mekka, where he found and knew his wife, the place being thence called 'Arafat' (recognition). Among the devices of Kossay to increase the honour paid to the guardians of the sacred territory, was the division of the pilgrims into two classes—the *Homsites*, or 'the Strong,' which included the Kuraish, their nearest relatives, and the tribes in alliance with them, and the *Hilla*, or 'the Unholy.' The first class did not visit Arafat, but only led the march as far as the limits of the sacred territory. The Homsites, moreover, unlike the Hilla, were not permitted during the ceremonies to reside under tents; they called themselves the 'house dwellers,' to signify that they were the permanent guardians of the sacred territory in contradistinction to those who had merely the privilege of visiting it. Muhammad put an end to these distinctions. He visited Arafat, although a citizen of Mekka; a tent stood ready for his reception, and he declared this part of the pilgrimage to be obligatory on all. He caused the ground to be marked out, and a fixed encamping ground to be allotted to each tribe.

At midday he delivered a discourse, in which he expounded the rites and duties required of a pilgrim, and impressed upon his hearers the absolute obligation laid upon the Faithful to accomplish the pilgrimage. Then he proceeded to warn them of the guilt of shedding Muhammadan blood, of dishonest trading, and more especially of the sin of usury. He quoted those verses from the Koran wherein this practice is denounced and forbidden. From usury he passed on to the duties which a man owes to his wife; to the laws laid down in the Koran respecting divorce, dowry, inheritance, infidelity to the marriage vows, and the prohibited degrees of relationship; and so, passing from one subject to another, he dwelt upon, expounded, and enforced all the laws of Islam, moral and ceremonial. Then the midday prayer was repeated, and the tribes dismissed to their encampments.

After sundown, Muhammad mounted his camel and rode to Mozdalifa, a halting place on the way back to Mina. He arrived there at the time of evening prayer. The traditions note down with loving accuracy the pace at which the Prophet rode—quickly, but not at a gallop. The next morning, at the same pace, he rode to Mina.

The tenth is the great day of the pilgrimage, and Muhammad gave out that whoever was in time for the morning prayer of that day must be regarded as having performed the entire pilgrimage. This day in the valley of Mina is the 'day of sacrifice,' in perpetual remembrance of the offering up of Ishmael as a sacrifice to God by his father Abraham. Three columns mark the spot where this occurred. Every pilgrim as he passes them flings seven small stones in that direction, in recollection of the stones hurled by the patriarch at Satan. On this day the victims are sacrificed. The Prophet immolated sixty-three camels—the number of the years of his life; his son-in-law Ali sacrificed thirty-seven. A portion of one camel was dressed for the Prophet and his household; the rest was distributed among the poorer pilgrims. Then such of the other pilgrims as had brought animals for sacrifice offered them up likewise, and the ceremonies of the pilgrimage were at an end.

The Prophet laid aside his *ihram*, shaved his head, put on his festive robes, and permitted Ayesha to incense him and anoint him with perfumes. He then rode to Mekka, made the seven circuits round the Kaaba, traversed seven times the distance between Safa and Marwa, and, without dismounting from his camel, returned to Mina. There he abode three days. They were days of feasting, and buying and selling. The only religious ceremony was the daily casting of the seven small stones. On the third day Muhammad rode back to Mekka, and on the next departed for Medina. 'The Pilgrimage of Farewell' was over.

Of the three months which elapsed between this pilgrimage and the breaking out of the fever which carried off the Prophet, the Muhammadan chroniclers tell us little. On Monday, May 25, 632, Muhammad delivered a discourse in the mosque at Medina, and warned the Faithful to prepare for an expedition against the Greeks. On the next day he sent for Osama, the son of his freedman Zaid, who had fallen in the disastrous battle of Mouta, and said to him: 'I appoint you leader of the army that is collecting; go to that quarter where your father fell in battle, but with such swiftness that you may take the dwellers by surprise. Burn their houses, their fields, and their palm-groves.' On the same day, at midnight, he went to the graveyard of the Faithful, and prayed for the blessing of Heaven on the members of this expedition. When his prayers were finished, he turned to a friend who had accompanied him—'To-night,' he said, 'the choice has been given to me of the treasures of this world or of the joys of Paradise; I have chosen the latter.' He returned to the hut of Ayesha and complained of a severe headache. From this time his sickness steadily increased upon him. In a few days he was unable (as had been his wont) to divide his time equally among his wives, but resided altogether in the house of Ayesha. The fever became so intense that the heat was perceptible through his clothes. He was extremely distressed in mind and body. His wives even reproached him with his want of fortitude and resignation. 'Do you not know,' he replied, 'that none have suffered so much as the prophets. Some have been devoured by insects; others have perished in such wretchedness that they had not a rag to cover their nakedness; but their reward has been so much the greater in the world to come.' To quench the burning of the fever his friends poured cold water upon his head from seven vessels at once. The immediate effect was refreshing, and he was able to go to the mosque and mount the pulpit. His first words were a prayer for those who had fallen at Bedr, at Ohod, at Mouta, and the other battle-fields. He then exhorted the soldiers of the Syrian expedition to be faithful and obedient to their commander. 'Whoever grieves him,' he said, 'grieves his father; and a braver soldier than he there was not among the Faithful.' But these exertions so exhausted him that on his return to Ayesha's hut he fell into a swoon.

On June 4 his illness reached its height. He asked for writing materials to execute a testament, but for some unknown reason his request was not complied with. He gave orders that after his death his corpse should be washed by his relatives, folded up in an Egyptian or Yemen shroud, and laid again upon the bed in which he had died. Then they were to leave it for a short space, when the angels would pray for him.

On June 6 he fell into a long swoon. His wives dropped into his mouth a preparation of olive-oil, Indian aloes, and saffron, to recover him. On coming to himself, he was very angry, as this preparation was supposed to possess magical properties, and to be in use among those who sold themselves to the Devil. His wives, to reassure him, took each a few drops of the liquid to show that there was nothing noxious in it. When the time for evening prayer came, he was too weak to go to the mosque, and he directed Abou Bekr to officiate in his stead, thereby, it is supposed, intending to indicate that he was to be his successor as the leader of the Faithful. On the next day, or the day after that (the exact date is uncertain), the Prophet ceased to breathe. He expired in the arms of Ayesha. His last words were—'To the worthiest companions in Paradise!'

There are two points of view from which we may estimate the character of Muhammad—we may regard him both as a successful Bedouin chief, and as the founder of a new religion. As the former the qualities must be without cavil conceded to him which have belonged to Sivajee, to Hyder Ali, and to every successful adventurer. He had a quick eye to perceive the elements of weakness in the conditions of life around him, and was prompt and dexterous in turning them to account. He had the power of attaching his followers to himself, and in the carrying out of his designs he knew when to be clement, and was rarely more ruthless or less scrupulous than his countrymen. But as a successful Bedouin chief, Muhammad is a character of small significance. His difficulties were smaller and his achievements less than many another Oriental adventurer who has figured in history. It is as the founder of a creed that Muhammad becomes a figure of world-wide significance, demanding and needing careful examination. As such he has been fiercely attacked, and of late years has been eulogised with almost equal extravagance. Of the sincerity of his belief in his own mission there can be no doubt. The great merit is his that among a people given up to idolatry he rose to a vivid perception of the Unity of God, and preached this great doctrine with firmness and constancy, amid ridicule and persecution. But there it seems to me that the eulogy of the Prophet ought to cease. When tried by the test of prosperity, his character lost its moral grandeur, his creed its spiritual elevation. At Medina, the religious teacher is superseded by the ambitious politician, and the idols of the Kaaba fall before the mandate of the successful chieftain, not under the transforming influences of a spiritual regenerator. To achieve worldly dominion, he has recourse to assassination; he perpetrates massacre; he makes a heathen superstition the keystone of his faith; and delivers to his followers, as a revelation from God, a mandate of universal war. With every advance in worldly power he disencumbers himself of that spiritual humility which was a part of his earlier faith. He associates himself with God on a footing approaching to equality. The angels, he declares, pray for blessings on the head of the Prophet. Disobedience to the Prophet is punished by hell-fire precisely as is disobedience to God. The names of God and his Apostle are linked together as those of beings who have equal claims upon the love and submission of men. The Apostle becomes a creature so exalted that even the easy drapery of Muhammadan morality becomes a garment too tight-fitting for him. 'A peculiar privilege is granted to him above the rest of believers.' He may multiply his wives without stint; he may and he does marry within the prohibited degrees.

It is often asserted that the legislation of the Koran by restricting polygamy did much to improve the condition of women. The supposition is erroneous. Muhammad limited the number of wives whom a Moslem might have *at one time* to four, but he applied no restrictions to the power of divorce belonging to the husband.

That was absolute. It never seems to have entered the mind of the Prophet that it could or ought to be subjected to rules. And the best commentary on the marriage laws of the Koran is the fact that his grandson Hasan contrived, by means of this power of divorce, to have seventy wives, or, according to some authors, ninety. In one particular only did Muhammad rise above the ethical level of his countrymen—he stamped out the crime of female infanticide. But in all else he was the Bedouin Arab, and in this fact lies the secret of his success. The predominant characteristics of the ancient Arab were an almost inconceivable vain-glory and self-conceit. He was never weary of contemplating and boasting of his own perfections. Muhammad was precisely the Prophet to win such a race. The Arab gloried in his language; Muhammad declared that it was a Divine language—the decrees of God had been written in it from all eternity. The Arab gloried in the traditional practices and customs of the desert—murder, predatory war, slavery, polygamy, concubinage. Muhammad impressed upon all these usages the seal of a Divine sanction. The Arab gloried in the holiness of Mekka. Muhammad affirmed it to be the single portal whereby men could enter into Paradise. In a word, he took the Arab people just as he found them, and declared all that they did to be very good and sacred from change. The fancied revelation gratified the vanity of the Arabs, but it pronounced on them a sentence of perpetual barbarism. Such as they were when the Prophet lived such are the Arabs now. Their condition is a proof that Islam is incapable of elevating a people to a higher level.

When Islam penetrates to countries lower in the scale of humanity than were the Arabs of Muhammad's day, it suffices to elevate them to that level. But it does so at a tremendous cost. It reproduces in its new converts the characteristics of its first—their impenetrable self-esteem, their unintelligent scorn, and blind hatred of all other creeds. And thus the capacity for all further advance is destroyed; the mind is obdurately shut to the entrance of any purer light. But it is a grievous error to confound that transient gleam of culture which illuminated Baghdad under the first Abbaside khalifs with the legitimate fruits of Islam. When the Arabs conquered Syria and Persia they brought with them no new knowledge to take the place of that which had preceded them. Mere Bedouins of the desert, they found themselves all at once the masters of vast countries with everything to learn. They were compelled to put themselves to school under the very people they had vanquished. Thus the Persians and Syrians, conquered though they were and tributary, from the ignorance of their masters, retained in their hands the control of the administrative machinery. The Abbaside khalifs were borne into power by means of a Persian revolution, headed by a Persian slave. Then began the endeavour to root the old Greek philosophy and the deep and beautiful thoughts of Zoroaster on the hard and barren soil of Muhammadanism. It was an impossible attempt to make a frail exotic flourish on uncongenial soil. It has imparted, indeed, a deceptive lustre to this period of Muhammadan history; but the orthodox Muhammadans knew that their faith and the wisdom of the Greeks could not amalgamate, and they fought fiercely against the innovators. Successive storms of barbarians sweeping down from the north of Asia tore up the fragile plant by the roots and scattered its blossoms to the winds. The new comers embraced the creed of the Koran in its primitive simplicity; they hated and repudiated the refinements which the Persians would fain have engrafted on it. And they won the day. The present condition of Central Asia is the legitimate fruit of Islam;—not the glories of Baghdad, which were but the afterglow of the thought and culture which sank with the fall of the Sassanides, and the expulsion of the Byzantine emperors. So also in Moorish Spain. The blossom and the fruitage which Muhammadanism seemed to put forth there, were in fact due to influences alien to Islam—to the intimate contact, namely, with Jewish and Christian thought; for when the Moors were driven back into Northern Africa, all that blossom and fruitage withered away, and Northern Africa sank into the intellectual darkness and political anarchy in which it lies at the present time. There are to be found in Muhammadan history all the elements of greatness—faith, courage, endurance, self-sacrifice. But enclosed within the narrow walls of a rude theology, and a barbarous polity, from which the capacity to grow and the liberty to modify have been sternly cut off, they work no deliverance upon the earth. They are strong only for destruction. When that work is over, they either prey upon each other, or beat themselves to death against the bars of their prison house. No permanent dwelling-place can be erected on a foundation of sand; and no durable or humanising polity upon a foundation of fatalism, despotism, polygamy and slavery. When Muhammadan States cease to be racked by revolutions, they succumb to the poison diffused by a corrupt moral atmosphere. A Durwesh, ejaculating 'Allah!' and revolving in a series of rapid gyrations until he drops senseless, is an exact image of the course of their history.

CHAPTER IV.

ALI AND HIS SONS.

A.D. 632—680.

Arabia, previously to the preaching of Islam, was not the home of a nation, but of a number of tribes, some stationary, some nomadic, and engaged in endless feuds among themselves. The political ability of the Prophet imposed upon these restless atoms the uniting influence of a common allegiance. But the period of a single man's life was too brief to allow the creed of Muhammad to root itself firmly in the mind of the Arab. The Arab, Mr. Gifford Palgrave tells us, is a believing animal rather than a religious one. He was not less so in the days of the Prophet. Gifted with an eager and vivid imagination, the universe of eye and ear which stretched around filled him with all 'the blank misgivings of a creature moving about in worlds not realised.' He heard voices other than human breaking the deep silence of the desert; forms beautiful to behold flashed across his eyes as he urged his camel over trackless wastes of sand; the supernatural was continually breaking into and commingling with the natural. Hence he gave an easy credence to any message which purported to come from the unseen world. There was nothing, to his mind, hard to believe in the fact of a Prophet having been sent by God into the world. But the very facility with which he conceded the demands of Muhammad had the effect of rendering him equally credulous of the pretensions of other prophets. No less than five prophets, two of whom were women, appeared in Arabia either before or immediately after the death of Muhammad. His death became the signal for a general revolt of the tribes whom his personal influence had hitherto held together. The new prophets relaxed some of the more stringent rules of Islam—the morning and evening prayer, the fast during the month Ramadhan, and the legal alms. These concessions were sufficient to win over the Bedouins, or Arabs of the desert—'most stout in unbelief and dissimulation'—as the Prophet had called them in the bitterness of his heart. They flocked round the new teachers. One tribe after another repudiated the creed of Muhammad. Islam, says the *Tareek-i-Tabari*, ceased to exist beyond the confines of Medina.

Even to that holy city the spirit of schism had penetrated. The people of Medina, on the ground that their city had given an asylum to the Prophet when his own had cast him out, asserted their right to elect a leader for themselves, Muhammad having died without nominating a successor. The men of Mekka might exercise a similar privilege if they pleased. 'Let each of the two great cities of Islam,' they said, 'have its own spiritual head.' It is needless to say that had the chiefs of Mekka accepted this suggestion, Islam would never have emerged from the deserts of Arabia to conquer the world. Mekka and Medina would have wrestled in endless conflict, to the extinction of the new faith altogether. The promptitude and resolution of Omar warded off the impending calamity. The Faithful of both Mekka and Medina were partly persuaded, partly compelled by him to acknowledge Abou Bekr as the khalif, or lieutenant, of the Prophet. One of the false prophets was murdered; the others fell before the fierce valour of Khaled; and then commenced that astonishing career of conquest which quenched for a time all remembrance of domestic feuds. The warriors of the Arabian deserts, bred in the midst of danger and hardship till their hearts were like steel and their muscles as iron, poured across the northern sandy waste to the conquest of Syria and Palestine. A few sieges, a few fierce battles, and these provinces were torn from the grasp of the Byzantine emperor. The ancient dynasty of the Sassanides was crushed on the field of Kadesia. In less than three years the Arabs were masters of Egypt. And still the tide of conquest flowed on with unabated speed. Eastward, the deserts of Sind, and northward the rocky defiles of Armenia, and the deep umbrageous forests of Azerbaizan, echoed with the victorious battle-cry of the Faithful. Nor were signs wanting of supernatural aid in these astonishing successes; angels fought on their side in the field of battle; messages from Heaven came to them in seasons of peril and extreme difficulty.

The Faithful looked back with wonder-smitten hearts over the few years which had passed since their Prophet abandoned Mekka—a homeless fugitive. It was all a marvellous period of predictions fulfilled. And that last and greatest prophecy, that the Faithful should possess the kingdoms of the earth and all the glory of them—that a thousand should cause two thousand to fly—what a speedy, what a marvellous confirmation had this, too, received! The new faith had been tried in a furnace seven times heated, and proved to be a weapon of surpassing sharpness and temper. It had not only shown itself stronger than every other Arab creed; but—north, south, east, and west—it had gone forth, and every foe the Faithful had encountered had gone down before their battle cry of 'God and His prophet.' This was just the demonstration calculated to convince the consciences of a people who confessed no principle of arbitration but that of force—whose god was an arbitrary Force issuing decrees to men. The Arab pretenders who had dared to set themselves up in opposition to the Prophet were swept utterly out of the remembrance of men. Jews, Christians, and Fire-worshippers, it was evident, had been created by the Merciful and the Compassionate to be the bondmen and the tributaries of the Faithful. The grain of mustard seed had become a majestic tree; the hills were covered with the shadow of it, and the boughs were like the goodly cedar trees. Henceforth, in consequence, there was no question of the verity of Islam, nor of the crushing power that dwelt in the confession of the Unity. But stronger to divide and rend asunder than the new creed was to unite, were the old deep-rooted and long-enduring family jealousies of the Arabs, the old tribal feuds which had been stilled for the time only by the brilliant prospect of plundering a world. The moment the tide of conquest was stayed they reasserted themselves in all their pristine vigour.

The posterity of the great Kossay had divided into

two branches, known from their progenitors as the Hashimites and the Ommayas. Many years before the birth of the Prophet, a quarrel had broken out between Hashim and Ommaya, which had resulted in the expulsion of the latter from Mekka. The feeling of unity which binds an Arab family together is hard for our Western minds to realise. Time is powerless to lessen its intensity. The loves and hatreds, the passions and emulations which coloured the lives of its first progenitors, are wrought, as it were, into the texture of the lives of all succeeding generations. Their hearts thrill with pleasure or pain over the old themes; their swords are ever ready to shed blood in the old long-past quarrels; and thus the recollection of the feud between Hashim and Ommaya had never ceased to rankle in the minds of their descendants. They had always remained bitter enemies. The Prophet was a lineal descendant of Hashim; and his ablest and most active enemy in Mekka had been Abou Sofyan, the grandson of Ommaya. Abou Sofyan had commanded the Kuraish at the battle of Ohod; it was owing to his personal exertions that the great army of the Confederates had been formed which besieged Medina for a fortnight; and he had even attempted to procure the murder of the Prophet. Muhammad, on his side, deemed him an enemy so formidable that he sent an emissary to Mekka to poison him; but the attempt was unsuccessful. Not less execrable to the devout Moslem was Hind, the wife of Abou Sofyan. Her father, her uncle, and her brother had fallen at the battle of Bedr, beneath the swords of Ali, the nephew, and Hamza, the uncle of the Prophet. Hind swore to be revenged. There was at Mekka an Abyssinian slave, named Wahshi, a very brave and able warrior, and skilled in the use of the javelin, after the manner of the Abyssinians. On the march to Ohod, Hind, who accompanied the Kuraishite army, promised Wahshi that if he slew Hamza she would give him all the jewels on her person. Wahshi bided his time, and in the thick of the battle transfixed Hamza with his javelin, flung from behind a rock. Hind, in savage glee, tore off her earrings and her bracelets, and flung them to the Abyssinian slave. But her thirst for revenge was not satiated by the simple death of her enemy; and when the field was won she caused the bodies of the fallen Moslems to be savagely mutilated; she made a necklace of their ears and noses; and the corpse of Hamza she caused to be cut open, and, tearing out the heart, rent it with her teeth.

Such acts it was hard to forgive; and when the Prophet made his triumphant march to Mekka he excluded both Abou Sofyan and his wife from the amnesty granted to the Kuraish. They were doomed to death. But on the day before the entry of the Prophet into the Holy City, Abou Sofyan entered the Moslem camp under the safe conduct of Abbas, the uncle of the Prophet, and professed his faith in the mission of Muhammad. This the Prophet accepted, and pardoned him and his wife. He knew he could count upon the submission of the Kuraish when their leading man had taken the oath of allegiance, while he understood his countrymen too well not to be aware that the blood of Abou Sofyan would create a spirit of division and a thirst for revenge which the new creed was impotent to remove or satisfy.

On their side the conversion of Abou Sofyan, his

relatives and friends, had been simply an act of necessity. They had resisted the new creed as long as they could; they accepted it when the alternative of submission or death was no longer to be evaded. How utterly their hearts were estranged from the words which they constrained their lips to utter was exhibited a few weeks after the capture of Mekka. A contingent of the Kuraish, under command of Abou Sofyan, accompanied the Muhammadan army, and was present at the battle of Honain. In this engagement the Faithful were at first driven back in utter confusion, and the men of Mekka could not refrain from loud expressions of delight at the spectacle of their overthrow. The Prophet, however, closed his eyes to what he did not wish to see. If his doctrines were incapable of penetrating their stubborn hearts, he trusted that the hopes of plunder to be gained under his banner would mollify the rocky soil, and so prepare it for the reception of Islam. Hence he allotted a portion of the booty acquired, not merely as though the men of Mekka had fought with the same single-minded devotion as the converts of an earlier day, but in such excess that his unjust profusion well-nigh caused a mutiny among the *Ansars* of Medina. They were with difficulty restrained from deserting the standard of the Prophet, and returning in a body to their homes. This open rupture was, it is true, averted, but the seeds of party divisions were then sown, to spring up a plentiful harvest hereafter. On the one side were ranged the 'companions of the Prophet' and the people of Medina; on the other the descendants of Ommaya and the Kuraish. During the reigns of Abou Bekr and Omar, the commanding character of the latter—who so long as he lived was the supreme spirit in Islam—held the spirit of internal feud in stern check. But with the accession of the third khalif, Othman ibn Affan, commenced a period of decline. He had been one of the first converts to Islam, and the only member of the family of Ommaya who had voluntarily become a follower of Muhammad. He was a man of gentle and amiable character, affectionate and liberal to excess, but weak in will, and under the dominion of favourites. Under his rule the companions of the Prophet and the great soldiers who had won distinction on the path of God under his two predecessors, were one by one removed from the places of trust and command which were then bestowed upon members of his own family. The khalif Omar had greatly feared lest the contact with Persian luxury should soften the iron hearts of the soldiers of God, and had attempted to enforce upon all governors of provinces and officials in high position the same austere simplicity of life which he practised himself. Despite his endeavours, however, even during his reign, the rulers of the more distant provinces had degenerated considerably from the rude life of the desert. They had become infected more or less with 'Khosroism,' as the Arabs termed it, after the official designation of the Persian monarchs. Under the feebler sway of Othman, these tendencies developed unrestrained. The khalif himself led the way. He built for himself a magnificent palace of vast extent at Medina, and many of the companions of the Prophet imitated his example. They had not only large sums of money stored up in these palaces, and hundreds of slaves, but were rich in flocks and herds, and troops of camels, and farms and springs. All this wealth had been acquired in actual war—the plunder of rich temples, the spoils of the palaces of emperors, kings, and nobles. It was, as we should say, stored-up capital lying idle, and its appropriation by the invading Arabs had inflicted little, if any, distress on the great mass of the population of those countries where it had been seized. Such hoards were no longer in existence when the House of Ommaya entered into the possession of power; but they brought with them an equally earnest desire to become rich at the cost of those they had been appointed to rule. One of them, indeed, to the profound disgust of the Faithful, had been heard to say in his insolent fashion that the hard-won conquests of Islam were a garden for the exclusive use and profit of this one family.

Othman, as if bent upon self-destruction, chose for his most lavish favours the men whose antecedents were the most distasteful to the Faithful. Muawia, the son of Abou Sofyan, ruled Syria and Palestine as an independent sovereign in all but name. Merwan ibn Hakem, who had been banished by the Prophet himself from Mekka and Medina, was recalled by Othman and installed as his chief favourite and confidential adviser. Abd Allah ibn Abou Serh—a man who having once been the secretary of the Prophet and employed in writing his revelations while at Medina, had apostatised, and, returning to Mekka, relapsed into idolatry—was selected by Othman to be governor of Egypt. Walid ibn Okbah, whose ultimate damnation had been authoritatively pronounced by the Prophet, was entrusted with the government of Koufa, where he conducted himself in a manner that scandalised the Faithful. He appeared in the mosque at the time of morning prayer, helpless, from intoxication, falling prostrate on the ground as he attempted to perform the duties of an Imam, or leader of the prayer; and when the bystanders hurried up to assist him to his feet, shocked them by demanding more wine, in a husky and stammering voice. He was also accused of having brought into the great mosque, at a time when the Faithful were assembled there, a Jewish magician, who performed a number of profane miracles, such as cutting off the head of a bystander and putting it on again without apparent injury to the person operated upon; producing the phantom of a gigantic donkey, down the throat of which he disappeared, to emerge again at the tail before the astonished eyes of the spectators. A Moslem who stood by, transported with indignation at this manifestation of satanic power, drew his sword and slew the sorcerer on the spot; whereupon Walid caused this eminently devout and zealous follower of the Prophet to be put to death as a murderer.

Such were the men whom Othman ibn Affan selected as his advisers and lieutenants. They fastened upon their provinces like famished leeches, heaping up wealth by means of pitiless extortion. Complaints came flowing in to Medina from all parts of Islam. But Othman was in the hands of certain favourites, who led him as they pleased, and the complainants were dismissed with no reply but hard words. The orthodoxy of Othman himself was deeply suspected. He had, it is true, done one thing which procured for him the unqualified applause of the Faithful. This was the destruction of the *Ghoumdân*, a superb palace in Yemen, which was supposed to be without equal in the world. Some of the Faithful who had visited it pronounced it to be superior in magnificence to the temple at Mekka. Othman accordingly destroyed it, to the great satisfaction of all true believers; and there is no Arabic chronicle in which stress is not laid upon the exceedingly meritorious character of this proceeding. But the khalif had also ventured upon an innovation in the ceremonies of the pilgrimage which awakened a profound fear and suspicion in the minds of the Faithful. In the recitation of a certain prayer, the Prophet, the khalifs Abou Bekr and Omar, had made only two prostrations. To the utter consternation of the orthodox world, the khalif Othman made four. This alarming piece of heresy filled the cup of discontent till it overflowed. The companions of the Prophet and the doctors of the law waited in a body upon the khalif. They bade him remember that they had taken the oath of allegiance to him on the understanding that he would walk rigorously in the footsteps of the Prophet and the two first khalifs. Four prostrations in place of two might in itself be a small matter, but it was the introduction of the thin end of the wedge; if the smallest departure were permitted from the practices of the primitive church, it was impossible to foresee whither the spirit of innovation would lead the generations who came after them. Any perseverance, therefore, in these practices would result in the deposition of Othman as one who had fallen away from the right path.

While Othman thus alienated from him the companions of the Prophet, the exactions of his lieutenants engendered a spirit of bitter wrath in the provinces. A wide-spread conspiracy was formed, including within its meshes the province of Egypt and the cities of Koufa and Basra. From these three quarters some twelve thousand men converged simultaneously upon Medina to lay their griefs before the khalif, and, in the event of a repulse, to slay him. Their numbers were greatly swelled by the disaffected of that city. Muhammad, a son of the khalif Abou Bekr, placed himself at their head. At this crisis Othman had recourse to the intervention of Ali, whose advice he had hitherto consistently set at nought. Ali induced the conspirators to return to their homes by giving them a pledge that their grievances should be redressed, but on their way back the Egyptians intercepted a slave bearing a missive to the governor of Egypt, written in the handwriting of Merwan ibn Hakem, and stamped with the seal of the khalif, which ordered that officer either to put them all to death, or, by cutting oft their hands and feet, to deprive them of the power again to come to Medina and pester the khalif with their grievances.

In high wrath the conspirators returned upon their footsteps. Expresses were sent off to overtake the parties who were returning to Koufa and Basra, to inform them of the treachery of the khalif, and summon them back to Medina. The whole of the twelve thousand were speedily re-encamped in the vicinity of the city. Othman, when he heard of the discovery which had caused their return, denied all knowledge of the letter, and refused to give up Merwan ibn Hakem, as the conspirators demanded. Ali declined to be again the intercessor between the khalif and his angry subjects. He considered that the intercepted letter showed that Othman did not scruple to fasten upon Ali the reproach of being false to his word, in order to maintain in their posts his favourites of the House of Ommaya, and rid himself from the clamours of those whom they oppressed. The other companions of the Prophet held aloof in sullen indifference. Othman, in despair, sent off expresses to Syria, to Egypt, to Irak, summoning the lieutenants of those provinces to march with all speed to his assistance. The conspirators felt that they must act promptly if they did not desire to be destroyed. They stormed the palace of the khalif. Muhammad, the son of Abou Bekr, was the first to enter the apartment where the aged khalif sat, reading the Koran. He had a dagger in one hand, and, seizing the old man by the beard, he cried: 'Son of Affan! what help to you now are Abdallah, the apostate; Merwan, the banished; and Muawia the accursed?' He was about to strike, when the khalif, fixing on him a calm, reproachful eye, replied: 'My son, if thy father Abou Bekr were alive, he would not be pleased to see my white beard in thy hand.' The young man, struck with sudden remorse, released the khalif and went out. The other conspirators were checked by no such tender recollections. The khalif fell beneath their knives and swords; his life-blood poured over the Koran he read, and dyed this verse—'Verily, God is sufficient for you; He understands and knows all.' One of his wives, who was near him when he fell, had her hand cut off by a chance blow in the confusion. The conspirators refused to permit the murdered man to be buried in the graveyard of the Faithful, and a tomb was dug for him in the ancient cemetery of the Jews.

Troops from Syria, Egypt, and Irak were only three days' march from Medina when they received the intelligence of the murder of Othman. They turned back at once, and Ali, the cousin and son-in-law of the Prophet, received the homage of the people of Medina as the spiritual head of Islam.

Ali is the Bayard of Islam—a soldier without fear and without reproach. But he lacked the qualities of a statesman, and these were the qualities he needed most sorely at the moment of his accession. The provinces were in the possession of his hereditary enemies, the House of Ommaya. These governors hated him as the head of the Hashimites, as well as the chief of a party which desired to expel them from office. Some of the friends of Ali earnestly counselled him to pursue a temporising policy with these provincial governors. They were, it was urged, worldly-minded men, and provided they continued to receive the emoluments of office, would not hesitate to transfer their allegiance from Othman to Ali. When Ali was secure in his seat, when his authority was established and confirmed, he might then remove them without danger to himself or the public peace. But there was too much of the wisdom of the serpent in this advice to commend it to the simple rectitude of Ali. The iniquities of these governors had, he said, been the cause of the death of his predecessor; how could he then, as a just ruler, retain them in their posts? So the decree went forth from Medina deposing them one and all. But the family of Ommaya was headed by a man too powerful, able, and unscrupulous to submit tamely to a decree of deposition. This was Muawia, the son of Abou Sofyan, and the governor of Syria.

He was the ablest man of his time, a skilful general and an astute politician. Courteous and accessible to all, thoroughly understanding the persuasive power of liberality, and gifted with eloquence and wit, he had attached his Syrian Arabs to his person with a truly remarkable enthusiasm. The ignorance of these Syrian Moslems regarding the creed they professed is a kind of standing joke with Muhammadan historians and divines. Some of them thought Muhammad himself to be God; others that Ali was a brigand who had risen to power in those disturbed times. But accuracy on such trifling matters they cared not for. It was sufficient for them to know that their beloved governor demanded their aid against an enemy. Their swords and their lives were at his disposal. Muawia knew he could reckon upon their unquestioning obedience. He accordingly denounced Ali as the murderer of Othman, and declared that he would not rest until he had avenged the blood of the slaughtered khalif. A slave of Othman had escaped to Damascus, bearing with him the bloody shirt of his master, and the hand of his wife, which had been cut off. Every Friday, when the people were assembled for prayer, the shirt and the hand were exhibited to their gaze. The whole assembly sobbed and wept at the harrowing spectacle. Thirty thousand of the bravest warriors in Syria bound themselves by an oath to drink no fresh water nor wash their bodies until they had avenged the murder of Othman. A messenger was sent to Medina to communicate this resolve to Ali. He obtained a guarantee of security before he dared to deliver his message. 'Thirty thousand men,' he then said, 'are assembled round the shirt of Othman, whose cheeks and whose beards have never been dry from tears, and whose eyes have never ceased from weeping blood since the hour of that prince's atrocious murder. They have drawn their swords with a solemn pledge never to return them to the scabbard, nor cease from mourning until they have extirpated all concerned in that detested action. This sentiment they have left as a solemn bequest to their descendants; and the earliest principle that mothers instil into the minds of their infants is to revenge the blood of Othman to the last extremity.'

Ali's peculiar position gave a plausibility to the charge made against him. He had been elected the Iman of Islam on the very spot where his predecessor had been murdered, and his sworn adherents were the men who had either actively participated in that murder, or by their apathy had virtually connived at it. When, therefore, Muawia and his party demanded that Ali should demonstrate his innocence from the crime of shedding the blood of the lieutenant of God by the prompt punishment of those who were undoubtedly guilty of it, they knew they demanded that which it was impossible for Ali to execute, but which, none the less, would fasten upon him the suspicion at least of the guilt with which they charged him. Nothing could be fairer, on the surface, than the demands of Muawia. 'Punish the murderers of Othman, and we lower the flag of rebellion and acknowledge your authority.' Only in withholding his allegiance until that punishment was inflicted, no one knew better than Muawia that he required an impossibility. This dexterous policy, however, had not merely the effect of throwing a cloud over the fair fame of Ali, but of attaching to the cause of Muawia a man, without whose cunning and fertility of resource his machinations would not, in all probability, have terminated in success. This was Amrou ibn Al-As, the conqueror of Egypt. He had been deprived of the governorship of that province by Othman, and had laboured assiduously, but in secret, to embitter the conspirators against the khalif. In so doing he was actuated partly by a desire for revenge, but more so by simple ambition. His was a character which rejoiced in troublous times, as giving freer scope and employment for his abilities; and he doubted not that the troubles which would certainly follow upon the murder of Othman would give his restless spirit the occupation he pined for in vain, in his compulsory inaction at Medina. He had hesitated for a while which side to espouse, but it did not require much time to convince him that the tortuous paths in which he delighted to tread were alien to the simple and candid mind of Ali. When intelligence reached him of the effect Muawia was producing in Damascus by his exhibition of the bloody shirt of Othman, Amrou broke out in an exclamation of delight, as of one who recognised a kindred spirit, and repaired to Syria without loss of time. Between these two arch-conspirators there was no attempt to conceal the real character of their cause, under a veil of specious pretences. Amrou said, candidly enough, that in espousing the cause of Muawia in preference to that of Ali, he had chosen the good of this world rather than the rewards of the next, and that he must be paid accordingly. He demanded the government of Egypt in perpetuity, with the revenues of that rich province entirely at his disposal. Muawia joyfully acceded to these terms.

But a nearer and more pressing danger confronted Ali than even the storm which had gathered in Syria. Ayesha, the favourite wife of the Prophet, resided in Mekka. She had long cherished a hatred of Ali. Years before, during the lifetime of the Prophet, the gossip of Medina had connected, in a scandalous manner, the name of Ayesha with that of a handsome young Muhammadan called Safwan. The Prophet himself had suspected his young wife, until assured of her innocence by the angel Gabriel. In his trouble he had asked Ali what he advised him to do. Ali, who was not in love with Ayesha, thought the matter a very trifling one. 'Apostle of God!' he is reported to have said, 'why distress yourself; there are many women in the world; if you suspect this one, divorce her, and choose another.' Ayesha never forgot or forgave these slighting words; and the present situation of Ali, with but few friends beside him, and girt by multitudes of enemies, seemed to open out the occasion for that revenge for which she had waited so long. She denounced him as the murderer of Othman, and declared it to be a duty on the part of the Faithful to refuse him obedience. Ayesha's hostility was a danger more formidable than the craft of Amrou and Muawia combined. As 'the Mother of the Faithful,' she occupied an unique position in the Muhammadan world. Her long and intimate relations with the Prophet were held to have given her a special understanding of the mind of Muhammad; she was the chief source whence the Doctors of the Law drew those 'sayings' of the Apostle of God which, under the title of 'Traditions,' are held of equal authority with the Koran itself; and her judgment upon all disputed questions was received everywhere with reverence, because her intellect had been formed and educated by years of intercourse with the Prophet.

Two of the most distinguished of the 'companions of the Prophet' allied themselves with her. These were Talha and Zobair. They had been amongst the first converts to Islam; and the Prophet had named them as predestined to enter Paradise. Talha was covered with wounds received at the battle of Ohod. 'Whosoever,' the Prophet had said, 'wishes to see a living martyr, let him look at Talha.' They had, both of them, fomented the angry feelings which led to the murder of Othman, in hope of the khalifate devolving upon themselves; and the bitterness of disappointed ambition now drove them into rebellion against their old friend and comrade. They were men of great wealth, and adventurers in consequence flocked readily to their standards. The triumvirate marched to Basra, and after some desultory fighting obtained possession of that city. Their army speedily swelled, according to the chroniclers, to 30,000 or 40,000 men.[1] But Ali, though deficient in political ability, was unequalled as a soldier. The men who had chosen him khalif were bound to his cause, not less by its justice than by the imperious instinct of self-preservation. They fought with their lives in their hands; and the defeat of

[1] I give numbers simply as I find them in the authorities; but I may as well say, once for all, that in Oriental histories statistics of every kind are simply worthless, especially those which have regard to the strength of armies in the field, and the killed and wounded in an engagement. They are exaggerated beyond the power of the most elastic credence to accept.

Ali involved their own immediate destruction. The city of Koufa, at this moment, also pronounced in his favour; and at the head of 30,000 men he marched rapidly against the insurgents, who had mustered their forces near Basra. Before engaging, he made a last attempt to persuade them to lay down their arms without affording to the infidels the delight of seeing Moslem shed the blood of Moslem. He chose as his envoy to carry this message of peace his cousin, Abdallah ibn Abbas. 'Do not,' he said, 'have an interview with Talha; for you will find him headstrong as the bull which twists up its nose; he will mount an unruly camel, and say it is perfectly broken; but meet Zubair, for he is of a more tractable disposition.' These negotiations were fruitless, and nothing now was left but to decide their quarrel by the dread arbitrament of the sword. In the terrible 'Battle of the Camel' (so called because Ayesha, in a litter, strapped on the back of a camel, was present during the engagement) 17,000 Arabs are said to have fallen; Talha and Zobair were both killed; and Ayesha became a prisoner in the hands of Ali. He treated her with the utmost forbearance and courtesy, and caused her to be escorted to Mekka. This signal victory made Ali the undisputed sovereign of Irak, Egypt, Arabia, Fars, and Khorasan.

The possession of Koufa and Basra did not, however, strengthen the cause of Ali so much as would appear at first sight. It rather weakened it. It swelled the numbers of his army, it is true, but it introduced into his ranks a number of theological fanatics, ever ready to quarrel on the dividing of a hair in matters of doctrine, and absolutely convinced of their own infallibility, and the everlasting damnation of everybody who differed, ever so slightly, in opinion from themselves. The type of character is a familiar one in Christendom, as well as in Islam. They fought for their creed, not for Ali; and the instant any divergence became apparent between that creed and the leader they had chosen, their swords turned against Ali, with as keen a desire for his heart's blood as for that of Muawia. And this, in the end, was what actually occurred.

Ali and Muawia met at Siffin, a broad plain extending along the banks of the Euphrates. The chronicler states that 80,000 men were ranged on either side. For more than a month fierce skirmishes were fought almost daily, until at length Ali forced on a general engagement. The Shia writers love to dwell upon the incidents of this great day, and have depicted with great minuteness the bearing and heroic acts of Ali. 'I saw,' Ibn Abbas is reported to have said, 'Ali before this day's battle; he was attired in a white turban; his eyes flashed like two jets of flame; he rode along the lines of the different tribes, exciting their ardour and their courage. "Moslems," he cried, "let your shouts strike despair in the hearts of the enemy; let your sabres dazzle their eyes, as they flash from their scabbards, and your looks freeze them with terror."' The action rapidly became general. The press was so close that the bows were flung away as useless, and men fought sabre to sabre. The sun gradually mounted to the zenith, and then gradually disappeared in the west, and still the conflict raged unceasingly. The clear stars of an Oriental sky shone all the night through upon the same stormy scene. The battle songs of the Arabs mingled with the crash of breaking lances and the noises of the battle. The morning sun rising, pierced the clouds of dust, and revealed the battlefield strewn thickly with the wounded and the dead. The times of prayer passed unheeded. Ali was to be seen wherever the battle was hottest. Every time he struck a blow he shouted, 'God is great;' and every blow he struck sent an infidel to Hell. Five hundred men are said to have fallen beneath his single sabre. 'Never,' said Muawia, as he watched the havoc he wrought in the ranks of his army, 'was there a man who crossed swords with Ali and returned alive from the encounter.'

The valour of Ali was brilliantly seconded by that of his favourite lieutenant—Malek al Ashtar—the Marshal Ney of the Arabian army. A tremendous charge of Malek at last forced a wing of the Syrian troops to give ground. Gradually the whole line was forced back; the retreat became a rout. Muawia, thinking all was lost, was mounting his horse to fly; when a device of Amrou destroyed the hopes of Ali at the very moment of success. He knew the fanatical character of the troops that followed Ali; and he ordered a number of Syrian soldiers to advance towards their line, bearing copies of the Koran fixed to the head of their lances. 'Let the blood of the Faithful cease to flow,' shouted the Koran bearers as they got within hearing; 'if the Syrian army be destroyed, who will defend the frontier against the Greeks? If the army of Irak be destroyed, who will defend the frontier against the Turks and Persians? Let the Book of God decide between us.' The effect was magical. The military theologians of Ali's army, though they loved fighting much, liked a theological disputation still better. Their swords dropped to their sides. 'God is great,' they shouted; 'we must all submit to the arbitrament of His Holy Book.' It was in vain for Ali to entreat and protest—to assure them that neither Amrou nor Muawia cared anything for the arbitrament of the Sacred Book, but only to deliver themselves from the jaws of death. His soldiers turned fiercely upon him, their drawn swords flashing in his face. 'If he did not,' they cried, 'recall Malek al Ashtar and stop the battle, they would inflict on him the punishment which had fallen upon Othman.'

Ali retired to his tent, with rage and despair in his heart, leaving the fanatics he commanded to make what terms they pleased. It was then arranged that the claims of Ali and Muawia should be submitted to the decision of two arbitrators—one to be chosen by each army. This arrangement was barely completed before a spirit of controversy took such violent possession of Ali's troops, and the lawfulness of this arbitration became the subject of such hot discussion, that he had to march in all haste to Koufa, in order to stay the controversialists from slaughtering each other in the presence of their Syrian antagonists. At Koufa 12,000 of his men declared him to be a heretic, and renounced their allegiance. They were those who had been most eager for arbitration, most clamorous for a suspension of hostilities, in order that the dispute might be argued out according to the principles laid down in the Koran. They now found that to do this was worthy of hell fire; that it was the business of the true Moslem to slay without mercy every one who advocated arbitration. But with the magnificent self-righteousness of religious bigotry, instead of turning their wrath upon themselves, they poured it upon the hapless Ali. They denounced him as one who had fallen into mortal sin, and incurred the penalty of hell fire. It was from an enervation of spirit engendered by misfortune that he had consented to submit to human arbitrators a cause which should have been submitted to the judgment of God alone upon a battle-field. Never would they march under the banner of such a heretic as this, or draw a sword in his defence. Not that Muawia, any more than Ali, was an Imam whom a true Moslem could recognise as such. They were both heretics; and it was lawful, and indeed obligatory, to slay them, if an occasion offered for doing so. For themselves, they would choose an Imam of their own, and declare war to the death against Ali. Ali, however, with that tender-hearted repugnance to shed the blood of men of his own creed which marked his career through life, forebore to attack them; and even succeeded in persuading them to await peacefully the issue of the arbitration. These men were the originators of the sect known as 'Kharegites,' or Separatists, of whose acts I shall have to give some account in a subsequent chapter.

The fortunes of Ali were doomed never to recover the blow given them at Siffin. The clouds gathered round him thicker and blacker; and his life, like a brief and bitter winter's day, went narrowing down and darkening to a close. The bigots who had compelled him to sheathe his sword at the moment of victory, forced upon him an arbitrator—a companion of the Prophet it is true—but a man vain, foolish and altogether incapable of coping with the astute and unscrupulous Amrou, who acted as the representative of Muawia. By a device of the latter, the representative of Ali was tricked into announcing solemnly the deposition of Ali, as his deliberate judgment. But the trickery was too manifest to deceive anyone, and Ali refused to accept the decision as valid. The war recommenced. The name of Muawia was regularly cursed on all occasions of public prayer from all the pulpits of Irak; the name of Ali from all the pulpits of Syria. But neither the ability nor the resources of Ali were equal to those of his rival. Invincible in battle, disinterested, merciful and generous, there must have been some radical weakness in the character of Ali which rendered him incapable of attaching his subjects to his person. The greater part of the 'companions of the Prophet,' with a foreboding of what would happen, abandoned him as rats do a sinking vessel, and took the oath of allegiance to his rival; the Kharegites broke into war against him; the people of Irak remained inert and apathetic to all his entreaties to march with him into Syria. The death of his brilliant lieutenant—Malek al Ashtar—cruelly poisoned by an emissary of Muawia, gave the mortal blow to his cause. Egypt, Mekka, and Medina were gradually occupied by Syrian troops, and administered in the name of Muawia. Ali, almost broken-hearted, withdrew into seclusion from the sight and commerce of men; and in the month of Ramadhan, A.H. 40, his sad and chequered life was brought to an end by the knife of a Kharegite assassin. With him perished the truest-hearted and best Moslem of whom Muhammadan history has preserved the remembrance.

Almost immediately after the death of his father,

Ali's eldest son, Hasan, made a formal renunciation of his claims, and took the oath of allegiance to Muawia. Muawia thus became the undisputed head of Islam. But anxious to bequeath the position to his son Yezid, he resolved to make away with Hasan; and nine years after the murder of his father, that unfortunate prince followed him to the grave. He died a victim to poison, administered by his wife at the instigation of Muawia, who persuaded her to the crime, by a promise that she should then become the wife of his son Yezid. On the woman claiming the fulfilment of this promise, he put her to death, as the murderess of the grandson of the Prophet.

Two years after the death of his brother, Ali's second son, Hosain, crowned the misfortunes of his family by a bloody death on the plain of Kerbela on the 10th day of Mohurrum, A.H. 61. This is the memorable 'Martyrdom of Hosain'—by reason of its consequences, the most important event in the history of the Muhammadan world, after the mission of the Prophet himself, and as such, requiring to be recorded in detail.

Ali had fallen in the city of Koufa. This place was the hotbed of Muhammadan bigotry. It was the favourite home of Koran readers, doctors of the law, disputants, and talkers of all kinds. The interpretation of the Koran, the rights of succession to the Imamate, all the multitudinous and bewildering refinements of Muhammadan theology, are in great measure due to the endless controversies of which Koufa was the theatre. The people breathed an atmosphere charged with religious fanaticism. Fierce gusts of theological controversy drove them this way and that, like a shifting gale which carries before it the sands of a desert. Eager, fierce, and impetuous, the people of Koufa were utterly wanting in perseverance and steadiness. They knew not their own minds from day to day. One moment ardent as fire for some cause or person, the next they were as cold as ice and indifferent as the dead. The fiercest conflicts that shook the Muhammadan world during these, the earliest, years of its history, raged round Koufa. The annals of that city are a series of narratives of causes taken up without calculation of consequences, and abandoned with the same thoughtless precipitation; of aspirants after power lured on by specious promises and then basely abandoned to their doom; of the people themselves rushing madly into excesses, to be savagely slaughtered back into a state of quiescence.

The crafty and able Muawia had died in the year 60, and was succeeded by his son Yezid. Before his succession, Yezid had deeply scandalised the Faithful. He drank wine openly; he was passionately fond of dogs, falcons, and other unclean animals. It was told of him that on one occasion intelligence was brought to him of the destruction of a Moslem army as he sat feasting with his friends. The young man turned indolently to a favourite slave girl, who reclined beside him, and chanted these verses:

What care I though death may have smitten our troops in the land of Roum,
When, softly reclined upon cushions, beside me is Omm Kolthoum.

Under this genial despot, a number of practices came into vogue which were utterly intolerable to the theologians of Koufa. The people of Damascus drank wine in the streets in humble imitation of their spiritual head. They, like him, passed their time with singing girls and musical professors. The sounds of musical instruments were constantly heard in the streets, and yet no one ever thought of stopping their ears, notwithstanding a highly authentic tradition which related that the Prophet did so when, on a certain occasion, he chanced to hear the profane sound of a shepherd's pipe. Finally, the votaries of other creeds, and the creeds themselves, were treated and spoken of by Yezid with a degree of indulgence hateful to the spirit which dictated the ninth Sura of the Koran, and which animated the people of Koufa. For this and other cogent reasons Koufa determined to revolt against Yezid.[1]

Hosain, the son of Ali, was residing at Mekka. He had refused to take the oath of allegiance to Yezid. A messenger was sent to him from Koufa, entreating him to

[1] Muhammadan historians represent Yezid as an Atheist; but the truth really is that he was a Sufi, who, believing in the presence of God everywhere throughout the universe, held that the rites and ceremonies whereby men acknowledged that presence were of very small importance. One way was as good as another. In Ibn Khallikan's 'Biographical Dictionary' there is preserved a fragment of his verses, couched in that mystical and allegorical strain whereby the Sufis were wont to express their yearning for unity with the Deity. It is important, as showing at what an early date the contact with Christian and Persian thought commenced to undermine the doctrines of the Koran. The passage runs as follows:—

'Separated from Laila, I longed for a glimpse of her figure, thinking that the flame which raged within my bosom would be calmed at her aspect; but the females of the tribe said: 'You hope to see the charms of Laila! die of the lingering malady of hope! How couldst thou look on Laila, whilst the eyes which you cast on other women are not yet purified by tears? How can you hope to enjoy her discourse since your ears have hearkened to the voice of strangers? O, Laila! thou art too noble to be seen! he only can see thee whose heart is humble and submissive.'

come to that city. The whole population, he was assured, were eager to espouse his cause, and pronounce the deposition of the Bani Ommaya. At first Hosain was distrustful of these advances, but such a number of invitations kept pouring in, with long lists of the chief men of the city, all of whom had taken a solemn oath to die in his defence, that he ultimately resolved to make the venture. His friends vainly counselled him not to do so. They urged that if the people of Koufa were so bitter against Yezid as they affirmed themselves to be, they could revolt without him being actually in their midst. When Hosain turned a deaf ear to these solicitations, they entreated him at least to go alone. But here also they failed. Hosain started on his perilous expedition, accompanied by all his wives, his brothers, and his children, and escorted by forty horsemen and 100 foot soldiers. Yezid, in the meanwhile, had received intelligence of what was intended, and taken measures accordingly. The governor of Basra—Obaidallah ibn Ziyad—was a man of stern resolution, and troubled with no theological sensitiveness. He was ordered to proceed in all haste to Koufa, hold that city in check, and at the same time send out a strong force to intercept Hosain. The alternative was to be given him of submission or death. These measures succeeded perfectly. Hosain had advanced by forced marches as far as the plain of Kerbela, when he found his route barred by a force of 3,000 men. The people of Koufa, forgetful of their promises—as cold now as they had been hot and devoted—stirred not hand nor foot to assist him. He was offered the alternative to yield himself up to

Obaidallah or die in battle. He chose the latter. 'We are,' he said to his followers, 'few in number, and the enemy is in force. I am resolved to die. But you—I release you from your oath of allegiance; let all those who wish to do so, leave me.' 'O! son of the Apostle of God!' was the reply; 'what excuse should we give to thy grandfather, on the day of Resurrection, did we abandon his son to the hands of his enemies? No; we have devoted our lives to you.' Before, however, the battle could join, Hourr ibn Yezid, an Arab of the tribe of Temim, spurred forth from the ranks of the enemy, and presented himself before Hosain, blessing him and the Prophet. 'Wherefore come you here?' asked the son of Ali. 'I come,' replied Hourr, 'to sacrifice my life for thee. I desire to fight to the death against thy enemies.' 'May God,' replied Hosain, 'grant to you a happy martyrdom; you will enter Paradise as a free man.'

Then the battle joined. One by one the little band that defended the grandson of the Prophet fell beneath the swords of the enemy. They had forbidden Hosain to draw sword or defend himself, until the last of them had fallen. There remained at last only Hosain and his five brothers. The five flung themselves in a body upon the enemy, were surrounded and cut down. Then the horse of Hosain fell to the earth, struck by an arrow. Hosain extricated himself. It was the hour of afternoon prayer. Tormented by thirst, the grandson of the Prophet sat down upon the ground without attempting to defend himself. Several of the enemy approached to kill him, but none dared to strike. They feared to have to answer on the day of Resurrection for the shedding of such sacred blood as his. Hosain had a child named Abdallah, only a year old. He had accompanied his father in this terrible march. Touched by its cries, he took the infant in his arms and wept. At that instant, a shaft from the hostile ranks pierced the child's ear, and it expired in his father's arms. Hosain placed the little corpse upon the ground. 'We come from God, and we return to Him!' he cried; 'O Lord, give me strength to bear these misfortunes!' Then, raising himself, he hastened towards the bank of the Euphrates to drink. Just as he stooped to touch the water, an arrow struck him in his mouth. He returned to his tent, the blood pouring from his lips. There his enemies rushed down upon him from all sides. Faint with thirst, and exhausted with wounds, he fought with desperate courage, slaying several of his antagonists. At last he was cut down from behind; at the same instant a lance was thrust through his back and bore him to the ground; as the dealer of this last blow withdrew his weapon, the ill-fated son of Ali rolled over a corpse. The head was severed from the trunk; the trunk was trampled under the hoofs of the victors' horses; and the next morning the women and a surviving infant son were carried away to Koufa. The bodies of Hosain and his followers were left unburied on the spot where they fell. For three days they remained exposed to the sun and the night dews, the vultures and the prowling animals of the waste; but then the inhabitants of a neighbouring village, struck with horror that the body of a grandson of the Prophet should be thus shamefully abandoned to the unclean beasts of the field, dared the anger of Obai dallah, and interred the body of the martyr and those of his heroic friends.

The great schism was now complete. The blood of the martyrs became the seed of a new Church. The body of Islam had been torn asunder, never again to be united; and 'the murdered Hosain' was henceforth a watchword of vengeance which again and again deluged with blood the empire of the khalifs, and ultimately brought it to ruin.

The following *Fatwa* on the (so called) 'Murder of Hosain' is a curious and favourable specimen of Muhammadan casuistry:—

'The Imam Abou Hamid al Ghazzali was once consulted on this subject. . . . . The questions proposed to him were these:—"Should a person who openly cursed Yezid be considered as a reprobate, or should he be treated with indulgence? Had Yezid the intention of slaying Al Hosain, or was it done in self-defence? Is it permitted to say, *God have mercy on him* when speaking of Yezid, or is it better to suppress the prayer? May the *Mufti* be rewarded with the Divine favour for dissipating our doubts!" . . . . His answer was as follows:—"It is absolutely forbidden to curse a Moslem, and he who curses a Moslem is himself accursed; the blessed Prophet having said: '*The Moslem is not a curser.*' And how should it be allowable to curse a Moslem when it is not permitted to curse the beasts of the field? The prohibition from doing so has been transmitted down to us, and, moreover, *the dignity of a Moslem is greater than the dignity of the Kaaba*, according to the positive declaration of the blessed Prophet. Now, it is certain that Yezid was a Moslem, but it is not certain that he slew Hosain, or that he ordered, or consented to his death; and so long as these circumstances remain undecided it is not allowable to believe that he acted so. Besides, it is forbidden to think ill of a Moslem, since Almighty God has said: 'Be not ready to entertain unfavourable opinions (of another), for sometimes these opinions are a crime;' and the blessed Prophet has declared that the blood, the wealth, and reputation of the Moslem are sacred, and of him no ill should be thought." Moreover, if any person assert that Yezid ordered Hosain's death, or consented to it, he gives thereby an evident proof of his extreme folly; for were he to endeavour to discover the true circumstances of the death of such great men—viziers and sultans—as perished in his own time; were he to essay to find out who ordered the deed to be committed, who consented to it, and who disapproved of it, he would not succeed; not even if the murder were perpetrated in his neighbourhood and in his presence. How, then, could he pretend to know the particulars of a similar occurrence which took place in a distant country and in a bygone age? And how can he know the truth (of Yezid's conduct) now that nearly four hundred years have elapsed, and that the crime was committed in a country far remote? It must be considered, also, that this event was taken up by party-spirit, and that (false) statements respecting it abounded on all sides. The true circumstances of it cannot therefore be known; and such being the case, it is incumbent on us to think well of every Moslem who can possibly deserve it. To this we shall add some observations. Suppose that there be positive proof of one Moslem having murdered another, the doctrine of the orthodox juris consults is that the murderer is not an infidel, because the act itself is not an act of infidelity, but of disobedience (towards God). It may also happen that the murderer repent before he dies. And if an infidel be converted from his infidelity, it is not allowable to curse him; how much the less is it allowable to curse him who repents of having committed murder? Besides, how can it be known that the murderer of Hosain died unrepenting? and *He (God) accepteth the repentance of his creatures* ("Koran," Sura ix. v. 105). Wherefore, inasmuch as it is not lawful to curse a Moslem after his death, he who curses him is a reprobate and disobedient to God. Suppose even that it were permitted to curse him; the abstaining therefrom would be no crime, according to the unanimous opinion of the Imams—nay, the man who never once during the course of his existence cursed Satan will not be asked on the Day of Judgment why he cursed him not. And as for him who cursed Satan, he shall be asked his motives for so doing, and how he knew that Satan was rejected and accursed. The accursed are those who are far removed from Almighty God; but who those may be is a mystery, except in the case of such persons as die infidels; for we know by the Divine law that they are accursed. As for the invoking of the Divine mercy on Yezid, it is allowable—nay, acceptable (in the sight of God); nay, it is included in these words which we utter in every prayer: "O, God! pardon the men and women who believe;" for Yezid was a believer. God knows if my opinion be right. Signed: Al Ghazzali.'—Ibn Khallikan's *Biographical Dictionary*, vol. ii. pp. 230–32. Slane's Trans.

CHAPTER V.

THE STRUGGLE FOR EMPIRE.

A.D. 680–718.

A CRY of rage and horror went up from Mekka and Medina when it was known in the Holy Cities that the grandson of the Prophet had been murdered by a profligate and a wine-bibber such as Yezid. And there happened to be in Mekka a man eager to take advantage of these angry feelings and possessed of the power to move the excited populations to open revolt. This was Abdallah, the son of that Zobair who had fallen at 'the Battle of the Camel.' Ambitious, crafty, and unscrupulous, he had long aspired to be the head of the Muhammadan world, and it was with ill-concealed delight that he had witnessed Hosain set forth upon the expedition which conducted him to the grave. So long as the son of Ali lived, the son of Zobair was eclipsed. But after his death there was no living Muhammadan who combined so many claims to the honour and affection of the Faithful. His father had been among the select few to whom the Prophet had expressly guaranteed the pleasures of Paradise. His mother was Asma, the daughter of the khalif Abu Bekr. His maternal aunt was Ayesha, the favourite wife of the Prophet, and the mother of the People of God.

His paternal aunt had been Khadija, the first and best-loved spouse of the Prophet, and the earliest of his disciples. He himself was a soldier who in Africa and against the soldiers of Byzantium had fought on the path of God with brilliant courage and success. Born at Medina—the first child born among the Faithful after their flight—the call to prayers had been repeated by his grandfather in his ear; his mother had laid him in the lap of the Prophet; and, after Ali and Ayesha, he was considered the foremost traditionist of the words and acts of Muhammad. He had, moreover, declined to take the oath of allegiance to Yezid, and, when threatened with violence, he had fled to Mekka and sought shelter in the sanctuary of the Kaaba. He signed himself the 'Refugee,' and, as though entirely withdrawn from the world, passed his days either in prayer or in making the circuits round the Kaaba.

When the news of the death of Hosain reached Mekka the people thronged in a tumultuous crowd to the House of God. Abdallah rose up in the midst of the congregation, and, after the customary praise of God and the Prophet, launched out in an eloquent discourse, bewailing the untimely fate of the son of Ali, and cursing the treachery of the people of Koufa. The oration was no sooner ended than his friends thronged around him and saluted him with the title of khalif.

The people of Medina were not slow to follow the example of Mekka. A large and turbulent crowd gathered in the great Mosque. There was a confused noise of tongues; voices blended discordantly, eulogising the fallen martyr, or heaping invectives on the head of his murderers. At length Moundsir, a brother of Abdallah, rose up and demanded silence. Then, taking his turban from his head, he flung it on the ground, saying: 'I reject Yezid as I reject this turban.' Another shouted: 'I reject Yezid as I reject this shoe.' The word and the action were like sparks of fire falling in the midst of dry stubble. The multitude were at once in a flame. The floor of the Mosque was covered with the cloaks, turbans, and shoes of those who rejected Yezid. His lieutenant was chased from the city; the members of the house of Ommaya, their clients, and their friends were threatened with instant massacre if they did not fly. They fled, in number 3,000. The whole of the Hejaz was in open revolt.

But Yezid, though a debauchee, was not the less a prompt, fearless, and determined Arab. Twelve thousand men, under a skilful and pitiless leader, were sent by forced marches against the rebel city. The rebels spurned the peaceful overtures which Yezid had directed his general to make before having recourse to arms. A fierce battle was then fought, and Medina, carried by storm, was given up for three days to the license of the Syrian soldiery. Four thousand Arabs fell in the fight and the subsequent massacre. Among these were ninety of the companions of the Prophet. The women were subjected to outrage, and, according to Ibn Khallikan, 'upwards of 1,000 unmarried girls of Medina gave birth to children in consequence of the infamous treatment they had undergone.' This, I think, without undue charity to the Syrian soldiery, may be set down as an exaggeration. Probably every lady in that part of the world who was guilty of an indiscretion at any time near to the period of the sack of Medina ascribed her unfortunate condition to the illicit violence of the Damascene army.

From Medina the Syrian army marched to Mekka. Muslim ibn Okba, the general who had commanded it, died on the march there. When he knew his end was near he called in Hosain ibn Nomair, and said to him: 'Come here, you ass; you are to know that the Commander of the Faithful ordered me, in case I was on the point of death, to give you the command; and now that I am dying, I am unwilling to disobey him, though I ought to do so.' He then prescribed to him a number of things which he should execute, after which he said: 'If I go to the fire of Hell after my good action of having slain the people of Medina, I shall be very unfortunate indeed.'

Arrived at Mekka, the troops of Abdallah were driven into the city by the Syrian army. The siege was formed and pressed with rigour for the space of two months. The Muhammadan historians relate with horror the fearful things that were done. War machines rained down a shower of stones, fiery darts and flaming naphtha upon the Kaaba. The covering of the Temple was consumed by the flames; the Kaaba crushed by the stones and reduced to a ruin. But the town still held out, when intelligence was received that the sacrilegious Yezid was dead. He had died suddenly in the flower of his youth —cut off, so said the Muhammadan divines, because of the abominable outrages he had perpetrated in the city of Medina. They quoted a saying of Muhammad: 'Whoever injureth Medina shall melt away, even as salt melteth in the water.'

In Muhammadan countries the death of the sovereign

is a critical moment at the most peaceful seasons. As all law and authority is supposed to reside in the heart of the ruler, and to flow from thence as a river from its source; as every official, high or low, is considered to be a servant of the king in the domestic sense of the word, the decease of the monarch is literally the commencement of anarchy. The action of the laws is suspended, the arm of the executive is smitten with paralysis; the pulse of life having ceased to beat at the seat and centre of authority, the whole body politic dies also. It is true that Yezid left a son, Muawia, who was instantly proclaimed khalif. But the new sovereign, a weak and sickly boy, died after a brief reign of forty days, and nominated no successor. Had Abdallah seized the propitious moment, he might have united under his rule all the countries of Islam. Everything was in his favour. The siege of Mekka had been raised the moment it was known that Yezid was dead. The commandant of the Syrian troops had even entreated Abdallah to accompany him to Damascus. The Hejaz, Yemen, Irak, and Egypt had proclaimed him khalif; even in Syria, the stronghold of the house of Ommaya, out of the five lieutenants who ruled that province, four, fearful of the anarchy of an interregnum, were ready to accept Abdallah. But at this supreme crisis he wavered; he feared to trust himself in Syria. The golden moment slipped by. The Ommayas, recovering from the consternation and perplexity which the death of Yezid, followed so closely by that of his son, had thrown them into, rallied round Merwan ibn Hakem, the friend and favourite of the murdered Othman. He was proclaimed in Damascus as the new khalif. The war of sects and religious leaders continued, notwithstanding, to rage with undiminished fury. There were four parties in the field—the house of Ommaya at Damascus; Abdallah ibn Zobair at Mekka; the partisans of Ali at Koufa; and, lastly, the Kharegites, or Separatists. These were the men who had broken away from Ali at the moment of victory on the plain of Siffin. The Puritans of Islam, these sectaries had grown into a tremendous host of warriors. Emerging from their fastnesses in the rocky country of Kerman, they swept through Fars, Ahwaz, and Irak, slaughtering, burning, and destroying all that came in their way—their hands against every man, and every man's hand against them.

Merwan died, and was succeeded by his son, Abdal Malek; but there was no pause or breathing space in the work of slaughter. Syria and Irak continued to be the theatre of bloody battles and bloodier reprisals. Koufa was the centre of this fanatical fury. The memory of their treacherous inaction on the day of Kerbela preyed upon the fickle, but sensitive, people like the worm which dieth not, and three years after Hosain's death (A.H. 64, A.D. 683) a portion among them determined to atone their crime by revenging his murder on the house of Ommaya. Suleiman, the son of Sorad, a leading disciple of Ali, was placed at the head of the movement. 'The Penitents,' as they called themselves, appointed a place of assembly outside of the city. Thence they despatched two of their number to ride through the streets of Koufa, shouting, 'Vengeance for Hosain.' Six thousand men responded to the summons. Their first step was to march to the plain of Kerbela. A day and a night they passed round the tomb of the martyr bewailing their sins and praying for forgiveness. One who was present affirmed that he had never seen such crowding and pressing even round the black stone of the Kaaba. When at last Suleiman gave the order to march, not a man would move until he had stood over the grave of Hosain and asked for pardon.

They plunged boldly into the waste which, scored with deep ravines and traversed by fierce hurricanes of wind, stretches away to the gardens of Damascus. But fatigue, hunger, and thirst are enemies more potent than the sword. The number of 'the Penitents' rapidly diminished the further they penetrated that parched land. The army of Merwan, 20,000 strong, barred their onward passage. They were given the alternative of surrender or death. They chose the latter, declaring they should never be so fit to die as they were at that moment. The struggle was long and obstinate; 'the Penitents' performed prodigies of valour which extorted the admiration even of their enemies; but in the end victory as usual was found to be on the side of the strongest battalions, and the avengers of Hosain were almost entirely cut to pieces.

Another champion was not wanting. Al Moktar seized the banner which had fallen from the grasp of Suleiman. Himself a man of daring and ability, he had as his lieutenant Ibrahim, the son of Ali's great lieutenant, Malek al Ashtar, and a soldier equal in skill and courage to his brilliant father. Thus seconded, Al Moktar waged for some time a successful war against both Abd al Malek at Damascus, and Abdallah at Mekka. Al Moktar claimed to be a prophet, and he propounded a rather ingenious theory regarding the Deity to account for the failure of his predictions. On the ground that there were certain verses in the Koran which were abrogated by later verses, he ascribed to God changes of purpose. What He wished and commanded at one time He prohibited at another. Consequently, while a fulfilled prediction was a satisfactory proof of prophetic power, an unfulfilled one did not establish the contrary. It betokened merely that in the interval God had changed His mind. Among other devices to stimulate the zeal and courage of his followers, he procured a chair which he affirmed to be the judgment-seat of Ali, the Prince of Believers. This he caused to be gorgeously decorated, enclosed in an ark, and always placed in the front line of the battle. 'This,' he explained to his followers, 'is to you as the Ark of the Covenant was to the Israelites. In it dwell the majesty and the terror of God, and on the day of battle the angels come down to help you.'

In this war quarter was neither asked nor given. Yezid, a general of Al Moktar, had defeated the army of the khalif, Abd al Malek. Three hundred prisoners were brought before him. He was in his litter, sinking under a mortal disease. Speechless, with the hand of death upon him, he had just strength sufficient to signify the order for death by drawing his hand across his throat. Retribution at last overtook Al Moktar. In A.H. 67 his troops were defeated in a pitched battle in the neighbourhood of Koufa by Mosab, the brother of Abdallah. With 6,000 men he escaped into his palace within the city. The palace was invested, and his followers destitute of food. Al Moktar proposed that they should sally forth and either cut their way through the enemy or perish with their swords in their hands. But his disheartened followers shrank from this dreadful alternative. Only nineteen of his most attached friends declared their readiness to follow him. Al Moktar took leave of his army with the assurance that they need not hope their pusillanimity would obtain for them the clemency of the victors. Then he and his companions, wrapping their winding sheets about them, rushed forth on the beleaguering army and fell fighting to the last. His followers surrendered; they were marched down to the market-place of Koufa with their hands tied behind their backs, and there slaughtered to the last man. Al Moktar is said to have executed 50,000 men during his brief and savage career, independently of the blood he caused to be shed on the field of battle.

The victory in the long struggle began at length to incline to the side of the khalif at Damascus. Not only was Abd al Malek a man of great ability and courage, but in the unquestioning steady devotion of his Syrian subjects he possessed a fund of strength which none of his rivals enjoyed. They relied solely on the religious zeal of the Arab; and this fanaticism rose and fell, swayed to this side and that with the suddenness and uncertainty of a sea vexed by contrary winds. At one instant it bore them aloft on a great wave of enthusiasm which seemed sufficient by its own unassisted power to carry them to the haven where they would be; but the next moment it had receded and left them helpless and forlorn, a prey to eager and merciless enemies. Thus it came to pass that step by step Abdallah ibn Zobair beheld Irak, Egypt, all his provinces, wrested from him. He indeed greatly aided in his ruin by the unaccountable apathy which caused him to cling abjectly to the sanctuary at Mekka, and never take the field at the head of his armies. At last his sway was recognised only in the Hejaz. At this juncture a man appeared upon the scene whose iron rule struck terror and amazement into the heart of even that iron age—a man, literally, of 'blood and iron.' This was Hejjaj.

Ali, so a tradition relates, on one occasion after a fruitless appeal to the people of Koufa to take the field under his banner, had, in the bitterness of his heart, prayed that God might punish them by placing them under a ruler as hard and unforgiving as he had been merciful and indulgent. In answer to that prayer, and on that night, Hejjaj was born. The infant refused the breast of his mother; nurses were brought, but the child resolutely rejected all nourishment, and they were at a loss what to do. At this crisis Satan appeared in human form and inquired what was the matter. They told him, and he said: 'Kill a black kid and give its blood to the child to drink; the next day do the same thing; the third day slay a black he-goat, and give the blood to be drunk by the child; then kill a snake, and make the child swallow the blood, and daub his face with some of it; if you do this the child will take the breast on the fourth day.' They followed these directions, and the effect (so it is said) of this first nutriment was such that he could not refrain from shedding blood. He said, or rather is reported to have said, of himself that his greatest enjoyment was to shed blood and commit actions which no other man could. A very characteristic act brought him to the notice of Abd al Malek. The khalif, in one of his campaigns, had been sorely vexed by the lack of discipline of his army; the soldiers neither marched nor halted at the same time as he did; and there seemed no officer who either dared or had the power to enforce order and obedience. The khalif complained to the commandant of his personal body-guard, Rouh ibn Zinba, who replied that there was a man in the Police Guards, Hejjaj ibn Yusuf, who, if placed in command of the army, would bring it into order. Abd al Malek adopted his counsel, and Hejjaj became commander of the army. Only the body-guard under Rouh ibn Zinba was exempted from his control. A few days after, the rest of the army having marched, Hejjaj came upon this body-guard, calmly enjoying their dinner. 'Dismount, you son of a slut!' said one of these jovial soldiery, 'and dine with us.' 'No, no,' replied Hejjaj, 'those days are gone by;' and he had the body-guard seized, paraded before the army, and flogged. Rouh ibn Zinba complained to the khalif of these high-handed proceedings, but the latter had too much discernment not to see that here was the very man he needed, and he treated Hejjaj with increased favour.

It was in the year 71 that Abd al Malek determined to carry the war against his rival Abdallah ibn Zobair into the Holy Territory itself. One day, after having made the prayer, he turned to his courtiers and asked who among them would lead an expedition to Mekka. There was no reply. They hesitated to engage in a duty which involved the violation of the Holy City. Hejjaj stepped forward. He was ready to go to Mekka or any other place where the khalif required his services. A picked body of 8,000 men was entrusted to him. The blockade of Mekka was established early in the following year. The investment lasted eight months. Abdallah ibn Zobair had, since the last siege, rebuilt the Kaaba. The war machines of Al Hejjaj once more laid the building in ruins. The sufferings of the people were extremely severe. The dearth of provisions was intensified by the avarice and parsimony of Abdallah. He had within the city large stores of wheat, dates, and other provisions. But so miserly was he that even to save his life he could not endure to part with his wealth. Every measure of wheat served out to his famishing soldiers wrung him with anguish. He grudged the very weapons with which his men had to be equipped, and dismissed from his service an Arab who had broken three lances in succession in the bodies of Syrian soldiers, on the ground that no arsenals could endure such wasteful extravagance. Half fed, ill armed, it is not surprising that his men flocked by hundreds into the enemy's camp. Hejjaj proclaimed an amnesty to all who abandoned Abdallah; and his sons, with one exception, sought an asylum in the enemy's camp. Nothing remained for Abdallah but to find a soldier's death. His mother Asma, the daughter of Abou Bekr, was a woman far advanced in age, and noted for her experience and wisdom. Abdallah, in all that he did, was guided by her counsels. He now went to see her. 'My mother,' he said, 'the world has abandoned me; even my sons have accepted the amnesty and gone over to the camp of the enemy. Hejjaj sends me word that if I surrender he will accord me everything I demand.

But what think you?' 'My son,' replied his mother, 'I think you ought to continue the conflict—at least you will find an honourable death.' 'Such,' said Abdallah, 'is also my resolution, but I desired to take leave of you before going to meet death.' He then embraced his mother and went out. All that night he passed in prayer in the Kaaba. When morning dawned, he and his few remaining friends donned their arms, and attacked the enemy. The fight continued till midday. Then Abdallah and his faithful few withdrew once more into the sanctuary to pray. The Syrian soldiers rushed into the streets, and crowded the entrance of the House of God. Abdallah, snatching up his sword, charged the foremost intruders. They gave way before his blows. But a stone struck him on his head and he fell. The soldiers surrounded him and cut him to pieces. His head was hacked off, and his body suspended to a gibbet.

Abdallah had a brother, named Orwa, noted for the sanctity and purity of his life. He went to the khalif, Abd al Malek, and said to him: 'I wish you to give me the sword which belonged to my brother Abdallah.' 'It is in the armoury,' answered the khalif, 'with the other swords, and I should not know it amongst them.' 'Let them be brought here,' replied Orwa, 'and I will point it out.' By Abd al Malek's orders the swords were brought in, and Orwa selected from among them one very much hacked on the edge. 'Did you know it before?' said the prince. 'No,' replied the other. 'How then have you recognised it?' 'By these words of the poet Nabigha:

> Their only blemish is in their swords,
> Which are jagg'd with striking hostile hordes.'

With Abdallah ibn Zobair perished the last rival of Abd al Malek, but he was still far from being in peaceful possession of his dominions. Irak, Fars, Ahwaz were in the hands of the Kharegites. Koufa and Basra remained, as they always had been, hotbeds of religious fanaticism. Mekka and Medina were crushed, not conciliated. But in Hejjaj, Abd-al-Malek recognised a man fit to cope with the dangers of the time, and he determined to station him at Koufa. At this time all the open country of Irak was overrun by the Kharegites. They had at one time penetrated to the walls of Basra, and, for a brief period, occupied the city. Mouhalleb—after the great Khaled, probably the best general Islam produced—had beaten them back; but his troops were drawn from the fickle and unstable populations of Koufa and Basra, and his progress checked by their mutinous and indolent behaviour. To bring this turbulent soldiery to order was to be the first duty of Hejjaj on his arrival at Koufa.

At some distance from that city, after giving his troops orders to march through the night, Hejjaj mounted a swift-trotting camel, and with none of the splendour belonging to his rank, but clothed only in a rough travelling dress, and with the Koran in his hand, he set out for Koufa. He entered the city shortly after daybreak. All along the streets he saw the soldiers, who ought to have been in the field with Mouhalleb, sitting at the doors of their houses, with their relatives and friends about them. As he passed these groups, Hejjaj held up the Koran and shouted: 'Come all to prayers.' The soldiers thought they would follow this strange man to the Mosque, and, if necessary, stone him. They had heard a governor was on his way to Koufa, but they could with difficulty believe that this rough Arab of the desert was the ruler of Irak. Hejjaj sat motionless in the chair of the Mosque. Jeers, threats, and insults were freely hurled at him; he remained silent, with his face muffled up in the folds of his dress. But when the court was filled, he rose, uncovered his face, and without the ordinary invocation of God and His prophet, plunged at once into his discourse.

'Men of Irak!' he said, 'servants of rebellion and perfidy; criminal souls! I am not a weak one. I have been chosen for my sagacity, sought out for my experience. But you—by God! I will strip you as the bark is stripped from the tree. I will scourge you as the camels are scourged which stray from the herd, and break you in pieces as stones are broken on the highway. People of Irak! too long have you walked in the paths of error and pursued the course which leads to destruction. You have habituated yourselves to crime, and persevered in ignorance. Slaves of the stick—sons of servants! I am Hejjaj, the son of Yusuf! If I promise, I perform; if I shave, I raze the skin. No more assemblies; no more reunions; no more useless chatter; cease to ask—"what now?—what has happened?" Children of prostitutes! what imports it to you what has happened? Let each one mind his own business, and woe to those who become my prey. Know that I am not one who cares to repeat my words or to make speeches. If once this sabre has started from its sheath, it will not return either in summer or winter, until that the Prince of Believers has, by the aid of God, chastised those among you who walk crookedly, and humbled those who exalt themselves. The Prince of Believers has ordered me to distribute to you your pay, and send you to fight under Mouhalleb. I call upon you to obey within three days; and may Allah hear and punish me if I keep not this oath. Every soldier of the army of Mouhalleb that I find here after that time, shall lose his head, and his goods shall be confiscated. Page,' he continued to an attendant at his side, 'read out the letter from the Prince of Believers!'

The Page commenced: 'In the name of God, the merciful and compassionate! The servant of God, Abd al Malek, the Prince of Believers, to the Faithful of Irak—greeting.' Here Hejjaj broke in with a roar of anger. 'Inhabitants of Irak!' he shouted; 'men of revolt and perfidy; partisans of schism and error; the Prince of Believers salutes you, and you do not return his salute. If God allows me to remain among you, I will cut and hack you like wood, and teach you politeness in another school than that of Ibn Nihyah.' (Such was the name of the former chief of the criminal police in Irak.) 'Page, recommence your reading.' This time, when the latter pronounced the word 'greeting,' the crowd responded with astonishing alacrity, 'Health to the Prince of Believers! May God bestow upon him His mercy and His blessings.' There was no more talk of stoning Hejjaj. The people of Koufa felt they were in the grip of a master. The reading ended, Hejjaj descended from the chair, and distributed pay to the soldiers. There was no further delay in despatching reinforcements to Mouhalleb's army. They poured into his camp as though the swords of the enemy were behind them. 'At last,' said that general, astonished and delighted, 'a man of energy governs Irak; now, God willing, the enemy is destroyed.'

From this time until close upon the death of Walid, the son and successor of Abd al Malek, Hejjaj ruled the two Iraks with all the power of an independent prince. So great, indeed, was the confidence reposed in him by these two khalifs, that Khorasan, Sind, Mekka, Medina, and even Northern Africa were virtually ruled by him. He nominated the governors of all these provinces, choosing them from his own family, as men on whose devotion and submission he could count. Of the art of government he and his lieutenants had no other conception than that of putting a sword to the throat of every one who had revolted or was suspected of a tendency to revolt. A frightful tyranny reigned throughout the empire of the khalif. The prisons were crowded with thousands of suspected criminals. In these wretched places men and women were crowded indiscriminately together; there was no roof to protect them from the heat of summer or the blasts of winter, and thousands of both sexes were in a state of utter nudity. The groans, the despairing shrieks, the cries of fear and anger which rose from these hideous dens filled the air with an unceasing and dismal clamour. 'Can they not rot together in silence,' asked the indignant governor of Irak, as one day he rode by one of these model prison-houses. Every independent or important person lived in hourly danger of being denounced by a spy, and summarily executed by the chief of the police, who had authority to act independently of the regular tribunals. The excessive severity of this rule naturally produced the very results they were intended to avert. Men desperate of justice or mercy, determined at least to perish with their swords in their hands, and more than one formidable rebellion caused the throne of Abd al Malek to totter. But Hejjaj was not lacking in military ability. The rebels were either slain in battle or fell beneath the sword of the executioner; and a dreary and hollow tranquillity at last prevailed throughout the Muhammadan empire; then the work of conquest recommenced. The pitiless severity of the administration at home had the effect of driving crowds of Muhammadans to recruit the armies on the frontier. If they were to die, they held it better to die fighting in the path of God, than to fall victims to the spies of Hejjaj. This second sweep of contest was hardly less astonishing than the first. In one direction the whole of Northern Africa, and Spain as far as the Pyrenees, were overrun by the Muhammadan generals, Mousa and Tarik. Another army marched into Sind, and conquered the whole of that province, crossed the Indus, and captured Moultan. A third army assembled at Merou under Kutaiba ibn Muslim, crossed the Oxus, and by a series of successful battles, and through romantic adventures of all kinds, added Samarkand and Bokhara to the dominions of the khalif, and carried the terror of the Muhammadan name into the distant lands of Ferghana and Kashgar. A fourth army, under the command of Maslama, a brother of the khalif Walid, attacked the territories of the Byzantine emperor, and wasted them, year after year, with fire and sword, almost to the gates of Constantinople.

These last invasions were, however, terribly avenged, when Leo the Isaurian mounted the throne. Of 180,000 Muhammadans who had formed the siege of Constantinople, only 30,000 returned to tell the tale of their defeat and the military skill of the new emperor.

PART II.

THE FATIMIDES.

CHAPTER I.

THE SHIA.

A.D. 687–988.

SOUTHWARD of Koufa and Basra, but separated from those cities, and from the cultivated parts of Central Arabia by the trackless waste of the Red Desert, the province of Hasa stretches along the black and sluggish waters of the Persian Gulf. Into this province the shattered wrecks of the Aliites had retreated. With the sea on one side and the desert on the other, they might defy even the deep hate of Hejjaj. That Red Desert, Mr. Palgrave tells us, is the terror even of the wandering Bedouin. So light, he says, are the sands, so capricious the breezes which traverse its surface, that no trace of preceding travellers remain to those who follow, while intense heat and glaring light reflected on all sides combine, with drought and weariness, to confuse and bewilder the adventurer, till he loses his compass and wanders up and down at random amid a vast solitude soon to become his grave. Beyond this unblest land rises a low range of hills; and on the further side of these lies the province of Hasa, thickly studded with oases, and green with groves of trees. The people of this part of Arabia had taken but a very superficial varnish of Islamism, and they speedily divested themselves of even that when at liberty to do so. Hence, whoever had fought against the religion of the Prophet was sure of a welcome here. The relics of the following of Moseilama the Liar, the Separatists who had broken away from Ali, the fire-worshippers from Persia, dwelt here in amicable intercourse. The followers of Ali brought with them an additional creed, but, diverse as were these forms of faith, their votaries were knit together by a common hatred of the orthodox Moslem; the province became, in fact, a kind of spiritual Alsatia, and in the action and reaction of the strange creeds which jostled one another there, we can trace the origin of those wild and mystical superstitions which were gradually engrafted upon the narrow and stern monotheism of the Koran.

Hither, then, the Shias[1] retired to brood upon their defeats and their wrongs. Originally there seems to have been no dispute between the two sections of Islam that the spiritual leader of the Moslems ought to be elected by a popular vote. But as calamity and misfortune thickened around the cause of Ali,—as he and his sons descended one after another into an untimely grave, his followers discarded this election by universal suffrage as heretical and profane. The dangers of the battle-field, the pains of persecution, clothed with a more than earthly splendour the objects for whom they were endured. It seemed impossible that so much zeal, so much courage, such a vast extent of misery, could have no higher originating cause than a simple question of election. Tradition was not slack to invest Ali and his sons with a

[1] 'Shia,' as a follower of Ali is called in Muhammadan history, signifies 'partisan,' 'companion,' or 'sectary.'

gorgeous halo of supernatural attributes. The death of Hosain on the field of Kerbela was embellished with a number of pathetic and strange traits. Plaintive voices, it was asserted, were heard at the moment the martyr died, denouncing the eternal wrath of God upon those who had done this deed. In such beliefs, in the recognition of a Divine right to command inherent in the family of Ali, the Shias found a consolation in the midst of disaster and death. And thus was gradually educed the fundamental tenet of the sect—devotion to the Imam as the divinely-appointed head of the Faith. It was incredible, they affirmed, that the supreme authority, both in spiritual and temporal affairs, should have been left to the chances of an election by vulgar and ignorant people. The Prophet could not have neglected to decide so weighty a matter himself. From this it was a short step to the conviction that he could have decided it in one way only, that he actually did decide it in that way, and that the position of Imam belonged and could belong only to Ali and his descendants after him. But if Ali and his son were so designated by the Prophet, he must have acted in obedience to a Divine command, seeing that he was under the guidance of God in all that he did. And then, it was not to be supposed for a moment that those who had been thus selected from the body of the Faithful to keep the people of God in the right path would be left to accomplish this gigantic task by their own unassisted intellect. What security could there be in such an arrangement that the Faithful would be guided in accordance with the will of God? In the Imam, as in the Prophet, there must be present the impulses of a higher wisdom and the light of a purer knowledge than ordinary human nature could attain to. The manner in which the various steps in this argument were deduced and established is a curious example of the theological dialectic of the Muhammadans and their method of interpreting the Koran.

The 118th verse of the Second Sura runs as follows:

> When his Lord made trial of Abraham by commands which he fulfilled, He said, 'I am about to make of thee an *Imâm* to mankind;' he said, 'Of my offspring also?' 'My covenant,' said God, 'embraceth not the evil doers.'

According to the Shias, the reading of this passage shows that the Imamate is a Divine institution, for, had it been otherwise—an institution, that is, which man could create or not as he pleased—the question of Abraham, when told that he had been elected, would have had no meaning. As it was, it implied that the Imam, in order to be legitimate, must be nominated by God. The rest of the Divine words—'My covenant embraceth not the evil doers'—proves that the perfectly righteous man alone is included in this pact with God. Consequently, the true Imam must, as part of his nature, possess the following attributes: impeccability, otherwise he would be liable to fall into sin, as other men, and so become deserving of chastisement. But who could administer chastisement to an Imam? For such a purpose another Imam would have to be nominated, superior to and above him; and then another to superintend this second Imam, and so on to infinity. The Imam must, too, be the most knowing of all men; otherwise, in the administration of justice, he would be liable to inflict the punishment of death when that of flagellation only was needed; or to flagellate when he ought to have put to death, and so apply the law in a manner contrary to the will of God. The Imam must also be the bravest of men, as otherwise he might fly from battle, and thereby expose himself to the wrath of God. In a word, the Imam, as the divinely-appointed leader and guide of the people of God, the being whom God has appointed to see that His will is executed upon earth, and His laws obeyed, must himself be without spot or blemish, or capacity to sin, as the necessary conditions for a perfect fulfilment of his high functions.

Having thus demonstrated the supernatural character of the Imamate, the next business of the Shia was to adduce proofs that these functions had been delegated to Ali and his sons. These proofs they declared had been handed down as traditional sayings of the Prophet, and they classed them under two heads—those of which the sense is clear, and those of which the sense is hidden. As an example of clear texts, they cite this word of the Prophet: 'He of whom I am master has Ali also for master;' and this: 'The best judge among you is Ali.' A third tradition is the following: 'Ibn Abbas (who had become blind) heard one day a number of men complaining against and speaking injuriously of Ali. He ordered his guide to conduct him to the spot, and then said to the men: 'Which of you dares to insult God?' 'Insult God!' they replied; 'Heaven forbid it.' 'Which of you insults His Apostle?' 'God preserve us from insulting the Apostle!' 'Which of you insults Ali!' 'As to Ali,' they replied, 'it is true.' Ibn Abbas replied: 'I bear witness that I have heard the Prophet say: "He who blasphemes my name blasphemes the name of God; he who blasphemes the name of Ali blasphemes my name."'

As examples of indications, of which the sense is concealed, they report that the Prophet, having received from Heaven the Ninth Sura during the pilgrimage, had charged Abou Bekr to signify the contents to the Arab idolators, when he received another revelation charging him to entrust this duty to one of his own relations. He thereupon made choice of Ali. This, they say, shows that Ali had obtained the preference. Moreover, the Prophet never placed Ali under the orders of anyone, while both Omar and Abou Bekr were so treated, the first having been placed under the orders of Amr ibn al-As, the second under those of Osama ibn Zaid.

A final demonstration was still needed. It had to be shown not merely that absolute perfection was the necessary qualification of an Imam, and that Ali had been chosen for this office, but also that he had been endowed with that gift of Divine life which elevated him above the category of ordinary men. This was effected by means of 'a tradition,'[1] reported, it is said, on the authority of Ali himself. According to this tradition, while as yet the universe existed only in the thought of God, He took a ray of light from the place of His splendour, the bosom of His royalty without companionship. This ray of light

[1] In a subsequent volume of this work I shall have to write in detail of the 'Traditions.' Suffice it to say here that they constitute the 'sayings' of Muhammad handed down on the authority of his 'Companions.' They are very numerous, and relate to an immense variety of subjects. The greater part of them are of exceedingly doubtful authenticity, but are held by Muhammadans to be as sacred and to possess as binding a force as the Koran itself. The traditions of the Aliites differ from those of the orthodox Muhammadans.

united itself to the form of the holy Prophet Muhammad. God then pronounced these solemn words: 'Thou art the Elect, the Chosen. I deposit in thee My light and the treasures of My grace. Out of My love for thee I will make the members of thy family the guides to salvation. I will reveal to them the mysteries of knowledge, so that for them there shall remain no more the secret and the unknown.' God then disposed the minds of His creatures to receive, in addition to the dogmas of His omnipotence and unity, that of the election of Muhammad and his family.

This having been done, God buried the form of His holy Prophet in the invisible world, and proceeded with the rest of His creative acts. He balanced the world, unrolled Time, raised the floods; the throne of God floated on the waves. Then he created the angels out of spirit and light, and taught them to believe in the mission of Muhammad as well as the unity of God. When God created Adam, He made known the high dignity reserved for man, and his superiority in knowledge over the angels, by causing Adam to give names to all the objects in creation. Nevertheless, the ray of light that had been taken from the place of his splendour was concealed under the veil of time until the birth of Muhammad. After him the celestial spark was transmitted to Ali, the noblest of his descendants, and by Ali to his sons and their sons. The Imams, then, are the Illuminated of Heaven, the hopes of salvation, the keys of knowledge, and to them should all men come. They are the first of all creatures, the kings of humanity, the living proofs that there is a Creator. Happy is he who acquiesces in their supremacy and permits them to guide him.

Such being the Divine decree written upon the everlasting table which stands before the throne of God, it followed as a logical consequence that the disorders and divisions in Islam were the results of casting aside the government of the legitimate Imam. Men had rejected the Heaven-sent Guide, and under leaders of their own choice were gravitating with fearful velocity into deeper and deeper abysses of misery and falsehood. Devotion, therefore, to the lawful Imam, whether visibly at the head of Islam or not, was the first duty of the true Moslem. The Shias clung to this tenet with an almost incredible fanaticism. It was held to constitute the whole of religion, and the moral precepts of the Koran were converted into allegorical injunctions of this single duty. The command to pray was declared to be only a mode of symbolising that entire devotion which was due to the Imam as the head of Islam. Fasting became the symbol of that silence and secrecy which it behoved the Faithful to keep regarding their faith in the presence of strangers and persecutors. The prohibition of fornication was refined away into a warning forbidding men to swerve even in thought from a single-minded submission to the lawful Imam. But the Arab, as we have already quoted, is a believing rather than a religious character. He feeds greedily upon chimeras. The old Sabœanism of Hasa and Oman, the witchcraft and magic of Africa, the dualism of the Persian, vague conceptions of the Incarnation and the Trinity, had entered into Hasa to mingle with the stern monotheism of the Muhammadan. The Shias accepted them all. Beyond the flaming walls of the universe, outside of the reach of human ken, who could tell what things the inscrutable God might not have prepared for the children of men? A swarm of wild beliefs assumed gradually some semblances of a system, and from Hasa as a centre 'rayed out' confusion, disorder, and perplexity into the regions of orthodox Islam. Some declared that Ali had never died; he had been simply withdrawn from mortal eyes; his voice it was that was heard in the thunder, and his scourge that glittered in the lightning. He would return to the earth when people least expected him, and fill the world with justice as it had been filled with wrong. Others appropriated the Christian doctrine of the Trinity. Their godhead was five persons in one; these were Muhammad and his daughter Fatima, Ali and his two sons Hasan and Hosain. They were termed the 'Sharers of the Glory;' the ray of light from the place of God's splendour dwelt in all equally, and none were before or after another. Secret societies sprang up in all parts of Asia, with a regular organisation of *dais*, or missionaries, to win adherents to the family of Ali, or to some modification of the tenets held by his followers. The 'Veiled Prophet of Khorassan' was one of these emissaries of disorder. Babek, who taught the indifference of human actions, and illustrated his teaching by acts of lust and cruelty during the reigns of Mamun and Mutasim, was another. These insurrections were productive of immense suffering; but the power of the khalifs was still too strong and closely knit together to be seriously endangered by them. Not so with the terrible outbreak of the Karmathians in the fourth century after the Hijrah. The dominions of the khalifs had then begun to crumble away and break up from within with the rapidity characteristic of Oriental politics; and the Karmathians shook to the very centre the already weakened fabric.

The foundation-stone of the Muhammadan polity was the absolute concentration of the supreme spiritual and temporal power in a single functionary. Everything that proceeded from the mouth of the Prophet had been declared by him to be a Divine message transmitted through the archangel Gabriel. This description was true of the least things as well as the greatest. Is his favourite wife Ayesha suspected of adultery? The angel Gabriel appears with a communication which not only restores her good name, but announces the exact punishment to be inflicted upon those who had dared to think otherwise. Is the Prophet smitten with an illicit admiration for the wife of his adopted son? The complaisant Gabriel again appears upon the scene and absolves the Prophet from the morality which chained smaller folk. Are his wives jealous and angry on account of his relations with a Koptic slave girl? The same messenger is at hand, and threatens them with the doom of Lot's wife unless they promptly repent. There was nothing too small or too trivial not to become a subject of Divine communication. And hence the Koran is not merely a revelation of God, but contains also a code of laws to regulate marriage, divorce, concubinage, inheritance, and all the other matters which the governor of an Arab tribe would be called upon to decide; and every such law was stamped with the seal of a Divine authority which rendered it incapable of change or modification. To these in after days were added 'the traditions'—in other words 'the sayings' of the Prophet, as handed down by those who had been his friends and companions—which in sacredness and authority were raised to a level with the precepts in the Koran. In short, the Muhammadan theory was, that before the death of the Prophet, a complete guide to conduct in all the concerns of life had been laid down for men by God Himself. There was only needed a single functionary to see that these laws were carried into effect. The khalif was that functionary. He was the vicar or lieutenant of God, and responsible to Him alone for the exercise of his authority.

The Church of Rome has always aspired to such a position; but there is this broad difference between her pretensions and the position of the khalifs—the Church of Rome claims to be in possession of a spirit of knowledge and light which gives her a co-ordinate power of jurisdiction with the scriptures of the Old and New Testaments. This has hitherto been the secret of her power. She has been able to adapt her teaching to the changing necessities of successive ages; and to incorporate into the Church every new manifestation of spiritual life which she found herself incapable of suppressing. The Muhammadan belief was quite otherwise. The khalif was simply the executor of a law which had been fixed finally and for ever. His rule was a highly centralised despotism, which fastened with an iron grasp on the inner life as well as on the actions of men. Progress either in thought or political freedom became impossible within the sphere of his authority, because change at all was tantamount to rebellion against the written decrees of God. No seeds of a newer or higher life were permitted to be sown; and any which chance might have wafted thither had to be destroyed before they brought fruit to perfection. Intellectual power, deprived of any legitimate sphere of activity, was driven perforce to feed upon the husks of casuistry, and expend itself in endless refinements and commentaries upon the law.[1] The religious

[1] Here are a few chance specimens of the barren frivolities which obtained for these Doctors of the Law the reputation of subtlety and learning:—

'Al-Ghazzali tells an anecdote of Al-Khaffal in the 'Wasit,' third chapter of the section on Faith, wherein he treats of the different modes by which perjury may be committed. Speaking of a subtle question on a point of law, he says—Question to which the proceedings give rise: If a person swear that he will not eat eggs, and he goes afterwards to a man and says, "By Allah! I will eat what thou hast in thy pocket! and behold it is an egg! what is to be done so as to avoid perjury?" This question was proposed to Al-Khaffal as he was seated in the chair, presiding at an assembly of his pupils, but he could not find an answer to it. On this his pupil, Al-Masudi, said: "Let him have a biscuit made with the egg and eat that; he will thus have eaten what was in the man's pocket, and not have eaten the egg." This answer received general approbation, and it was certainly a most ingenious solution of the difficulty.'—*Ibn Khallikan*, vol. ii. p. 618. Slane's Trans.

'Ibrahim al Harbi related the following anecdote:—"Mukatil Ibn Suleiman took his seat in order to teach, and said: 'You may question me concerning whatever is beneath the throne of God.' On which a man said to him: 'When Adam performed the pilgrimage, who shaved his head?' 'Nay,' replied Mukatil, 'such a question does not proceed from your own mind; but God meant to humble me for my presumption.'"—*Ibn Khallikan*, vol. iii. p. 409.

'The Shaikh Abu Ishak as-Shirazi relates the following anecdote. . . . . He gives it in the words of Nâfé himself:—"I was walking with Abd Allah Ibn Omar, and he heard the sound of a shepherd's pipe. On this he stopped his ears with his fingers and went off the high road. Every now and then he would say to me: 'Do you hear it still, Nâfé?' and when I at length answered that I did not, he removed his fingers from his ears and returned to the high road. He then said to me: 'It was thus I saw the Prophet act on a similar occasion.' This tradition presents a difficulty which gave rise to a discussion among the Doctors of the Law; it is this: 'Why did

life, either petrified into a lifeless formality or lost in a self-seeking mysticism, ceased to be a factor in the ordinary

Ibn Omar stop his ears so as not to hear the sound of the pipe, and yet instead of ordering his client Nâfé to do the same, he authorised him to listen, inasmuch as he asked him every moment if the sound had ceased or not?' The solution given of this difficulty was that Nâfé, being at that time a mere boy, and not responsible for a breach of the law, it was not necessary to forbid him to listen. This answer gave rise to another question, namely, 'Is it perfectly certain that a declaration made by a boy is not receivable in law? Why, then, did Ibn Omar put his trust in Nâfé's declaration touching the sensation of the sound?' This matter formed the subject of a famous controversy." '—*Ibn Khallikan*, vol. iii. p. 521.

Similar examples might be given to almost any extent. I insert one more, because, besides being a curious example of Muhammadan casuistry, it appears to me to present a very remarkable picture of the social and family life of the ancient Muhammadan world:

'Muhammad Ibn Abi Laila was one of those Imams who decided certain points of law by their own private judgment, and he exercised the functions of *kadi* at Koufa for thirty-three years; first in the name of the Ommayides, and afterwards in that of the Abbasides. A slight degree of coolness subsisted between him and Abû Hanifa. It is related that as he was one day returning from the Mosque at Koufa, wherein he had been sitting in judgment, he heard a woman say to a man: "Thou son of a prostitute and a fornicator!" on which he caused her to be arrested, and having returned to his tribunal he ordered her to be flagellated twice, inflicting on her each time the number of strokes prescribed by the law, and this punishment she underwent standing. When Abû Hanifa was informed of this proceeding, he said: "In this single affair the *kadi* has committed six faults; first, in returning to the Mosque after the sitting was ended, which it was not requisite for him to do; secondly, in inflicting the punishment of flagellation in the Mosque, a thing expressly forbidden by the blessed Prophet; thirdly, in flagellating her and she standing, whereas women should be flagellated in a sitting posture and their clothes on; fourthly, in inflicting the flagellation twice, whereas the calumniator incurs only one flagellation, even if he address the insulting words to a number of persons; fifthly, were the double flagellation incurred, he should have waited before inflicting the second till the pain caused by the first had ceased; sixthly, he caused her to be flagellated although no prosecutor had made a complaint against her." When this came to the ears of commerce of humanity. During the khalifate of Mamun an effort was made to relieve the world of this horrible incubus of a dead revelation, and give some freedom to the intellect and conscience. A party which numbered the khalif among its adherents denied that the Koran was the Word of God, uncreated and eternal. They affirmed it to be the composition of the Prophet only, and as such liable to correction and modification. But their endeavours failed to make any wide or lasting change of thought, and the orthodox Muhammadan's creed remained, as before, 'stiff as a dead man's hand.' This hard inflexible rigidity it is which has rendered the Muhammadan world incapable of profiting by the experience of history, and powerless to heal the ravages of storm and decay.

The governors of the various provinces were clothed with powers as broad and sweeping as those of the khalif; but they derived all their authority from him, and the smallest deflection from the straight path of

Muhammad Ibn Abi Laila he sent this message to the Governor of Koufa: "There is here a youth called Abû Hanifa who attacks my judgments and gives opinions in opposition to them, and insults me by saying that I have erred. I wish you would prevent him from so doing." On this the governor sent to Abû Hanifa, ordering him not to give opinions on points of law. They then relate that Abû Hanifa was one day in his house, and his wife beside him, and his daughter and his son Hammad, when his daughter said to him: "Papa, I am keeping a fast of abstinence, and some blood has come out from between my teeth, but I spat it out till my saliva became clear, without any trace of blood. Should I break the fast if I swallowed my saliva now?" To this her father replied: "Ask thy brother Hammad, for the governor has forbidden me to give opinions on points of law." This anecdote is cited as an example of Abû Hanifa's signal merits and of his respectful obedience to the constituted authority, so much so that he obeyed even in private, and abstained from giving an answer to his daughter; this is the utmost extent to which obedience could be carried.'—*Ibn Khallikan*, vol. ii. p. 584. Slane's Trans.

obedience—so long at least as the central authority was strong and energetic—was visited with swift and often fearful retribution. The plan generally adopted was to depose the offending governor, and send his worst enemy to occupy his place, whose first act would be to destroy a possible rival. There was no regular mode of execution. Beheading was most common, but khalifs and governors exhibited a truly devilish ingenuity in devising torments for their enemies. Oriental history abounds with stories of almost incredible cruelty; and these impress the reader with the more horror because they are told without any expressions of wonder and reproach. They were too common to provoke such feelings. But a despotism of this kind, just because it succeeds so completely in crushing the patriotism of its subjects, can never be other than a fair weather government. It has no reserve fund of affection to the ruler or loyalty to the law, on which it can draw to supplement the mercenary force it wields. It stands upon force pure and simple, and therefore must fall the moment a stronger power takes the field against it. The khalifs suffered from this. A rebellious governor could only be coerced by a loyal one. But the loyal governor of a neighbouring province would hazard his life and his power only by the promise of an extension of wealth and authority. That extension once granted, the governor became virtually independent. There was no one left strong enough to coerce him, and the khalif had to be content with a nominal submission. Mamun, one of the greatest of the khalifs, was the first who was compelled to make one of these concessions. He granted Khorasan in perpetuity to his general, Taher. It was like the letting out of waters.

The Soffarides drove out the family of Taher; the Samanides supplanted the Soffarides; the Ghaznivides these; and so the turmoil of Eastern history whirls and spins unrestingly on as 'in dry Sahara, when the winds waken, and lift and winnow the immensity of sand. The air itself is (travellers say) a dim sand air; and dim looming through it, the wonderfullest colonnades of sand pillars rush, whirling from this side and from that like so many spinning dervishes of a hundred feet stature; and dance their huge desert waltz there.' What happened to the silent and suffering people while these spinning dervishes of conquerors danced their desert waltz on slain encumbered battle-fields, and by the light of burning cities, is not hard to guess. Occasional passages in the old chronicles reveal them to us perishing of famine and pestilence, or groaning under the iron heel of some tremendous tyrant. And we can easily understand how all faith in any divinely appointed order of the universe must have perished under the weight of these accumulated sufferings. It is by contemplating them that we penetrate to the inner springs of Oriental thought and action—of Sufism, which strives to seek for consolation by complete abstraction from a world racked by all the powers of evil; of Eastern poetry, which finds its fount of inspiration, its type of human joys, in the transient beauty of Spring, or the fleeting splendours of a full-blown rose; and, lastly, of those wild and desperate efforts to utterly destroy the foundations of all order, to set men free from the tyranny of all moral laws, and all religious creeds, of which the Karmathian insurrection was one, and the 'Sect of the Assassins' another and more terrible result.

A great number of sects are included under the designation 'Shia,' but the greater part of these sectaries ranged themselves into two divisions, namely, the Imamites, or Believers in the Twelve Imams, and the Ismailiens, or Believers in the Seven Imams. The Imamites trace the succession of Imams to the twelfth in descent from Ali—Muhammad, the well directed. He, while still a boy, becoming the object of the persecution of the Abbaside khalifs, disappeared down a well in the courtyard of the house in which he was living at Hillah, near Baghdad. At the end of time he will reappear and fill the world with justice. For this reason he is termed 'the Expected.' The Shias base this expectation, as usual, upon a tradition reported by one of 'the Companions' to the effect that the Prophet had declared that the world would not come to an end until a man of his family, and bearing the same name as himself, reigned over the Arabs; and Ibn Khaldun states in his *Prolegomena* that so late even as his time, groups of devout Shias assembled every evening after sunset at the mouth of the sacred well, and passed the night in prayer to the Imam, entreating him to come forth and take possession of the world. When the stars began to pale they retired to their homes, going through the same ceremonies on the next night.

The Ismailiens, like the Twelvers, make profession of an exclusive attachment to Ali and his descendants; they recognise no Imam as legitimate if he be not a member of that family, and in all the externals of religion they adopt the customs of the Shias. The schism was occasioned by a dispute on the question of succession to the Imamate. Djafar Ibn Sadik, the sixth Imam, had four sons, the eldest of whom was Ismail, whom also he designated as his successor. One day, however, Ismail had the misfortune to be discovered in a state of inebriety, and Djafar Ibn Sadik disinherited him, declaring that he could not be his son, but a demon who had assumed his similitude. His second son, Mousa, was then declared to be his successor to the dignity of the Imam. The greater part of the Shias accepted this decision, and on the death of Djafar Ibn Sadik transferred their allegiance to Mousa. But a small number, who applied the allegorical method of interpretation to the ordinances of the Koran, remained attached to Ismail, and on his death to his son Muhammad. To their minds the inebriety of Ismail was a virtue rather than otherwise, as a positive proof of his acceptance of an inner and hidden meaning in the precepts of religion. Djafar Ibn Sadik died A.H. 148; the origin of the sect therefore cannot date from a much earlier period than that event.

The doctrine of the Ismailiens was as follows: The world never has been nor ever will be without an Imam. Whoever is an Imam, his father and his grandfather had been so before him, and similarly his ancestors until the line terminates with Adam. The son of the Imam is also Imam, and his descendants after him to the end of time. It is not possible for an Imam to die until a son has been born to him to carry on the succession. The Imam is not always visible; at times he manifests himself; at times he withdraws into seclusion. When the Imam is manifest, the doctrine is concealed; when the Imam is hidden, the labours of the missionary commence. The Prophets possess the gift of revelation; the Imams that of interpretation. From the time of Ali until that of Muhammad, the son of Ismail, the seventh Imam, the Imams were visible. Then commenced the succession of concealed Imams.

The fourth of these concealed Imams (so called because they had to 'conceal' themselves from the inquisition of the khalifs of Baghdad) was a certain Abdallah, the son of Mamoun, who lived about the middle of the third century after the Hejira. In utter weariness, it would seem, of the wrangling of religious factions round him, he cast aside all theological beliefs, and conceived the project of founding human life and human society upon a basis of pure materialism. At the same time he perceived clearly enough that any open or sudden avowal of this audacious resolution would result in his instant death by the hands of his own followers. They were too fanatically attached to the chains which were eating into their souls, to welcome as an emancipator the man who would strike them off. He was obliged, therefore, to mask his purpose under the cloak of religion, and he adopted as this covering the affectation of a fervent zeal for the House of Ali. Obedience to the Imam was, however, only the portal, so to speak, of the Temple of Knowledge. The neophyte who desired to penetrate to the innermost circle of truth must pass through nine stages of initiation. But before describing these, it will be well to try to picture to ourselves the mental condition of that world to which Abdallah made appeal.

The discoveries of modern science have so wrought into our minds the conception of the universe as a vast orderly whole, subject to fixed laws—the torch of knowledge has so completely dispelled that vast host of secondary agencies—djinns, divs, genii, fairies, and the like which perplexed and tormented an earlier world—that we find it difficult to feel that the Arabian Nights, for example, really represent the convictions which once possessed all men regarding the unseen universe, which still hold sway over the larger portion of the earth. Still, there are moments even in our lives when we are conscious of feelings as if those old beliefs were attempting to re-establish themselves. On lonely mountain tops, in silent woods, whenever we are alone with Nature,

> The fair humanities of old religion,
> The power, the beauty, and the majesty
> That had their haunts in dale or piny mountain,

revive, and the world seems, as in days of old, to be endowed with a conscious life. But most of all do we understand such beliefs when we are in any danger from the fury of the elements. Then we can readily apprehend how the untutored intellect of an earlier world should have imagined a conscious purpose to be directing the *fury* of the sea, or the *pitiless* pelting of the blinding rain. And so it is that, to this day, the men who are most prone to this —shall we say—superstition are those who are most exposed to moving accidents by flood and field. There has rarely been a great general without his 'lucky day' or his 'star of destiny,' or some other *deus ex machina* to lighten the obscure and give hope in seasons of difficulty; while sailors have constructed quite a Pantheon of lesser deities out of Mother Carey's chickens and materials of a like kind.

In the times and countries of which I am writing,

everything combined to give a morbid activity to such exercises of the imagination. Science, as we understand it, had not yet been born, and the life of the Arab was one long struggle with the ruthless forces of Nature—'plague and famine, blight and earthquake, roaring deeps and fiery sands.' The imagination roamed at will amid the awful forces of Nature, and constructed a truly marvellous theory of the origin of things. Water was supposed to have been the first thing created by God, and the Eternal Throne was sustained on that element. From this water God caused a vapour to ascend out of which He fashioned the sky. Then He solidified a portion of the liquid mass and transformed it into earth, which He divided into seven parts. God then created a fish, on which the earth was supported; the fish and the water were borne up by blocks of stone; the stones rested on the back of an angel; the angel on a rock, and the rock on the wind. The movements of the fish causing the earth to be violently agitated, God fixed mountains upon it to give it stability. The heavens also numbered seven; that nearest to the earth was formed of green emerald; the next of silver; the third of ruby; the fourth of pearl; the fifth of pure gold; the sixth of topaz; and the seventh is an illimitable expanse of fire, covered with angels chanting the praises of God. They sing, 'There is no god but God, the Lord of the Glorious Throne.'

Around the earth was the 'circumambient ocean,' and around this again were the mountains of Kaf, formed of green chrysolite, and peopled with innumerable djinns. Previously to the creation of Adam these djinns had dwelt upon the earth. They had been forbidden to shed the blood of animals or quarrel with each other. They did both continually; so God in His anger sent down troops of angels, who in part exterminated them and in part shut them up in the mountains of Kaf. The inhabited portions of the earth compared with the unknown regions given up to deserts and demons were as a tent pitched in the midst of a wilderness. And even here such favoured spots as the gardens of Damascus were merely patches of verdure springing out of a vast expanse of barren waste. The appalling solitude, and still more appalling dangers of these sandy wastes, were the parents of countless superstitions. Every chamber of the great wilderness (to borrow the language of De Quincey) which with little interruption stretches from the Euphrates to the western shores of Africa, had its own peculiar terrors as to sights and sounds. Far away beyond Ségelmessa, in Northern Africa, on the other side of a large river extended the land of gold. The people of this mysterious region had never been seen by mortal eyes. The merchants who traded in gold deposited their merchandise on the banks of the river and departed. The next morning beside every article thus deposited they found the amount of gold the gnomes were willing to give for it. At the other extremity of the world, on the confines of China, rose a mighty circular temple from a massive block of rock, steeply scarped. It was furnished with seven gates, and crowned with an heptagonal dome marvellous for size and elevation. From the summit of this dome, what seemed to be a gigantic precious stone flashed a blinding radiance all around the temple. King after king had striven to get possession of this stone. But all who approached to a distance of ten cubits from it were stricken with instant death. Within the temple was a well, around the margin of which ran an inscription which said: 'This well leads to the archives of the Books, wherein are to be found the chronology of the world, the history of the past, and the revelation of the future.' But whoever, lured on by this inscription, was tempted to look down this well, was dragged into the abyss by an unseen but irresistible force, and disappeared in its fathomless depths. Between these two extreme points the world was all one wild and inexplicable marvel. The Muhammadan became a slave to his imagination. The air rustled with the invisible wings of supernatural beings. He was hedged in on every side by occult and malignant powers. His wellbeing—nay, his very existence—depended upon the properties of charms and amulets, the power of magicians, the intercessions of the pious. The historian al-Wakidi recommends the following as a charm for the cure of fevers: Take some olive leaves, and on a Saturday, being yourself in a state of purity, write on one of these leaves, *Hell is hungry;* on another, *Hell is thirsty;* and on the third, *Hell is refreshed.* Put them into a rag, and bind them on the left arm of the person suffering from fever. 'I made,' says al-Wakidi, 'the experiment myself, and found it successful.' 'When,' Ibn Khallikan informs us, 'Ibn al Khattan, the Poet, was sitting down to dinner with his wife, he told her to uncover her head. When she did so, he repeated these words of the Koran: *Say God is one.* She asked him what was the matter, and received this answer: 'When a woman uncovers her head the angels do not remain present, and when that verse of the Koran is pronounced, the demons take to flight. Now I do not like being at table with a crowd about me.'

Men, as it is not hard to understand, found it difficult to endure the burden and the mystery of such an unintelligible world as this, and eagerly grasped at anything which promised to illuminate the darkness. What was the secret of it all? what the ultimate power which assumed these innumerable forms? 'A hair,' so writes Omar Khayam—

> **A hair, they say, divides the False and True;**
> **Yes, and a single Alif were the clue,**
> **Could you but find it, to the Treasure House,**
> **And peradventure to the MASTER too.**

The search for that 'single Alif' was the great spur to enquiry in those days. A doctrine which required nine stages of initiation exactly suited the temper of the time. It struck the imagination as a kind of vista which narrowed the further one advanced, by the progressive elimination of all unimportant accidents from the vast and complex phenomenon which had to be investigated, until at the far end the enquirer was brought to the philosopher's stone, the single Alif, the narrow portal which gave admission to the temple of universal knowledge.

The nine stages were as follows:—The *Dai*, or missionary, having accosted this or that man, and engaged him in theological discussion, would take occasion to point out that the Koran and human life abounded in riddles which the unassisted intellect of man was powerless to solve. He would ply him with such questions as these:—Why had God created the world in seven days? Why had he thought proper to make seven heavens and seven climates? Why did the first chapter of the Koran contain only seven verses? Why were there twelve months in the year? How could it be true that the skins of the damned should be changed for other skins in order to make them suffer sharper torment, seeing that these new skins had done no evil? Why had Hell seven gates, and Paradise eight? Why was man alone upright among animals? Why had he ten fingers and ten toes, no more and no less? What meaning was involved in certain enigmatic expressions to be found in the Koran? with many others too numerous to mention. In general, such questions shook the soul of the enquiring Moslem with fear and wonder. He knew that in the sound of the word 'Allah' there were marvellous powers whereby men could annihilate time and space, liberate themselves from the prison house of flesh, and traverse the realms of air as disembodied spirits. He knew, or at least he believed, that magicians and enchanters could peer into the secrets of the heart, could make the forms of the absent appear by the power of their art, could compel beings of supernatural power to fetch and carry for them, like household drudges bought in the slave market; and that these marvels were wrought by the virtue hidden in strange collocations of words, by the repetition of enigmatic incantations or spells. The puzzling queries of the *Dai* seemed to place him at the very gate of similar mysteries. But how to enter in? The *Dai*, as soon as he saw that the shaft had struck, became as reserved as he had been communicative. The mysteries to which he had alluded were, it is true, known to a few elect and exalted spirits; but they were of too awful and tremendous a character to be revealed to any casual enquirer whose curiosity had been stimulated for a moment. It was not after this fashion that God proceeded when he selected a prophet to be a mediator between Himself and the world. He exacted a solemn engagement of fidelity and devotion. What says the Koran on this subject? 'We have entered into a covenant with the prophets and with thee, and with Noah and Abraham, and Moses, and Jesus, son of Mary: and we have formed with them a strict covenant.' If, then, the enquirer desired to enter into these most holy mysteries, he must conform himself to the example ordained by God. He must place his right hand in that of the missionary, and swear solemnly never to divulge the secrets about to be communicated to him; and never by thought, word, or deed to swerve from an unquestioning obedience to the missionary. The oath being taken, the second degree was entered upon.

In this the enquirer was instructed that to the Imams alone had been entrusted the duty of teaching the Faithful, and that all the calamities which had fallen upon Islam were due to the abandonment of these true teachers for so-called doctors, who had neither knowledge nor authority.

The third degree aimed to establish why there were seven Imams and no more, by argument from the analogy of the seven planets, the seven climates, and so forth; but chiefly because to Ismail and to none other of the descendants of Ali had been revealed the science of allegorical interpretation, the knowledge of the things hidden under those puzzling queries which the *Dai* had originally propounded to the neophyte.

The fourth degree was of great importance. Herein the enquirer was made acquainted with the special tenets regarding the Imamate held by the Ismailiens. These are, that the world since its creation has passed through seven 'periods,' each distinguished by its own peculiar religion. Each religion has had its own special promulgator or prophet, and each prophet has been accompanied by an Imam, or interpreter, whose function it has been to consolidate and establish the new religion which has been revealed, upon the ruins of the old. The number of such Imams, or interpreters, has in every case been limited to seven. Thus there have been seven religious 'periods,' seven prophets, and seven Imams to each prophet. The first prophet was Adam, and his Imam, Seth; the second Noah, and his Imam, Shem; the third Abraham, and his Imam, Ishmael; the fourth Moses, and his Imam, Joshua; the fifth Jesus, and his Imam, Simon Peter; the sixth Muhammad, and his Imam, Ali; the seventh Ismail, the son of Djafar as-Sadik, and his Imam, his son Muhammad. In Muhammad, the son of Ismail terminated the cycle of old faiths with their positive precepts and inculcation of the letter; and with him began the knowledge of that allegorical significance latent in all the preceding religions. The proselyte who passed through this grade ceased by that very act to be a Moslem; since, contrary to the express declarations of the Koran and the universal belief of the Muhammadan world, he acknowledged a prophet posterior to Muhammad, and a revelation which abrogated that contained in the Koran.

In the fifth degree the mind of the enquirer was imbued with a contempt for the traditions and the letter of the written word. All moral commands, he was instructed, and all religious ceremonies were to be explained allegorically. Then some faint adumbration of the Pythagorean doctrine of numbers was brought in to strengthen the special doctrines of the sect God, it was urged, never created anything without a design and special purpose. The arrangements of the external world contemplated by the discerning mind became the index to the nature of His spiritual supremacy over men. Thus the seven Imams, the seven prophets, the seven religious 'periods,' were figured and foreshadowed in the seven heavens, the seven planets, the seven climates, the seven apertures in the human face, and so forth. Each Imam had, moreover, twelve principal ministers to make him known throughout the world; and these were symbolised in the twelve signs of the Zodiac, the twelve months of the year, the twelve tribes of Israel. Few of the proselytes were, however, permitted to advance as far as this degree; and only certain hardy and resolute spirits even among the missionaries were deemed able to digest the strong meat provided for them in the sixth degree. For at this stage began the work of detaching the enquirer from all religious beliefs whatever. Hitherto the Prophets, the Imams, and the religions they taught and interpreted, had been mentioned with all due reverence. Though one religion was held to supersede another, there had been no question but that all were of Divine origin. But in this sixth degree, the opinions of the philosophers were for the first time opposed as superior to those of the prophets, because they were grounded upon the reason of man, whereas in the legal and ceremonial observances of religion it was impossible to discover anything reasonable. The fact being, as the missionary now ventured to suggest, that the laws and prohibitions of all religious creeds were cunningly devised artifices on the part of acute men to fetter the reason of men, and so make them orderly, submissive, and obedient; and the fiction of a Divine origin had been invented in order to give them authority. But they were suited only for the childhood of the race. The man arrived at the full stature of humanity, bore within himself, in his reason, the supreme criterion of his actions. He rose superior to the creeds of an earlier world, by becoming his own god, and, as such, discerning between good and evil.

In the seventh degree, the proselyte was made to observe that each one of the great prophets had had an assistant to preserve and propagate his doctrine: thus Abraham had his son Ishmael; Moses, Joshua; Jesus, Simon; Muhammad, Ali; and finally Ismail, the last of the Imams, had his son Muhammad. He was made to perceive that this dualism is an essential condition of the potential being transmuted into the actual. There must always be two living principles—the higher, *that which gives*; the lower, *that which receives*; the one male and life-giving; the other, female and life-bearing. The Deity Himself must have been subject to this condition. He could not have fashioned the world according to His thoughts unless the raw material (so to speak) had existed previously. The object of this grade was to destroy the doctrine of the Unity by asserting the co-eternity of matter.

The eighth degree developed this doctrine further. The two co-eternal principles under the designation of *that which precedes* and *that which follows*, were fused together into a vast and shadowy system of Pantheism, which represented good and evil, joy and sorrow, pleasure and pain, as manifestations of one changeless essence—a constant *becoming* or everlasting process of evolution, not unlike the operations of Hegel's famous principle of identity. Before this last revelation the entire fabric of past faiths crumbled into ruins. The miracles by which prophets were said to have supported their teaching were merely an allegorical account of the rising of one religion on the ruins of that which preceded it; the resurrection, the end of the world, the final judgment, were figurative expressions to signify the recurring cycles of the stars—the death and new birth of all living things from the inherent affinities and organic properties of matter. The veritable prophet is not the worker of miracles, but the founder of a political order in harmony with the nature of man; not the preacher of some doctrines about God, but the setter forth of a philosophical system concerning the primitive formation of the heaven and the earth, the substance and the accidents of the universe.

Arrived at the ninth degree, the proselyte was welcomed to the spiritual emancipation prepared for him. He passed behind the veil, and found there—blank negation. There was no God; there was no such thing as a law, moral or ceremonial, binding on the passions of men. Self-restraint, prayers, alms, pilgrimages, were all parts of a gigantic falsehood palmed off by the few upon the many in order to hold them in subjection. A society, like Muhammadanism, erected upon such manifest falsehoods, must be extirpated root and branch before men could obtain that portion of happiness which was to be snatched from the fleeting hours of life. Coleridge has remarked on the appalling power the most insignificant man could put forth who was completely emancipated from the control of a moral law. Such were the instruments which Abdallah sought to frame for his war against Islam; and with what terrible success, is recorded in the history of the Karmathian insurrection and that of the Assassins.

The Karmathians were so called from Karmath—a name given to the *Dai*, or missionary, whose preaching in the country round Koufa led to the formation of the sect. The disintegration of the Muhammadan empire had advanced with rapid steps, but the khalif was still a potentate of considerable power when this sect broke out into revolt. Mutadhid was the Abbaside khalif reigning at Baghdad. The disorders they at first excited were inconsiderable; but they continually increased in strength; and with every accession of strength their blows fell heavier on the tottering fabric of orthodoxy. In the course of six years they had laid waste with fire and sword the provinces of Irak, Syria, and Mesopotamia; they had stormed the cities of Baalbec and Salenico, and massacred the citizens. The armies of the khalifs were defeated again and again. The karavans proceeding to the Holy City were repeatedly plundered and the pilgrims murdered. All the country which lay between Baghdad and Mekka became a scene of smoking ruins, weeping, and bloodshedding. The leaders of the Karmathians assumed the state of powerful princes. In the province of Hasa, shut in on every side by the burning sands of the Red Desert, they ruled secure from invasion. The remains of their magnificent palace is still to be seen on the shores of the Persian Gulf. It was in A.H. 317 that these ruthless sectaries committed their most dreadful outrage—an outrage which filled Islam with horror, and awakened an intensity of hatred which at length effected the suppression of the Karmathians.

The karavans had arrived safely at Mekka—an unusual occurrence—and the Holy City was filled to overflowing with the numbers of the devotees. On the 8th Dzul Hajj the great pilgrimage is made to the mountain of Arafat. The city and all the narrow valleys were crowded with the concourse of men, horses, and camels; each karavan striving to fall into its appointed station. Suddenly, the gleam of swords and spears flashed in a line of fire above the hills overlooking Mekka. The Karmathians, under their fierce chieftain, Abou Tahir, had marched rapidly across the desert, over the uplands of Nejd, and now stood mustered in battle array, with the devoted city at their feet. The vast multitude, wedged into the narrow streets, could neither fight nor fly. The swords of the Karmathians hewed their bloody way through an unresisting mass. The slaughter did not cease till thirty thousand corpses lay rotting in the sacred valley. The holy well of Zem Zem was choked with the bodies of the slain. The pavement of the House of God was torn up and the slaughtered devotees buried in the holy precincts, in promiscuous heaps, without any of those rites which are held essential at the interment of a true believer.

Mekka was pillaged; the cloth covering of the Kaaba removed; and the black stone, split into pieces by a blow from a sacrilegious Karmathian, was conveyed away to Hasa, and not restored for a space of twenty-two years. 'On the whole,' says Ibn Khallikan, 'no Moslems, either before or after them, committed such crimes against Islamism as they; most of Irak and of the land of the East (i.e. Mesopotamia), the province of Hejaz, Syria, and the country up to the gates of Misr (Egypt), fell into their power.' But this last outrage had the effect of uniting the orthodox against the common enemy. It became a struggle not merely for the preservation of Islam, but of society against anarchy. The conflict raged with intermittent severity till nearly the close of the century, when the Karmathians yielded up the struggle. They were driven back and cooped up in the narrow strip of cultivation that runs along the Persian Gulf. The Red Desert, they trusted, would remain the insuperable barrier it had always been; but even in this they were disappointed. In the year 378, an Arab named Asfar passed the desert, destroyed the palace of the Karmathian chiefs, and dispersed or exterminated the feeble remnants of their followers; and from this time there is no further mention of the Karmathians in Muhammadan history. Nevertheless, the people of Hasa and Bahrein have never since returned in heart to Islam. The district, Mr. Gifford Palgrave tells us, has remained permanently estranged,—a heap of moral and religious ruins, of Karmathian and esoteric doctrines. The Wahabee at present reigns supreme there and compels an external orthodoxy, but 'the Karmathian reaction burns secretly on, and waits but an occasion to break out afresh into a blaze sufficient to consume, perhaps for the last time, the superstructure of Wahabeeism and Islam.'

It was a seed flung from this teeming nursery-ground of heresy and abomination which, lighting on the soil of Northern Africa, developed into the empire of the Fatimide khalifs of Africa and Egypt.

CHAPTER II.

THE ARAB AND THE BERBER.

A.D. 647–893.

AMONG the Arabs there was no division of the world known under the name of 'Africa.' Egypt was not included in that continent at all, and the name of 'Afrikia' applied only to the northern parts of Africa which at present include the kingdoms of Morocco, Algiers, Tunis and Tripoli, known generally as Barbary. This tract of country was divided by Muhammadan geographers into three parts—*Further Magreb*, extending from the shores of the Atlantic to Telemsan; *Central Magreb*, which included the tract of country lying between Oran and the district of Bagaia; and *Afrikia* proper, which extended from the eastern limit of *Central Magreb* to the Egyptian frontier. The Great Desert formed its southern boundary. The Atlas Mountains were its most remarkable natural feature. These extend across the whole of Northern Africa, or, to speak more correctly, they form a series of parallel chains running north-east and south-west, and separated from each other by level valleys of varying width. The highest parts of this range are the snow-capped mountains which separate Morocco from the Desert. Next in height to these are the mountains of

Auress, which extend nearly to the frontier of Tunis; and between these are several minor ranges, having rich sheltered plains running up between them, the abundant harvests of which made Numidia in the old time one of the granaries of Rome. As the mountain land approaches Tripoli, the hills and the valleys between them become parched and sterile, and ultimately reach the frontiers of Egypt as a chain of naked rocks. All the western and more fruitful parts of this strip of Africa were known to the Arabs as 'the land of dates,' from the abundance of that fruit which they produced. The date-trees clustered round the feet of the hills, and for miles and miles between the southern slopes of the Atlas and the inhospitable waste of the Great Desert, the interminable groves threw a broad and grateful shadow over the land. To early historians and geographers, the people of these countries were known as Libyans; by the Arabs they were called *Berbers*—a tall, noble-looking race of men, fair skinned, though embrowned by the scorching rays of an African sun, and with an air of pride and indomitable love of freedom stamped upon their faces, their action, and their speech.

While the broad belt of desert which encloses the central regions of Africa has secluded them from any notable part in the world's history, the northern regions have repeatedly been the theatre of great events. Here the great Carthaginian Republic flourished and fell. From the brave and hardy mountaineers of the Atlas she recruited her famous Numidian Horse, whose swords did such fearful execution on the battle-fields of Thrasymene and Cannœ. Mounted on their small Barbary horses, they needed no saddles, and a halter of twisted rushes served them for bridle. The skin of a lion or tiger was their dress by day and their couch at night. When they fought on foot a piece of elephant's hide served them as a shield. Their onset was dreadful by reason of the speed and cunning of their horses. If unsuccessful, they eluded pursuit by scattering like so much chaff before a gust of wind, till a fresh opportunity arose, when the broken fragments would reunite with astonishing rapidity, and in one compact body swoop down upon their prey. These mercenary troops were at once the strength and the weakness of the Carthaginian Republic. They were irreclaimable barbarians, with the usual virtues and faults of the savage. Severed into a vast number of tribes, divided from each other by hereditary hatreds, they repelled every attempt to make them abandon this savage and bloody independence. They hated all order, and all masters, good, bad, or indifferent. Greedy of plunder and reckless of life, they fought with great courage in the armies of the Republic. But they had no love for the mistress they served. At any offence given, their swords were ready to sheathe themselves in the bosom they were intended to defend. The Carthaginians, on their side, treated these mercenary troops with that callous indifference to the rights and feelings of 'barbarians' which was characteristic of the old world. The mutual hatred, long smouldering, broke out at the close of the first war with Rome. The army of Carthage rose against the city and nearly brought her to destruction. The 'war of the mercenaries,' though ultimately brought to a successful conclusion, inflicted a wound upon the Republic, from which she never recovered. It revealed the secret of her weakness. The wandering tribes of the Atlas discovered that they held her fate in their hands, and they flocked to the banners of Scipio as soon as he landed in Africa. And so Rome triumphed and Carthage fell. The one power was founded upon the rock of patriotism; the other upon the shifting sand of a mercenary army. Nothing less than the matchless genius of Hannibal could have succeeded in maintaining the unequal struggle so long.

Carthage fell; the wars against Jugurtha were fought out to their bloody conclusion; the Vandals drove out the Romans; the Romans drove out the Vandals; Northern Africa from one end to the other became a theatre of religious persecution, wasted with fire and sword; but through all these tempests and vicissitudes the mountaineers preserved untainted their barbarism and independence. They continued as of old to wander over the desert, and build their villages in the valleys running up between the parallel ranges of the Atlas. The poorer classes devoted themselves to the cultivation of the soil; the richer wandered with their flocks and herds from one pasture land to another; each tribe had its own chiefs, and they were in unison upon one matter only—no government should ever be allowed to restrict the liberty they so dearly loved. Their matchless and innumerable cavalry was at the disposal of any one who would aid them in casting off an existing yoke, whether imposed by Carthaginian, Vandal, Roman, or Arab.

It is necessary to keep these traits in recollection to understand the history of Northern Africa under the domination of the Arabs. The conquerors of Asia found themselves in these regions confronted by an enemy unlike any they had hitherto encountered. In Syria and Persia they had fought against populations physically weakened by luxury, and spiritually enfeebled by despotism. The highly centralised form of government existing in those countries had concentrated at a single point all the springs of resistance. That point mastered, the country was defenceless. But in Northern Africa every valley was the home of a teeming population who rated liberty higher than life, who were as inured to hardship, as bold, vigorous, and active as the Arabs themselves. Greek met Greek, and the tug of war was terrible indeed. Money and treasure were poured into these regions without stint by the khalifs. The Arab's brilliant courage was nowhere illustrated by more brilliant deeds, but he never held more of the soil than what his armed foot was planted on. Even from that he was repeatedly cast out. The Arab armies cut like the keel of a ship into the masses of their Berber enemies. Like the waves of the sea, these masses reunited and closed up behind them, and army after army was engulfed. 'The Berbers,' said the great Arabian general, Mousa, the conqueror of Spain, —'the Berbers, Commander of the Faithful, are of all foreign nations the people who most resemble the Arabs in impetuosity, corporal strength, endurance, military science, and generosity; only that they are, Commander of the Faithful, the most treacherous people on earth.'

The first expedition of the Arabs was made A.H. 27 (A.D. 647–8). Othman was at that time khalif, and had entrusted the government of Egypt to his brother

Abdallah. Abdallah sent parties of horsemen into Afrikia to report upon the country, and the accounts they brought back of its wealth and fertility determined Othman to undertake a regular invasion. The khalif furnished from his private funds a thousand camels for the use of the poorer soldiery, as well as horses and arms, and bestowed a gratuity upon each soldier enrolled in the expedition. The army was composed of detachments from several Arab tribes, and these, on arrival in Egypt, were further strengthened until they reached a total of twenty thousand men. The governor of Egypt took command of the whole. He marched swiftly across the desert of Barka, left the walled cities of Tripoli and Kabes in his rear, and attacked the Byzantine prefect, Gregorius, in a plain, twenty-four hours' journey from Carthage—'a vast city,' says the Arabian chronicler, 'enclosing lofty edifices, with walls of white marble, and thronged with colonnades and monuments of various colours in immense numbers.' The Greek army was completely defeated, and Gregorius slain. By the payment, however, of a sum of money, the Greek government prevailed upon the Arabs to withdraw into Egypt. The interval of peace was a short one. The rapacity of the Greek government drove the Berbers into rebellion; they invited the Arabs to come to their assistance,—an invitation eagerly accepted. It is unnecessary to follow the incidents of the war. Suffice it to say that by A.H. 55 (A.D. 675) the Arab rule was established in Afrikia proper. The governor was the celebrated Okba, and he had built a city—Kairoan—as a point of support from which to push into the interior of the country. The Greeks still occupied Magreb, and had collected an immense number of Berbers as auxiliaries to their regular troops. In the year 55, Okba, at the head of a large army, crossed the boundary line of Afrikia, and entered Magreb. The open towns surrendered as he approached; the Greeks and Berbers hung about the flanks of his army and tried to impede his advance; but he made his way, by dint of hard fighting, through all obstacles, until he reached the furthest coast of Africa, and beheld before him the tumbling billows of the Atlantic. Spurring his horse, chest deep, into the waves, he raised his hand to Heaven, and exclaimed: 'O God! but for this sea I would have gone into still remoter countries, like unto Zulkarnein, fighting for Thy religion, and slaying such as believe in other gods than Thee!'[1]

This triumphant advance of Okba had the effect of stilling the turbulent Berbers into an alarmed quiescence. The land had rest for a brief space. Okba himself was the means of arousing the storm again. He grossly and wantonly insulted Koseila, a leading Berber chieftain. At his summons the clans resumed the weapons they had just laid aside, and a countless host poured forth from all the valleys of the Atlas on the handful of Arabs that garrisoned Kairoan. Okba disdained to endure a siege. He broke the scabbard of his sword in token of his resolution to conquer or die, and, leading out his small force, charged into the centre of the Berbers who

[1] Okba here alludes to the following passage in the seventh sura of the Koran, entitled 'The Cave' (Zulkarnein, it must be premised, is supposed by the majority of commentators to be Alexander the Great):—'The Jews will ask thee concerning Zulkarnein. Answer, I will rehearse unto you an account of him, &c. &c.'—Vide Sale's *Koran*, p. 246-7.

encompassed his capital. He fell fighting; only a very few of the Arabs effected a retreat into Egypt; Koseila took possession of Kairoan; and the domination of the Moslems appeared to be at an end.

The khalif Abd al Malek was at this time struggling with a number of formidable enemies. Abdallah ibn Zobair ruled in the Hejaz; the fierce and crafty al-Moktar held Koufa, and dealt out a bloody revenge for the death of Hosain; the Kharegites scoured Irak, leaving wherever they passed ruin and desolation. It was impossible, so long as these enemies were unsubdued, to attempt the recovery of Northern Africa, and for the space of four years Koseila ruled in Kairoan as an independent king. At length, in A.H. 69 (A.D. 619), Abd al Malek found himself sufficiently secure on his throne .to undertake the reconquest of Afrikia. In that year Zobair, the lieutenant of Okba, who, after the fall of his chief, had with a few troops maintained himself in Barka, entered Afrikia with an army larger and better equipped than the one which had been destroyed with Okba. Koseila abandoned Kairoan at his approach, falling back in order to give the Berbers time to leave their mountain homes and rally round him. The Arabs followed closely, and, according to their own account, made immense havoc amid the retreating mountaineers. But their success was short-lived. Zobair had not advanced far when he heard that a Greek army, encouraged by the late expulsion of the Arabs, had appeared upon the coast of Barka. He hastily retraced his steps, rashly attacked these new invaders with very inferior forces, and he and his troops were cut to pieces almost to a man. Afrikia had again cast out the Muhammadan invader.

The khalif, however, was not to be discouraged. In A.H. 74 a third army, 40,000 strong, and commanded by Hasan ibn Noman, made good its footing upon the hardly-contested soil. For awhile it carried all before it. Kairoan was recaptured; the city of Carthage was stormed and pillaged; and the Greeks and Berbers defeated in a great battle in the open field. The remnant of the Greek army hastily abandoned the country; the Arab was once more supreme, but only for a very brief while. Koseila had died; but his vast influence had passed undiminished to a woman—*El Kahina*, or the Divineress—who was supposed to have the power of prediction, and to be gifted with other supernatural attributes. She descended from the highlands of Mount Auress at the head of an immense multitude, defeated the Arabs with great slaughter, and compelled them for the third time to relinquish their hardly-gotten prize.

For five years *El Kahina* remained the queen of Northern Africa. At the expiration of that time Abd al Malek despatched a fourth army to attempt the recovery of the province. On receiving intelligence of the march of this new army the Berber queen formed the desperate resolution of turning the entire province of Afrikia into a desert. It was the wealth of the country, the grandeur and luxury of the cities which the Greeks had left behind them, which, she supposed, attracted thither these pertinacious invaders. But all this wealth was in the hands of aliens, Muhammadans, Jews, and Christians; for the Berbers it had no attraction. They needed nothing but their flocks and grazing grounds. So, in a speech to her troops, she informed them that if they really desired to stay these repeated invasions, and preserve unmolested their old immemorial freedom, they must utterly destroy the attractions which lured the enemy thither. Immediately the hordes of the Berbers spread all over the country, more destructive than an army of locusts. The cities and the villages were laid in ruins; the groves were cut down; the precious metals, and all that was valuable and could not be destroyed, were carried away into the recesses of the mountains. From Tripoli to Tangiers there was not a town or a village which did not suffer in a greater or less degree from the effects of this destroying fury. These stern measures materially aided the re-conquest of the province. As Hasan ibn Noman advanced into the country he was hailed as a deliverer by all the mercantile and agricultural populations. The gates of the cities were flung open to him; the people thronged into his camp to take the oath of allegiance, and swell the strength of his army. The Sibyl was defeated and slain in a great battle; and the Berbers, exhausted by the indomitable perseverance of the Arabs, sued for peace. They obtained it on the condition that they should furnish a contingent of 24,000 men to aid in the invasion of Spain.

'From this time,' says the chronicler, 'Islam spread itself among the Berbers.' But the change of faith worked no change in the national character. They remained as deeply enamoured as before of their savage independence; they hated the Arab more bitterly now that his foot was planted on their necks than when they confronted him on equal terms in the field of battle. They waited only for an opportunity to assume their old attitude of active hostility. The materials for an explosion were all ready; it needed only a chance spark to fall and ignite them. The spark soon fell. A new sect appeared in Northern Africa—the sect of the Separatists. These were the descendants of the men who had forced Ali at the moment of victory to submit his claims to arbitration; and then denounced him as a heretic for having done so. Ali defeated them in two battles with such crushing severity that for many years after they made no third appeal to arms. The character of their tenets, for a while, underwent a complete change. They became the adherents of Islam as it was preached at Mekka. They asserted that mere faith unaccompanied by works—an intellectual confession of the unity without a corresponding observance of the moral law—was powerless to save. They declared that the quarrels which rent the Muhammadan world on the subject of the Imamate or lawful head of Islam were about a matter of no spiritual importance. The true Imam was neither, of necessity, a member of the tribe of Kuraish, nor of the family of the Prophet, but the devoutest and purest believer among the Faithful. The Faithful, however, could manage perfectly well for themselves whether this—the only true and lawful Imam—was visibly at their head or not. Into this sect, during these years of its peaceful propagation, were gradually attracted all those spirits who were disgusted by the debaucheries and cruelties of the khalifs of Damascus, and weary of the endless hair-splitting controversies of Muhammadan doctors. They became the subjects of a cruel persecution, which they endured for a time with rare fortitude and resignation. But at last, maddened by the relentless cruelty with which they were hunted out and killed wherever they were found, they proclaimed the *jehad*, or 'sacred war,' against all unbelievers. They passed from one extreme to the other. They alone were the 'children of light;' all other (so-called) Muhammadans were unbelieving dogs to be slaughtered without mercy. They carried on their war with an awful ferocity; women and children fell before their indiscriminating fury; and it was only after enormous cruelty, fighting, and blood-shedding that they were driven out of Irak, some into Hasa, others through Egypt into Afrikia and Magreb.

These were precisely the leaders the Berbers were in search of. Hitherto they had always commenced one of their fierce outbreaks with a general renunciation of the Muhammadan faith, and a return to the national worship of their hills. But their uniform ill-success had generated the belief that this Arabian god was stronger far than any they worshipped—that they must have him on their side if they hoped for success. The Separatists seemed to have brought this secret with them. The Berbers hated the government that was over them; the Berbers deemed that these Arab rulers were an accursed race, fit only to be devoured by the sword; and now these sectaries came among them with the glad tidings that such feelings and such acts were exactly those most grateful to the deity they wished to have upon their side. These Separatists, like themselves, rejected the authority of all khalifs indifferently. They cursed Othman; they cursed Ali; they cursed Ayesha Talha and Zobair; they cursed the House of Ommaya; they consigned to everlasting torments the most venerated of the companions of the Prophets. They alone were the true Muhammadans, and it was their business to exterminate idolators, hypocrites, and misbelievers from the earth they contaminated. This was the true Holy War; and whoever refused to take part in this pious work became a heretic, who was to be slaughtered without pity, and his wife and children reduced to slavery. The Berbers, to their great joy, found that they had been Muhammadans all along, without knowing it. All these tremendous doctrines had been revealed to them, as it were, by the light of nature, and embraced with ardent enthusiasm. They were, in fact, the true believers, and their Arab conquerors the outcasts and heretics. The Separatist leaders, who had been hunted like partridges upon the hills, found themselves all at once the leaders of formidable hosts.

In two successive battles the Arabs were defeated. In the latter of these the Arab general and his chief officers, in the usual heroic fashion of their nation, scorned to fly when their army was broken and routed. It is no exaggeration to say of an Arab general of that day that he died, but never surrendered. The battle was known as 'the fight of the nobles,' from the number of distinguished men who perished in it. The khalif Hisham ibn Abd al Malek broke out in fierce wrath when he heard of the disaster. 'By Allah!' he cried, 'I will make them feel the wrath of an Arab. I will send an army such as has never been seen in their country. The head of the column shall be entering Afrikia while the rear is still with us. I will not leave a Berber fort without establishing at its side a standing camp of warriors of the tribe of

Kais or that of Temim.' The menace proved to be an idle one. A fresh host, it is true, was poured into Afrikia, but only to be cut to pieces like those which had preceded it. The rule of the Damascus khalif was limited to the walls of Kairoan. And in A.H. 124 the Berbers determined to wrest from him this solitary possession.

Two large armies came down from the hills to make a joint attack upon Kairoan. The Arab governor, Hanzala, a man who combined all the religious enthusiasm of the Muhammadan with a gentleness of heart unwonted in that savage age, acted with resolution and promptitude. He sallied forth from the city, and, assailing one of the two armies—that commanded by Okasa, the Safrite—before it could effect a junction with the other, routed it with heavy loss. He then fell back on Kairoan to repel the second army. But the force he sent out to stay its advance, after a great deal of hard fighting, which continued for the space of a month, was driven back upon Kairoan, seriously weakened in numbers. Okasa, in the meanwhile, had recovered from his defeat, and the two hosts beleaguered the devoted city. The chronicler, with the usual exaggeration of the Oriental, numbers them at 300,000 men. Hanzala, however, was not dismayed. He drew out of the magazines all the arms stored up in them, and made an appeal to the inhabitants, giving to each person that enlisted a complete suit of armour and fifty *dinars*. This attracted so many volunteers to his ranks that he diminished his gratuity first to forty, then to thirty *dinars*, rejecting all recruits but the young and vigorous. It was a crisis never to be forgotten by those who, with beating hearts and straining eyes, watched till the torches of the night had burned out, and day stood tiptoe on the misty mountain tops. All round the city the twinkle of the innumerable watch-fires marked out the lines of the beleaguering host. Within, in the great square in front of the mosque, the glare of the lights showed Hanzala and his chief officers engaged hour after hour in the distribution of arms for the morrow's battle. It was for all a question of life and death. A Berber victory would instantly convert the city into a human shambles, where men, women, and children would be slaughtered indiscriminately. At the break of day the besieged troops broke every man his scabbard—the usual Arab symbol that death or victory was the only choice before them—and marched forth to engage the enemy. There was a terrible struggle; but the courage of despair proved at the last stronger than the force of numbers. The vast Berber host broke and fled; their numbers encumbered their flight, and rendered impossible either order or resistance. The Arabs pressed their rear, and slew them by thousands. One hundred and eighty thousand in all are said to have perished. This, of course, is wildly exaggerated. The statistics of Oriental historians are pure and unalloyed products of the imagination; but there can be no doubt that the victory wrought a marvellous and unhoped-for deliverance. It was accounted one of the 'great days' of the Arabs. 'After the battle of Bedr,' said a warrior of that time who was not present, 'I should wish to have fought in the battle in front of Kairoan.'

But this brilliant victory brought no lasting peace. As soon as the Berber hosts were scattered, the Arabian emirs commenced to quarrel with each other. A few years after the battle of Kairoan occurred in Asia the great revolution which overthrew the House of Ommaya, and replaced it by that of the Abbasides. The rights of one house or the other furnished a convenient pretext for the revolt of any ambitious chieftain who hungered after power. If defeated, he sought and obtained shelter among the Berbers. These eagerly availed themselves of the divisions among the Arabs to recover their independence. Partial revolts and sanguinary battles kept the province in a state of perpetual turbulence, and exhausted even the long-enduring courage of the Arabs; and in A.H. 154, another universal and terrific outbreak occurred.

Abou Djafar al Mansour, the second of the Abbaside khalifs, was at this time reigning at Damascus, and his representative in Afrikia was Omar ibn Hafs, a descendant of the great Muhallab, the conqueror of the Kharegites, and himself a soldier of brilliant courage. He had acquired by his deeds the cognomen of *Hazarmerd* (equal to 1,000 men). How well he deserved that title we shall soon see. He had commenced to govern Afrikia A.H. 151, and for three years nothing had occurred to disturb the tranquillity of the country. Deluded into a false security, Omar, leaving Kairoan under charge of a relative, Abou Hazem Habib, repaired to Tobna, a distant town on the coast of Magreb, to superintend the re-building of the walls. Immediately, as by a common impulse, the Berbers arose in revolt at a dozen different points. The Arab detachments scattered about the country were buried beneath the human avalanche that rushed down the hills. Abou Hazem was killed in a great battle in front of Kairoan, and that town blockaded. Tripoli was seized. A host of 300,000 Kharegites, made up of levies from different Berber tribes, blockaded Omar ibn Hafs in Tobna. He had with him only 5,000 men. Seeing himself invested by this huge multitude, Hazarmerd assembled his principal officers, and demanded their advice. They were all of opinion that it would be madness to attempt a sortie; and he determined to have recourse to bribery to break up this formidable league. He sent into the camp of the enemy a native of Northern Africa, to whom he entrusted a sum of 40,000 dinars and a large number of rich vestments, and instructed him to purchase therewith from Abou Karra—a Kharegite leader at the head of 40,000 men—a promise to abandon his allies. These proposals were scornfully rejected by the Kharegite chief, but his son undertook to do all that was needed on receiving a sum of 4,000 dinars and some rich clothing. Abou Karra was a stranger to these negotiations, and obtained his first intimation of them by the breaking up of the force under his command, and the dispersal of the men to their homes. Having in this way got rid of one portion of the enemy, Omar sent a detachment of 1,500 men to surprise a body of 15,000 cavalry under Ibn Roustem, another of the Kharegite chiefs. This enterprise was completely successful, and the huge Berber army despairing of success withdrew from the walls of Tobna.

These events had occupied eight months, and during all this time the city of Kairoan had been held closely besieged. There remained not a single *dirhem* in the treasury, nor any food in the granaries. The inhabitants were eating dogs and the baggage animals, such as mules and donkeys, and were exhausted by their labours in repelling the almost daily assaults of the Berbers. Already a large number of the townspeople, despairing of relief, had abandoned Kairoan, and yielded themselves prisoners to the besiegers. Omar ibn Hafs, learning their extremity, took with him 700 men and hastened to their relief. His departure was the signal for a fresh assault on Tobna by the Kharegites. But the lieutenant he had left behind him made a sortie with such effectual vigour that the enemy were forced back in the utmost confusion. Omar, in the meanwhile, had reached Arbés, a place situate a three days' journey from Kairoan. The Berbers, ignorant of the force he had with him, raised the siege when they heard of his approach, and marched to attack him. Omar retired upon Tunis, drawing the Berbers after him. This gave the exhausted garrison the time and opportunity to refill their empty granaries. Omar, in the meanwhile, by a swift and skilful movement, marched unperceived round the flank of the unwieldy Berber army, and joined the defenders of Kairoan. He had barely time to complete the provisioning of the place, and strengthen the outworks, when an immense wall of dust, moving across the level plain on which the city of Kairoan stands, showed that the enemy were at hand. They were 130,000 strong.

Omar attacked them with fury; but by sheer weight of numbers the Berbers, though suffering tremendous losses, succeeded in cooping up the fiery little band of Arabs within the circle of their defences. Day after day, from that time Omar harassed the besieging army by fierce attacks, till the strength of his little garrison was well-nigh exhausted. Soon, too, famine re-appeared, and cats, dogs, mules, and donkeys were the only articles of food left to the wretched townspeople. The people lost heart. Omar then proposed to take a band of chosen men, cut his way through the enemy, and, after collecting provisions in the country beyond, force his way back into the town. At first the people consented, but the Berber host had now increased to double the strength which it possessed when it commenced the siege; hatred of the Muhammadan and the hope of plunder had drawn thither thousands of hardy recruits from all the tribes of Northern Africa; and when the people of Kairoan gazed forth upon the enormous multitude which begirt their city, their hearts sank within them at the thought of losing their heroic leader. They entreated him to stay, and depute to another the charge of the sortie. Omar consented. But here a new difficulty arose. The soldiers refused to make the attempt unless they had Omar at their head. At this moment, angry at the opposition he encountered, Omar received a letter from his wife, in which she informed him that the khalif, angry at receiving no intelligence, had recalled him and sent to Afrikia Yezid ibn Hatem at the head of 60,000 men. This, then, was to be the reward of his labours. His wife had added in her letter that to survive such a disgrace would be dishonourable. Omar felt that it would be so. He ordered the troops to make ready for the grand sortie which had been determined on. He would lead them himself, he said. 'Then,' relates one of his friends, 'he demanded to see me. On coming into his presence, I saw he was deeply moved with anger; the sweat stood on his forehead; he gave me his wife's letter; I wept when I read it. "What evil is there," I said, "that a member of your own family should come to deliver and give you rest?" "Yes," he replied, "a rest that will continue till the day of resurrection. Be attentive now to my last wishes." He dictated them to me; then, rushing out like a furious camel, he flung himself on the besiegers and ceased not to strike with lance and sword till he received a mortal wound,'[1] Dzul Hajj. A.H. 154 (October, A.D. 771).

Kairoan seemed to be lost; but the courage and tenacity of the defenders had impressed even the ruthless Kharegites with admiration. They offered honourable terms to the city, which were joyfully accepted. Kairoan threw open her gates; and for the fifth time since the first coming of the Arabs, the Berbers were masters of their native hills and valleys.

We do not purpose to follow the eventful, but monotonous, narrative further, or to tell how Yezid ibn Hatem—a soldier of the same family, and cast in the same heroic mould as his predecessor—re-established the authority of the khalif in Afrikia by a series of splendid military successes. He is said to have fought upwards of sixty battles in achieving this arduous task. But his death (A.H. 170)

[1] One is reminded of the passage in Scott's 'Rokeby'—

And now my race of terror run,
Mine be the eve of tropic sun!
No pale gradations quench his ray,
No twilight dews his wrath allay;
With disk-like battle target red
He rushes to his burning bed;
Dyes the wide wave with bloody light,
Then sinks at once—and all is night.

was the signal for the old confusion to recommence. The khalifs, in fact, never succeeded in conquering the northern provinces of Africa throughout their entire extent. Their authority never extended beyond the limits of Afrikia Proper. And even this, in the year 183, was virtually ceded by the khalif Haroun al Rashed to the family of the Aghlabites. Hitherto an annual subvention of 100,000 dinars had been sent to Kairoan to defray the cost of governing Afrikia. In the year above mentioned Ibrahim ibn al Aghlab—a soldier who had won fame in these African wars—wrote to the khalif, undertaking, if invested with the government, not only to relinquish the annual subsidy, but to pay into the treasury at Baghdad a yearly revenue of 40,000 dinars. The khalif, not without reluctance, accepted this proposal, and the province of Afrikia became a kind of hereditary fief held by the Aghlabite family.

The Aghlabites held the province in truly military fashion. Ten thousand watch-towers, or forts, were erected along the frontier line to protect Afrikia from the inroads of the Berbers of Magreb. The dismantled towns were surrounded with walls; a system of signals, by means of beacon-fires, could in a single night carry intelligence from the Straits of Gibraltar to the frontier of Egypt; and regular postal routes knit together the most distant parts of the province. Along these routes horses and couriers were always in readiness to carry news to the capital; and their maintenance in an efficient state was one of the most important duties of the Administration. Finally, to protect them from the turbulence of their own subjects, the Aghlabites imported immense numbers of negro slaves from Soudan, which, to the number of many thousands, formed their personal body-guard.

They were splendid princes of the Oriental type, rejoicing in erecting magnificent mosques, excavating enormous tanks, and building spacious and sumptuous palaces. They carried their arms into Sicily and wrested that rich island from the Byzantine empire. Themselves of Persian extraction, the Aghlabites spread through the province the sciences, the arts, the public education which the great Persian revolution in Asia caused to flourish with (unhappily) such transient brilliancy at Baghdad. Ibrahim ibn al Aghlab received, at his favourite residence Kasr al Kadim, the ambassadors of Charlemagne; and the young doctors of his capital travelled to the holy cities to study theology and jurisprudence.

Beyond this province, however, the Berbers either retained their old lawless independence, or successful adventurers established principalities which professed some variety of the Muhammadan faith, but acknowledged no allegiance to the khalifate at Baghdad. A brief sketch of the chief of these is necessary to make intelligible the rapid progress and easy conquests of the Fatimide missionaries:

Tahart.—Tahart, situated in Central Magreb, was the capital of a small kingdom known to the Muhammadans as 'the Irak of Northern Africa.' It was the home and central point of Kharegite fanaticism. Its founding was in this wise. Amid the incessant turmoil and confusion of African history, it chanced that in A.H. 140, a Berber tribe—the Werfadjouma—obtained possession of Kairoan. They gave themselves up to the cruellest excesses. They stabled their horses in the great mosque of the city; they put to death every Arab they could find; and practised such pitiless extortion upon the townspeople, that the traders almost entirely deserted the city. One day, a Kharegite, belonging to the sect known as the Ibadhites, whose business brought him to Kairoan, saw some of these Berbers outraging a woman in the public streets, without attracting any particular attention, far less condemnation. Carried away by his indignation, he forgot the business on which he had come, and hastened away to the camp of Abou 'l Khattab, a great Kharegite chief, to whom he related what he had seen. The chief was transported with fury; he rushed out of his tent, exclaiming: 'Behold me, O God! ready to serve Thee! I respond to Thy appeal.' He collected his forces, and marched to Kairoan. In a great battle, the Werfadjouma were almost altogether destroyed, and Kairoan fell into his hands. He entrusted the charge of the city to Abd al Rahman ibn Roustem, and settled himself at Tripoli, from which place he gradually brought under his sway the whole province of Afrikia. Affairs remained in this state until A.H. 144, when the khalif Abou Djafar al Mansour sent Muhammad ibn Ashath to recover the province. In the campaign that ensued Abou 'l Khattab perished, with 40,000 of his followers. When the news of this disaster reached Abd al Rahman he abandoned Kairoan. The relics of the army of Abou 'l Khattab joined him during his retreat, and, acknowledging him as their chief, they resolved to build a town, hereafter to become the capital of a Kharegite kingdom. They halted on a bare bit of land in the centre of a dense forest. The following Friday Abd al Rahman made the prayer with his companions. They had but just completed this act of piety when the congregation was startled by the angry roar of a lion close at hand. The beast was captured alive, brought back in triumph, and slain upon the spot where the prayer was made. It was a sign, Abd al Rahman told his followers, that the city they were about to build would be continually exposed to war and the shedding of blood. They then set to work and built the mosque, the beams of which were formed of the timber cut in the surrounding forest. Gradually a flourishing town arose round the mosque, with gardens, plantations, baths, and karavanserais. The district was remarkable for the abundance of its flocks, and the excellence of its cattle, horses, mules, and other beasts of burden. 'Honey, butter, and all sorts of provisions,' says the geographer, Ibn Haukal, 'are found here in abundance.' The sovereignty thus founded by Abd al Rahman was retained by his descendants for the space of 130 years.

Segelmessa.—South of the Atlas range, and on the very edge of the Great Desert, was the large and populous city of Segelmessa. Large suburbs surrounded it on every side; it was encircled by a magnificent wall, having eight iron gates, and within were lofty houses, spacious public buildings, and beautiful gardens. It owed its beauty and fertility to a peculiarly happy situation. At a short distance from Segelmessa was the source of a river fed by a multitude of smaller brooks; this stream, as it approached the town bisected, one stream flowing to the east of the town, the other to the west. The soil thus fertilised produced in abundance dates, grapes, and all kinds of fruits. Segelmessa was also a great trading depôt. Commerce was the chief source of its wealth. Rich karavans passed incessantly to and from Soudan, and brought great wealth to the city, in the shape of amber, silk, cloths of very fine wool, iron, lead, quicksilver, and eunuchs drawn from the country of the negroes. The geographer Ibu Haukal is loud in his praise of the people of this place. 'In all their actions,' he says, 'they conform themselves scrupulously to the precepts of the law, and distinguish themselves by their charity and humanity. I have never seen in any part of Magreb so many sheikhs of profound knowledge and religious habits as in Segelmessa. The wealth of the inhabitants is marvellous. I have myself seen a paper by which a native of Segelmessa acknowledged himself the debtor of a person in the same town for a sum of 40,000 dinars, the like of which I have never seen in the East; and when I spoke of it afterwards in Khorasan and Irak it was regarded as an unique fact.' The women were remarkable for their beauty and plumpness, which they attributed to their practice of feeding upon dogs. The Segelmessa dog which produced so agreeable a result must have been a beast altogether different from the dog eaten in China.

Segelmessa, like Tahart, was the seat of a Kharegite kingdom. The family of Medrar ruled there for 160 years. The originator of this dynasty was an owner of flocks and herds, which he had been in the habit of conducting to graze on the lands where Segelmessa was afterwards built. Struck by the natural advantages of the place, he and about forty other Kharegites commenced to build the city in A.H. 140; and before the close of the century it had become the richest and most populous place in Northern Africa. Its very situation is now unknown.

The Edrisides.—In the month of Dzul Kada, A.H. 169 (May 786), Hosein, a lineal descendant of Hasan, the son of Ali, revolted against the Abbaside khalif Hadi. He took up arms at Mekka, and there rallied round him several members of his family, among whom was his uncle Edris. Hosein was slain in battle at Fekh, a place situated about three miles from Mekka. A great number of his relatives were killed; his partisans fled, and many of them were made prisoners. Edris contrived to effect his escape, and, through the fidelity of his freedman Rashed, succeeded in eluding the vigilance of the khalif, who caused diligent search to be made after him. Rashed, a man of great intelligence and courage, and remarkable as well for his physical strength, disguised Edris as his servant, and they left Mekka together, with a karavan of home-returning pilgrims. During the journey Edris scrupulously performed all the offices of a servant, and his disguise was not suspected by their fellow-travellers. Arrived at old Kairo in Egypt, they passed a well-built house, the aspect of which showed that the possessor was in easy circumstances. They sat down to rest in a shop close at hand. The master of the house, perceiving from their general appearance that they were strangers in Kairo, courteously addressed them. This man was a client of the Abbasides; nevertheless, Rashed, attracted by his look and manners, determined to make an appeal to his piety and generosity. He made known to him the true character of his seeming servant, and conjured him as a true believer to aid in preserving the life of a descendant of the Prophet. 'I am,' he added, 'conducting him to the country of the Berbers; in that remote country he will perhaps find an asylum from the vengeance of his enemies.' The appeal was not made in vain. The man took them into his house, and kept them concealed there till a karavan which was shortly to proceed to Kairoan was ready to start. Then he hired a camel for them, furnished them with provisions and clothes; and when the karavan was about to set out, he said to them: 'The Governor of Egypt has military posts all along the frontier, so that no person can pass without being questioned and examined; but I am acquainted with an old deserted road; I will guide the young man along that until the frontier is passed'—and he indicated Edris with his finger. Rashed accordingly set out with the karavan; the good Egyptian and the young Edris following the circuitous route, rejoined the karavan safely at a point beyond the frontier. Here the citizen of Kairo took leave of the two men to whom he had rendered such signal service; Edris and Rashed, not daring to enter Afrikia, traversed the country occupied by the Berbers, and arrived at last in Further Magreb, where they placed themselves under the protection of Ishak ibn Muhammad, the grand emir of the Auréba tribe.

Shortly after (A.H. 172, A.D. 788–9) Edris announced openly his pretensions to the Imamate in virtue of his descent, and a large number of the Berber tribes in that part of Africa acknowledged him as their chief. His authority grew apace; either by force or persuasion he brought nearly the whole of Further Magreb under his authority, and in the following year established himself in Telemsan as his capital city. The news of the uprising of this new power having reached the khalif Haroun al Rashed, he consulted his vizier, Yahya ibn Khaled, the Barmekide, what he should do. Yahya told him not to be troubled, that he would soon relieve him of anxiety on this score. He summoned to his presence an Arab of the tribe of Rebyah—Suleiman ibn Horeiz—a man soft and engaging in his manners, brave upon occasion, learned in theology, and eloquent in the exposition of doctrine, and not at all disinclined to commit murder if properly paid for it. Him, Yahya induced to undertake the hazardous enterprise of murdering Edris in his capital. He gave him a large sum of money, and a phial containing poison so strong and subtle that a person died by merely inhaling it. A companion of tried valour and fidelity was selected to accompany him. The two emissaries reached Magreb in safety. Suleiman presented himself before Edris, as a refugee from the wrath of Haroun on account of his devotion to the family of Ali. He was cordially received, and his engaging manners and pleasing conversation soon made him a great favourite with his intended victim. Suleiman spared no pains to conceal the true purport of his mission. He held conferences with the Berbers, in which he eloquently expounded the great duty of supporting the descendants of the Prophet. In all he did or spoke he acted as an enthusiastic adherent of the House of Ali.

One day when Rashed was absent, Suleiman, taking with him the poisoned flask, entered the presence of the young prince, and presented him with the phial, saying it contained a very rare and exquisite perfume, such as was not to be found in Northern Africa. He then left the apartment. For months past he had kept two horses in severe training; Suleiman and his companion now mounted these, and rode away at full gallop. Edris in the meanwhile had inhaled the poison, and fallen on the ground senseless. His servants found him in this state, but were at first unable to divine the cause. The flight of Suleiman, however, speedily divulged both the crime and the criminal; and Rashed, with a band of friends, set out in pursuit. One after another, the horses of his companions gave up exhausted, but the steed on which Rashed was mounted held bravely on, and at last he had the gratification of seeing the two fugitives ahead of him. He made straight at the traitor Suleiman. With one stroke of his sword he severed the hand of the murderer, so that it dangled from his wrist by a strip of flesh; a second blow inflicted a wound on his head, a third slashed his face; but here the horse of Rashed, utterly spent, came to a dead stop; and Suleiman, riding an animal which had been trained, was able to rejoin his companion, who, anxious only for his own safety, had not attempted to aid or protect his chief.

Edris died at the close of the day on which he inhaled the poison (A.H. 175, A.D. 791–2). The crime proved to be an useless one. Shortly after his death one of his concubines gave birth to a son, who was recognised by the Berbers of Magreb as succeeding to all the rights of his father. The monarchy now passed from father to son with not more of confusion and uncertainty than is usual in Muhammadan kingdoms. In A.H. 192 (807–8) the reigning prince laid the foundations of his new capital —Fez—which speedily became one of the most flourishing cities of Northern Africa.

Besides these three kingdoms, other smaller principalities were dotted over Northern Africa, which need not be specified more particularly. Between these independent states extended either vast stretches of forest land, rocky hills, or bare, desolate plains. The wandering Berbers roamed over this country, levying black mail on the karavans which wound their difficult way between Kairoan, Fez, and Segelmessa. Other communication there was little or none. It was a country, in fact, where a preacher of heresy, persecuted everywhere else, could disseminate his doctrines in perfect security. The Berbers, as credulous as the Arabs, were always ready to receive and listen to a new religious teacher. Sheltered in the encampments or the villages of one of these tribes, the missionary could make hundreds and thousands of proselytes, without attracting the attention of any of the potentates around him. Only when he was the leader of an armed force, eager and able to strike a crushing blow, was the effect of his teaching manifested to the startled sovereign whose territories he invaded.

CHAPTER III.

THE RISE OF THE FATIMIDES.

A.D. 900–916.

TOWARDS the close of the third century after the flight to Medina, the representative of the Ismailien Imams was Said, the son of Ahmed, surnamed Obeidallah. His father had been the seventh in the line of the concealed Imams. Among the most zealous and successful missionaries of the sect was a certain Ibn Hausheb, originally a believer in the twelve Imams, who had been converted in a sudden and mysterious manner to a recognition of the rights resident in Ismail and his descendants. His centre of operations was in Yemen, and he and missionaries working under his orders spread a knowledge of the faith and made numerous proselytes in Yemen, Yemamah, Bahrein, Egypt, and Afrikia. In the last-mentioned province they had been signally successful; and the Ketama, the largest and most powerful of the Berber tribes, who had their settlements in the province of Constantine, had been converted.

Among these missionaries was one known in Muhammadan history as Abou Abdallah, the Shia, a man deeply versed in all the learning of that age, subtle and wise in the formation of plans, bold and adroit in carrying them into effect, and possessed of a remarkable power to attract and fascinate the minds of those who were brought under his influence. To judge from his career, he had not been allowed to penetrate to that void of blank negation which served as foundation for the Ismailien doctrines. He believed in the manifestation of the Imam descended from Ismail, as a veritable redeemer who would fill the earth with his justice. It so happened that a few years before the termination of the third century the missionaries who resided in Afrikia died almost simultaneously, and Ibu Hansheb made choice of Abou Abdallah as their successor. He accordingly set out from Yemen to travel to Afrikia by way of Mekka and Egypt. It was the season of the pilgrimage, and on his arrival at Mekka he established himself in the quarter of the city occupied by the pilgrims from the Ketama. Without making himself known as an Ismailien missionary, he managed to insinuate himself into their confidence. The pilgrims were charmed by the fascination of his conversation, and awed by his piety and spiritual detachment from the world. He learned from them the condition of Northern Africa—the political situation, the religious parties, the character and strength of the different tribes, and the degree of authority which belonged to the Aghlabite princes. He journeyed with the Ketama pilgrims as far as Kairo, and then made as though he would have gone another way; but they earnestly entreated him not to leave them. He must, they said, accompany them to Africa, where he should be received as an honoured guest; and Abou Abdallah, secretly rejoicing, yielded to their solicitations.

He found the tribe of Ketama zealous for Ali and the Imams of the House of Ismail. There he declared his true mission as the messenger sent before to prepare the way for the coming of the *Mehdi*, or the Expected One. The period had passed, he said, in which the true Imams had to remain hidden; the Mehdi was at hand, and every eye would behold him, and great signs and wonders would be wrought by him. The dead would be raised; the course of the sun would be reversed, and he would set in the East. The tribe of Ketama were filled with warlike enthusiasm at these wonderful tidings. Abou Abdallah, however, was too wary to rush precipitately into action till he could strike with effect. He assumed the garb and demeanour of an austere recluse, to lull the suspicions of the Aghlabite prince, to whose ears vague rumours had come of the stir and excitement amid the Berbers beyond his frontier. When at last he took the field it was as the leader in a sacred war. The Ketama were designated the 'true Believers.' A herald went before the troops on the line of march, proclaiming to all the villages and encampments through which they passed: 'To horse! to horse! soldiers of God!' The banners and the caparisons of the horses were embroidered with the words from the Koran: 'Victory belongeth unto God!' 'Their hosts shall be put to flight, and turn their backs.' On the signet-ring of Abdallah was engraved: 'Put your trust in God, and you will rely upon a manifest truth;' and the seal used for stamping official documents was inscribed with these words: 'The orders of the Lord have been executed with truth and justice.'

The plans of Abou Abdallah had been greatly aided

by the disorder into which the province of Afrikia had fallen since the arrival of that missionary among the Ketama. When Abou Abdallah first appeared in Northern Africa, Ibrahim Ibn Ahmed, of the house of Aghlab, was ruling Afrikia, in the name of the khalif at Baghdad. In the beginning of his reign this prince had distinguished himself by the justice and benevolence of his acts. Every Friday after prayer he was accustomed to hold an open durbar, and it was proclaimed throughout his capital, Requada, that all who had complaints to make or petitions to present would then have free access to the ear of the sovereign. He used to declare that the people were the chief stay and support of a king; and that every injury inflicted on them, or oppression endured by them at the hands of a noble, however highly he might be placed, was in fact a wrong done to the king, which the latter was bound to punish in order to preserve his crown from danger. All high-handed acts, accordingly, by which the people suffered unjustly, he punished with extreme severity, even when the wrongdoer was nearly related to himself. But the intoxication of absolute power wrought in him as it has done in so many Eastern sovereigns. Insurrections put down with merciless severity begat a fiendish delight in shedding blood which converted him into one of the most appalling monsters who figure in the annals of Muhammadanism.

The people of the town of Belezma had revolted against him. Ibrahim marched against them in person, but having failed to reduce the place he feigned to make peace with the rebels, and invited the leading citizens to Requada to agree upon the conditions. They came with their friends and followers to the number of a thousand men. Ibrahim received them with magnificent hospitality; lodged them in a huge building erected specially for that purpose, and gratified them with rich banquets and lavish presents. But in the night he surrounded the building with his soldiers, and caused the whole of his unhappy guests to be massacred. This butchery was perpetrated A.H. 278. The murder of these men ultimately proved the ruin of the Aghlabites. The city of Belezma had subdued the tribe of Ketama, and imposed a heavy tribute on them. But the murder of their leading men so enfeebled the place that they could no longer control the turbulent Berbers, and in delivering the Berbers from this yoke Ibrahim enabled them to rise at the bidding of Abou Abdallah. The immediate effect, too, was the revolt of all Afrikia in a fit of indignation at the atrocity. For a time Ibrahim possessed hardly a foot of land in the province except where his capital stood. Want of concert, however, among the rebels, and Ibrahim's army of negro slaves, enabled him to drown the insurrection in a deluge of blood.

A few years after (A.H. 283) Ibrahim marched to invade Egypt. He was opposed on the way by the Nefousah, a Berber tribe. After a bloody battle, the Nefousah were defeated. Ibrahim pursued so closely on their heels, that numbers of the fugitives sought shelter in the sea, and were massacred there. The waves as they broke on the bank were reddened with the carnage, and Ibrahim cried as he saw it: 'Oh! would that so great a victory had been gained fighting in the path of God! How glorious it would be!' An officer who was standing by suggested that he should interrogate some of the prisoners on their belief. They proved to be Kharegites. Ibrahim was rejoiced. The victory then was a sacred one, and Ibrahim determined to celebrate it as such a mercy deserved to be celebrated. Seating himself upon a throne, with a lance in his hand, the prisoners were led to him one by one. As they approached the royal seat, their left sides were laid bare, and the royal lance was driven into the hearts of the victims. Ibrahim did not cease from this humane pastime until 500 bloody corpses were piled up round him.

It was after this surfeit of blood that a kind of homicidal madness seized upon Ibrahim; he slaughtered his companions, his faithfullest servants, his sons, and his daughters. He was racked by a truly insatiable thirst for blood. A napkin with which he used to wipe his mouth after dining, having been mislaid, he put 300 servants to death as a punishment for their remissness. On a vague suspicion, he killed his son Abou al Aghlab, and eight brothers who were his servants. All his daughters were killed the moment they were born. His wives he tortured in a variety of ways. Some were built up in walls, and left to perish of hunger and thirst; some were strangled; others had their throats cut. He had a body-guard of sixty young men, of whom he seemed to be very fond, and who slept every night in the palace. It was told to Ibrahim that during the night these young men occasionally paid visits to each other's apartments. He immediately ordered them into his presence, and questioned them whether or not the accusation was true. One of the young men, a special favourite of

Ibrahim, asserted that the charge was false. Ibrahim, without uttering a word, struck him with an iron mace which he held, and crushed his skull. He then caused a large brazier to be filled with coals and lighted, and every day he ordered five or six of his unhappy body-guard to be flung into it, until all were consumed. His mother, hoping to charm away the sanguinary devil which had taken possession of her son, brought one day into his presence two beautiful slave-girls, who read the Koran, and sang and played with remarkable skill. Ibrahim seemed pleased, and thanked his mother. Scarcely had the mother returned to her apartments when a domestic entered, bearing a covered tray—a present, he said, from her son. The mother raised the veil, and beheld, horror-struck, the heads of the two girls she had just presented to her son. On another day, his mother seeing him in a good humour, said: 'I wish you to see, if you will, some young maidens who will please you.' As he expressed a wish to see them, she sent for the girls. They were sixteen of his daughters, who, when the mandate went forth to kill all his female children, had been hidden away and secretly brought up. Ibrahim greeted them kindly, but on leaving the apartment he ordered his executioner to bring him the heads of the girls. This order was at once executed, and the sixteen heads flung down at his feet as he sat.

The career of this homicide was brought to a close A.H. 289. The account of his atrocities had aroused indignation as far even as Baghdad, and the Abbaside khalif, Al-Motadhid, sent an envoy to recall Ibrahim to Asia. The emir had an interview with this messenger on the salt plains round Tunis. The khalif had charged the latter to express his anger at the manner in which Ibrahim had treated his subjects, and especially those of Tunis, ravishing their wives and forcibly abducting their daughters. He, in consequence, deprived him of the government of Afrikia, naming in his stead his son Abou'l Abbas, and ordered him (Ibrahim) to return to Baghdad. Ibrahim appeared submissive; he put on the coarse garments of a recluse who had taken his farewell of the pomps and vanities of the world; he set free the crowds of captives that were groaning in his dungeons, and recalled his son from Sicily, to deposit in his hands the supreme power. But all this being done, instead of repairing to Baghdad, he crossed over into Sicily to carry on the holy war against the Greeks. Five months after his arrival in that island, he was carried off by a bowel complaint, dying (it is satisfactory to be able to record) after suffering horrible agonies.

The son of Ibrahim, a firm and equitable prince, skilled both in war and the administration of affairs, might well have defeated the ambitious plans of Abou Abdallah, the Shia. But nine months after his accession he was murdered. Suspecting his son Ziadet Allah of a design on his life, he had placed him under arrest. Ziadet Allah, by way of retaliation, instigated three of his father's eunuchs to murder him in his sleep. As soon as the deed was done, the murderers hastened to Ziadet Allah, and saluted him with the title of Emir; but he, suspecting a snare, refused to come out from his place of arrest. The assassins then hastened back to the palace, severed the head of the slaughtered prince from his body, and carried the grisly trophy back to Ziadet as a proof of their good faith (A.H. 290.) Ziadet Allah was now the sovereign of Afrikia. His first act was to crucify the murderers of his father in order to remove suspicion of complicity from himself. This method of rewarding such services was so habitual with Oriental princes that one wonders how people were so infatuated as to commit murder for their benefit. The next act of the new sovereign was also truly Oriental. He arrested as many of his uncles and brothers as he could surprise or decoy into his power, and put them to death. Having, as he supposed, established his power upon a firm foundation by thus sweeping away all actual or possible rivals, he abandoned himself to debauchery with that utter single-mindedness which is not to be found outside of the pale of Muhammadanism. He took no thought of the movements beyond the frontier, but in the society of buffoons and the vilest of men, passed his time in gambling, drinking, and all manner of riotous excess.

These confusions in the interior of Afrikia had been of the greatest service to Abou Abdallah. He was at the head of a formidable army. Meila, Setif and several other towns had either been stormed or surrendered to him, and the danger became so pressing that Ziadet Allah was compelled to pause in his debaucheries, and take account of the political situation. He set on foot 40,000 men, under the command of one of his drinking companions, Ibrahim ibn Habish. For six months this army loitered away its time in the town of Constantine, and when at last it came in contact with the enemy, the troops abandoned their leader and fled. Ibrahim himself fled to Kairoan. Abou Abdallah followed up his success with vigour, and the customary atrocities which characterise wars of religion. One town after another was captured; the inhabitants of those which were stormed were massacred without pity. In the year 295, Ziadet Allah contrived to collect a second army, which he placed under the command of one of the principal chiefs of his family, Ibrahim ibn Abi al Aghlab; but this too was defeated in two great actions, and Ziadet Allah possessed neither the courage nor the perseverance to struggle any more against adverse fortune.

He was at Requada when the news of this second defeat reached him. Requada was situated three miles from Kairoan. The spot was renowned for the extreme salubrity of the air, and the delicious climate. There, it was said, a man was happy without cause and gay without motive. The place was not so much a town as an immense cluster of fortified palaces, enclosing beautiful gardens, baths, fountains, and vast reservoirs. The Aghlabite princes had there collected all their wealth, and freely indulged their taste for costly and magnificent structures. When the news of Ibrahim's defeat reached him, Ziadet Allah gave out that he had won a great victory. In order to confirm this statement, he sent executioners into the prisons, and putting to death those who chanced to be confined there, caused their heads to be paraded through the streets of Requada as those of the Ketamiens slain in battle. In the meanwhile, he commenced to pack up his riches, and sent confidential servants to inform his relatives of the veritable state of his affairs, and prepare them for his flight. In vain his vizier, Ibn al Saigh, advised him to remain in Africa, urging that were he only to make proper use of his wealth, he would speedily be at the head of such a vast army that the Shia would not dare to attack him. In vain he strove to kindle the courage of the faint-hearted prince by recalling to him the memory of his ancestors and the great deeds they had done in the old time. His sole reward was to be suspected of being a secret ally of the enemy engaged in luring his sovereign to death. And Ziadet Allah, collecting together his treasures, his jewels, his arms—in a word, all of his wealth that was capable of being moved; and his chief officers having done the same, they abandoned Requada as night was beginning to set in. The prince had selected 1,000 men from the slaves in his service; to each of these was entrusted a sack containing 1,000 dinars; he brought away with him also some of his wives. Just as the train was setting out, one of the girls whose fate it was to be abandoned, took her lute and sang—

> I have not forgotten the day of farewell; when, with eyes bathed in tears, she said, as the camels moved away: 'You leave me, O, my master! and you go yourself.'

This plaintive appeal touched the heart of the flying prince. He took the load from off one of the baggage mules, and seated the fair singer there instead. The news of the defeat of Ibrahim had arrived just after the midday prayer, and the prayer of evening had not yet been proclaimed from the minarets of Requada, when the long procession issued from the gates of the capital. The inhabitants followed it, detachment after detachment, directing their march by the light of torches; and before midnight the city was deserted.

The defeated Ibrahim, in the meanwhile, had reached Kairoan almost unattended. He alighted at the palace of the emir, and immediately summoned the doctors of the law and the chief men of the place to wait upon him. A dense crowd soon blocked up the square in front of the palace. Ibrahim harangued it. He accused Ziadet Allah and his debaucheries as the cause of the ruin of his house; then he spoke against the Ketama and the Shia, conjuring the people to make one more effort to defend their women and their homes against this pitiless enemy. The appeal was fruitless. The people, in terror at their situation, were only anxious to win the favour of the conquering Shia by evidences of their zeal against the enemy he had overthrown. A great cry rose up from the crowd: 'Get out from our gates; we have for you neither respect nor obedience.' Fearful of their lives, Ibrahim and his few followers left the palace and made for one of the gates of the city. The mob followed, hooting and shouting, and at last hurling stones at the fugitives till they had passed through the gates. They were not pursued further. There was a richer booty to be got elsewhere. The speech of Ibrahim had made known the fact that Requada had been abandoned the day before, and the population of Kairoan rushed over in a tumultuous body to plunder its rich palaces. They found the streets, lately so thronged, as silent and abandoned as the wilderness. The ladies of the Harem, deserted by Zaidet Allah in his precipitate flight, had withdrawn to the inner apartments of the palace; and remained unmolested. But nothing else did. For six days the work of pillage and destruction went on. The palace of the emir was gutted; the rich furniture carried away; the beautiful iron gates were torn off their hinges; and the flooring of the apartments torn up in order to search for concealed treasure.

On Saturday, 1st Rajeb, A.H. 296, Abou Abdallah made his triumphal entry into Requada. His army marched in seven divisions, chanting the following verses from the Koran:

> How many gardens, and fountains, and fields of corn, and fair dwellings, and advantages which they enjoyed, did they leave behind them!
>
> Thus we dispossessed them thereof, and we gave the same for an inheritance to another people.

Abou Abdallah dismounted at the palace. A number of negroes belonging to the body-guard of the Aghlabite sovereigns was brought before him. These men had been the instruments of Ibrahim's cruelty. Ziadat Allah, when flying, had deprived them of their arms, and abandoned them to the vengeance of the people they had so fearfully oppressed. Abou Abdallah caused them to be massacred to the last man; and their corpses were flung out into the street. He then proclaimed a general amnesty; no inquisition even was made into the perpetrators of the plunder of Requada; but governors were at once despatched throughout the province to assume charge of the cities and preserve order. This wise and merciful policy had the effect of making the conquered people cordially welcome their new ruler. The ladies whom Zaidat Allah had left behind him were brought into the presence of the successful general. Many of them were of ravishing beauty; but, to the inexpressible amazement of the spectators, the ascetic soldier deigned not so much as to cast a glance on them. He coldly ordered that they should be entrusted to the custody of an old woman until the Mehdi appeared.

In the meantime Ziadet Allah, having been rejoined by Ibrahim, and by a great number of other persons who remained faithful to his cause, had reached Tripoli and taken up his residence in the palace. He caused search to be made for his vizier, Ibn al Saigh, and not finding him, became convinced that his suspicions were correct, and that that officer had gone over to the Shia. The vizier had, in fact, gone on board a ship to fly to Sicily; but the wind drove his vessel into the harbour of Tripoli shortly after Ziadet Allah had arrived in that place. Ziadat Allah rejoiced that the traitor, as he supposed him to be, should have fallen thus unexpectedly in his power, and caused him to be arrested and instantly beheaded. After a stay of seventeen days at Tripoli, Ziadet Allah continued his flight towards Egypt; and from thence to Rakka in Mesopotamia. Here he sent a letter to the vizier, demanding the permission of the Chief of Believers to enter Baghdad; but the khalif al-Moktadir, indignant at his pusillanimous flight from Afriḳia, refused to admit him into his presence; and he was ordered to remain in Rakka until further orders. Ziadet Allah accordingly sojourned there for the space of a year, passing his time with a number of boon companions in drunken orgies and the vilest immoralities, so much so that he drew upon himself the censure of the kadi of Rakka. At the end of a year he received orders to return to Egypt, and the governor of that province was instructed to furnish him with men and money and all things needful to attempt the recovery of Afrikia. Ziadet Allah entered the capital of Egypt in great pomp, traversing the streets girt with two swords; but instead of applying the funds supplied to him for the object intended he expended them in debauchery. He even sold his arms to feed his convivial tastes and those of his companions. The result of his excesses was a complete prostration of mind and body; broken in health, he went to Jerusalem and there died; and in him the family of the Aghlabites became extinct.

Meantime, the man for whom this signal revolution had been accomplished was in a dungeon, in danger of death. The father of Obeidallah, when at the point of death, had invested his son with the imamate, adding these words: 'You are he who will be the Mehdi; after my death you will fly to a distant country, where you will undergo severe trials.' As soon as Abou Abdallah had convinced himself that he had welded the tribe of Ketama into an ardent Ismailien army, he despatched messengers to Salamia in Syria, where Obeidallah resided, conjuring him to come to Afrikia and place himself at the head of the movement. Obeidallah set out with all speed; but his journey was beset with perils. Secretly as Abou Abdallah had worked, the air was full of rumours that the long-expected Mehdi of the Shias was about to be manifested; and these had not only reached Baghdad, but suspicion had fixed itself on Obeidallah as the coming Mehdi. His flight from Salamia confirmed these suspicions; and the khalif of Baghdad circulated through all the provinces of the empire a description of the fugitive, with orders to seize and imprison anyone at all resembling it. The governor of Egypt in particular was warned to be on the alert. Obeidallah had passed from Syria into Irak, and thence into Egypt. He was disguised as a merchant, and accompanied by his young son, Abou'l Kasim, Abou'l Abbas the brother of Abou Abdallah, and a few devoted adherents. Guards were posted on all the routes leading in and out of Old Kairo; and parties of horse scoured the country in every direction to seize all strange or suspicious-looking travellers. Obeidallah and his friends fell into the hands of one of these parties, and were brought before the governor of Egypt. The governor had no doubt that he had seized his man; but by means of lavish bribery Obeidallah persuaded him to release him. No rulers are so badly served as despots. Arriving safely at Tripoli, Obeidallah directed Abou'l Abbas to proceed on to Kairoan, and from thence join his brother and the army. But when the latter reached Kairoan, Ziadet Allah, who had received intelligence of his movements, had him seized and thrown into prison. There he was subjected to torture in order to wring a confession from him as to his true character and that of his companions, and the veritable object of their coming into Africa. Abou'l Abbas bore his torments with firmness, and obstinately adhered to his original account, that he and his companions were traders, who had come to Afrikia on business, and knew nothing whatever of the movements of Abou Abdallah and the Ketama. The suspicions of Ziadet Allah remained unallayed. He retained Abou'l Abbas in confinement; and despatched orders to the governor of

Tripoli to seize the rest of the party. Obeidallah, however, had learned the ill-success of the mission of Abou'l Abbas, and had fled from Tripoli, accompanied only by his son. They passed the frontier undetected, and entered the district of Constantine. Obeidallah might now have easily joined the army of Abou Abdallah. But he knew that his doing so would immediately tear off the disguise of Abou'l Abbas, and consign him to the sword of the executioner. He was unwilling thus to sacrifice a faithful servitor; and with a generous magnanimity, rare in Oriental history, he passed, still disguised, through Constantine, and took up his abode in the city of Segelmessa (A.H. 296, A.D. 909).

The sovereign of Segelmessa was Elisa ibn Medrar. At first he gave a kindly reception to the strange merchant; but having learned by a letter from the emir Ziadet Allah that the new comer was the Mehdi whose emissaries were creating so great a stir in the country of the Ketama, and who purposed to establish his throne on the ruins of all the existing dynasties of Northern Africa, he threw him and his son into prison, confining them in separate cells. Abou Abdallah was profoundly troubled when the news reached him of this disastrous incident. Leaving his two brothers in charge of the government of Afrikia, he put himself at the head of a large army to march on Segelmessa. The fame of him had by this time spread abroad through all Magreb, and the tidings of his coming struck terror into the hearts of the most turbulent Berber tribes. None knew against whom the advance was made; and all hastened by an early submission to avert an attack from themselves. When the army drew near to Segelmessa, the prince of that place interrogated Obeidallah as to who he was, whence he came, and whether he was the cause of the hostile advance of Abou Abdallah. Obeidallah protested with an oath that he had never so much as seen Abou Abdallah (an assertion entirely true), that he knew nothing of him, being, as he seemed, a simple merchant. Then the son was subjected to a similar examination. When simple questioning could extract nothing from him he was beaten, but he bore the punishment with constancy, and revealed nothing. Abou Abdallah, who, by means of his spies, had intelligence of all that passed, was sorely grieved and perplexed. He sent a deputation to Elisa ibn Medrar to try to arrange an accommodation; but that prince replied by putting his envoys to death, and marching forth at the head of all his troops to give him battle. In the battle that ensued the Segelmessa army fled; and Elisa ibn Medrar, with a few friends, abandoned his capital. Abou Abdallah, ignorant of this flight, passed the night in a state of profound anxiety respecting the fate of his master; but on the morrow the chief men of Segelmessa repaired to his camp, and conducted him to the prison in which the Mehdi and his son were confined. He placed them on horseback, and, proceeding on foot in front of them, accompanied by all the chiefs of the Ketama, conducted them to the camp, shedding tears of joy as he went, and exclaiming to the wondering multitudes who thronged the streets: 'Behold your master!' Elisa ibn Medrar was captured and put to death (A.H. 297, A.D. 909).

Obeidallah's first care, in true Oriental fashion, was to destroy the ladder by which he had ascended to his present elevation. Abou Abdallah and his brother Abou'l Abbas were arrested on a charge of treason against the sovereign they had just raised from the dust. They were accused of instigating the Ketama to revolt against Obeidallah, pretending that he was not the veritable Mehdi, because he worked no miracles as the true Imam undoubtedly would. The brothers were put to death in the garden of the palace, and interred in the presence of Obeidallah. He approached the corpse of Abou Abdallah. 'May God pardon you,' he said, 'and reward you in the next world, for you have laboured zealously in His cause.' Then turning to the body of the brother, he said: 'May God have no pity upon you, for you it is who caused your brother to sin.' He then repeated from the Koran the words: 'He who shall live in forgetfulness of God, I will place him under the yoke of a demon.' A number of Ketama chiefs who were accused of having plotted with the brothers were put to death at the same time (A.H. 297, A.D. 910–911).

The new monarch breathed more freely as soon as his powerful subject was no more, but he was too well acquainted with the shifting and changeable character of African politics to suppose that his present supremacy would long remain unquestioned. The Arabs of Afrikia, though they accepted his authority, declined to become converts to his creed. Among the Berbers, the tribe of Ketama alone acknowledged him as their legitimate ruler. The other tribes of Central Magreb were almost wholly Kharegites. Tahart, the centre of their power, had been stormed, and the dynasty overthrown by the man whom he had just put to death; but Segelmessa, a

Kharegite principality also, had cut to pieces the Berber garrison, and recovered its independence fifty days after the departure of Obeidallah from the place. In Further Magreb, the Edrisides reigned unhurt and hostile. The work of conquest, moreover, had been effected with a prodigal shedding of blood which had left a deep hatred and desire of revenge burning in the bosoms of the survivors. When, for example, the town of Laribus fell by assault, the inhabitants took refuge in the great mosque, and the crowd was so great that men and women were literally wedged together and unable to move. All through the night the swords of the Berber army hacked away at this helpless unresisting mass of human life. The blood, it is said, flowed out through all the doors of the mosque like little brooks swelled by a summer shower. At Tahart, treason was added to cruelty; Abou Abdallah having obtained entrance to the city by means of a capitulation, the terms of which he violated in order to wreak his wrath upon the Kharegites. Similar massacres were perpetrated in Tunis, Bakarma, and other cities. Nor did the bloody work cease with the expulsion of the Aghlabites and the establishment of Obeidallah at Requada. His fierce and savage Berber allies signalised their zeal in his cause by horrible cruelties upon the conquered people. Pious and learned doctors were scourged, mutilated, or crucified, because they had spoken with respect of the three first khalifs, forgotten a Shiite formula, or pronounced a *fatwa*, according to the code of the orthodox Malek. Odious and almost incredible tests of loyalty to the new dynasty were enacted. Men, under pain of being put to death as rebels, were compelled to witness the violation of their wives, and to submit to gross personal outrages on themselves. At Barka, a Ketama chief cut in pieces and roasted some of the citizens; then he forced others to eat the flesh thus prepared, and ended by casting these involuntary cannibals into the fire. It is to the credit of Obeidallah that he did his utmost to check these atrocities, but he was, unhappily, powerless to do so. It is always the fate of a despot to be the passive tool of those who have borne him to power. Obeidallah possessed sufficient sagacity to foresee that these acts would culminate in some general outburst against the dynasty which permitted them, and he determined to build a city so strongly fortified by nature and art, that, should his partisans be expelled from the surrounding country, they might find there an impregnable rallying point. Setting out from Tunis (A.H. 300), he visited Carthage, and several other towns, and traversed the entire sea-coast to choose a fit spot whereon to erect his capital. After long hesitation, he fixed upon a slip of land jutting out into the sea, and connected, says Abu'l Fœda, with the mainland as the hand is joined to the arm. On this spot rose a city, called after himself—Mehdia. A strong wall, with gates of iron, enclosed it; and within were built splendid marble palaces, and vast tanks and underground storehouses, which were filled with provisions. The works were commenced A.H. 303 (A.D. 916) and completed A.H. 306 (A.D. 918–19). 'I am now at ease,' said Obeidallah, when he saw the finished city, 'regarding the fate of the Fatimides.'

CHAPTER IV.

THE CONQUEST OF EGYPT.

A.D. 919–1093.

OBEIDALLAH brought a long reign to a prosperous end, but the storm which he had dreaded and provided for burst in fury over his son and his successor, Abou Muhammad al Kaiem. Abou Yezid Maklad was the son of Keidad, and a native of Castilia. Educated at Tahart, where subsequently he kept a school, he had been brought up in the straitest sect of the Kharegites. Worn out with the weight of sixty years, with disease and infirmities, this man contrived to persuade the Berbers of Mount Auress that he was a prophet sent by God to sweep the Fatimide khalifs out of the land. In the year 332 (A.D. 943–44) they burst from their mountain fastnesses, and swept like a destroying deluge over the open country. The Fatimide troops were defeated again and again. City after city was taken by storm, and became a scene of the most frightful atrocities The men and the children were massacred, the women reduced to slavery. The empire of Al Kaiem fell to pieces with even greater rapidity than it had been built up. The khalif was shut up in his capital and closely besieged. But here the success of Abou Yezid terminated. Four times he delivered desperate assaults upon the town, and each time he was bloodily repulsed. The siege had been converted into a blockade, when Al Kaiem died, and his son, Ismail al Mansour—a young man of rare energy and ferocity—mounted the vacant throne. Step by step, under his conduct, the fierce sectaries were driven back to their mountain homes. They had shown no pity in their hour of success, and none was shown to them in the day of defeat. The leaders who fell into the hands of the Fatimide khalif were flayed alive, and their skins stuffed with straw, and nailed to crosses in the sight of the army; the rank and file were roasted to death, or their hands and feet were cut off, and the mutilated, but still breathing bodies, fastened to crosses to linger out the painful remains of life. The heads of those who fell in battle were hacked off and sent to Kairoan, where they served as playthings for the children. Ten thousand of these grisly trophies were, it is said, distributed as balls among these amiable young creatures. These atrocities obtained for the ruthless young prince the name of 'the flayer.' They caused the followers of Abou Yezid to change sides with great rapidity, and all such tenders of submission were cordially accepted by Ismail. Abou Yezid fled to Djebel Selat, a precipitous and inaccessible rock, rising from a parched desert, which needed eleven days to traverse. Ismail plunged boldly into this sandy solitude, but his soldiers perished of thirst; his horses and beasts of burden died from want of forage, and he extricated himself with immense difficulty and severe loss. It was after four years' fighting (A.H. 336, A.D. 947–48) that the sectary and his followers were at last cooped up in the mountain of Kiana, with every passage of escape barred by the armies of the khalif. The struggle round this last position was long and terrible, and marked by the usual hideous cruelty. The khalif caused an immense oven to be constructed, above which a pulley was suspended. Whenever a Berber was captured, he was bound hand and foot, and hung by the feet from the pulley, with his head in the heated oven, and thus slowly roasted; when death seemed imminent, he was withdrawn, and as soon as he had a little recovered once more lowered down to taste the torment of burning till he died. At length, seeing his troops diminishing every day, Abou Yezid issued from his entrenchments, in a desperate endeavour to cut his way through the besiegers. His followers were mostly cut to pieces, and he fell covered with wounds upon the field of battle, and was made prisoner. He died that same night, but his body, stuffed with straw, was carried in solemn procession from city to city. Notwithstanding the death of this formidable heretic, the crisis was far from past, and the rule of the Fatimide khalifs still trembled in the balance, when Ismael died, A.H. 339 (A.D. 950–51), or, as some say, A.H. 341.

Ismail was succeeded by his son, known in history by the title of Moezz-li-din-Allah. Among the freedmen of the prince was a Greek, named Djauher. He had been a favourite of Ismail, who had caused him to be carefully educated; Moezz regarded him with even greater partiality, and Djauher passed rapidly from one office to another, till he became vizier and generalissimo of the kingdom. In this last capacity, the task of completing the subjugation of Northern Africa, which the preceding khalif had left incomplete, was entrusted to him. This he accomplished with equal skill and success, and after the lapse of a few years Moezz found himself the undisputed sovereign of all the country from the shores of the Atlantic to the confines of Egypt. But it was not Africa only which the Fatimides coveted. The real goal of their wishes was Baghdad; their heart's desire was to expel from thence the heretic who pretended to be the supreme head of Islam, and substitute themselves in his place. Accordingly, Northern Africa having been subdued, Egypt was the next province to be conquered. Egypt, like the other provinces of the Muhammadan empire, had become virtually independent of Baghdad, and it was at this time governed by a hump-backed African eunuch—Kafour—who had raised himself from the position of a slave to his present eminence. This man had shown himself equally great as a soldier and a statesman, but he was now well stricken in years, and Moezz deemed it his wisest policy to defer the execution of his plan of conquest until after Kafour's death. This occurred A.H. 357, and the province at once fell into a state of the utmost confusion. The Turkish soldiers mutinied, and, under the pretence of arrears of pay, demanded immense sums of money. As these were not paid up immediately they pillaged the palace of the vizier and the houses of his principal friends, some of whom sent off messages to Moezz entreating him to restore order in the province, and engaging to aid him to the utmost of their power. To crown all, one of those terrible famines peculiar to Egypt descended upon the province. There are several such visitations recorded in the Arabic chronicles; and the sufferings and mortality were such as to be well nigh incredible. 'The river,' says Benjamin Tudela, who visited Egypt about a century after this time, 'overflows once every year, in the month of Elul (August), and inundating the whole country, irrigates it to the extent of fifteen days' journey. The water remains standing on the land during that and the following month, whereby it is moistened and made fit for agriculture. A marble pillar, constructed with great skill, has been erected in front of an island; twelve yards of this pillar protrude above the level of the river, and whenever the water rises to a height sufficient to cover the pillar, people know that it has inundated the whole land of Egypt to the extent of fifteen days' journey; whereas if one-half only of the pillar be covered, it shows that one-half of the country is yet dry. A certain officer measures the rise of the river every day, and makes proclamation in these words:—"Praise God, for the river has risen so and so much." The measurement and the proclamation are repeated every day. Whenever the water submerges the whole pillar, it produces great plenty in the whole land of Egypt. . . . . Whenever the overflowing of the Nile is suspended, they can neither sow nor reap, and the famine is sore in the land.' Then, to quote the figure of Abd al Latif, describing one of these terrible seasons of dearth, the year presented itself as a monster whose wrath must annihilate all the resources of life and all the means of subsistence. All who could, fled the devoted country. The poor ate carrion, corpses, dogs, little children. The traveller passed through towns and villages tenanted only by the dead. Those guilty of the crime of cannibalism were burned to death, but in the agonies of hunger the very executioners have been known to tear fragments from the roasted flesh and devour them. It is needless to say that at such seasons all the bonds of order were unloosed. Civil government was in fact at an end. Murder and rape were perpetrated in open day. Bands of kidnappers infested the principal cities, who caught up passengers by means of hooks let down from the upper windows, and murdered them either for their wealth or for food.

No conjunction of circumstances could have been more favourable to the designs of Moezz, and he hastened to send back an affirmative response to the requests of the mutinous Turkish militia. The army of invasion was placed under the command of Djauher, and the expedition set forth from Kairoan on Saturday, 14th of the first Rebi, A.H. 358. The khalif spared no labour or expense to ensure success. Each separate soldier received a gratuity in addition to his pay; and an immense treasure, and abundant munitions of war followed the army. On the day of departure the khalif, attended by his chief officers, rode to the camp to bid adieu to the commander-in-chief. After some conversation he ordered Djauher to mount his horse, and then caused his sons, even the heir presumptive, his brothers, and the emirs of his court, to dismount and pass on foot before the departing general, as the highest mark of honour and confidence he could confer upon him. On returning to his palace the monarch sent to Djauher his robe and all his apparel, with the exception of his ring, to signify that he was in every respect the representative of his sovereign, and possessor of the same unquestionable authority. The khalif wrote also to every city on the line of march, ordering the governors to receive Djauher with the honours usually paid only to himself; and caused a number of vessels to be laden with grain and provisions for the relief of the distress in Egypt. These were to sail along the sea-coast, regulating their movements by those of the army.

The inhabitants of Fostât—the ancient capital of Egypt—were terror-stricken at the tidings of this invasion. They sent messengers to Djauher, before he had crossed the frontier into Egypt, to treat for the surrender of the capital, and preserve it from pillage. Djauher conceded all their demands, but continued to advance steadily upon the city. There, all was confusion. The partisans of the former dynasty, and a part of the Turkish militia, renouncing their pacific intentions, determined to oppose the entrance of Djauher. A citizen of Baghdad, and consequently a partisan of the Abbasides, and an enemy of the Fatimides, rising up in the mosque just before the Friday prayer, cried aloud: 'O, men of Islam! you have given yourselves over to the man who plundered Fez, and reduced its people to slavery.' Then he passed in review all the evils that Djauher had inflicted upon the people of Northern Africa; and adjured them to drive out from among them those evil counsellors whose pusillanimous advice had brought them to their present evil strait. This discourse made a lively impression upon the fickle multitude. They were now for fighting to the death. All the approaches to the city were occupied in force. But this newly-born valour oozed rapidly away when the banners of the Fatimide army appeared in sight. An insignificant skirmish placed Djauher in possession of the city. He refrained from plundering it, and caused proclamation to be made that he would adhere to the terms of the original treaty. This calmed the fears of the people; the shops remained open, and business went on as usual; and the only remarkable incident was that the exuberant gratitude of the inhabitants caused them to murder the leaders of the war party, and present their heads to Djauher.

On 18th Ramadan, Djauher made his triumphal entry into Fostât, with banners borne before him and trumpets sounding; he was clothed in a silken robe broidered with gold, and mounted upon a superb charger caparisoned in the finest cloths of Egypt. He established his camp on the site of modern Kairo, and proceeded at once to trace out the outer boundary of a new city, and to lay the foundations of the khalif's palace. He decreed the abolition, throughout Egypt, of all forms or ceremonies which might recall the domination of the Abbasides. He removed their names from the public prayers, and called in the coin stamped with their superscription. He forbade the wearing of black—the colour of their family—and ordered that all preachers should be clothed in white, and should repeat this formula at public prayers: 'O God! shed Thy blessings upon Thy chosen servant Muhammad; upon Ali, the object of Thy affection; upon Fatima, the virgin; upon Hasan and Hosain, the grandsons of the Prophet, whom Thou hast purified and preserved from all taint of sin; and, O my God! upon the

Imams, the progenitors of the chief of believers, Moezz-li-din Allah.'

But the power of the Fatimide khalifs was as yet far from secure. They were surrounded by implacable enemies. The adherents of the Abbasides—divided though they might be on other points—were at one in regarding this new dynasty as the very abomination of desolation standing where it ought not. The 'Twelvers'—the true servants of Ali, as they held themselves to be—viewed with the profoundest indignation the dominion for which they had suffered so much and waited for so long, handed over to a race of heretics and impostors by the inexplicable caprice of destiny. The Karmathians were still at the height of their power. They had laid Egypt under tribute. The weakness of the government there had enabled them to make with impunity the terrible raid upon Mekka described in a previous chapter. This apparition of a power, still in its youthful vigour, and backed up by all the resources in men and money of Northern Africa, was like the first warning note striking their hour of doom.

Insurrections soon broke out in half-a-dozen different parts of Egypt. Rebellion, hydra-headed, was destroyed in one place only to spring up in another. But Djauher was a man of surprising energy, promptitude, and military skill. He seems, also, to have been gifted with rare discernment in the selection of fitting instruments to execute his plans. Egypt was quieted by a series of rapid and crushing blows; Syria was invaded, and that province added to the dominions of Moezz. But now a more formidable enemy appeared. Hassan ibn Ahmed, the Karmathian ruler, had had the amazing effrontery to solicit the co-operation of the khalif of Baghdad—Moti—in destroying the Fatimides. The khalif rejected the proposal with indignation; but Hasan, not discouraged, determined to make the attempt alone. Gathering together a large army, which was further recruited by the relics of the Egyptian insurrections, he advanced against Damascus. For awhile the Karmathian carried all before him. After a brilliant victory the gates of Damascus were thrown open to him, and he advanced against Ramlah. Djauher, in the meanwhile, had despatched a force into Syria to support the troops already there. But before its arrival these troops had been cut to pieces in the battle before Damascus, and the reinforcement was compelled to seek refuge in Jaffa, and was there closely blockaded. Leaving a detachment to maintain the blockade, Hasan marched against Fostât. Djauher was awaiting him. He had encircled the capital with a deep trench; arms had been distributed to the populace; and spies were sent out in all directions to bring the earliest intelligence of the approach of the enemy. On Friday, the first day of the first Rebi, A.H. 361, the Karmathians came in sight. The battle raged for two days, but ultimately the Karmathians were defeated with prodigious slaughter. They fled, abandoning their camp, their provisions, and all their treasure. They had never received such a crushing blow. It confirmed the power of the Fatimides; and Moezz, after much hesitation, determined upon coming in person to take possession of his new province. He made his entry into Fostât on the 7th Ramadan, A.H. 362, accompanied by his brothers and his children, and all the descendants of the Mehdi Obeidallah. On the 15th of the same month the khalif, seated on a throne of gold, received the most distinguished men of the province. Djauher presented them in the order of their precedence. Lastly, he came forward himself to offer the presents he had prepared in honour of his master's arrival. These were: 1. One hundred and fifty horses, with saddles of gold, and bridles studded with precious stones, and inlaid with amber. 2. Thirty-one silken pavilions borne upon as many Bactrian camels. 3. Nine riding camels covered with cloth of gold. 4. Thirty-three mules, seven of which were equipped with saddles and bridles. 5. One hundred and thirty baggage mules. 6. Ninety dromedaries. 7. Four open caskets containing gold and silver vessels. 8. One hundred swords, enriched with gold and silver. 9. Two silver caskets filled with precious stones. 10. A turban studded with gems. 11. Nine hundred boxes containing a selection of the most precious objects to be found in Egypt.

Thus had the whirligig of time brought back its revenges; and the hunted Shia seated himself as a sovereign in the richest province of the Muhammadan empire. By reason of its influence on the destinies of Europe, this conquest of Egypt by the Fatimide khalifs is perhaps, so far as the West is concerned, the most important episode in the history of Islam. The disunited provinces of the Baghdad khalifate were shortly to be welded together in the vast empire of the Seljukides; when, but for the rising of this hostile power in Egypt, the entire weight of the Muhammadan world would have descended upon the tottering empire of Byzantium, and indubitably have crushed it. The Fatimide khalifs were the allies of the Crusaders;

and to them, hardly less than to the hosts of the Red Cross, Europe owes that interval of precious time which enabled her to consolidate her nationalities and roll back the tide of Muhammadan invasion, when at last Constantinople—the bulwark of the West—succumbed to Othman and his Turks.

The Fatimide khalifs, though nominally Muhammadans, denied the fundamental tenets of the Prophet. According to Muhammad, he himself was the seal of the prophets, and the Koran a complete rule of conduct. No further communications were to be expected from God, either in writing or through the agency of prophecy. The successors of Muhammad were but the executors of a law entrusted to them; they had no authority to alter it one jot or one tittle; they were gifted with no inspiration making them wise above what was written. They were themselves bound by the mandates of the sacred book, as rigidly as the meanest Muhammadan on whom they inflicted the penalties of the law. The Fatimide khalifs, on the contrary, held themselves to be incarnations of the Divine Reason. Their doctrine was that all the phenomena of this sensible and material world were types or symbols of corresponding realities in the spiritual and unseen world. Every positive precept of the Law was an allegorical statement of some unseen verity; and as one pure and universal Reason presided over the spiritual world above, so was it necessary that in this lower world also this pure Reason should be incarnate in a person. It had been so in Ismail and his descendants; it was so in the Fatimide khalifs of Egypt. They were, to use the words of the Koran, 'a fire lighted by God, which penetrated the hearts of men.' They could discern that which was hidden from the eye and dwelt within. All the course of the preceding history of the world had tended to the manifestation of the Mehdi. No messenger who had been sent from Heaven in bygone ages but had indicated this great event in his writings and discourses, in the emblems of his doctrine, and the allegorical figures of his teaching. To know, then, the Imam was indispensable to a knowledge of God. 'If any among you'—is the statement of a preacher discoursing to a congregation of women—' say, "I have acknowledged the Unity of God; I have never failed to make this confession of faith, and I can have no need of a Mediator," the perception of the truth is hidden from that woman. Have you not heard in the conferences of wisdom that which has been spoken of a *torch*, which in its perfect state represents the religion of Unity, but which ceases to be a torch as soon as its several parts are divided from each other. Then the wax by itself is called "the wax," the wick "the wick," the flame "the flame" the chandelier "the chandelier;" but when all are united—the wax, the wick, the flame, and the chandelier—these together constitute a complete torch. Know then, O female believers in the Unity! why this parable has been set before you. It is in order that you may know you cannot attain to a right apprehension of the religion of Unity unless you include in that apprehension all the ministers of that religion. Has it not been delared to you in these conferences that the Koran is a living being? When its chapters, its grand divisions in ten and in five parts, and its verses are all combined into one, then the Koran is complete; but when its chapters are divided and parted from one another, no one would call that a complete Koran. When entire it is the symbol or representative of the Imam, and men call it the "Word of God."'

We of the West may at first experience some difficulty in comprehending how multitudes of rational creatures could have persuaded themselves that a spirit of pure reason and infallible knowledge was incarnate in these poor weak khalifs of Egypt. But we ought not to find it difficult. It is true that the founders and many of the chief propagators of this belief were at heart utterly sceptical; but such a frame of mind in the guides and teachers of a Church is not unknown to Western history. For the immense majority of men in those lands belief in Islam had become a part of their nature. They might act counter to its precepts; they might disregard its prohibitions; but they never questioned its authority or doubted the reality of its rewards and punishments. For such men the proclamation was a very welcome one: that Paradise was to be won by acknowledging the sovereign of Egypt as the legitimate Imam. Multitudes of devout souls, too, there were, to whom the belief in a divinely-gifted guide to conduct men in the right way was like the beam of light which Milton's Satan beheld in his journey through the realms of chaos, sending far into the bosom of dim night a glimmering dawn. They clung to it convulsively, as the one sign remaining that God had not entirely forsaken the world He had created.

Nor are the arguments by which this belief was enforced in any way unfamiliar to Western ears. They were briefly as follows: Either, said the Ismailiens, a man must maintain that he can attain to a knowledge of God by the unassisted reason, without the intervention of a mediator divinely commissioned, or that he cannot do so. But if he maintains the first thesis against an opponent who holds the second, in the very act of enforcing his opinion he demonstrates its falsity; for he cannot deny that so far as his opponent is concerned an instructor is needed to guide him to the knowledge of God. Of what kind, then, must this instructor be? It evidently cannot be anyone who chooses of his own will to assume that character. This deification of the private judgment has torn to pieces the body of Islam, and filled the Muhammadan world with a multitude of sects who teach men to tear and devour one another, but are impotent to bring them to a knowledge of the truth. And yet the avidity with which men follow these false guides, the tenacity with which they cling to the errors they have been taught, show what a hunger there is in the human heart for a truly inspired leader and head. Clearly, then, this guide must be one elevated above the frailties of the flesh, and incapable of falling into error. He must be able to teach as one having authority to do so. Where, lastly, should such a teacher be found except in the family of the Prophet? It is not enough, as is proved by the state of the Muhammadan world, to possess an infallible book. To preserve men from error there is needed an infallible interpreter of that book; and this wisdom and knowledge can be possessed by none but those who by right of blood inherit them from the Prophet.

It was under the khalifate of Hakem, the grandson of the conqueror of Egypt, that these doctrines attained their fullest expansion and their most systematic propagation. The intoxication of absolute power never engendered a more marvellous combination of the grotesque and the terrible than this prince. Utterly convinced of his own impeccability, and his right divine to rule over his subjects, he indulged every fantastic whim, and revelled in every species of cruelty with a callousness and supreme contempt for the rights of humanity worthy of a Hindoo deity. On one occasion he caused to be constructed an immense magazine, which he stowed brimful of acacia wood, brambles, and straw. The construction and storing of this work occupied many months. No one knew for what purpose it was intended; but all sorts of vague and horrible rumours flitted about, until at length it became generally known that the khalif intended to cast into this building all the Koran readers of the capital, and all the writers and other subordinate officials employed in the offices of the administration, and make a huge bonfire of them. All Kairo was smitten with terror. The intended victims assembled together, and advanced in a long procession through the streets, filling the air with their groans and lamentations. At every step the concourse prostrated themselves as one man, and kissed the earth. Thus they advanced to the palace of the khalif, and were admitted into his presence. They flung themselves on the ground at his feet, and entreated him to have mercy, and the khalif was graciously pleased to relinquish his amiable intention. But determined to glut his thirst for blood somewhere, he turned upon the wretched grooms who served in the royal stables. He ordered them to be slain without mercy; and so hot was his fury against them that the miserable creatures provided themselves with swords, carefully sharpened, which they handed over to the executioners, in order to make their sufferings as brief as possible. As soon as he was weary of butchering these, the khalif fell upon the eunuchs, the writers, and the slaves attached to the royal establishments; and a great number of these were put to death; their arms being first chopped off with a hatchet. Then the dogs of Kairo became distasteful to him, and he waged a war of extermination against them, so that not one was to be seen in the streets. Simultaneously with these atrocious proceedings, he issued a number of fantastic decrees. He forbade the sale of beer in the streets, because the khalif Ali disliked beer; he forbade also the sale of certain vegetables, because the khalif Muawia was said to be particularly fond of the one, and Ayesha was supposed to have introduced the eating of the other. He commanded that inscriptions cursing the Companions of the Prophet should be written on the walls of all the mosques of Kairo, the bazaars, and the streets; and he wrote to the governors of the provinces commanding them to do the same. But a year or two after he changed his mind. The inscriptions were ordered to be effaced; and anyone who dared to utter a malediction against a Companion was first flogged, and then paraded ignominiously through the streets. He recommenced his prohibitive decrees. He forbade the sale of raisins, and prohibited their importation into Egypt; a great quantity of this fruit was then collected and burnt by his orders. In the same year he forbade the sale of grapes, and caused a number of vines to be cut down, thrown on the ground, and trampled under foot by oxen. He had all the jars of honey in the storehouses of the Kairo merchants collected together, and their contents poured into the Nile. Any-one transgressing these ordinances, and daring to vend the prohibited articles, was beaten with whips, paraded through the streets, and then beheaded. Then, suddenly, his sanguinary impulses drove him to persecute the Jews and Christians, who formed a considerable part of the population of Egypt. For five years they endured the fires of persecution. Their chief men were beaten to death, and the bodies flung to the dogs. The churches and synagogues were destroyed all through Egypt and Syria; the lands belonging to them were given away to the favourites of the khalif; and the furniture of the sacred buildings, the vases of gold and silver, and the sacramental plate were put up for sale in the streets. When, at last, he became weary of slaughter, he gave orders that the Christians and the Jews should wear black because that was the colour of the Abbasides; that the Christians should suspend from their necks crosses, one cubit in length and ten pounds in weight; that the Jews should wear in like manner logs of wood of the same weight, but carved into the similitude of a calf's head, to remind them of their apostasy under the shadow of Mount Sinai. He forbade the people of both religions to ride with embroidered saddles, and their stirrups were to be of wood. They were forbidden to have Moslem servants; to ride on asses hired out by a Moslem, or to embark in a vessel having a Moslem crew. When they entered a public bath, in order to distinguish them from the Faithful, the Christians had to wear their crosses, and the Jews bells. Subsequently, however, he assigned to them separate baths, and forbade them to contaminate by their presence those in which the Faithful performed their ablutions.

Not less fantastical and whimsical were the personal habits of this terrible madman. At the beginning of his reign he wore magnificent dresses embroidered with gold, and turbans adorned with precious stones of immense value, and rode upon horses of price; then he took a whim to abandon all that external display, rode only upon a donkey, and wore a simple woollen garment. At one time he ordered that no special mark of respect should be paid to him, either in speaking of him or in his presence; then he issued orders that whenever his name was uttered either in conversation or any other way, all who were within hearing should prostrate themselves and kiss the earth; and the police were enjoined to enforce this regulation strictly. He passed several years in his palace, surrounded day and night with burning torches; then he took a fancy to pass a like time enveloped in perpetual darkness. He raged like a pestilence amid his ministers and the officials of his household. They were imprisoned, beaten, mutilated, and put to death, apparently without any pretext whatever beyond the sanguinary impulses of their master. He seems to have regarded the killing of a man as a pleasant pastime. One day he descended from his donkey at the door of the grand mosque, seized one of his attendants, threw him on the ground, and there and then disembowelled him; then washing his hands, went on as though nothing had happened. On another occasion, desiring to signify to a minister his displeasure and the doom that awaited him, he slew a beautiful slave in his presence. This tyranny endured for five and twenty years (A.H. 386–411). All Egypt trembled before this fantastic monster, and yielded an implicit obedience to his commands. He was in the habit of making nocturnal peregrinations through the streets of Kairo, to see that his ridiculous orders were duly observed. He was on such occasions very slenderly attended, and his attendants committed horrible outrages on the passengers they encountered; but no one dared, by a stroke of a dagger, to avenge himself, and rid the world of a monster. Each fresh act of cruelty only served to increase the abject prostration of his subjects. They bowed before this hideous incarnation of evil as a god manifest in the flesh; until at length the creed was actually promulgated and won numerous adherents that Hakem was God. They deduced his divinity from the utter inhumanity of his life; and addressed him—strangely enough—in the words of the Koran, as 'the Merciful and the Compassionate.' Hakem accepted this creed in perfect good faith. He put an end to the rites and ceremonies of the Muhammadan religion; he forbade his subjects to go on pilgrimage to Mekka; the Deity, he said, was manifest in Kairo, and there was no need to seek for him elsewhere.

Unhappily for this Egyptian god, he entered into a conflict with the women of Kairo; and this put an end to his life. The Egyptian ladies, then, as now, were celebrated for the extreme license of their manners, and the Khalif, in his character of an Egyptian Providence, determined to put a stop to this scandal. He had in his pay a number of old women whose business it was to worm themselves into the confidence of these gay dames, and then make known their delinquencies to the khalif, whereupon he caused the culprits to be arrested and thrown into the Nile. His nocturnal wanderings were also in a great measure undertaken in order to seize unwary lovers stealing to the place of assignation; and all such offenders were summarily put to death. But, dissatisfied with the result of these endeavours, he had recourse to more heroic measures. He published a decree forbidding women to appear in the streets, either by day or night, under pain of death. They were never to leave their homes; and to ensure the order being obeyed, he prohibited the shoemakers of the capital, and throughout all Egypt, from making any shoes for women. These orders remained in force for seven years, and many women who disregarded them were put to death. Passing one day by the baths, known as 'the baths of gold,' Hakem heard the sounds of merriment within. He inquired what occasioned it, and hearing there were women there, he ordered the doors of the bath-house to be bricked up, and the wretched bathers to be left to perish of hunger. The women of Kairo took a characteristic revenge for this atrocity. During his promenades through the city the khalif was accustomed to receive all petitions presented to him, and either examine them on the spot, or reserve them for future inquiry, according to the desire of those who presented them. The Egyptians more than once took advantage of this custom to present him papers, apparently petitions, but filled with invectives against him and his family. The women of Kairo dressed up the figure of a woman, which they placed at the corner of a road by which the khalif was certain to pass. In its hand was placed a paper filled with the most outrageous accusations against Sitt ul Mulk, an unmarried sister of the khalif. When Hakem approached and saw the figure, he supposed it to be a woman who had left her home in defiance of his orders, and he instantly ordered his attendants to rush upon her and cut her to pieces with their swords. The guards ran up, but finding it was merely a figure, they took the paper and brought that back to Hakem. When Hakem opened the paper and read what it contained, he was extremely furious. He let loose his slaves and his African body-guard upon his own capital, and for four days the streets were a scene of fighting and rapine. The inhabitants fought desperately in defence of their homes. Every morning Hakem came from his palace to watch the fighting. About a third of the capital was burned with fire, and fully one-half of it plundered; and the wives and daughters of the citizens were carried off and violated by the soldiery. At last, however, the townspeople, aided by a portion of the troops, succeeded in beating off the guards of the khalif and rescuing the rest of their city from destruction.

The wrath of the khalif was not assuaged by the destruction of the offending city, and he threatened his sister with death, on the ground that her immorality was the primary cause of the insult he had received. She determined to be beforehand with him, and, in concert with one of the chief nobles of the court, who, having offended the khalif, lived in hourly expectation of death, she formed a plan to murder him in the course of one of his nightly excursions. This plan was successfully carried out, and the khalif Hakem brought his reign to a close on the night of the 27th of the month, Shawal, A.H. 411.

The Fatimide khalifs, from the commencement of their power, had organised a vast army of missionaries, or *dais*, as they were called, for the secret propagation of their tenets through Asia. With the conquest of Egypt, this work of proselytising had been pursued with greater energy than ever; and the khalif Hakem built in Kairo a college for the regular education of these propagandists. It was named the 'Hall of the Sciences.' A large sum of money was annually set aside for the payment of the professors and other officials. At the head of the whole establishment was an official known as the chief *dai*, or missionary. The office was hereditary, descending from father to son, and its duties were manifold. The incumbent had to be thoroughly learned in all the doctrines regarding the descendants of the Prophet, and to give instructions in them. He received all subscriptions for the propagation of the faith. He held regular assemblies in the palace for the exposition of the doctrines of the sect. These were designated 'Conferences of Wisdom;' one special sitting was for the *devotees* or the *initiated*; a second for the officers of the court; a third for the general public and chance visitors to the city; a fourth was held in the grand mosque of Kairo for women; and a fifth in the palace, for the benefit of the ladies and female slaves resident in the harem.

Among the many who year after year crowded to the 'Hall of the Sciences' came Hasan ibn Sabah, the first grand master of 'the Assassins.' Hasan ibn Sabah, while yet a youth, was the companion and friend of two eminent men—Nizam ul Mulk, the illustrious prime minister of the Seljuk Sultans, Alp Arslan, and Malek

Shah; and Omar Khayam, the astronomer and poet, whose name is familiar to English readers, through the beautiful translation of his *Rubaiyat.* The prime minister has given an account of this early friendship, which has been preserved for us in Mirkhond's 'History of the Assassins.' 'The Imam Muafiq of Nishapore,' he writes—'one of the most illustrious doctors of Khorasan—was everywhere held in honour, and his society sought out as a source of good fortune. It was the general opinion that all young men who were educated by him in the knowledge of the Koran and the traditions, obtained the favours of fortune. It was this belief which induced my father to send me from Thous to Nishapore. Two young men of my own age—Hakim Omar Khayam and the unfortunate Hasan ibn Sabah, had also been entrusted to the care of the Imam a short time before I came. They were both gifted with excellent abilities, and we struck up a close friendship. Omar had been born at Nishapore, and Hasan ibn Sabah had as his father, Ali, a man who led an austere and ascetic life, but who professed erroneous opinions, and was, in a word, suspected of heresy. Abou Moslem Razi, governor of the province of Rei, where Ali dwelt, was remarkable for the purity of his faith, and his zeal in the cause of orthodoxy. He openly declared himself the enemy of Ali, and the latter sought by lying words and false oaths to exculpate himself from the accusations of the governor. As the Imam Muafiq of Nishapore was held to be a model of right thinking and orthodox belief, this unfortunate man, to remove from himself all suspicion of heresy, sent his son to Nishapore to study under the

Imam. As for himself, he retired into a monastery, and devoted himself to a life of religious seclusion; at times, nevertheless, he was accused of an heretical attachment to the doctrines of the Motazales, and at other times of scepticism and atheism. He claimed to be of Arabic extraction, of the family of Sabah Homäiri, and said that his father first settled in Koufa, then at Kom, and finally at Rei. But the people of Khorasan, and particularly those of Thous, wholly discredited this statement, asserting that his ancestors had all along been inhabitants of that province. To come, however, to my tale: One day Hasan said to Khayam and me: "It is a generally held opinion that the pupils of the Imam come to greatness; and doubtless, although the three of us cannot hope for equal good fortune, some one among us will verify the universal conviction regarding the Imam. In such case, what agreement shall we three make together?" "Whatever you propose," we replied. "Well," said he, "let this be our engagement, that whoever among us shall attain to wealth or honour, shall hold his possessions as common to all three." We agreed to this proposal, and bound ourselves by promises. The years went by, and I became prime minister to Alp Arslan; Hakim Omar Khayam came to me, and I did my utmost to fulfil the letter and spirit of our engagement.' Omar Khayam, however, would take nothing but permission to live at peace in Nishapore on a small pension. 'At Nishapore,' adds the vizier, 'thus lived and died Omar Khayam, busied in winning knowledge of every kind, and especially in astronomy, wherein he attained to a very high preeminence.'

The wise poet had no wish to stretch himself on the rack of this tough world. He has left us his philosophy of life—

> Some for the glories of this world, and some
> Sigh for the Prophet's Paradise to come.
> Ah! take the cash, and let the promise go,
> Nor heed the music of a distant drum!
> Were it not folly, spider-like to spin
> The thread of present life away, to win—
> What? for ourselves, who know not if we shall
> Breathe out the very breath we now breathe in!

The philosophy of Omar Khayam was that of Sardanapalus—'Eat, drink, and be merry, for to-morrow we die'—though it is clear enough that the feasting and the merriment without never excluded the consciousness of an aching heart within. It is a cry of anguish and despair which rings through the beautiful poem from which I have taken the lines quoted above. There was no purpose to be discovered in the movements of humanity; men, so it seemed to the poet, were the sport of a capricious and pitiless Destiny—

> —pieces of the game He plays
> Upon this chequer-board of nights and days,
> Hither and thither moves, and checks and slays,
> Then one by one back in the closet lays.

Speculation as to the future was unprofitable—the endeavour to amend the present a wasted labour; the business of the enlightened man was to bow to the inevitable, and get what happiness he could. The temperament of Omar Khayam led him to find this happiness in 'winning knowledge of every kind;' but given the same utter scepticism in a mind of a different cast—one devoured by the lust for power—and we have such an one as Hasan ibn Sabah, the first Grand Master of the Assassins.

'As for Hasan,' proceeds the vizier, 'he had remained obscure and unknown during the entire reign of Alp Arslan, and it was not until the time of Malek Shah that he came to Nishapore and made himself known. I received him with the greatest honours, and strove in every way to acquit myself honourably of the engagement I had contracted towards him when we were both young men.' In short Nizam ul Mulk obtained for his old schoolfellow an influential place at court, and Hasan at once commenced to make use of his new position in order to plot the ruin of his benefactor. A long series of plots and counterplots terminated in Hasan bringing himself into a position whence nothing but flight availed to rescue him from the sword of the executioner. He fled from the court of Malek Shah, and after escaping many dangers and long wanderings passed into Egypt. The khalif Hakem had long been dead; but the reigning sovereign, Mostansir, gave him a gracious reception, assigned him a residence in Kairo, and distinguished him by other marks of favour. At one time his prospects were so bright that people spoke of him as about to become the prime minister. These changed with the swiftness characteristic of an Eastern court. 'A man is not perfect,' was the remark of a vizier of those days, 'unless he have abilities sufficient for elevating to the pulpit his friend, though a simple soldier of police, and for sending to the gibbet his enemy, though a vizier.' A rival who had both the will and the capacity to act upon this rule of conduct converted for Hasan the prospect of a viziership into the reality of a dungeon in the castle of Damietta. He managed, however, to obtain his release; and returning to Syria spent three years in preaching the tenets of the Ismailiens in Baghdad, Ispahan, and other places, and making a great number of converts, until A.D. 1090, when, partly by force, partly by stratagem, he obtained possession of the Castle of Alamut. Alamut, or 'the Vulture's Nest,' so called from its impregnable position, is the largest and strongest of fifty castles which lie scattered about the district of Rudbar, at the distance of sixty parasangs north of Kasvin. This he resolved to make his capital; and he proceeded at once to strengthen the fortifications; he caused a canal to be dug, bringing water from a considerable distance to the foot of the castle; and planted groves of fruit trees around the cliffs on which the fortress was built. It was here, too, that he reduced to a system the vague plans of aggrandisement he had cherished through so many years of misfortune and obscurity.

Hasan perceived that in Central Asia, torn and distracted as it was, it needed only a ruthless tenacity of purpose for a man, situated as he now was, to become a formidable potentate. The endless confusions of that period had filled Central Asia and Syria with hordes of armed men similar to the 'Free Lances' who roamed over Europe during the long wars between France and England. Their military skill and practised rapacity were at the disposal of anyone who could hold out pay or prospects of plunder; and they flocked eagerly to offer their services to the lord of the fortress of Alamut. But this, the established method of carving a way to a throne, was too coarse and uncertain for his political subtilty.

Hasan had seen all his life that thrones supported by a mercenary soldiery alone never survived a single defeat. Their armies fought for plunder, not from any regard for the potentates under whose flag they were accidentally arrayed. And a defeat was the signal for desertion, in order to range themselves under some more fortunate leader. He must contrive some plan whereby he would, at one and the same time, fix himself deeply in the hearts of his subjects, and the fear of him not less deeply in the hearts of his enemies. The semblance of devotion, he resolved, should effect the one; and the secret use of the dagger, the other. It should be his work to weld together into one cutting and irresistible weapon the unquestioning devotion of religious fanaticism, and the cold calculating prudence of utter inhumanity. He perceived that hitherto the missionaries of the Fatimide khalifs had committed a fatal error in their method of proselytism. They had not been sufficiently careful to conceal the atheism and anarchy which lurked at the root of their teaching. Hasan determined this should no longer continue. These tenets were withdrawn into an obscurity impenetrable even to the mass of his own followers. To the world in general he stood forth as a follower of Ali, it is true, but also as a Moslem adhering strictly to the positive teaching of the Koran; demanding from his subjects a rigorous abstinence from wine, and the due and proper fulfilment of all the rites required of the Faithful. But the central tenet of his teaching was the manifestation of the Mehdi, or the Expected One. Incarnate, at present, in the khalif of Egypt, he was, so he taught, shortly to emerge from that muddy vesture of decay, and appear before the eyes of his faithful subjects as the monarch of the world. This coming of the Mehdi was to the devout Muhammadan what the second advent of Christ has been to many a weary and suffering Christian. It gave him hope; it painted on 'his straight prison walls, beautiful, far-stretching landscapes;' it spoke peace to his soul in the midst of carnage and oppression; it was, as it were, a rope flung to a spent swimmer struggling for life amidst storm and darkness—a rift in a mass of piled-up cloud, revealing the blue sky and the calm stars beyond. And as in the annals of Christendom it will be found that during periods of darkest calamity the belief in a second advent has most become a living power, so was it with its counterpart in the history of Islam. The promise of a Mehdi to lighten the burden of existence had a fascination in it which never failed to win the heart of the Muhammadan.

For the purpose of winning proselytes, Hasan created a hierachy of seven grades, which spread themselves through all Asia, doing the work of missionaries. But behind these, and concealed from the knowledge of the world—an inner circle within the larger—were carefully selected proselytes, initiated into the secret knowledge which should fit them to become the co-operators and lieutenants of the Ismailien chief. This, as at Kairo, consisted in the passing through a variety of stages up to the inculcation of the utter indifference of human actions. Hasan was himself Grand Master of the Order; next to him came his Grand Priors, or Lieutenants, scattered through Persia and Syria as the sect won adherents in those countries; then came the *Dais*, or missionaries—the teachers of the secret doctrines; the *Rafeeq*, or those engaged in learning; then the *Devotees*, or those who had taken the oath of unquestioning obedience; and lastly the *Aspirants*, who waited for the permission of the Grand Master to commence the process of initiation.

Of these different classes, the one with which history is chiefly concerned is that of the *Devotees*. These were 'the Assassins.' They were young men, selected on account of their physical strength and courage. The whole object of their training was to inspire them with a spirit of absolute submission to the Grand Master, founded upon a conviction of his Divine authority. The practice of murder in a just cause was justified by the most valid precedents. Had not the blessed Prophet slaughtered a whole Jewish tribe, numbering some 700 men, after they had surrendered themselves to his mercy? Had not the blessed Prophet on more than one occasion made use of the secret dagger and the midnight assassin to rid the world of enemies dangerous to himself and the true faith? Hasan ibn Sabah would not, therefore, lack instruments to execute his purposes if he could only convince them of his right to command them, and his power to reward their devotion. The Muhammadan conception of Paradise rendered this a not very difficult matter. The process of manufacturing a devotee was in truth exceedingly simple. He was asked to the table of the Grand Master, and when there, laid under the influence of a strong opiate. While still unconscious, he was conveyed away to a delicious garden, and there awoke amid the perfume of flowers and the cool splashing of fountains, with crowds of dark-eyed and obsequious damsels flitting around him. After a few days passed in this Paradise, he was again rendered insensible, and retransferred to the light of common day. To the credulous, unquestioning mind of a bigoted Muhammadan, what further proof was needed of the supernatural power of the Great Master? Paradise was no longer an anticipation; he had actually seen it, and tasted of its pleasures. The momentary agony of death alone divided him from their unbroken fruition. He was only asked to obey and die—a small thing when faith had been turned into sight.

Hardly, however, had Hasan established himself in Alamut when he was assailed. The Sultan Malek Shah despatched a force with orders to take the castle and exterminate the defenders. Hasan was on the point of capitulating when one of his lieutenants, who was making proselytes in Kasvin, sent a force to his relief. This effected a junction with the garrison, and in a night attack completely dispersed the besieging force. The check only stimulated the determination of Malek Shah. He ordered another body of troops to march—this time against Hasan's lieutenant, Hoosain Kainï, who was preaching with great effect in the mountains of Kohistan. Hasan took shelter in one of the hill forts, and was blockaded. To extricate his lieutenant, Hasan had recourse, for the first time, to the dagger. Nizam ul Mulk, the aged minister of Malek Shah, was stabbed to death; and Malek Shah followed him to the grave a few weeks after. This occurred A.H. 485 (A.D. 1093), and the anarchy that immediately ensued enabled Hasan ibn Sabah to consolidate his power. The vast kingdom of the Seljukides was torn in pieces by the struggles of rival claimants, and Asia, from Herat to the Caspian Sea, resounded with the tramp of marching armies.

PART III.

THE KHALIFS OF THE HOUSE OF OMMAYA.

CHAPTER I.

THE ARABS BEFORE ISLAM.

A.D. 120–716.

HEJJAJ, as was related in a previous chapter, had either slaughtered or suppressed all opponents of the khalif Abd al Malek. During his reign and that of his son and successor Walid, the broad dominions of the kha lifate lay stunned into the appearance of internal peace. But this interval was merely a period of suspended animation. There were no healing processes going on to obliterate by insensible degrees the gaping wounds which ruthless civil war had left behind it; there was no fusion of different races into a homogeneous whole. The dynasty of the Ommayas was a purely Arabic dynasty, the product of the conditions of Arabian society as it existed anterior to Islam, and subject therefore to the weakness and rapid decadence inseparable from the peculiar character of that society. Before relating, then, the story of its downfall, it is necessary to give a brief sketch of the Arabs before Islam.

The Arabs anterior to Muhammad formed two distinct nations—the most ancient of which traced back its origin to Kahtan, who is generally identified with the Joctan of Genesis; the other, and more recent one, claimed to have sprung from Ishmael, the son of Abraham and Hagar.

The cradle of the first was Yemen; that of the second, the Hejaz.

'Yemen' (properly so called) is the country which forms the south-west extremity of Arabia, and which is washed by the waters of the Red Sea on the west, and by the ocean on the south. The northward boundary is the Hejaz, and the province of Hadramaut extends along the eastern frontier. The Arab historians love to enlarge on the grandeur, richness, and prosperity of Yemen under the rule of their national sovereigns—the Himaryite Tobbas as they were called. The territory of Saba or Mareb in particular was the most verdant, the best watered, and the richest part of Yemen. It was covered with monuments, bridges, and magnificent trees. A cavalier, well mounted, would require a month to journey from one end to the other of the broad expanse of cultivated land. The inhabitants led the most agreeable life conceivable. They enjoyed a pure air, a refreshing climate, abundant irrigation. The beauty of their country passed into a proverb. Their empire attained the highest pinnacle of magnificence. A sudden and awful catastrophe overthrew their greatness.

There existed near Mareb an immense dike, intended to store up the water which collected at the foot of two mountains, and which, confined as in a well between their precipitous slopes, could escape by a single aperture only. According to Masoudi, this aperture was an enormous floodgate, with thirty circular openings bored in it, through which the water was permitted to flow. Insensibly, however, the waters heaped up behind it sapped the foundations of the dike, without the people of Saba being aware of their danger. A sudden rise in the reservoir at last broke down the weakened barrier, and a deluge of water was poured over the country sweeping everything before it. The people, the city, the rich cultivated lands were involved in one common ruin.

The tribe which inhabited the city of Mareb or Saba, and cultivated the rich lands surrounding it, was the tribe of Azd. Shortly before the inundation (which Muhammadan historians carry back to the time of Alexander the Great, but which Western criticism has fixed at about A.D. 120), the chief of the Azdites was one Amir, the son of Amir. This prince had a brother, named Amran, who was gifted with the faculty of divination. The first foreshadowing of the coming calamity was a prediction on the part of Amran that his fellow tribesmen would leave their native land, and be dispersed in countries far removed from one another. But the wife of Amir—Darifah—was a seer as well as the brother of her husband. She beheld a vision in her sleep which clearly announced a near and terrible catastrophe. 'Go,' she said to her husband, 'and examine the dike; if you see a rat whose fore feet leave deep impressions, and whose hind feet detach large stones from the mountain, know that the calamity which threatens us is now at hand.' Amir repaired to the dike, and saw with horror a rat detaching with his feet a huge stone which fifty men could not have moved. He determined to sell all that he possessed, and with his family abandon the doomed spot. But fearing lest conduct so extraordinary should awaken the suspicions of his countrymen, and thereby diminish the value of his property, he contrived a plan to conceal the real reason of his departure.

He prepared a grand feast, to which he invited all the inhabitants of Mareb. Then he summoned a young man, named Malik; according to some, one of his sons, according to others an orphan brought up in his family. 'When,' he said to the young man, 'I am seated and busy entertaining my guests, seat yourself near me; and understand, you are to contradict whatever I say to you, and in every respect to treat me as I shall treat you.' The time arrived; the guests were assembled; the young man seated himself near Amir as he had been told to do. Whatever Amir said, the young man contradicted. The former in an apparent excess of rage gave the young man a blow; Malik instantly returned it. 'O! disgrace,' shouted Amir, 'to the honour of Amir! to be struck and abused by a child!' And he swore he would put the young man to death. The guests interceded, imploring him to forgive Malik. Amir gave way, but added, 'God is my witness; I will remain no longer in a place where I have been so shamefully humiliated. I will sell all I possess, and find elsewhere a home.' The people were not displeased with this. They said one to another, 'Let us profit by the anger of Amir, and buy up his property before his wrath has time to appease;' and they purchased all that he possessed in the country of Mareb. As soon as Amir had received the price of his property, he announced to the tribe the doom with which they were threatened. Only a few families, however, determined to emigrate with him.

Though setting out as a single horde from Mareb, the emigrants soon broke up into a variety of parties, and sowed the germs of Yemenite tribes throughout all Arabia. Thus a portion of them under the name of the

Khozaa (separated) fixed themselves at Batn Marr near Mekka, and after the expulsion of the Djorhomites obtained the guardianship of the Kaaba. Two families after much wandering in many lands finally made their way to Yathrib, and developed in the course of years into the tribes of Aus and Khazraj—so memorable for the part they played in the career of Muhammad. Others again wandered to Syria and Irak, the former under the title of the Ghassanides, passing under the domination of the Roman; the latter to lay the foundations of the city of Hirah, and to establish a monarchy which endured till close upon the conquest of Irak by the Muhammadans, acknowledging, however, the Sassanides of Persia as their paramount power. One detachment separating from the main body almost immediately after it had quitted Mareb established itself in Ḣamadan; another turning eastward entered Oman on the shores of the Persian Gulf, where subsequently they were known as the Azdites of Oman. In this manner, starting from Mareb as their point of departure, the children of Kahtan, or, as they are more commonly called, the Yemenite tribes spread over the entire peninsula of Arabia.

The Ishmaelite tribes of Arabia are better and more accurately known as the tribes descended from Maad, the son of Adnan, or the Maadique tribes. Adnan or Maad (it is doubtful whether or not they are one and the same person) is the true father of the tribes, who assert that they are descended from Ishmael. To these tribes belongs the Kuraish. Between Muhammad and Adnan the Arabian genealogies count twenty generations; from Adnan to Ishmael there is pure night and the blankness of

T 2

ignorance. The Kuraish inhabited Mekka, and with the exception of the Aus and Khazraj, the whole of the Hejaz was peopled by tribes belonging to the Maadique federation. Their common father was Modhar, the grandson of Maad. In Muhammadan history they are collectively termed 'the tribes of Modhar.' Sprung from the same Maadique stock were the powerful tribes of Bakr, Taghlib, and Temim, which wandered over the uplands of Nedjd in the times anterior to Islam.

In addition, however, to their origin these two Arabic nations are distinguished by peculiar characteristics. The Yemenite tribes were the most civilised: wherever we find them located, in Yemen itself, in Hira, or in Medina, we find the rudiments at least of a civil administration and regular government; but the Maadique tribes were purely nomadic with the exception of the Kuraish after the time of Kossay. Each tribe formed a distinct and separate unity, finding its chief by a kind of silent popular vote in the man among them most distinguished for courage, wisdom, and wealth. This divided condition rendered them of necessity weak against an organised enemy. And hence, so long as the empire of the Himaryite Tobbas lasted, the Maadique tribes acknowledged their supremacy and paid them tribute. Now and again, driven by some sudden impulse of wrong, they forgot their internal feuds to combine against the common oppressor. Such efforts were spasmodic; the alliances they created weak and transitory. Nevertheless, from peculiarities in the circumstances and character of the Arabs, the recollection of these struggles sank deep in the minds of the two nations. They kindled a spirit of rivalry, a keen and constant antagonism between them, which Islam was wholly powerless to efface, which never needed more than a spark to flame forth in civil war.

A Muhammadan writer has said, 'I should like much if we had with our Islamism the nobleness of character which belonged to our fathers in the "days of ignorance." Antara was a pagan, and Al Hasan, son of Hani, a Moslem; well, Antara was restrained within the limits of duty by his honour, and Al Hasan, son of Hani, was not so by his religion. Antara says in his poetry—

> And I lower my eyes if the wife of my neighbour I see,
> Until the tent curtain descending conceals her from me.

While Hasan has said in the bosom of Islam,

> Ah! youth was the tempter who led me astray—
> When the eyes of the world were weary with sleep
> She impelled me at midnight to stealthily creep
> To the house of a lov'd one whose spouse was away.'[1]

The particular virtue which this writer has selected for eulogy was, it must be confessed, conspicuous by its absence among the ancient Arabs. Nevertheless there was in them a nobleness of character, a free, frank, and genial courageousness, a sort of child-like gaiety and enjoyment of life, which Islam either destroyed by conversion into a gloomy and cruel fanaticism, or branded as impious.

The deserts of Arabia have once or twice witnessed the march of invading armies. The Roman troops of Ælius Gallus perished to a man in those pitiless solitudes. And dim legends are to be found in early Arabic literature

[1] Quoted in Fresnel's *Prem. Lettre.*

of the passage of a Babylonish army through the Hejaz on its way to the conquest of Egypt. That was in the days of the great Nebuchadnezzar. The sacred city lay in the track of this host. It was levelled with the ground. The entire posterity of Ishmael was destroyed; and it is to this complete extermination that the Arab genealogists attribute the want of the missing links between Maad and Ishmael. As Maad, however, lived several centuries subsequently to the reign of Nebuchadnezzar, the legend is not of much historic value. Be, however, its authenticity what it may, certain it is that the broad belt of desert which forms the northern boundary of Arabia was a barrier which excluded the peninsula from the great changes witnessed by the rest of Asia. The Arabs formed a little world of their own. They were not unacquainted with the splendid and luxurious court of the monarchs of Persia. They had relations with the emperors of Byzantium. The trade routes which crossed their deserts in every direction brought them in frequent and intimate intercourse with men of different speech and religion from their own. But these glimpses of the world beyond, though they gave to the Arabs a brightness of intellect which is not to be found among the wandering races of Northern Asia, never in the slightest degree weaned them from their love of the free life of the desert. Centuries passed over their heads leaving them precisely as they found them.

The elements of good and evil in the character of the desert Arab did not, as in ordinary men, blend together like the dyes in tangled skeins of silk. They were in distinct and striking contrast like the squares on a chess board. Outside of the limit of his tribe the Arab could revel in crimes of every description, not merely without incurring reproach, but in most cases with the warm approval of his compatriots. Robbery was his sole occupation and means of livelihood. Revenge was a sacred duty. Murders, in pursuit of this end, of the most cowardly description—the slaughter, for example, of sleeping men, the massacre of helpless children, not under a momentary excess of passion or in the heat of battle, but deliberately and in cold blood, entailed no stigma upon the murderer. They were acts in which he gloried. They became the favourite theme of his songs. His tribe would lavish their blood like water rather than abandon him for such laudable acts as these. To pounce down upon a defenceless or unsuspecting tribe, to slaughter as many men as they could, to carry off the wives and children, reducing the former to concubines, the latter to slaves—such acts constituted 'an expedition.' To make successful 'expeditions' was the highest glory of the Arab chief. In short, murder, robbery, rape, and slave-catching formed the active elements of his life. They constituted the profession by which he lived. This is the dark side of the Arab character.

Happily there is a somewhat brighter side. The Arab hospitality has passed into a proverb. There is no doubt that even here there was much of ostentation and self-glory. The Arab was troubled by no modest scruples. If he was a mighty man of war, he frankly proclaimed that fact to all the world. If he was profuse in his hospitality, he sounded a trumpet before him as vigorously as ever did Pharisee in the distribution of alms. But after deduction made on this account, there was much that was truly admirable in the old Arab hospitality. The notion of indebtedness on the part of the guest was utterly eradicated. It was the host who was obliged, who was bound to be grateful. The hospitality of the Arab was rooted in a conviction that to shower blessings upon others, and never to turn from him that would borrow of him, was the highest privilege man could enjoy. Thus Hatim Tai—the most generous of all the Arabs—made a vow never to refuse anything that was asked of him. In the heat of a fight he had disarmed an enemy, and was pressing him close—not to kill (for he had also made a vow, which he kept through life, never to take a human life) but to capture him, when the Arab turned upon his pursuer. 'Hatim,' he said, 'give me thy lance.' At once Hatim Tai flung him his lance, remaining unarmed himself. It is a rare and refreshing fact to have to record that the Arab respected his generous antagonist, and refrained from plunging the lance he had acquired in the bosom of the donor.

The perils too he had to encounter—perils in the wilderness as well as from men—evoked in the Arab an unequalled hardihood and courage. Carrying his life, as it were, always in his hand, he learned to contemplate death with a calm and indifferent eye. Not that life was of small value to him. The Arab drank in the joy of existence with a deep and eager thirst, which gives to his poetry an exulting vitality that almost saddens European minds, groaning under the burden and the mystery of an unintelligible world. But this joy in life arose from that inward sense of fearlessness which could look the whole world in the face, because it feared not any man. The stigma of cowardice would have rendered life intolerable. There was, it is true, little of chivalry in the courage of the Arab. If he scorned to ask for quarter, he seldom gave it. He hardly ever shrank from killing a wounded foe. But with this ruthlessness there was always a frank recog nition of a more excellent way. An act of mercy on the part of a generous foe never failed to win for the doer the approbation of the poets—which constituted the highest meed of glory. But the mere courage to face death was not the only virtue that the Arabs required of a man. They demanded that he should be affable in prosperity, patient and strong in adversity. They considered suicide as cowardly and disgraceful; nay—they could cordially admire the virtues they were most reluctant to practise. The very men whose ardent susceptibility was always tremblingly alive, whom a biting word could plunge into a career of homicides, could eulogise in their poems the long suffering of the Bani Zimman, who endured a thousand wrongs rather than war against a brother tribe. 'They are our brothers,' they said at each fresh insult; 'perhaps they will return to better sentiments; perhaps we shall see them again as they once were.'

The strongest passion, however, in the ancient Arab was pride of race. His camels and his horses constituted his wealth. He had observed in the propagation of these animals the absolute need of good parents to produce good offspring. No breeder of English race-horses has a more settled belief in the value of 'blood' than had the ancient Arab. And arguing from analogy, he applied the same principles to the human race. He was convinced that in men as in horses qualities good or bad transmit themselves in the blood. Hence the stress which the ancient Arabs laid upon genealogies; hence the jealous care with which they were preserved. The courage, the vigour, the wisdom of some bygone chief did not sleep in his grave. It was an everlasting possession enjoyed by his children. The daughters of such men became 'the mothers of heroes' in virtue of a natural law. There was no higher honour possible for man than to have the pure Arab blood flowing in his veins. To unite an Arab maiden with even the monarch of Persia was held to be a humiliation; and a reluctance to incur this disgrace cost one of the last kings of Hira his kingdom and his life. The social position of men of mixed blood—those whose mothers were African slaves—was, in consequence of this pride of race, an extremely melancholy one. Their compatriots of pure Arab blood looked down upon them from an infinite height. No exploits however brilliant, no qualities however great, sufficed to wipe out this primary stigma. Antara, the typical poet and hero of Arabia, was a man of mixed blood; and his life is one long series of heroic actions and desperate perils to make himself worthy of the hand of a pure Arab maiden. Shanfara, another of the Arabic poets, was like Antara a man of mixed blood. Having ventured to address a familiar observation to an Arab girl, she was so indignant at the presumption on the part of a man of mixed blood that she gave the poet a box on the ear. Shanfara swore that he would revenge himself by the slaughter of a hundred men of her tribe. And he kept his word. He was an unerring archer; and his first act was to fashion an arrow of peculiar construction, so that the Salamanides (the tribe to which the maid belonged) might recognise the slayer of their compatriots. Ninety-seven of the Salamanides fell pierced with these arrows, and every attempt to seize or slay Shanfara had failed. At last the Salamanides learned in good time of the approach of Shanfara, and the spot where he lay hidden. They set out immediately, in the hope of surprising him. Shanfara had quitted his lair, but his enemies followed on the track. In his flight the poet met a woman belonging to the tribe of the Salamanides, and demanded from her something to drink. The woman having recognised who the speaker was, gave him at first a piece of extremely salt cheese to aggravate his thirst, and then, when he asked for water, pretended to have none, but proffered in its stead some inebriating liquor. Shanfara, after taking a draught, hastened on, and those who were tracking him, having come up with the woman, learned what had occurred. Certain then that the first need of the fugitive would be to quench his thirst, they posted themselves close to a well—the only one there was in that part of the country.

The night fell, and soon after Shanfara was seen stealthily drawing near the spot. 'I see you,' cried the poet as he approached; actually perceiving nothing, but endeavouring to disclose an enemy if any chanced to lie concealed near the well. The Salamanides lay flat on the ground; they stirred not a limb; but remained with breath suspended, silent as the dead. Nevertheless Shanfara perceived a black mass marked out against the back-ground of sand. The Salamanides had grouped themselves round the well in parties of two; and they had agreed that should any of their number be struck by an arrow from Shanfara's bow before the favourable moment for springing upon the revengeful poet, the wounded man was to suppress every sign of pain or emotion, so as not to reveal the ambuscade. Shanfara saw the black mass, and fitted a shaft to his bow. Straight and true went the shaft, and one of the Salamanides died without a cry or a movement. He had now slain ninety-eight of the hecatomb he had vowed to offer up. The perfect immobility of the black mass, the profound silence which reigned around the well, reassured Shanfara. He approached the well, laid aside his weapons, and stooped down to drink of the water. In a moment up rose the Salamanides; a portion of them seized his arms; the rest flung themselves on the poet. He was a man of enormous agility; swifter of foot than the best of the horses of the desert. 'A better runner than Shanfara,' was a proverb among the Arabs to signify a horse of exceptional speed. He made one gigantic bound to escape his enemies; but one of them struck at him in mid air and severed his left hand. Shanfara picked it up with his right hand, and flung it, like a stone, at the chest of his adversary. The latter grappled with Shanfara; they rolled together on the sand; Shanfara, rapidly disengaging himself from his enemy, rose to his feet, and trampled with all his might upon the neck of his enemy. The Salamanide rolled over in the dust dead. It was the last of Shanfara's exploits. The next moment he fell dead beneath the blows of twenty sabres. They attached the corpse to a cross, where it remained suspended for a year or two.

Nevertheless a debt weighed upon the corpse, for Shanfara had sworn to immolate one hundred men of the tribe of Salaman, and at the moment of his death he had slain but ninety-nine. It so happened that a Salamanide, returning to his tribe after a long absence, passed the spot where the skeleton had fallen to the ground. He accidentally struck his foot against the skull. The sharp bone inflicted a wound, which turned into an ulcer, and from the effects of this, after a brief while, the man died. That man completed the hundred.[1]

Not less remarkable than the passionate pride of blood was the Arab's passionate love of poetry. It is not too much to say that we cannot understand the early history of Muhammadanism unless we have appreciated the part which poetry played in it. The genius of the Arabic language lends itself readily to rhymed compositions; and the early Arabs literally lisped in numbers. The spell that resides in harmonious verse exercised over them an almost irresistible power. A poetic satire wounded them far more keenly than a knife; an eulogy moved their souls with unspeakable delight. These poetic compositions were rarely written; but the tenacious memory of the Arab found no difficulty in retaining them without this artificial aid. A popular poem passed with the speed of light from mouth to mouth, and was known and repeated over the whole extent of the deserts of Arabia. The poets were the national historians. They glorified the exploits of their tribes. They covered with ridicule the character of their enemies. And hence the appearance of a great poet in any tribe was a signal for rejoicing of the most enthusiastic kind. That tribe,

[1] Fresnel's *Prem. Lettre.*

thenceforth, knew that the beauty and chastity of its women and the heroism of its men would be familiar as household words in every camp and city of Arabia. And fame and glory were the very life-breath of the ancient Arabs. But not only so. A first-rate poet was a barrier against aggression for the tribe so fortunate as to possess him. The Arab's love of praise was of necessity accompanied by a sensitiveness to ridicule equally keen; and one tribe hesitated to attack another, when the moment of aggression would be the signal for an outpouring of savage satire that would make them a laughing-stock to their countrymen. These satires lasted; and the Arab reflected with dismay that, ages after he had passed away, the lines which declared him to be a sot, a coward, or a fool, and his wives and daughters ugly and abandoned prostitutes, would remain indelibly burned into the memory of posterity.

I have spoken of the Arab tribes as being continually engaged in 'expeditions' against each other. The reader will, perhaps, have wondered how, under such circumstances, society of even the most rudimentary character was possible. By a very rapid kind of natural selection, the weaker members of the community, it would seem, must be expunged, and the population of Arabia reduced to a single tribe which had devoured all the others. The Arabs felt that this was the inevitable issue of their practices. And more than once they voluntarily elected a king, or solicited one from Yemen or Persia, to keep themselves in order. But a more effective remedy still was the institution of the three sacred months during which, by common agreement, war was suspended and homicide interdicted. This was the season of the Pilgrimage and of the Fair of Okazh. It is with this last that we are concerned here.

The Fair of Okazh was a large market, open annually to all the tribes of Arabia. It was held in the neighbourhood of Mekka, between Taif and Nakhlah, and commenced at the new moon of Dhúl Kada, i.e. at the commencement of the three sacred months. It lasted for a period of twenty days. All the tribes mingled there amicably. Feuds were for the time supposed to be laid aside, and the man who had committed a murder might approach without fear the man whose duty it was to revenge it. But it was also a great congress of literature. The Fair of Okazh was the Arabian substitute for booksellers and advertisements. The poets from all parts of the continent went thither to recite their compositions; the lovers of literature crowded thither to hear them. 'Expeditions' being everywhere suspended, and hospitality a sacred duty which no true Arab could evade, not only were all the roads safe, but the poorest wayfarer was certain of board and lodging all along his route. The concourse, therefore, was immense; and from Okazh, as a centre, the knowledge of the events of the past year was disseminated throughout Arabia. The holiday-makers carried back to their encampments the glory or the shame of the different tribes as embodied in the odes to which they had listened.

These poems, even through the mists of a translation, give a singularly vivid picture of the ancient Arabs and the life in the desert. The desolate grandeur of the sandy wastes is depicted with a force and vividness that evince the 'seeing eye' of the true poet. The midnight march, the swoop down upon the defenceless camp as the sun peeps above the horizon, the fury of an equal battle—all these incidents are depicted with a fresh and living reality. And not less so the more amiable characteristics of the Arab—his sensibility to the loveliness of women, his hearty and ardent friendship bred out of danger and hardship encountered together, his thorough enjoyment of life, and, lastly, the reckless scepticism which formed the basis of his character, and which it is a great mistake to suppose that Islam succeeded in eradicating. It was these recitations which achieved that fusion of dialects that furnished Muhammad with a language which carried his message to every tribe in Arabia. But—and this is the point which I wish to insist upon here—these recitations had the effect of inflaming tribal feuds, of keeping raw and tender, old wounds. These poetic insults rankled like poison in the minds of those they struck. These poetic eulogies rendered still more arrogant and aggressive the tribes which happened to be lauded. And so the annual congress at Okazh became a means of keeping alive and perpetuating the heritage of hate which already divided the tribes of Yemen from those belonging to the Maadique confederation.

The creed of Muhammad failed altogether to remove this spirit of rivalry; it succeeded only in suspending it for a few years. The rapid conversions which followed his teaching were due to causes anterior to it. Amid all their rivalries and intestine feuds the Arabs had never entirely forgotten that they were a single nation. The universal observation of the three sacred months, the institution of the Fair of Okazh, were acknowledgments of this fact. The point, however, on which the two branches could not agree was, the place which ought to be selected as the metropolis of Arabia. The tribes of Yemen insisted that Mareb ought to be so considered. They supported this claim on the ground that they had the purer Arab blood in their veins; that Mareb was the richest and most populous place in Arabia; and that, in point of fact, all the tribes of Arabia acknowledged the supremacy of the Himaryite Tobbas. The tribes of Modhar admitted that they were engrafted on the Arab stock by the marriage of Ishmael with a daughter of the Djorhomites, a Yemenite tribe, and they frankly acknowledged the greatness and splendour of the Himaryite Tobbas, but they asserted that the spiritual glory of Mekka obscured any merely terrestrial magnificence. As containing the Temple built by Abraham, as the spot whither all the tribes went up every year to worship, they contended that no other spot but Mekka could be the metropolis of Arabia. So long as the empire of the Himaryite Tobbas lasted, this dispute remained undecided. But when Yemen was invaded (about A.D. 525), and conquered by the Abyssinians, and an Abyssinian king ruled there, there could no longer be any question that the Arabian metropolis was not to be looked for in Yemen. Mekka rose to undisputed pre-eminence. And when the Abyssinian monarch marched against the sacred city at the head of an immense force, swearing that he would level the Temple of Abraham with the ground, when he and his army were smitten with a mysterious death just as they were on the point of entering the undefended city, the sacred city became a spot more holy than ever. It was clear to every Arab in the peninsula that the place was under the Divine protection. When, therefore, Muhammad incorporated with his creed all those rites and ceremonies which from immemorial times had been held in reverence by his countrymen, he achieved, it is true, a superficial kind of religious unity; but he did so, not by converting the Arab to his creed, but by lowering his creed to the spiritual level of the Arab. He sacrificed the religious teacher to the exigencies of the ambitious politician. Once lord of Arabia, and the doctrine of *jehad* became a necessary consequence of his position. He had purged the old Arab creed of a number of impurities which time and the ignorance of its professors had caused it to contract; he had given the impulse of a divine sanction to the nascent aspirations of the people after religious unity; but he had wrought no change in the character of the Arab nor the social conditions of his life. He contemplated none. After, as before, Islam, the Arabs were to be a predatory nomad and blood-shedding race. And his two immediate successors, Abu Bekr and Omar, strove their utmost to preserve these national characteristics unalloyed by contact with the manners and habits of more civilised races. The consequence was, that when Muhammad interdicted the Faithful to prey upon each other, he was compelled to find occupation for their swords elsewhere. Out of this necessity sprang the command to inherit heaven by fighting on the path of God. This is the doctrine which has rendered Islam so fascinating a faith to savage and barbarous races. It exacts from them no endeavours after a higher life. It tells them that they can win an immortality of sensual bliss by merely giving free scope to their most imperious passions.

Among the Arabs the first effect of the new doctrine was marvellous. The recollections of domestic feuds were quenched in the bright hopes of plundering a world. An united Arabia poured across the northern sandy waste to the conquest of Syria, Palestine, and Persia. But the feelings of enthusiasm, evoked by an unprecedented career of conquest, by the acquisition of wealth and magnificence far beyond the highest reach of the Arab's imagination, speedily spent themselves by reason of their very excess. They were fed from without; not the effect of any well-spring of conviction within. And, as I have shown in a previous chapter, with the accession of Othman to the khalifate, the old tribal feuds asserted themselves with all their former bitterness and intensity. There was, moreover, another and even more potent influence keeping alive the memories of the old wars and struggles for supremacy between the tribes of Yemen and the tribes of Modhar.

According to Muhammadan divines, the Koran is in itself the greatest of all miracles. In most cases, they say, miracles have not occurred at one and the same time with the revelations committed to the Prophet. They have been intended to confirm and bear witness to the revelations, and have in consequence been subsequent to the divine message. But the Koran is a miracle and revelation in one. It is otherwise with regard to the Pentateuch, the Evangel, and other Divine books; they are revelations received under the form of ideas. When the writers of these books returned from the ecstatic state to the normal human condition, they clothed the revelations they had received in their own language. And consequently, in the style of these books there is nothing miraculous. But not so in the case of the Koran. The actual text of the Koran came to the Prophet through the ear, as is shown by the following among other passages:

> Move not thy tongue in haste to follow and master this revelation:
> For we will see to the collecting and the recital of it;
> *But when we have recited it*, then follow thou the recital,
> And verily afterwards it shall be ours to make it clear to thee.
>
> Sura 75, v. 16–19.

These verses were communicated to the Prophet to quiet the anxiety he manifested to fix by constant repetition the words of the Koran in his memory. There are many other like passages which clearly show that the Koran was made known to the Prophet under the form of a reading delivered in a high voice; and thus every line of the Koran is a miraculous revelation of Divine eloquence surpassing the power of men.

To interpret, therefore, this text aright became nothing less than a question of eternal life or death for the devout Muhammadan. The work of exegesis divided itself into two branches: the traditional and the philological. The former comprised a knowledge of the circumstances under which any particular revelation was made, and of the later passages which abrogate earlier ones—knowledge which was supposed to have been communicated by the Prophet to his companions, and handed down by tradition to succeeding generations. The latter was confined to an investigation of the precise and exact meaning attaching to phrases and idioms. By reason of the imperfect fusion of the dialects at the time of Muhammad, the Arabic language had a wealth of synonyms, and an abundance of idioms and peculiar turns of phrase which rendered its complete and perfect acquisition beyond the power of any single mind. The true signification of many of the phrases used in the Koran were known frequently to none but some remote and petty tribe, from whose dialect the Prophet had borrowed a few expressions. Yet, as I have just said, the risk of leaving any point obscure or uncertain was too dreadful to be endured patiently. It became needful, in consequence, to enter upon a systematic study of the dialects of Arabia as they existed previously to Islam. All the old chivalric stories, all the old poems, were invested with a new and almost divine significance. They were collected from every quarter, preserved with the utmost care, commented upon with the minutest industry; and so the wounds and divisions of the days of ignorance were kept bleeding and open, by reason of the care with which the records were preserved in which they were related.

The succession, too, of the poets had never ceased. Farazdak, Jarir, Omar, Akhtal, and many another, modelled their writings on the style of the giants of former times. They, like them, sang the glories of the tribes to which they belonged, and poured forth slander and abuse upon everyone else. Many a sanguinary and bitter feud was the consequence. The following narrative will suffice as an illustration, and will prove also how completely

Islam failed in welding the Arabic tribes into a united nation.

Akhtal was famous for his powers as a satirist, and the exercise of this power brought him upon one occasion very near to death. He was a great favourite with the khalif Abd al Malek, who liked to listen to poets reciting their poems against each other. The Bani Taghlib, to which tribe Akhtal belonged, had killed near the city of Tekrit a certain Omair ibn Khachab, belonging to the family of Bani Kais, a branch of the tribe of Bakr. The enmity between the Taghlibites and Bakrites dated from a period more than a century anterior to the birth of Muhammad. At that time they wandered over the uplands of Nedjd; and their residence there was rendered memorable in the annals of the Arabs before Islam by a war of forty years, known as the 'War of Bassous.' They now dwelt in Mesopotamia, and the old enmity merely slumbered; it was not extinct. Temim, a brother of the murdered man, vowed vengeance. He obtained the assistance of the Bani Bakr and their chief, Zofar, son of Hareth. Parties of horse were sent into Syria to plunder and harry the families of the Taghlibites located there. All who could not fly were put to the sword. Zofar marched in person against the sections of the tribe which dwelt in Mesopotamia. They fled across the Tigris, but were overtaken at a spot some distance to the south of Mosule. After a bloody struggle the Taghlibites were defeated, the conquerors sparing neither women nor children in the pursuit. The war lasted for several years with varying success and invariable ferocity. But at last, in A.H. 63, the rival tribes, exhausted rather than pacified, suspended hostilities, and the chiefs met together in apparent amicability at the court of Abd al Malek. But the khalif, instead of seeking to strengthen these symptoms of returning friendship, inflamed the old hostility by causing to be recited before him the songs composed on the events of the recent war. On this occasion Akhtal recited a poem which vaunted the courage of the Taghlibites and lavished contempt on the Bani Kais. Referring to a battle in which his tribe had vanquished their opponents, he said :

> 'Fame! has she made known how between Razail and Khadr, the Arakems have slaughtered the children of Kais, of those men who hesitated not to commit injustice, who knew no difference between good faith and perfidy?'

A warrior-poet of the Bani Kais, Hadjaf, rose in anger at these verses, and wished to leave the presence-chamber. Abdal Malek ordered him to remain, and extracted a promise that he would do nothing to rekindle the flames of war.

A few days after Akhtal quitted Damascus and returned to his own people. Hadjaf got together a thousand horsemen; he repeated to them the insulting verses of Akhtal, and asked if they were willing to forego vengeance. Of course they were not willing. They marched all that day and the night, and with the first streaks of daylight they reached the valley where resided the Taghlibite family of which Akhtal was a member. They burst in upon the sleepers; men, women, and children were massacred indiscriminately; a child of Akhtal was killed; Akhtal himself was captured, but saved his life by his presence of mind. He cried out that he was only a slave, and owing to the darkness, and the coarse garments he chanced to be wearing, he was spared as such. The deed done, Hadjaf ordered his party to disperse; they hid themselves in the Greek provinces till the khalif's first outburst of fury should have time to cool down. They had not long to wait. Abd al Malek granted them a free pardon at the intercession of the leading men of the Bani Kais.

In the end, however, Akhtal obtained a small revenge for all the evil which Zofar, the chief of the Bani Bakr, had inflicted upon the Taghlibites.

In the first part of this volume I have described the anarchy that reigned in Syria on the death of Muawia, the son of Yezid, after a brief reign of forty days. The Yemenite Arabs of Syria were known as the Kelbites, those of the Ishmaelite stock as the Kaisites; the Bani Bakr were included in the Kaisites. In the struggle for power, the Kaisites, under the leadership of Dhahak ibn Kais, had declared for Abdallah ibn Zobair, and when Merwan ibn Hakem appeared in the field, the circumstance that they had done so was sufficient to cause the Kelbites to rally round Merwan. At their head Merwan marched against Dhahak ibn Kais, and in a great battle at Merdj Rahit, near Damascus, which lasted two days, completely defeated him. Dhahak was killed, and a terrible slaughter made of the vanquished Kaisites. Zofar was present in this battle, and fled, accompanied by two friends. The Kelbites followed hard upon their track. Zofar was mounted upon a horse of great speed and strength; his friends were not so fortunate, and seeing the pursuers gaining upon them, they entreated Zofar to save himself and leave them to their fate. Zofar reluctantly consented, and giving his horse the rein was soon out of danger; but his two friends were surrounded and killed. The memory of that desertion was gall and wormwood to the heart of Zofar, and he relieved the bitterness of his feelings by recording in verse the unappeasable enmity he bore to Merwan and the Kelbites. 'Shall,' he asks in this poem, 'shall a single day of weakness efface then all my exploits, all my heroic actions? Shall we allow the Kelbites to repose in peace. Shall not our lances transfix them? Our brothers slain at Rahit, shall they not be revenged? Doubtless the grass will grow again upon the newly heaped earth which covers their bones, but never will we forget them, and ever for our enemies shall we have an implacable hatred. Give me my arms, woman! to my thinking the war should be perpetual. Assuredly, the battle of Rahit has dug an abyss between Merwan and us.'

He was as good as his word. With the wreck of the army that had been beaten at Merdj Rahit, Zofar took possession of Karkesia, a fortress of Mesopotamia situated to the east of Kinnesrin at the point where the Khabour falls into the Euphrates. The disordered state of the times hindered Abd al Malek, the son and successor of Merwan, from besieging the place; and Zofar and the Kaisites for many years carried on a war of 'expeditions' against the camps of the Kelbites, stained by acts of horrible atrocity. At length, however, Zofar surrendered, on honourable terms being granted to him. These were, a complete amnesty for his companions in arms, and for himself the government of Karkesia. Lastly, as the pledge and seal of amity, it was arranged that Maslama, the son of the khalif, should espouse the daughter of Zofar. These terms having been settled, Zofar waited upon Abd al Malek, who received him with great distinction, and seated him by his side on his throne. Akhtal was at the time drinking in another room of the palace, and hearing of this honourable reception, he said, 'I will go and bring down the high looks of this Zofar.' He immediately entered the presence of the khalif, and after regarding him fixedly for some seconds, he declaimed these verses:—

'The wine that fills my cup has the brilliant sparkle that animates the eye bright and animated of the cock. It exalts the spirits of the drinker.

He who drinks three brimmers of it without admixture of water, feels arising within him a desire to spread benefits.

He walks, balancing himself lightly, like a lovely daughter of the Kuraish, and lets his garments float lightly to the wind.'

'Abou Malek,' said the khalif, 'what is the meaning of these verses? You have without doubt some idea in your head.' 'It is true,' Commander of the Faithful!' replied Akhtal; 'many ideas crowd in upon me when I see seated near you on your throne, the man who said but yesterday,

'Doubtless the grass will grow again upon the newly heaped earth which covers their bones.

But never shall we forget them, and ever for our enemies shall we have an implacable hatred.'

At these words, and the facts they recalled, the khalif sprang up in wrath from his seat. He aimed a kick at Zofar which struck him in the chest and sent him headlong to the earth, crying out at the same time, 'God destroy your hatreds in your heart!' 'In the name of God,' said the terrified Zofar, as he picked himself up, 'remember, my lord, the safe-conduct you have granted to me.' Zofar avowed subsequently that he never thought himself nearer his last moment than when he heard the above lines proceed from the lips of Akhtal.[1]

[1] This Akhtal, curiously enough, was a Christian; but notwithstanding his religion he never lost the affection of the Khalif Abd al Malek. In the 'J. A.' 2nd series, vols. xii., xiii., xiv., there is a very interesting notice of him and his two celebrated contemporaries, Farazdak and Jarir, translated by M. Caussin de Perceval from the 'Kitab al Aghani.' The above incidents are in part extracted from that notice, and the following as well, which gives a very amusing account of the rivalry between Arabic poets and the delight which the early Muhammadans experienced in hearing their praises sung. It illustrates, too, what I have been trying to explain in this chapter—the power of poetry over the Arab:—'Akhtal and Jarir had for a long time exchanged sarcasms and outrages, but had never met until chance brought them together at the court at Damascus, in the presence of Abd al Malek. Akhtal was already present when Jarir was announced, and when the latter entered Akhtal looked at his rival with a curious eye. Jarir enquired his name. Akhtal replied, "Jarir; I am he who frequently robbed you of sleep and humiliated your family." "In that case," replied Jarir, "may misfortune light upon you whoever you are;" then turning to the Khalif, he asked of him who this man was. Abd al Malek laughingly told him. Jarir threw upon the Christian a look of infinite scorn, and said: "May God curse you, son of an Infidel! If you have hindered me from sleeping, it would have been better for you had I slept quietly than remained awake to crush you with my satires. You have, you say, brought disgrace on my family. How could you do that, you sprung from a race condemned to opprobrium and subject to shameful tributes? What humiliation could a family like mine, whence have sprung khalifs and the Prophet himself, endure from so vile a slave? Commander of the Faithful," he continued, "permit me to recite some verses against this Christian." But the Khalif refused to hear them, and Jarir left the presence-chamber in a huff. "Jarir," said Akhtal, "has pretended that he could compose a panegyric on you in three days. I—I have laboured at one for

This story exhibits to perfection all that I have been attempting to explain in the present chapter—the fiery and merciless character of the Arab, which a taunt could provoke to cowardly murder, that utter social disintegration which Islam was powerless to reform, and the incapacity of the ablest khalifs (for Abd al Malek was undoubtedly among the ablest) even to conceive of a society knit together by the supremacy of law. It is easy to pick out from the Koran excellent moral precepts, even prudent political maxims, and by insisting on these to endeavour to show that the universal decadence of Muhammadan lands is not due to the religion they profess. But this is an idle and erroneous method of judging a creed. The strength or weakness of a creed arises from the dominating idea which runs through and pervades the whole. Is that idea one which kindles hope, or engenders despair? Thus in no sacred books are beautiful moral precepts more abundantly scattered than in the religious writings of the Hindoos, but these have been practically of little or no avail against the Pantheism which is the dominant idea, the all-pervading spirit, that runs through their religious faith. The effect of this has been to obliterate the sharp

a whole year, and am not yet content with it." "Let me hear it," said the Khalif. Akhtal obeyed. Abd al Malek was so delighted with the sound of his own praises that he cried aloud, "I will publish a decree declaring you to be the first poet of the age." A large goblet stood beside him; the Khalif commanded it to be filled with gold pieces and given to Akhtal; he then caused the poet to be clothed in a robe of honour, and accompanied through the streets of Damascus by one of his officers, who proclaimed in a loud voice, "Behold the poet of the Commander of the Faithful! the greatest bard among the Arabs!"'

dividing line between right and wrong, and to convert the stress laid upon the former by philosophers and sages into merely an ingenious device for obtaining the submission of the multitude. In the Koran the root-conception is the idea of God as an immovable Fatality. This is the tenet that has been burned indelibly into the heart and brain of the Muhammadan world. And under its withering shadow the idea of 'order' has been unable to strike root downwards or bear fruit upwards. What the Muhammadan world understands by order is simply repression. The right of a king to rule depends upon his power to massacre all dissentients.

The chief of the Kaisites and the khalif Abd al Malek might agree upon conditions of peace, but the feud between Kaisites and Kelbites was not quenched thereby. The blood shed at the field of Rahit had kindled the Arabs' insatiate thirst for revenge. The fire kindled in one province passed on from country to country till the whole vast empire of the khalifate, from the Pyrenees to the furthest limit of Khorasan, became a prey to the conflagration. Everywhere Yemenite and Ishmaelite wrestled in a death-struggle; and every 'expedition' and every battle lost and won were as fresh fuel added to the flame. But for the timely aid of the Kelbites, the father of the khalif Abd al Malek would never have reached the throne. The arrogance and pretensions of that tribe, in consequence, compelled his successors to lean more and more on the Kaisites as a counterpoise. During the long tenure of power by Al Hejjaj—a Kaisite—that branch of the Arab race became supreme throughout Asia. The government of the provinces, the care of the finances, were monopolised by them; the leading men of the Yemenites were either out of employ, or languished in dungeons. And could the House of Ommaya have remained at unity in itself, they might have striven successfully against the enmity of half their subjects. But this unity it was impossible to preserve. The question of the succession was the inevitable rock on which it was doomed to go to pieces. The khalif Abd al Malek had nominated as his successor his son Walid, and on his death his second son, Sulaiman; and this testamentary disposition had been ratified by the concurrence of the Muhammadan world. But Walid, become khalif, desired, as a matter of course, to set aside his brother Sulaiman in favour of his own son, Abdou'l Aziz. He revealed the project secretly to Hejjaj and Kutaiba, who engaged to support him. With their aid, and those of their friends and relations, he hoped without much difficulty to wrest from Sulaiman a concession of his rights. All these lieutenants were members of Modharite tribes. The consequence was that Sulaiman was compelled, by the necessity of self-preservation, to throw himself in the arms of the Yemenites. They, smarting under the rigid and cruel rule of Hejjaj and his subordinates, impatient, too, of the monopoly of power by a single branch of the Arab race, eagerly embraced the hand held out to them. At each revolution of power, the race which rose for the moment to eminence trampled on its fallen kinsmen with pitiless exultation; till from the clash of their opposing rivalries resulted the memorable revolt of Yezid ibn Mouhallab, the Azdite. This, though unsuccessful, gave a blow to the dynasty of the Ommayas from which it never recovered. For awhile, indeed, it swayed unsteadily amid faction and discord, like the falcon banner of Lord Marmion in the field of Flodden, and then—

> Like pine-tree rooted from the ground,
> It sank amid the foes.

CHAPTER II.

THE REVOLT OF YEZID IBN MOUHALLEB.

A.D. 714–720.

AL HEJJAJ was a type of the Muhammadan Puritan. He was eminently devout after the manner of his creed. His knowledge of the pure language of the desert was remarkable for its extent and accuracy; and such knowledge of the divine tongue invariably invested the possessor with a certain amount of sanctity. His discourses in the pulpit were famous for their eloquence and edification. A number of misreadings having crept into the Koran in use at his time, he caused to be prepared a new and carefully corrected copy with a system of diacritical points to preserve the Faithful from again falling into similar errors. In short, despite of the blood he had shed, he would in all probability have descended into the grave leaving an excellent name behind him, but for an act committed just before his last illness. This was the execution of Said ibn Jobair.

Said was an eminent saint, as holiness was understood in that day. He knew all the seven authorised methods of reading the Koran. He had learned a multitude of traditions from two of the greatest masters in that lore—Ibn Abbas, and Abdallah, the son of the great khalif

Omar. He had been known (so it was said) to repeat the entire Koran as a single prayer. But after having taken an oath of allegiance to Abd al Malek, he took part in a revolt against him. This brought down upon him the wrath of Hejjaj. Said was arrested while in hiding at Mekka, and sent as a prisoner to Wasit. Hejjaj, on seeing him, said: 'Wretch, son of the Wretched! didst thou not come to Koufa when a vile Arab of the desert was Imam there, and did I not put thee in his place?'—'Yes.' 'And did I not appoint thee kadi? and when the people of Koufa murmured, and said that none but an Arab of the desert was fit for that office, did I not replace thee by Abû Burda Ibn Abi Musa, ordering him, however, not to decide any question without consulting thee?'—'Yes.' 'Did I not admit thee to my evening parties as a companion, though the company were all Arab chieftains?'[1]—Yes. 'The first time I saw thee, did I not give thee 100,000 dirhems to distribute among the needy without questioning thee afterwards about the manner in which the money was employed?'—'Yes.' 'What then made thee revolt against me?'—'An oath which bound me to Ibn al Ashath.' Here Al-Hejjaj grew angry, and said, after a pause: 'And before that, wert thou not bound by an oath to the Commander of the Faithful, Abd al Malek? By Allah! I will put thee to death: guard, strike off his head.'

Groans and curses from all the devout in Islam responded to this execution. 'Al-Hejjaj,' said Ahmed ibn Hanbal, the great Muhammadan doctor, 'killed Said ibn

[1] The favour here arose from the fact that Said ibn Jobair was of mixed blood and an enfranchised slave.

Jobair, yet there was not a man on the face of the earth who did not stand in need of Said and his learning.' 'O God!' exclaimed Hasan al-Basri (a citizen of Basra famous for his holy and ascetic life), when he heard the dreadful intelligence, 'O God! be turned against this reprobate of the tribe of Thakif! Almighty God! if there be any persons on earth, from east to west, who were accessory to his death, lay them prostrate in the fires of hell.' The tomb of the martyr became a sacred spot for pilgrims to resort to. Hejjaj himself was terrified at what he had done. He died forty days after his victim; and, during that interval, 'God' (we are told) 'did not put it in his power to slay another human being.' His malady was cancer in the stomach. He entreated Hasan al-Basri to pray for him. 'I forbade you,' was the answer, 'to attack men of holiness, but you persisted.' 'O Hasan!' replied the dying chief; 'I ask you not to pray to God that He may deliver me from my pains; beg of Him only that He hasten to take my soul from my body, and terminate my tortures.' Hasan on this wept bitterly; and Hejjaj continued to suffer under his malady for fifteen days; he then expired in the month of Ramadân, A.H. 95 (A.D. 714). During this period, whenever he fell asleep, he saw Said come up, and seize him by the girdle, saying: 'Enemy of God, arise! why didst thou murder me?' On which he would awake in terror, and exclaim: 'What business has Said ibn Jobair with me?' When Hasan heard of his death he made a prostration in thanksgiving to God, saying: 'O my God! Thou hast caused him to die; let also his example die from among us.' It was also related that a person saw Hejjaj in a dream after his death, and asked him what God had done to him. 'He put me to death,' replied Hejjaj, 'once for each person whom I put to death, and seventy times for Said ibn Jobair.'

Hejjaj is a type of the stern, relentless Muhammadan bigot. But it would be a great mistake to suppose that all, or nearly all, of the Arab conquerors of Asia were men cast in this mould. Cruel they all were. Indifference to human suffering, and harshness to a fallen foe, were the characteristics of all the Arabs. But in many of them an undoubting belief in the doctrines of Islam was combined with a joyous and reckless scepticism, which made their characters not unlike some of the Cavaliers of England. 'Life,' says one pre-Islamite bard, 'is a treasure which lessens every day. Man, while death forbears to strike him, is as the animal attached to a loose cord, which permits him to feed, but the end of which is always within the hand of his master. The tomb of the ascetic, and the tomb of the generous-hearted man who has drunk deep draughts of life, do not differ the one from the other. They are both small mounds of earth covered with flat stones placed one upon another. Thou who blamest my passion for the battle and for pleasure, canst thou make me immortal? If thy wisdom cannot delay the fatal moment, let me at least revel in enjoyment until the blow strikes me. There are but two things which in my judgment constitute the charm of life:

If a friend in danger be,
To his aid I love to flee,
Mounted on an eager steed,
Like the frighted wolf's, his speed—
Flying from the fountain's brink,
Whither he had come to drink.

Lastly, on a rainy day
(Not the least delightful they !)
I love to wile the hours away
Folding in embraces warm
Some fair beauty's rounded form.'

Precisely such a man was Yezid ibn Mouhalleb. His father, Mouhalleb, was, with the exception, perhaps, of the renowned Khaled, the most consummate soldier the Arabs had produced. When the Kharegites were sweeping all before them, and general after general had fled ignominiously before their fanatical fury, his prudence, courage, and skill had checked their career, and step by step either driven them out of Asia, or compelled them to take refuge in remote and inaccessible countries. Subsequently he had become governor of Khorasan ; and there also he had acquired the love of all his subjects by his equitable and gentle rule, his lavish profusion, his open-handed liberality. He had ten sons, all of them renowned for their courage and skill in arms ; all of them men who had fought and conquered in numerous pitched battles. Yezid was the eldest. When the old hero was on his death-bed he summoned all his sons to his side. Some arrows tied up so as to form a bundle were brought in by his order. 'What think you,' said he, 'could you break them all, now that they are tied together?' They answered that they could not. 'And if they were separated?' 'Certainly,' said they, 'we could break them.' 'Such,' continued he, 'is the effect of union.' He then made a long exhortation, advising them, under all circumstances, to hold together in act, word, and thought, and nominated Yezid as the one among them whose authority they were all to acknowledge. One of his sons replied: 'Had you not placed him at our head, we ourselves should have done so.' Yezid was just such a man as the Arabs admired. Foremost in the fray, he shrank from no odds, and he rarely knew defeat. In peace time, hospitable, lavish, affable, his praises were the theme of all the poets; his rule in Khorasan—which he governed after the death of his father—was likened to a fertilising rain on parched land; stories of his generosity were on every tongue. One of his intendants sold for the sum of 40,000 dirhems (1,000*l.*), the melons produced in one of his farms. When Yezid was informed of the circumstance, he said to his intendant: 'You have converted us into green-grocers! Were there not old women enough in the tribe of Azd among whom you might have shared them?' Having made the pilgrimage, in order to conclude the rites and ceremonies, he sent for a barber to shave his head. When the operation was finished, he ordered him a recompense of 1,000 dirhems. The man was amazed and astounded, but at length said: 'With this sum I shall go and ransom from slavery my mother.' Yezid said: 'Give him another thousand.' The barber exclaimed: 'May my wife be divorced from me if I ever shave anyone's head after this.' 'Give him two thousand more,' said Yezid. In all this there was working the Arab's passionate love of glory, and his delight in praise. Yezid confessed this. 'By Allah!' he is reported to have said, 'I prefer life to death, and an honourable reputation to life; could I obtain a gift never yet granted to mortal, I should wish to have an ear by means of which I might hear what people say of me after my death.' But he knew also that the pursuit of reputation in those stormy times was one beset with danger; and that the higher he ascended, the deeper he was likely to fall. Being asked by one of his friends why he did not build himself a house, he replied: 'What should I do with it? I have always a dwelling ready prepared for me.' 'Where is that dwelling?' asked his friend. 'If I hold a command it will be the state palace; and if I be out of place it will be the state prison.'

While Yezid was governor of Khorasan Hejjaj ruled the two Iraks. He had married Hind, the sister of Yezid; nevertheless, he regarded his brother-in-law with extreme dislike and jealousy as the one man in the empire of the khalifs who stood at all on a level with himself. He perceived that Yezid's position on the frontier of Islam gave him an opportunity of illustrating his government by conquests over the infidel which might enable him to supplant even Hejjaj. And he desired to have this province also under the rule of a chief, who owing his elevation to his intercession would not easily be persuaded to use his authority against him. In accordance with the practice of the time he consulted astrologers and other persons skilled in the art of divination in order to learn who should succeed him in the government of the two Iraks. These people, forecasting the future much as Hejjaj himself, constantly replied, 'By a man named Yezid,'—a prediction which, it is needless to say, confirmed Hejjaj in his original intention. He addressed the khalif Abd al Malek continually on the subject, affirming that Yezid, carried away by the popularity he had acquired, was meditating a declaration of independence. At first the khalif, mindful of the great services the Muhallebides had rendered to him in the early days of his reign, turned a deaf ear to these complaints. Subsequently, however, he yielded. Yezid was deposed from authority, and the government of Khorasan entrusted to Kutaiba ibn Muslim. This occurred in A.H. 83.

Yezid was summoned to Irak. On his arrival there, he was, with two of his brothers, flung into prison by Hejjaj, and detained there eleven years. This long captivity was in order to exact money from Yezid. Finding, however, that Yezid would surrender none, Hejjaj had recourse to torture. A sum of 100,000 dirhems (2,500*l.*) was daily demanded from the prisoner, and he was subjected to grievous torments so long as it was not paid in. To Hejjaj's great exasperation, Yezid neither paid the money nor allowed a sign of suffering to escape from him. Hejjaj consulted his friends what to do under these distressing circumstances. He learned that in an expedition beyond the Oxus, Yezid with sixty men had had in former years a desperate encounter with 600 Turcomans. In the fray he was wounded by an arrow in the thigh. The arrow-head remained imbedded in the flesh, and if Hejjaj were pleased to order the torturers to beat Yezid on the wounded thigh, he would have the satisfaction of hearing the groans of his enemy. Hejjaj lost no time in acting upon this advice. Yezid was at this time confined in a tent close to his own, and Hind, the wife of Hejjaj, hearing the cries of her brother, rushed out and began to weep and lament. Hejjaj was so furious at this expression of sympathy for his rival, that he divorced her on the spot.

Yezid at last contrived a means of escape. He had at Basra a number of horses under the charge of his brother Merwan. These he caused to be brought to the camp of Hejjaj under the pretence of selling them in order to satisfy the daily demand made upon him ; but at the same time demanded a price so high that no purchaser came forward. In reality he wished to have them at hand should he succeed in eluding the vigilance of his guards. He then caused a grand dinner with abundance of wine to be prepared, to which he invited his guards. He plied them copiously with the wine till they ceased to take heed of their prisoner. Then Yezid slipped on the garments of his cook, put on a sham white beard over his own, and went out. The guards, fuddled with drink ing, did not recognise him. One, indeed, attracted by his halting gait, caused by the arrow-head in his thigh, said, 'That is Yezid's manner of walking,' and went up to take a nearer look at the seeming cook. But the night was dark ; he could see little but a long white beard, and saying, 'This is an elderly man,' he turned away.

It was not until the dawn of day that the guards discovered that Yezid, as well as his two brothers in captivity, Al Mufaddal and Abd al Malek, had fled. Hejjaj was profoundly alarmed. He knew Yezid's popularity in Khorasan. He knew that the Arab army in that province was largely recruited from the tribe of Azd (Yezid's own tribe), as well as others of the tribes of Yemen, and that these would respond eagerly to the summons of one whose name was as a household word among them. He sent off an express to Kutaiba Ibn Muslim, warning him of Yezid's approach, and directing him to send instructions to the commandants of all frontier posts to be on the alert and arrest all suspicious-looking travellers. The khalif Abd al Malek had died during Yezid's long captivity; his son Walid now reigned in Damascus. To him also Hejjaj despatched messengers to inform him of Yezid's escape and prepare him for the gathering storm. Yezid and his two brothers in the meanwhile had ridden off in the direction of Syria. After enduring great fatigue, and passing through more than one serious peril, they reached the confines of Syria. There they obtained rest and protection in the house of an uncle of Yezid—Wohaib ibn Abdalrahman—a person whom Sulaiman, the brother of the khalif, held in high esteem. Wohaib conveyed them to Sulaiman, recounted the history of Yezid, and solicited his protection for his nephews until the khalif Walid had accorded them an amnesty. Sulaiman responded cordially to this appeal. He understood at once that in becoming the protector of Yezid he bound to himself by the strongest ties of gratitude, not merely the most brilliant soldier in Islam, but also all the tribes of Yemen—the very counterweight he needed against the designs of his brother, and the enmity of Hejjaj and the tribes of Modhar. He gave Yezid a gracious reception, and presented him with a robe of honour.

The reception of his rival by the heir-apparent alarmed Hejjaj more seriously than even his supposed flight to Khorasan. In those days of plague, pestilence, and famine, battle, murder, and sudden death, any moment might see his master hurried to the grave, and Sulaiman seated in his place with the injured Yezid as his chief friend and adviser. Such a revolution implied of course the ruin and the death of Hejjaj. The torments he had so pitilessly applied to Yezid and his brothers he would then have to endure in his own person. He wrote to the khalif Walid urging him to demand the surrender of Yezid. The khalif perceived the need of depriving his brother of this strong ally, if the succession of the throne was to be regulated as he wished. On the other hand, setting aside the political motives which urged Sulaiman to non-compliance, the surrender to an enemy of one who had sought the shelter of his roof was the most dishonourable action of which an Arab could be guilty. Death was preferable far to such a disgrace, and Sulaiman firmly resisted the importunity of his brother. At last Yezid himself interposed. He demanded to be delivered up to the khalif rather than be the cause of animosity between the two brothers. Sulaiman then directed his son Ayoub to accompany the prisoner to Damascus, and as Walid had commanded that Yezid should appear in his presence chained, he enjoined Ayoub to appear before the khalif bound by the same chain as Yezid. Ayoub was also the bearer of a letter in which Sulaiman entreated his brother to spare not only him, but the family of the Ommayas, the intolerable disgrace of being known through all Arabia as people incapable of affording protection to those who solicited their hospitality. Walid was moved by the reading of this letter and the sight of his nephew in chains. Yezid seized the favourable moment; he asked leave to speak, and in an eloquent speech set forth the achievements of his father, his brothers, and himself. It could not fail to be a moving recital, however told. If to fight on the pathway of God was a sure means of cutting a believer's way into Paradise, there were surely none of the Faithful who deserved a more loving welcome from the Houris in those blissful gardens than Muhalleb and his soldier-sons. Walid could not resist the appeal. 'I acknowledge,' he said, 'your innocence, and that Hejjaj has used you unjustly.' He caused 30,000 dirhems to be presented to Ayoub, and 20,000 to Yezid, and sent them both back to Sulaiman. From that time Yezid rose into such favour with Sulaiman that the latter never received a present the half of which he did not send to his friend.

Two years after this occurrence (A.H. 96, A.D. 715), Walid died suddenly. He had not relinquished his design of securing the khalifate to his son, Abd al Aziz. In fact, at the moment of his death he was on his way to Ramla, where Sulaiman resided, to seize the person of his brother and compel him under pain of death to resign his claims. Sulaiman was proclaimed khalif on the day of his brother's death. Hejjaj, fortunately for himself, had preceded by a few months his master to the grave; but the two Iraks, Khorasan, Sind—in short, all the richest provinces of the empire—were in the hands of his creatures or his friends. The transfer of power carried dismay among them. It must be confessed that in their selection, Hejjaj had given proof of a singularly accurate perception of the worth of men. They were all possessed of striking ability; under their rule the peace of the empire had been preserved, and its frontiers vastly enlarged; but they were, too, cast in the mould of their pitiless master. They had never spared their political rivals, and could look for no mercy in return. To quote the words of an old dramatist, 'That was no world in which to pity men.' Vengeance fell upon them, swift and crushing. In the two Iraks, the family of Hejjaj, his creatures and dependents, were arrested, and put to the torture to wrest from them their wealth. The conqueror of Sind was deposed and executed. Kutaiba at Meru, hopeless of life, determined to revolt. 'Think you,' he said to some who tried to dissuade him, 'that I fear death? What I fear is that the government of Khorasan should be given to Yezid, the son of Mouhalleb, who would summon me before him, and disgrace me in the eyes of the world. I prefer death to that.' He counted upon his glorious victories to carry his troops away with him; but he calculated erroneously. They declined to follow him. A report was spread abroad that he had expressed his resolution to exterminate to the last man the contingent of the tribe of Azd which served under him. This sealed his fate. 'We must,' shouted a member of the threatened tribe, 'breakfast on Kutaiba before he sups upon us.' They rushed in a tumultuous crowd to the palace where he dwelt. They forced the doors; the guards were either slain or fled; they penetrated to the room where Kutaiba awaited them seated in sullen majesty upon his throne. An arrow pierced his brain, and the brilliant and successful soldier fell dead. The ruin of the party of Hejjaj was complete. The Persians, when they heard of the death of Kutaiba, said, 'Had he been one of us, we should have placed his body in a coffin to be carried at the head of our armies, in order to ensure us victory; for never has man accomplished in Khorasan such deeds as he, or won so many victories.'

Yezid succeeded the murdered Kutaiba. He felt that he must eclipse the glories of his predecessor by some signal achievement if he was to retain his position and power among his countrymen. The achievement he selected was the reduction of the city and fortress of Gurgan. This fortress was situated at the south-east extremity of the Caspian, and the ruins are still to be seen. At that time it was deemed impregnable. The most powerful of the Persian kings had retreated discomfited from before its walls. The Turks, in their endeavours to penetrate to Kharezm, had been broken in pieces before this insurmountable barrier. Kutaiba had frequently entreated the permission of Hejjaj to try his strength against the fortress, but the latter had withheld it. Yezid himself had been used to say, when mention was made in his presence of the splendid achievements of Kutaiba, 'Let him make himself master of Gurgan; then he will in truth have achieved a conquest.'

I shall not follow the chronicler through the details of this arduous campaign. Suffice it to say that Yezid succeeded. Gurgan and all the surrounding country fell into his power. His victory was sullied by acts of atrocious cruelty. In addition to the slaughter in battle, four thousand of his prisoners were hung, twelve thousand put to the sword. An incalculable booty fell into his hands. He wrote an exulting letter to Sulaiman, in which he stated that the fifth of the booty which belonged to the khalif amounted to several millions of dirhems. It was in vain that his secretary, a prudent man, cautioned

Yezid against this imprudent admission, pointing out that, though Sulaiman might not demand the full amount to be paid to him, Sulaiman's successor might. Yezid persisted, and this was the primary cause of his ruin. For a very few months after the receipt of this epistle, Sulaiman died, after a brief reign of two years and eight months (A.H. 99). He had several sons, but in his testamentary dispositions he set these aside, and bequeathed his power to Omar ibn Abd al Aziz, and after him to his own brother Yezid ibn Abd al Malek.

Omar ibn Abd al Aziz was a royal saint. Concerning him it is related that one night, as the khalif Omar was patrolling the streets of Medina, he heard a woman say to her daughter, 'Rise, my girl, and water the milk.' The other answered, 'O mamma, did you not hear the Commander of the Faithful's public crier forbid the mixing of milk with water?' To this the mother replied, 'His crier is far from you now.' But the daughter replied, 'If he see me not, the Lord of that crier will see me.' Omar wept, and when the morning set in he sent for the two women and asked the daughter if she was married. The mother answered that she was not, and Omar then said to his son Abdallah, 'O Abdallah! marry that girl. If I stood in need of a wife, I myself would take her.' Abdallah replied that he was already suited; and the khalif, turning to his other son, said, 'Abou Aasim, do you marry her.' Abou Aasim did so, and she bore him a daughter, whom they named Omm Aasim. This daughter became the wife of Abd al Aziz ibn Marwan, and bore him Omar ibn Abd al Aziz. Other prognostications were not wanting of the piety of the future khalif. When he was a little boy he received a kick from a horse. He was taken to his mother, who clasped him in her arms, and began to wipe the blood off his face. She had not finished, when, seeing his father come in, she turned towards him in a passion and began to reproach him. 'You have killed my child,' she said, 'because you would not give him a servant or a nurse to protect him from such accidents as this.' He replied, 'Be silent, Omm Aasim! What a benediction will it be for you if this boy turn out to be the Ommaya with the scarred forehead.' There was a prediction afloat that a descendant of Ommaya, having a mark on his face, should fill the world with his justice.

The conversion of Omar to a humble and faithful servant of Allah was effected in this wise. While yet a young man, he was on the point of inflicting corporal punishment on a black slave who had been guilty of some fault. 'Master,' asked the slave, 'why are you going to beat me?' Omar reminded him of the fault he had committed. 'And you,' replied the slave, 'have you never, by some wrong that you have done, exposed yourself to the wrath of your master?' Omar assented that he had done so. 'And did he hasten to chasten you?' 'My God! no.' 'Then, wherefore are you so eager to punish me, who have but done to you what you have done towards your master?' 'Rise,' said Omar, 'in the name of God I pronounce you a free man.' This circumstance was the cause of his conversion; and in after life he would recall it in his prayers, murmuring to himself, 'O the gentleness of God! who hastens not to punish those who have offended Him.'

There was great dismay among the poets when this

austere and pious khalif ascended the throne. Their pensions they felt to be in great danger. A man of this stamp could have little partiality for men who sang the delights of wine-bibbing and other forbidden practices. His desire was to suppress all superfluous expenditure, and so lighten the burden of taxation laid upon the people. Pensions to poets he might with certainty be expected to consider among those items of expenditure for which there was no justification. The poets pensioned by the preceding khalif came, in consequence, to pay their respects to the new sovereign in a very depressed frame of mind. They were headed by Jarir, the first poet of the time. Omar refused to receive them. As they stood in the ante-chamber, a doctor of the law passed through on his way to the khalif, to whom Jarir addressed himself as follows :—

> 'Doctor with the floating turban, the good time has come for you; for me it is passed.
>
> Say to the Khalif, if you have the honour to see him, that I am at the gate, as one chained, with my companions in misfortune.'

The doctor obtained from the khalif permission for Jarir to come into his presence. When Jarir was admitted, after the manner of poets, he commenced to recite verses setting forth the sorrow that afflicted the Muhammadan world, and how all eyes were turned towards the Commander of the Faithful, and all hearts trusted in his benignity and justice. Omar was moved to tears; and Jarir, thinking the moment propitious, requested that his pension should be continued. This the khalif refused to do, but, 'I have,' he said, 'forty dinars and two dresses, one of which I wear while the other is being washed. I will share them with you; though, God knows, I have more need of them than you.' Jarir declined this munificent offer. 'Had you not done so,' added the good khalif, 'I confess you would have inconvenienced me greatly.'

One of Omar's first acts after his accession was to address a circular letter to the governors of provinces, cautioning them against admitting *Zimmis* (i.e. Unbelievers) to any of the State offices, because, as he said, there could be 'neither judgment nor experience among those who provoked the anger of God and of the Prophet.' Haian, his lieutenant in Egypt, replied to this circular in these words: 'O prince of believers! if such a state of things endures for any time in Egypt, all the Zimmis will become Moslems and the revenues will be lost which they bring into the imperial treasury.' Omar thereupon sent a special commissioner into Egypt charged with this order: 'Strike Haian thirty blows on the head with a whip as a punishment for the wicked words he has spoken; and tell him that every soul who shall embrace Islamism shall be exempted from the capitation tax. I should be beyond measure happy if all the Zimmis became Moslems, for God sent his Prophet to do the work of an apostle, not to act as a collector of taxes.'

To a man like this, a gay, pleasure-loving, lavish and vain-glorious soldier like Yezid was an abomination. And his family he disliked no less. 'They are a proud lot,' he said; 'and I like not people of that sort.' Yezid, on his side, detested Omar, and was perfectly convinced the man was a hypocrite. Subsequently, however, he confessed that in this he was mistaken. Between two such men a good understanding was impossible. Yezid was deposed from the government of Khorasan; the Yemenite officials were speedily replaced by members of the tribes of Modhar; and Yezid was summoned to deliver up the sums of money which he had promised to Sulaiman. As he would not, probably could not, do this, Omar had him arrested. At first the khalif intended to treat him with great severity. He had him clothed in a woollen cloak, with his hands chained to his neck, and gave orders that he should be removed to Dahlak. Dahlak was an island in the Red Sea which was used as a prison for the most scandalous criminals. But when Yezid was led through the streets thus disgracefully fettered, the indignation of the people rose to such a height that Omar revoked the order, and Yezid was detained in a species of honourable restraint. So long as Omar lived Yezid made no effort to escape. He knew that his life was safe. He nevertheless had made arrangements to escape the moment that there was any need to do so. For he had everything to fear from Omar's successor, Yezid ibn Abd al Malek. This prince had married a niece of Hejjaj, and when, on the succession of Sulaiman, the wrath of the Yemenites fell upon the officials who had for so many years oppressed them, the future khalif registered a vow that, if Yezid ibn Muhalleb ever fell into his power, he would hew him limb from limb. The gradual carving of a man to death, by detaching his members one by one from the trunk, was a popular method of revenge among the early Muhammadans. And Yezid, like his predecessor of the same name, was a debauchee to whom pity was unknown.

Omar died (A.H. 101), having reigned only two years and four months. As soon as his illness became serious,

Yezid effected his escape. His guards were already bribed, and swift-trotting camels awaited him at a spot not far from his prison. He distributed a thousand dinars as a parting present to his guards, quitted his prison and fled to Irak. As soon as he reached a place of safety, he addressed a letter to Omar, in which he said: 'If I had felt assured that the Prince of Believers would recover his health, I should not have fled; but I know he is very sick, and if Yezid, son of Abd al Malek, ascends the throne, I have reason to fear for my life, by reason of the enmity which, as you are aware, exists between me and him.' The new khalif perfectly understood the peril he was in. Unless Yezid was seized and executed before he had time to gain a place of safety, all the Yemenite tribes would rally to his call. The two branches of the Arab race would once again, as in the days of old, stand embattled one against the other, and a lost battle would be the utter ruin of the House of Ommaya. Never was the khalifate in greater peril.

The governor of Basra, Adi ibn Arta, was a bitter enemy of Yezid. He was the man who, at the command of the khalif Omar, had in the first instance arrested Yezid. He had bound him in chains, his legs fettered together, and his hands chained to his neck. This was an indignity which the high spirit of Yezid could not but bitterly resent; and his vengeance was certain to descend heavily on Adi at the earliest opportunity. On the fidelity, therefore, of this governor the khalif could confidently depend. He sent off an express to inform him of the flight of Yezid, and ordered him to cast into prison all the members of the family of Muhalleb who were to be found in Basra. A number of clients and relatives and three brothers of Yezid—Abd al Malek, Habib, and Merwan—were thrown into prison. In the meanwhile Yezid had reached a spot a day's march from Koufa, and halted there. The governor of Koufa had been warned of his approach, and had sent out a force to intercept him. But the troops shrank from attacking Yezid, and he and his small party passed on unmolested to Basra.

Adi, the governor, sallied out to stay him. But the bulk of his troops were Yemenites, and the popular leader was no sooner seen than they passed over to his standard. A band of Thakifites—the tribe of Hejjaj—offered some resistance, but they were beaten back without difficulty, and Yezid made his entrance into the city. His first measure was to plunder all the mosques in the city of their chandeliers. These he had broken up and recast into coins wherewith to pay his troops. The soldiers of Adi were in arrears, and the intelligence that pay was being distributed to their brethren in the opposite camp caused them to flock to Yezid in great numbers. Notwithstanding this great accession of strength, Yezid appeared at this moment to have experienced some hesitation in assuming an attitude of open revolt against the existing government. It was contrary to the traditions of his family and to his own antecedents. He had laid down without a remonstrance the government of Khorasan when summoned to do so by Hejjaj, though knowing well that in so doing he was going to captivity, perhaps to death. He had acted in the same loyal manner when deposed by the khalif Omar, though he had then just achieved an exploit which no Arab general before him had attempted to undertake, and might have counted with confidence on the support of the tribes of Yemen. He now addressed a message to the governor of the city, engaging to recognise his authority and to make no further attack upon him provided his brothers and friends were set at liberty, and he himself was permitted to remain unmolested till he had solicited the pardon of the khalif. Adi rejected these offers. He could still depend upon the fidelity of the Syrian troops and the Arabs of Modhar. With these he ventured to attack Yezid. The fighting in the streets continued for several days. But the troops of the governor were gradually dislodged from all the positions they occupied, and driven back into the citadel. This, too, was carried by escalade. Adi was made a prisoner; but Yezid spared his life. These occurrences had not turned Yezid aside from his original intention of attempting to make his peace with the khalif. He had despatched a mission for that purpose, and the envoys were actually on their way back to Basra bearing the 'aman' (pardon) of the khalif, when they met parties flying from Basra. From these they learned the particulars of the fighting in the streets, the storming of the citadel, the capture of Adi the governor, and the flight from the city of those of the inhabitants who were fearful of disorder and tumults, or who had no liking for the cause of Yezid. The tidings induced the deputation to turn back to Damascus. It was in vain that a nephew of Yezid, who formed one of the party, entreated them to proceed, affirming that it would be found that Adi and not Yezid was responsible for the disturbances in Basra. Of him they made a prisoner, and returned with all haste to Damascus to inform the khalif of the revolt of Yezid.

There was no prospect then of reconciliation with Yezid ibn Abd al Malek. The die was thrown, and Yezid must stand the hazard of the cast. He convoked the people in the great mosque of Basra, mounted the pulpit, and after having paid a tribute of praise to God, he spoke in these terms: 'I call you to the observation of the book of God and the law of the Prophet, and entreat you to make the holy war against the people of Syria—a war which is more meritorious than that against the Turks and Deilemites. Trust me that it is so; for these Syrians, they are the men who have massacred all the descendants of the Prophet they could approach, and obliged others to seek refuge in Hindostan and Turkestan. They have murdered Hosain the son of Ali, and all his family; they have fixed his head on a spear and cursed Ali from all their pulpits.' This sudden change of front on the part of Yezid ibn Mouhalleb was certainly startling. The pleasure-loving sceptical Yezid, the wine-bibber, the friend of poets and sinners, calling upon the people of Basra to observe the Book of God and obey the precepts of the Prophet—there was an irony in all this which struck at least one of his hearers with extreme force. That one was Hasan the Basrite.

I have already spoken of him in connection with Hejjaj. He was noted through all Islam for his self-mortification, fear of God, and devotion. His mother had been a slave belonging to Omm Salama, one of the Prophet's wives; and it happened occasionally while he was an infant, that when his mother was kept away by some occupation, Omm Salama would give him the breast to quiet his crying until his mother returned. To the blessed influence of that milk were attributed the wisdom and eloquence for which he was afterwards distinguished. His sayings were noted for their originality and epigrammatic terseness. Among others recorded of him is this: 'I never saw a certainty of which there is no doubt bear a greater resemblance to a doubtful thing of which there is no certainty than death does.' When at the point of death he had a fainting fit, and on coming to himself he said, 'You have awaked me out of gardens and fountains, and an honourable place.' A believing spirit such as his could not but be moved with righteous indignation when he beheld the garment of religion donned with such transparent effrontery by a ruffling soldier full of strange oaths and seeking only for a bubble reputation. He was as fearless as he was devout, and gave free vent to his scorn and anger. 'Glory to God!' he cried; 'Yezid, son of Mouhalleb, call the people to the observance of the Book of God and the precepts of the Prophet!' Then turning to that chief he exclaimed in a loud voice: 'By God, we have seen you both as governor and subject. How dare you, then, come here and hold such language?' Some friends rushed upon Hasan and stopped his mouth before he could utter another word. But the speech had not been unheard by Yezid, and a relative of his drew his sword to cut down on the spot the audacious speaker. 'Sheath your sword,' said Yezid, 'for by Allah! if you kill him, the people who are now for us will turn against us;' and he affected to have heard nothing.

Hasan, however, did not desist from his remonstrances. When Yezid and his friends had quitted the mosque, he again took up his parable. 'This Yezid,' he said, 'is a reprobate among the reprobates, an impious man from among the impious. He is the very man who but yesterday was cutting off your heads and sending them to the sons of Merwan in order to gain his favour by making you perish. Now that he has revolted against them, he ties a white cotton rag at the end of a long staff, calls this his standard, and says, "I summon you to obey the Book of God, and the precepts of the Prophet." He says, "I summon you to follow the path traced by Omar ibn Abd al Aziz!" but were that path followed, he would be fettered in chains and cast into the place where Omar had already put him.' At these words cries rose from all sides: 'What, Abou Said, are you become the apologist of the Syrians?' meaning the Ommayas. 'I make their apology,' replied the sturdy saint. 'May God never forgive them! Said, the son of al-Abbas, related as follows: "The Prophet of God said: 'Almighty God! I declare sacred in Medina all those things which You declared sacred in your town of Mekka." And yet the people of Syria entered into it for three days, and not a door was locked, but they burned the house and all that was in it; things went so far that vile Kopts and Nabatæans intruded upon Kuraishite women, tore their veils off their heads, and their bracelets off their ankles. Their swords were suspended from their shoulders, whilst the Book of God was trodden by them under foot! Shall I let myself be killed for one or other of two reprobates who dispute the possession of worldly authority? By Allah! I should be delighted if the earth were to swallow them both up.'

The fickle and excitable people of Basra paid little heed to the cautious counsels of the sturdy sage. They consisted in the main of the Arab tribes who had formed part of the ancient kingdom of Hira. They had not succumbed to the yoke of the Kuraish without a hard and bloody struggle. The flight, too, of the inhabitants had purged the city of all but a Yemenite remnant. And these were ever ripe for revolt. The dethronement of the khalif was decreed with acclamation. The example of Basra ran like wild-fire through the provinces which had formerly constituted the kingdom of the Sassanides. They groaned under religious persecution not less than mere political tyranny. Such a leader as Yezid raising the standard of revolt against their oppressors, seemed to them like the first dawn of a coming emancipation. The provinces of Fars, Kerman, Mekran, Sind and Ahwaz revolted one after another, and proclaimed their adhesion to the party of Yezid. One of his brothers, Habib, urged him strongly to take advantage of this movement and establish himself in the hilly and difficult province of Fars. He reminded him of the shifty and uncertain character of the people of Irak; whereas by retreating into Ahwaz he would not merely draw the Syrians away from their own frontiers into the heart of a hostile country, but would be aided by a population animated by the enduring spirit of political hatred, not subject to the changing currents of religious emotion. An idle scruple, based upon a military punctilio, induced Yezid to reject this prudent counsel. He could not endure to appear to retreat before an enemy, and determined to meet the troops of the khalif on the frontier line between Irak and Syria. This resolution occasioned his ruin. At the commencement of A.H. 102 Yezid, leaving his son Muawia as his lieutenant, marched against the Syrians. His brother Abd al Malek commanded the advanced guard. The Syrian troops were under the command of Maslama, the brother of the khalif—the general who had conducted the Faithful to the walls of Constantinople. He threw a bridge over the Euphrates at Anbar, and passing the river, established his camp not far from that of Yezid. For eight days, with only some trifling skirmishing, the armies remained inactive; but the interval was sufficient to convince Yezid what a broken reed was the support of the men of Irak. He had planned a night attack on the enemy which, if successful, would have hurled them into the Euphrates, when all at once he was amazed to learn that his troops refused to move. They had been seized with precisely the same conscientious qualms which broke the heart of Ali, and occasioned the death of his son on the plain of Kerbela. They wanted to try the force of a moral appeal on their misguided brethren in the opposite camp. By means of korans affixed to the heads of lances they must appeal to them to act according to the Law of God before they had recourse to the sword. It is not difficult to imagine the wrath and despair of Yezid. 'May a curse light upon you!' cried that sorely-tried general; 'how can you think the Bani Ommaya will act according to the Book of God, after all they have done? Have they not attacked the sanctuary of God, and destroyed the kaaba? Have they not slain the grandsons of the Prophet and Abdallah ibn Zobair, whom they have tied to a gibbet?'

His remonstrances were of no avail. The conscientious scruples of his followers were not to be stilled. The night attack had to be given up. 'It is thus,' says the chronicler, 'that the Kharegites have always acted.'

The issue of the struggle was now virtually decided. On Friday, Safar 14, A.H. 102 (August 24, A.D. 720), Maslama ordered the bridge of boats by which he had crossed the Euphrates to be burned, so as to cut off from his troops the hope of safety by flight. The precaution was needless. When Yezid's troops saw the smoke and were told that the bridge of boats was burning, they fled in disorder. Yezid asked why they did so, and, on being told, he exclaimed, 'May God curse them for mosquitos that fly away before smoke!' One of his friends rode up to his bridle. 'See you,' he said, 'our troops have fled; let us fly to Wasit; and there you can hold out till the people of Oman and Bahrein come to you in their ships.' 'Confound your advice!' replied Yezid; 'do you pretend to say that death will be easier there than here?' The other answered, 'I fear for your life; see you not the mountains of iron (*the masses of armed men*) which surround you?' 'I care not for them,' exclaimed Yezid; 'no matter whether they be mountains of iron or of fire. They cannot delay death if my hour be come, or hasten it if destiny has not so decreed. If you wish to fight, come on!' At this moment intelligence was brought to Yezid that his brother Habib had been slain in another part of the field. 'Life,' said the chief, 'has no value for me after the loss of Habib; I abhorred the idea of retreating when my troops took to flight, and now, by Allah! I abhor it more than ever! March forward!'

Before him stretched a wide plain covered with the masses of the Syrian army. Far away beyond these the banner of Maslama floated in the breeze. That was the point to make for. If he could slay Maslama, the battle might yet be won; or, if not, he would at least find a soldier's death. There is nothing finer in the Arab's character than the calm, unconquerable resolution with which he faced death. He always carried in his heart the noble sentiment of Virgil's hero, 'One hope there is for vanquished men, to cherish hope no more.' As he spoke Yezid gave his horse the rein. It was a beautiful white Arab. A band of chosen friends gathered round him, and, like the six hundred at Balaclava, they rode unfaltering into the valley of death. Detachments of the Syrian cavalry dashed at the little phalanx; bodies of infantry strove to bar their way; but the troop swept on, cutting their path through all obstacles. They neared the spot where Maslama stood surrounded by a picked cohort of Syrian cavalry. The officer in command of this body-guard was Kahl, the son of Ayash the Kelbite. As the white charger of Yezid came sailing gallantly onward, he gave the signal to charge. 'By God,' he shouted to his followers, 'stand by me, and I will kill Yezid this day!' The two troops met in mid career; clouds of dust closed over the conflict; and for the space of an hour from the thick pall of sand came the momentary flashes of steel, the trampling of steeds, and the shouts of the combatants. Nothing more was to be seen or heard.

The dust gradually cleared off; the clangour of conflict ceased, and then, where the slaughter had been thickest, the body of Yezid was found stone dead. Beside him lay Kahl, the son of Ayash, mortally wounded. He signalled with his hand to say that he had killed Yezid and Yezid him. Three hundred of Yezid's men remained prisoners in the hands of the Syrians. These were beheaded.

On learning the death of Yezid, his son Muawia abandoned Wasit, first putting to death all the prisoners that were in his hands. He fell back on Basra. There Moufaddal, the brother of Yezid, who had escaped from the battle, took command of the relics of the rebellion. Boats were prepared which conveyed the beaten army to Kerman, and thence to Kandabil, a town in Sind. In this town Yezid had placed a man of his own tribe as governor, for the purpose of securing an asylum for himself and his friends should he be defeated at Basra. This governor proved a traitor. He refused admittance to the fugitives, and when the Syrians, who followed hard upon their track, assailed them in front, he made an attack upon their rear. Shut in thus between two fires, nothing was left for the Mouhallebides but to sell their lives as dearly as they could. Not a man asked for quarter. They fought on till the last of them lay dead amid a heap of Syrians. A number of women and children remained in the hands of the victors. Furious at the losses inflicted on his troops, Maslama swore that every one of them should be sold in the market as slaves. A generous and wealthy Arab who was present rose and said, 'I buy them, and release you from your oath;' and he proffered Maslama one hundred thousand dirhems. The brother of the khalif answered not a word, but set free the captives. And thus terminated the revolt of Yezid ibn Mouhalleb.

Not so, however, the consequences of it. The heroic death of Yezid became a favourite theme of the Yemenite poets. They kept alive the desire for revenge. The khalif Yezid knew neither moderation nor pity in his hate against all who had participated in the rebellion. And so the feud between the two races of Arabs, drowned for a moment in blood, waited only a fitting opportunity to break out more fiercely than ever. Not many years elapsed before the opportunity came.

CHAPTER III.

THE DECLINE OF THE OMMAYAS.

A.D. 720–747.

History records few stranger freaks of fortune than that which seated the son of Abou Sofyan on the throne of the khalifs. Abou Sofyan was the bitterest and ablest opponent of the Prophet. His wife, Hind, was one of the few specially excluded from the mercy of the Prophet when he made his triumphant entry into Mekka as the greatest chieftain in Arabia—an exclusion richly merited by her conduct after the battle of Ohod. The conversion of Abou Sofyan himself was merely a political manœuvre, the insincerity of which was transparent. The children of Abou Sofyan made some clumsy endeavours to smooth over the awkwardness of these antecedents by putting certain sayings in the mouth of the Prophet attesting the zeal and devotedness of Abou Sofyan. One of these was, that the Prophet hoped to find in him 'one capable of replacing Hamza Ibn Abd al Muttalib,' the very Muhammadan martyr his wife had caused to be slain and then savagely mutilated. Another tradition asserts that the Prophet nominated Abou Sofyan as one of those who were certain to enter Paradise. But even to the almost unbounded credulity of the Arab these traditions must have come under the bead of '*munkir*,' i.e., traditions proceeding from a reporter of feeble authority. Muawia, the son of Abou Sofyan, seems to have been in almost every respect the duplicate of his father. Faith in Islam he had none; in his contest against Ali he was spurred on simply by worldly ambition, as also was his friend and colleague Amru, the conqueror of Egypt. Astute, unscrupulous, and pitiless, the first khalif of the Ommayas shrank from no crime necessary to secure his position. Murder was his accustomed mode of removing a formidable opponent. The grandson of the Prophet he caused to be poisoned; Malek al Ashtar, the heroic lieutenant of Ali, was destroyed in a like way To secure the succession of his son Yezid, Muawia hesitated not to break the word he had pledged to Hosain, the surviving son of Ali. And yet this cool, calculating, thoroughly atheistic Arab ruled over the regions of Islam, and the sceptre remained among his descendants for the space of nearly one hundred and twenty years. The explanation of this anomaly is to be found in two circumstances to which I have more than once adverted. The one is, that the truly devout and earnest Muhammadan conceived that he manifested his religion most effectually by withdrawing himself from the affairs of the world. The other is, the tribal spirit of the Arabs. Conquerors of Asia, of Northern Africa, of Spain, the Arabs never rose to the level of their position. Greatness had been thrust upon them, but in the midst of their grandeur they retained in all their previous force and intensity the passions, the rivalries, the petty jealousies of the desert. They merely fought again on a wider field 'the battles of the Arabs before Islam.'

The great sovereigns of the House of Ommaya are the khalifs Muawia, Abd al Malek, and Walid; but even here we look in vain for any of those elements of greatness which have given such a peculiar lustre to the memory of Akbar in India and our own Alfred in England. They founded nothing; their administration was guided by no general principles which they could transmit to their descendants. And if we pass beyond these three sovereigns, setting aside Omar ibn Abd al Aziz, and Hisham, the successor of Yezid II. (neither of whom, however, had any of the characteristics of great rulers), we find only idle and debauched profligates. The first Yezid, Sulaiman, the second Yezid and his son Walid, who succeeded the khalif Hisham—these were one and all royal rakes of that thorough-going type which is to be found only in Oriental countries. The first Yezid I have described already. Sulaiman was noted for his gluttony. The second Yezid passed his life in wine-drinking and feasting, and became so desperately enamoured of a slave-girl, that on her death he seems to have literally died of a broken heart. At least he refused to be comforted; he passed days in conversing on the merits of his beloved with a young girl who had been her servant, and in a few months followed her to the grave. It would be a mistake to attribute this excess of grief to a corresponding depth of love. The passions of Oriental sovereigns derive their destructive force, not from the strength of the nature from which they proceed, but from the weakness of its will. Incapable of self-restraint in any direction, they give way utterly to grief, just as they give way utterly to pleasure. Walid II. was surnamed 'the Reprobate.' He was dissolute in his life, revolting in his language, and disgusting in his habits. In one of his orgies a chamberlain said to him, 'Prince of Believers, the approaches to the palace are filled with delegates from the Arabs and the Kuraish, and your condition is not becoming the dignity of the khalif.' By way of reply the prince ordered the chamberlain to seat himself among the drinkers, and on the latter refusing to do so, he had him seized and bound, a tube forced between his teeth, and wine poured through it till the wretched man fell down dead drunk. On another occasion, happening to repeat the following verse of the Koran, 'Then sought they help from God, and every proud rebellious one perished; Hell is before him, and of tainted water shall he be made to drink,' he ordered a copy of the sacred book to be brought before him, and, setting it up as a mark, pierced it with arrows, while he recited verses to the following effect:—

> You threaten the man proud and rebellious; well, that man proud and rebellious is me.
>
> When you appear before your Master on the day of Resurrection, say to Him, 'Lord! it is Walid who has cut me into shreds.'

Under such sovereigns it is not hard to conjecture the condition of the populations they ruled. Sunk in pleasure, the khalifs trusted blindly to the governors of the provinces. These, knowing the precarious and uncertain tenure by which they clung to power, rarely had but one object—to amass as much wealth as possible before the hour of their deposition struck. Thus the pay of the army was always in arrears; lands fell out of cultivation, and the treasuries stood empty. The people, despairing of justice, rose everywhere in rebellion. All through the reign of Yezid and of his successor Hisham, from one end of the khalifate to the other, there was unceasing disorder and blood-shedding, and in Northern Africa the governor, a favourite official of Hejjaj, was murdered by the maddened Berbers. The regions lying beyond the Oxus, Armenia and Azerbaijan, all rose against their oppressors; two Muhammadan armies were cut off to a man; and only after very severe fighting were the risings temporarily suppressed. To crown all, an act of Walid's revived the sleeping rivalry between the Yemenites and the tribes of Modhar, which this time did not cease till the power of the Ommayas had sunk to rise no more—at least in Asia.

The khalif Yezid died A.H. 105, after a reign of four years, and was succeeded by his brother Hisham. The latter perceived the impolicy of bestowing all the high offices in the kingdom upon officials belonging to a single branch of the Arab race. He saw that Irak and Khorasan, being largely occupied by Yemenite tribes, ought to be governed by one of their own kin, and he appointed as governor of Irak, Khalid ibn Abdallah who, since the overthrow of the family of Mouhalleb, was reckoned among the foremost of the Yemenite chiefs. The wisdom of the policy was abundantly proved by its results. For fifteen years, during a period of tremendous agitation elsewhere, Irak, hitherto the stormiest part of the khalif's dominions, enjoyed unbroken repose. But Hisham's ruling passion was avarice. During these fifteen years he knew that Khalid must have amassed incalculable wealth. He longed to have this wealth in his coffers; but for this purpose it was necessary to depose Khalid. This was a matter requiring delicate treatment. A sudden discovery of his purpose would not improbably lead to an insurrection similar to that which had placed his predecessor in such great danger. A fitting successor was not wanting. A cousin of Hejjaj, Yusuf ibn Omar, ruled in the province of Yemen. He was a bitter enemy of Khalid, and would spring with greediness at any chance of wreaking his spite upon him. The difficulty was to bring him from Yemen to Irak without disclosing the purpose of his mission to Khalid. The manner in which this was accomplished discloses a curious picture of Muhammadan rule.

When Hisham ibn Abd al Malek (so says an author quoted by Ibn Khallikan in his 'Biographical Dictionary') wished to dismiss Khalid ibn Abd Allah from the government of Irak, a courier came to him from Yusuf ibn Omar, the Thakifite, the governor of Yemen. He had the messenger brought in, and spoke to him in these terms: 'Your master has passed the bounds in asking for a thing much above his merit.' He then ordered the man's clothes to be torn off, and had him flogged with a whip. 'Now,' said he, 'go back to your master, and may God treat you as you deserve.' He then called in Salim the Yemenite, who at that time was chief of the correspondence. 'Here,' said he, 'is an order of mine which must be sent to Yusuf ibn Omar; write it out, and bring me the letter.' Salim retired, and drew up the despatch whilst Hisham, who remained alone, wrote with his own hand to Yusuf ibn Omar a short note, containing these words: 'Go to Irak, for I have appointed you its governor. Take care not to let anyone know what you are about, and rid me of that Christian woman's son (Khalid's mother was a Christian) and of his intendants.' This note he held in his hand, and when Salim returned and presented to him the despatch which he had written, the khalif slipped his own note into the cover of the other letter without being perceived, and having sealed all up, he gave orders that the packet should be delivered to Yusuf's messenger. Salim obeyed, and the messenger departed. When Yusuf saw him arrive, he said to him: 'What news?' The other replied: 'Bad! The Commander of the Faithful is incensed against you, and caused my clothes to be torn off and myself to be whipped. He wrote no answer to the letter which you sent him, but here is a despatch from the chief of the board of correspondence.' Yusuf broke the seal, read the despatch, and on finishing, perceived the little note. He in consequence proceeded to Irak, and left his son As-Salt to act as his lieutenant in Yemen. Salim was by this time replaced in the board of correspondence by Bashir ibn Abi Talha. This officer, being very intelligent, understood what Hisham's intentions were, and said to himself: 'This ill-treatment of the messenger is a mere stratagem; he has certainly appointed Yusuf ibn Omar to the government of Irak.' He, in consequence, wrote the following lines to Iyad, the intendant of the territory called Ajma Salim, for whom he had a sincere affection: 'Your people have just sent you the Yemenite cloak; when it reaches you, put it on, and let thanks be given to God.' Iyad told this news to Tarik, the intendant who had been charged by Khalid ibn Abdallah with the administration of Koufa and its dependencies. Bashir then regretted what he had done, and wrote again to Iyad saying: 'They were thinking of sending you the Yemenite cloak.' Iyad communicated this news to Tarik, who said: 'The truth is in the first letter, but your friend repented what he had written, fearing that his conduct might be discovered.' He immediately rode off, and informed Khalid of what was passing. Khalid said to him: 'What think you best to be done?' Tarik replied: 'My advice is that you ride off this very instant to the Commander of the Faithful; your presence will make him ashamed of what he is about, and dissipate that prejudice against you which weighs on his mind.' As Khalid did not accept this advice, Tarik said: 'Allow me in that case to go and appear before him; I shall then take the engagement that all the revenue of the province for the present year shall be paid to him immediately.' Khalid asked to how much it would amount, and the other replied: 'To one hundred millions of dirhems. I shall then bring you a diploma confirming you in your place.' 'Where will you get the money,' said Khalid; 'by Allah! I do not possess ten thousand dirhems,' Tarik replied: 'I and Said ibn Rashid will undertake to pay forty millions of dirhems; az Zainabi and Abban ibn al Walid will engage to furnish twenty millions, and we will make up the rest from the other intendants.' Khalid replied, 'I should be considered a low-minded man were I to recall favours already granted.' 'Nay,' said Tarik, 'we save not only you but ourselves by giving up a part of our property; the advantages which you and we enjoy will then continue, and it is better for us to renew our efforts in the pursuit of wealth than to let you be prosecuted for the non-payment of the money. The merchants of Koufa have cash of ours in their hands; let us force them to give it up, for they will be tempted to delay the payment, and wait to see what may become of us; in that case we shall be the authors of our own ruin; and when we lose our lives they will keep the money and spend it.' Khalid refused to follow this advice, and Tarik then bade him farewell, saying: 'This is the last time we shall see you.'

In the meanwhile Yusuf with a few attendants was making his way to Irak with the best speed he could. He reached Koufa after a march of seventeen days, and halted for the night in the neighbourhood of the city. Tarik, to whom Khalid al Kasri had confided the collectorship of the land tax, had just circumcised his son. A man came to him, and said: 'I have just seen some people whose looks I do not like, and who pretend to be travellers.' In the meantime Yusuf ibn Omar went to the quarter where the Arabs of the Thakif tribe were residing, and told one of them to assemble and bring to him as many Modharite Arabs as he could. This was done, and at the dawn of day Yusuf entered into the mosque, and ordered the Muezzin to recite the *ikama*, and thus indicate that the Imam was already at the head of the congregation. The Muezzin replied: 'Wait till the Imam comes;' but, being intimidated by Yusuf's threats, he at length obeyed. Yusuf then placed himself at the head of the assembly. He could recite the Koran with great elegance, and having repeated the verses: *When the inevitable shall come*; and, *A person asked to see God's vengeance arrive*, he accomplished the prayer of daybreak. The kadi then stepped forward, offered to God praise and thanksgiving, and a prayer for the khalif. He asked also the name of the new emir, and, being told it, prayed for his welfare also. All the people of the city had joined the congregation before it separated.

There was to Muhammadan minds a sacramental virtue proceeding from the act of presiding at public prayer, which invested him who did so with a kind of sacredness. It is hard to make this feeling intelligible to us who live under such widely different conditions, intellectual as well as emotional. The way in which they reasoned seems to have been this. All the rules and ordinances which preside over and regulate the conduct of the Faithful are the utterances of the voice of God. Whoever be in possession of power, he cannot deviate one jot or one tittle from the written law. But to administer the law of God the administrator must be fortified with a Divine sanction. The khalif, then, as the source and channel whence this God-given authority is imparted to men, must, to use our language, 'ordain' the Imam, before his acts or his judgments could have any binding force on the conscience. Hence it was that long after the khalif had been stripped of every shred of worldly power, and was simply a prisoner in the hands of his Turkish guards, conquerors, like Mahmud of Ghuznee, still solicited from him the insignia of authority—the consecration, we may call it, of their power. The mystical significance, it is true, of this sanction developed mainly after the great Persian revolution which brought the Abbasides into power, but it was felt, though not perhaps reasoned out, from the very commencement of the khalifate. And hence it was that when once a duly authorised governor had presided at the public prayer, the power of him who would oppose him withered away, as if struck by a sudden blight. His force had been extracted from him. He could no longer summon spirits from the vasty deep; at least they would not obey him if he did. The would-be rebel was as conscious of this as anyone else; and therefore we always find that his first act is to deny the Divine legitimacy of the reigning khalif, and so render null and void all that proceeds through a channel tainted at the source. The sudden change of front effected by Yezid ibn Mouhalleb, which provoked the indignant derision of Hasan the Basrite, is an illustration of this. Khalid ibn Abdallah was not prepared to take so decisive a step. The blow which had struck him had been given with too little warning to allow of any such preparations for warding it off. He and his intendants were arrested without resistance, and cast into prison. Yusuf ibn Omar was cruel by nature, and at present his natural feelings were intensified by the desire of revenge. When on the accession of Sulaiman, the retribution long delayed had fallen upon the family of Hejjaj, he had been one among those arrested. He had had his gains wrung out from him by the pitiless persuasion of the torturers; but now these hated Yemenites were in his grasp. He set to work without delay. The sagacious Tarik, who had foreseen all, was tortured to death; several others of the intendants also perished under the hands of the executioner. A sum of ninety millions of dirhems was in this way extracted from them. Khalid was not spared. Hisham, who at first thought the above sum sufficient, had written to Yusuf, saying: 'I declare solemnly before God that if Khalid receives from you even the scratch of a thorn, I shall have your head struck off.' This was a bitter grief to the amiable Yusuf. He entreated pathetically for permission to put him on the rack, asserting that there was still some of the public revenue in his hands. Hisham seems to have felt that it would be ungracious in him not to concede so trifling a favour to so devoted a servitor. He might, too, get a little more money; and so he granted permission to Omar to torture his enemy, but only once, taking at the same time precautions that the governor of Irak did not pursue his pleasures too far. A soldier of the royal guard was deputed to witness the operation, and the khalif swore that if Khalid died, the head of Yusuf would be forfeited. Khalid was accordingly tortured at Hira in the presence of the people, but, to Yusuf's great disgust, refused to gratify his ears by a single groan. He was then taken back to prison, and remained there for eighteen months. At length in the year 121 (A.D. 739) Hisham wrote to Yusuf, ordering the prisoner to be set at liberty. He departed with his family to Syria, and resided there till the death of Hisham, accompanying every summer the expeditions made in the provinces of the Byzantine empire.

Yusuf was a man who delighted in cruelty and oppression. It is related of him during his government of the two Iraks that having weighed a dirhem, and found it too light by one grain, he wrote to all the coining establishments in Irak, ordering the persons employed there to be chastised; and it was reckoned that one hundred thousand lashes were given in all for the deficiency of a single grain.

His hospitality was great, but even here his cruel humour comes out in a curious way. He used to have five hundred tables set out, and to these were admitted people from all quarters far and near; the native of Irak would partake of the repast with the native of Syria. On every table was placed a cake of bread sprinkled with sugar. The guests at one of the tables happening one day to complain that their cake was not sugared, Yusuf ordered the baker to be chastised, and three hundred lashes were inflicted on him whilst the company were at their meal. Ever after, the luckless baker would go about with the sugar boxes, and add sugar wherever it was wanted.[1] Though compelled for the moment by the mandate of the khalif to spare the life of his enemy, the Thakifite governor of the two Iraks was not one to forego the sweets of vengeance. Walid, the son of Yezid, and the successor designate of Hisham, was related by the mother's side to the family of Hejjaj. From him it would be easy to obtain the full gratification of that revenge which the scruples of Hisham had obliged him to postpone.

The khalif Hisham died A.H. 125 (February, A.D. 743).

[1] I have taken these anecdotes (as the Orientalist will know, if any such do me the honour of reading these pages) from that comprehensive, most instructive, and most amusing compilation, Ibn Khallikan's 'Biographical Dictionary,' which the learning and industry of Baron MacGuckin de Slane have made accessible to the uninstructed English reader. There is another anecdote there connected with Yusuf ibn Omar, which I cannot refrain from quoting:—

'Yusuf ibn Omar said to a man whom he nominated to the government of a district: "Enemy of God! you have eaten up the wealth which belonged to God!" The man replied, "Tell me whose wealth I have been eating from the day in which I was created until now. By Allah! if I asked from Satan a single dirhem he would not give it to me.'—*Ibn Khall.*, *De Slane's Trans.*, vol. iv. p. 444.

His nephew Walid was already known as a debauched and impious profligate, for whose sensuality the wide license of the Muhammadan creed was all too narrow, and who held the Koran in contempt. But he was known also as lavish and open-handed. The court, the army, the poets had all suffered grievously from the severe parsimony of the khalif Hisham, and they knew that vast treasures had been amassed by the deceased sovereign, which, under the auspices of the new, would descend in golden showers upon their parched and thirsty souls. There was, in consequence, no opposition to the succession of Walid II.; nor were they disappointed in their expectations. The pay of the army was increased. Damascus became a scene of magnificent festivity. Singers and musicians from all parts of Asia were summoned thither to grace the banquets of the khalif. The people were delighted with exhibitions of horse-racing on a scale of grandeur never before beheld. In these spectacles as many as a thousand horses—all Arabs of the desert—were started in a single race. True it was that the private life of the khalif was sullied by a number of disgraceful acts. The ladies of his own family were not secure from his outrages. The sons of his predecessor were, on the most trifling pretexts, cruelly treated, flogged, and imprisoned. But so long as he showered gifts upon the soldiers, and delighted the people by his shows and his feasts, the khalif could afford to disregard the murmurs of his own family. And he took advantage of his popularity to proclaim throughout his dominions, in an exceedingly pious and edifying letter, that he nominated his two infant sons to succeed him in the khalifate. This was contrary to an old precedent. Not only were these sons merely children, who, should their father die, would be incapable of presiding at the public prayer, or giving testimony in a court of justice, but since Abd al Malek, no khalif had ventured to nominate his own son as his successor. The attempt on the part of Walid was a blow struck at the rights of his uncles. The sons of Hisham and Walid I. now combined together against the khalif, denouncing him as a blasphemer, and accusing him of incest. But they would have failed, in all probability, to find supporters, but for Walid's own imprudence.

Since his deposition from the government of the two Iraks, Khalid ibn Abdallah had resided at Damascus. As the man of greatest influence among the Yemenites, the khalif was eager to obtain his support for his two sons. But Khalid refused to take the oath of allegiance to two children incapable of either understanding or performing the functions of an Imam. At the same time he rejected the solicitations of the enemies of the khalif to enter into a conspiracy against him. He even went so far as to warn the khalif of his danger, and advised him to give up his intention of making the pilgrimage to Mekka, lest there should in his absence be a revolt in Damascus. Walid, nevertheless, exasperated by his opposition to his pet scheme, had him thrown into prison.

A short while after this Yusuf ibn Omar came from Irak, on a visit to the court at Damascus. He brought with him, as presents to the khalif, 'such a quantity of treasure, merchandise, and vases as was never before brought from Irak.' The khalif was delighted, and on

Yusuf offering a further sum of 40,000,000 dirhems if the prisoner Khalid was given up to him, accepted the offer at once. Yusuf then caused Khalid to be enclosed in a litter without cushions, and bore him back to Irak. He put him to death in Hira; first, he placed the feet of his prisoner between two pieces of wood which he then forced together until the feet were crushed to pieces; he next placed the pieces of wood on the legs which he broke in the same manner, then on the thighs, and lastly on the back; when the back was broken Khalid died. During these tortures he neither uttered a groan nor spoke a word.

This barbarous murder was perpetrated in the month of Mohurrum, A.H. 126 (A.D. 743). It gave the decisive blow to the declining power of the Ommayas. The Yemenite tribes rose up as one man in angry revolt against the sovereign who had permitted the cruel deed. The conspirators at Damascus suffered no longer from any lack of supporters. The Kelbites sprang to arms. Yezid, a son of Walid I. and grandson of Abd al Malek, placed himself at their head. He marched by night into Damascus at the head of a band of chosen men, and seized a mosque in which a large quantity of weapons had been stored up. Many of the citizens of Damascus now joined the conspirators, and from all the country round Yezid's partisans flocked to join his standard.

The khalif Walid was at this time absent from Damascus with a force of only a few hundred men in attendance upon him. His friends advised him to seek refuge in Palmyra or Emessa, as in either place he could find shelter until the regular soldiers were drawn together.

He rejected the advice, and shut himself up in the fortress of Nadjra, a place not far from Damascus. He knew that Abbas, the brother of Yezid, had done his utmost to dissuade the latter from creating dissensions in the family. And he had ascertained that he was now on his way at the head of an armed force to support the khalif against the insurgents of Damascus. Walid did not doubt that he could maintain himself in the fortress until Abbas came to his relief. The promptitude of Yezid baffled these expectations. He intercepted Abbas in a narrow defile, scattered his troops in irretrievable rout, and making his brother prisoner, compelled him to take the oath of allegiance to himself.

The fortress was then assaulted. The few followers of the khalif made a gallant stand against ten times their number. The khalif exhibited a degree of personal courage in this last act of his life, hardly to have been expected from such a voluptuary. But when his troops saw Abbas in the ranks of the enemy they knew that there was no hope of succour, and laid down their arms. The khalif withdrew into the castle, and from the ramparts endeavoured to enter into negotiations with the insurgents. He promised to the troops an increase of pay, to the people a remission of the revenue; and to the poor a prodigal almsgiving. But his proposals were flung back with scorn. It was not material interests, the insurgents shouted, which had banded his subjects against him, but indignation at his dissolute life and zeal for the purity of the Faith. Then Walid appealed to the Koran, and demanded that a new election should be held in accordance with the provisions of the Law. But this offer also was rejected, and he retired into an inner room of the castle, muttering as he went, 'A day like that of Othman's.' Then he read the Koran, with some strange thoughts one would think, for only a few days had elapsed since he had made the sacred volume a butt for his archery, until the rebels bursting in slew him (27th Djoumada'l Ashir, A.H. 126, 16th April, A.D. 744). On the following day, his head fixed on a lance was paraded through the streets of Damascus, and his own brother Sulaiman refused to pronounce the funeral prayer over the body of the murdered khalif.

Yezid did not long enjoy the power he had wrested from his cousin. He died six months afterwards (Dzul hajj, A.H. 126, 12th October, 744), and was succeeded in the khalifate by Merwan ibn Muhammad, a descendant of that Merwan ibn Hakem who had already reigned in Damascus.

Merwan II. (as he is known in Oriental history) was the most distinguished general of his day. During the reigns of Hisham and Walid he had governed the provinces of Armenia and Azerbaijan. His period of rule had been a stormy one. The people under their national sovereigns had made desperate and persistent efforts to throw off the Muhammadan yoke. And in the long and arduous campaigns which preceded the suppression of these attempts Merwan had given signal proofs of his valour, endurance, and military skill. He had endeavoured without avail to dissuade Yezid from rebelling against Walid. And no sooner had he received the intelligence of Walid's murder than he left the Kaukasus, and marched into Mesopotamia at the head of 20,000 men.

Yezid, hopeless of making head against this formidable soldier, proposed a division of power—Merwan to govern, with plenary power, Armenia, Azerbaijan, and Mesopotamia. Merwan had signified his acquiescence in this proposal, when Yezid died, and all was again in confusion.

Ibrahim, a brother of Yezid, was proclaimed khalif by the Kelbites of Damascus. But Merwan refused to acknowledge this nomination. The two sons of Walid were imprisoned in Damascus, and Merwan marched from Harran at the head of a strong army, ostensibly to liberate the young princes and carry on the government in their name. In Kinnesrin he defeated and took prisoners two brothers of the late khalif. From thence, strengthened by many Arabs of the tribes of Modhar, commanded by Yezid ibn Omar ibn Hobaira, he turned in the direction of Emessa. This city had already revolted against Ibrahim, and an army of Yemenites were besieging it. These fell back upon Damascus at the approach of Merwan, and the latter entered Emessa in triumph. Without halt he marched towards Damascus. At Ain Aldjarr, a small quarter between the Libanon and the Anti-Libanon, on the road from Baalbec to Damascus, he was encountered by the khalif's army, numbering 120,000 men, and composed almost entirely of Yemenites. Merwan had but 80,000 troops to oppose to this host. But they were seasoned soldiers, accustomed to act together, and inured to danger in many a terrible battle against Armenians, Greeks, and Turks. The Yemenite army was nothing but a crowd of men with arms in their hands. The battle, moreover, was fought in a narrow pass where their huge numbers were an incumbrance rather than an advantage. A murderous battle was fought which lasted the entire day. Merwan remained on the defensive until a force which he had despatched to attack the Yemenites in the rear had had time to reach their position. The slaughter then was terrible, as wedged in between two fires the unwieldy masses of the Yemenites could neither fight nor fly; 17,000 fell upon the field; a like number flung down their arms, and yielded themselves prisoners; the remainder fled in small parties, so completely routed and broken up that they could not rally for the defence of the capital.

The news of this crushing defeat was a signal for the flight of Ibrahim from Damascus. He had reigned four months (Second Rabi, A.H. 127, January, February, A.D. 745). But, apprehensive that if Merwan entered the city, he would deliver from prison Hakem and Othman, the sons of Walid, and that these two princes would have no mercy on any of the persons who had contributed to their father's death, he gave orders before his flight that they should be put to death. These wretched boys were accordingly beaten to death with clubs. It is, however, a satisfaction to have to record that at the same time Yusuf ibn Omar, the cruel murderer of Khalid al Khasri, met with a richly-merited doom. On the murder of Walid, and the accession of Yezid, he had fled from Irak disguised as a woman. But search was made after him, and he was seized, while seated in female attire among his women and children. Since then he had remained in prison in Damascus. The son of his former victim was now deputed to execute justice upon Yusuf ibn Omar. He beheaded him with his own hand; a rope was tied to the headless trunk, and the little boys began to drag the headless corpse through the streets of Damascus. Yusuf was exceedingly small in stature, and a woman, seeing the diminutive body lying covered with dust and blood, exclaimed, 'Why did they kill that unfortunate boy?'

Merwan was now master of Damascus. He had hitherto appeared in the field as the protector of the sons of Walid; but, those princes being no longer alive, he assumed the title of khalif. To give, however, the semblance of a legitimate sanction to his seizure of power, a fellow-captive of the murdered princes attested upon oath that Hakem, the eldest, had, before his murder, designated Merwan as the heir of his rights. Could a mere soldier have given stability to the tottering throne of the Ommayas, Merwan would have been the right sovereign for the crisis. Unlike so many of his predecessors, he was sternly ascetic in his habits. The celerity of his movements, the crushing blows he dealt his enemies, the wonderful energy, daring, and promptitude with which, during the few years of his tempestuous reign, he made head against enemies which swarmed around him one after another like waves of the sea, attract our sympathy and admiration to a degree unusual in Muhammadan history. But Merwan was destitute of the large outlook required of a statesman. Instead of endeavouring to soothe and pacify the feuds between the two great branches of the Arabs, he flung himself into them with the blind zeal of a partisan. A Modharite himself, he regarded a Yemenite as his bitterest enemy, and his harshness and partiality kindled to a kind of frenzy the hatreds of the tribes. The quarrel waxed hotter continually. The spirit of rivalry spread among the nomads of the desert not less than among the dwellers in the cities. The poets, it is needless to say, rode on the whirlwind and fanned the storm. They raked up the memories of long past years—the slaughter at Merdj Rahit, the pillage and violation of Medina, the debts of vengeance which a long series of 'expeditions' on either side had left behind them—and launched them forth in an incessant stream of song. I have spoken of the sensibility of the Arab to poetry. A well-aimed satire poisoned all his springs of enjoyment: at night it robbed him of rest; by day he heard continually the jeers and laughter of those who listened to the recitations of the bard. Every couplet was like a barbed arrow quivering in his flesh. This deluge of poetic satire was as oil added to flame. Wherever a few Arabs met together snatches of these satirical odes were chanted, and Yemenite and Modharite swore to obliterate with blood the insults they heaped upon each other. The Yemenites, as the subjected race, were the first to strike the blow.

The Yemenites in Oman and Bahrein assailed the Modharite tribes established in those countries, and slew a great number of them. The Kharegites of Yemen itself invaded Mekka and Medina, and took possession of the Sacred Territory. Koufa was occupied by the Kharegite Dhabbak ibn Kais, and the governors appointed by Merwan were expelled from Irak. The principal towns in Persian Irak, Fars and Ahwaz, were seized by Yemenites headed by Ismail, a brother of the murdered

Khalid al Kasri, and acting under the orders of another Kharegite leader, Abdallah ibn Muawia. Even Emessa, the town which three months ago had flung open its gates to admit Merwan, now rose in revolt against him. Merwan remained resolute and unappalled in the midst of this turmoil and confusion, like some huge bison baited by troops of hungry wolves.

Emessa was the first spot to feel his wrath. He dashed upon the rebellious town, fought his way into it with irresistible inpetuosity, and crushed the insurrection. Five hundred of the rebels were hung round the walls of the city. But the country meanwhile had risen in his rear. Under the leadership of Yezid, the son of Khalid al Kasri, the Yemenites of 'the Ghutah' had shut up in Damascus the governor, the khalif had left behind him. Merwan swooped down upon them with the swiftness of a hawk. Taken by surprise, the rebels were cut to pieces; Yezid, their leader, was taken prisoner and promptly hung. A like fate overtook the governor of Palestine, who had taken advantage of the general confusion to proclaim his independence.

These swift and crushing blows quieted Syria, and the khalif had a brief breathing space to devote to the affairs of Irak. He appointed his most able officer, Yezid ibn Omar ibn Hobaira, governor of the two Iraks, and ordering him to set off at once and collect together the relics of the khalif's troops who had been beaten by the Kharegites, he made arrangements to send off after him as speedily as possible a reinforcement of ten thousand men.[1]

[1] This Yezid ibn Omar ibn Hobaira was one of the great chiefs of the day, who made a profound impression on the popular imagination;

But these troops had barely started on their march, when they mutinied in a body and proclaimed as khalif Sulai-

and Ibn Khallikan, in his notice of him, has preserved a curious picture of his daily habits, which I transcribe here, both because it is interesting as a glimpse into the private life of those strange and far-off times, and also as an agreeable change to the dreary catalogue of battles and sieges with which I am obliged to fill this part of the book. The passage is as follows:—'The *hafiz* Ibn Asakir says in his greater history, "Every morning when Ibn Hobaira awoke they brought him a large bowl containing some honey or else some sugar on which milk had been drawn from the camel. He would drink it off, and towards the hour of morning prayer would remain seated in the oratory, till the proper time for saying it came. After that he would retire and call for breakfast. At this repast he ate two fowls, two young pigeons, half a kid and flesh meat dressed in a variety of ways. He then went out, examined into the applications made to him, and, at noon, when he retired he would send for some of his officers and the chief men of the place, and then call for dinner. Placing a napkin over his breast he would swallow large morsels without stopping. When he finished the company retired, and he went in to the women, with whom he remained till the hour of afternoon prayer. He would then come out to pray, after which he would give audience to applicants, examine into their affairs, and say the *asr* prayer. A throne being then set up for him and chairs placed for the others, all sat down, and bowls of honied milk and other drinks were brought in. The cloth being spread for the people, and covered with dishes of meat, a table was set on an estrade for himself and his companions. They ate with him, and after sunset they went to attend the evening prayer. When the prayer was over, the persons who were to pass the evening with him would assemble in a room and sit there till called in. Conversation would then be carried on till the night was far advanced. Every evening he allowed ten services to be asked of him, and these were all granted the next morning. His yearly salary was six hundred thousand dirhems (15,000*l.*) Every month he would distribute large sums to his companions, to the legists, and to the members of respectable families. Abd Allah ibn Shuburna ad Dabbi, the Kadi and jurisconsult of Koufa, who was one of those admitted to his evening conversations, said—

'When the night was advanced and sleep was overcoming us,
Ayad would bring to us one of the two reliefs.'

Ayad was his doorkeeper, and the two reliefs were the permission of man, the son of the khalif Hisham. This Sulaiman had commanded the Yemenites at Ain Aldjarr, but after that victory he had made his submission and taken the oath of allegiance to Merwan, who had until recently permitted him to reside near him. Just before this incident he had, on some pretence or other, obtained leave to depart from Harran, and now lost no time in assuming command of the mutinous soldiery. He seized Kinnesrin, which became immediately the rallying-point for all the discontented spirits in the realm. Merwan met the new danger with his usual terrible promptitude. A few forced marches carried him to Kinnesrin, and Sulaiman's army was destroyed in a great battle. But a portion of the routed troops succeeded in throwing themselves into Emessa, and another battle had to be fought and a tedious siege to be prosecuted before the embers of the revolt were altogether extinguished.

First towards the end of A.H. 128 (September, 746) was it possible to send Yezid ibn Omar back to Irak. It was high time to do so. All that province, all the Hejaz, and all Yemen were occupied by the Kharegites. But Merwan was a really glorious soldier. In three great battles he defeated the Kharegites, killing their leaders

going in to the emir or of retiring. At these social meetings he had no napkin, and when he called for one it was a signal for the company to rise up and retire." A *shaikh* of the Kuraish tribe related as follows:—"On a very hot summer's day Yezid ibn Omar ibn Hobaira admitted some people who were waiting to be introduced. He had on an old tunic, the breast of which was patched. They looked at him with wonder, and he, remarking their astonishment, recited this verse of Ibrahim ibn Harma's, applying it to himself:—

'A gallant youth can attain to glory though his robe be torn and his tunic patched.'"'—*Ibn Khall., De Slane's Trans.* vol. iv. p. 211.

and opening a way to Koufa, of which city he took possession in the month of Ramadan, A.H. 129 (May–June, A.D. 747). The remains of the Kharegites had entrenched themselves on the eastern bank of the Tigris. Merwan, strongly reinforced after the acquisition of Koufa, stormed their defences and drove them in hideous rout back into the province of Fars.

Simultaneously with these operations the khalif had detached a force under Abd al Malek ibn Muhammad to recover Arabia. The first encounter took place at Wadi'l Kora, not far from Medina. The Kharegites were utterly defeated and their leader killed. They fell back on Mekka; Abd al Malek following hard on their traces, compelled them to hazard another engagement. The Kharegites were again defeated, and another of their leaders was killed. These two victories cleared the Hejaz of the enemy. Yemen was still in their hands. Abd al Malek, who seems to have been inspired with all the energy of his chief, marched into that province, and in a third battle, which lasted from morning till night, utterly defeated the enemy. They abandoned Yemen and sought shelter in Hadhramaut, a province of which they retained possession ever afterwards.

Syria, the two Iraks, the Hejaz, and Yemen were by these operations cleared of the enemy. But much remained to be done. These campaigns had denuded the frontier provinces of troops, and the Kaukasus was a scene of universal disorder. In North Syria and in Asia Minor the Byzantine armies were making raids across the undefended frontier. Fars was strongly occupied by the Kharegites. Yet there is little doubt that Merwan would in time have made head against these enemies, had not another and more formidable tempest gathered in Khorasan. This was the great Persian revolt, long and skilfully matured, which bore in triumph the black banners of the Abbasides from Meru to Damascus.

CHAPTER IV.

THE ABBASIDES.

A.D. 500–745.

I HAVE spoken in a previous chapter of Kossay, the revolution he accomplished at Mekka in favour of the Kuraish, and the preeminence he acquired in the tribe. His great ambition was to transmit his power undiminished to his eldest son. He had in all four sons; the eldest of whom was named Abd al Dar, the second Abd Menaf; the latter being the most vigorous and enterprising in character. The consequence was that on old Kossay's death the real power and influence passed into the possession of Abd Menaf, though on his elder brother was concentrated all those offices of dignity which Kossay had devised for exalting himself among his compatriots. Abd Menaf managed all the affairs of Mekka, and to him was entrusted the important duty of laying out fresh quarters for the increasing population of the city. Upon the death of Abd al Dar the five offices passed to his sons, but they all died within a few years after him, leaving children too young to perform the functions, and consequently to defend the privileges which had descended to them (A.D. 500). Meanwhile the sons of Abd Menaf had reached man's estate; they inherited the lofty qualities of their father, and the respect in which he had been held by the tribe of Kuraish was enjoyed in equal measure by them. The two eldest were Al Mutallib and Hashim. Between them and the grandchildren, relatives, and clients of Abd al Dar there was bitter and perpetual feud. The one side, in possession of the titular honours, chafed at the power having passed in such great measure into other hands. The other side were eager to give that power the legal sanction obtainable only by the appropriation of the titles of dignity. Mekka at one time seemed in danger of becoming the theatre of a civil war, when a compromise was effected which averted the calamity. To Hashim and his party was conceded the office of providing food and water for the pilgrims; and the descendants of Abd al Dar retained the custody of the Kaaba, the right to preside in the Hall of Council, and that of raising the banner. Hashim, a man of great wealth, greatly increased his authority by the lavish scale on which he entertained the pilgrims, and by the munificence with which during a famine he relieved the wants of his fellow-citizens. He died early in the sixth century, leaving one son, who was brought up at Medina under the care of his mother.

Hashim left his right of entertainment to his elder brother, al Muttalib, who continued to discharge that function in such magnificent fashion that he received the appellation of 'Munificent.' After the lapse of some years he went to Medina, returning with his nephew, the only child of Hashim. He reached Mekka during the heat of the day. As the inhabitants, sitting in the shade of their houses, saw him pass with the lad at his side, they took the latter for a slave he had purchased. '*Abd al Muttalib*,' they exclaimed. 'Look at the servant of Muttalib;' and this name clung to the son of Hashim ever after.

On the death of his uncle, Abd al Muttalib succeeded to the office of entertaining the pilgrims. But he was poor, and for a long time remained destitute of power or consideration. He had, however, the good fortune, after a time, to discover the celebrated well of Zem Zem, which had been choked up centuries before, but the recollection of which had been preserved by tradition. The scarcity of water at Mekka rendered this discovery one of great value; while the tradition which identified it with the spring miraculously discovered by Hagar when she and Ishmael were perishing of thirst caused his superstitious countrymen to look upon Abd al Muttalib as one specially favoured of Heaven. From that time, at any rate, his position changed, and he became and continued until his death the chief man in Mekka.

He had ten sons. The youngest and best beloved was Abdallah, the father of Muhammad. Abdallah died while his son was still unborn, and the guardianship of the future Prophet devolved upon the venerable Abd al Muttalib. This guardianship lasted only a few years. Abd al Muttalib died A.D. 578, at the ripe age of four score and two. The right of entertaining the pilgrims passed to Zobeir, the eldest son of Abd al Muttalib, and after him to Zobeir's youngest brother, Abbas, the progenitor of the Abbaside khalifs. But since the death of Abd al Muttalib, the influence of the family had greatly declined; and that of Abou Sofyan, a lineal descendant also of the great Kossay, had acquired preeminence. Abbas succeeded in retaining the privilege only of supplying the pilgrims with water. This was held by him until the introduction of Islam, and confirmed to him and his family by the Prophet.

Abbas was a man in no way remarkable, and was never held in much account by his fellow-citizens. When the Prophet had resolved to abandon Mekka, and went out beyond the city for that momentous midnight interview with the Medina converts which resulted in 'the Flight,' Abbas was his sole companion. But he was not at this time a believer in the Prophet, nor, indeed, did he feign to be such until long after. He feared lest a profession of the new faith should draw down upon him the hostility of the tribe and eject him from the single privilege he enjoyed. He even took part in the battle of Bedr on the side of the Kuraish, and remained a prisoner in the hands of the victors. The Prophet allowed him to purchase his freedom, and return to Mekka. From that time he played the part of a trimmer, and contrived, not without dexterity, to preserve the goodwill of both parties. Only when the Prophet set out on that triumphant march which carried him unopposed to Mekka did Abbas openly espouse his cause. He met the Prophet half way between Medina and Mekka, and pronounced the confession of faith.

Notwithstanding these dubious antecedents the Prophet received him with favour and affection, and always treated him with marked consideration. His example was imitated by the khalifs Abu Bekr, Omar, and Othman. They dismounted if they met him walking; and not unfrequently would accompany him to his residence. For the last five years of his life he was blind. He died, according to some, A.H. 32; according to others, A.H. 34.

He left behind him four sons—Abdallah, Fadl, Obaidallah, and Kathan.

Abdallah, better known in Muhammadan history as Ibn Abbas, was born three years before the flight from Mekka. His father carried him to Muhammad, who embraced and implored a blessing upon him. 'God,' he said, 'be pleased to enlighten this infant, fill his mind with intelligence, and make him one of thy most virtuous servants.' Ibn Abbas had reached the age of thirteen when the Prophet died.

To the efficacy of that prophetic prayer pronounced over the unconscious infant, the Muhammadan world attributed the wisdom and piety which in after life Ibn Abbas displayed. He was profoundly wise in the interpretation of the Koran; and it was said of him that none knew better than he, the traditions, the legal decisions of the three first khalifs, the law and the sciences of poetry and arithmetic. Crowds flocked to him from all parts to hear his lectures; and he it was who gave the great impulse to the study of the history of the Arabs before Islam, and the preservation of all that could be collected of their literature. In his lectures on grammar he was accustomed to explain and illustrate obscure or difficult passages in the Koran by verses from the ancient poets, and he was accustomed to say: 'When you meet with a difficulty in the Koran look for its solution in the poems of the Arabs, for these are registers of the Arabic nation.' On being asked how he had acquired his extensive knowledge, he said: 'By means of an inquiring tongue and an intelligent heart.' When he died it was said of him: 'To-day is dead the Doctor of the people and the sea of learning.'

His merits were acknowledged by the three first khalifs. They held his learning in such high esteem that in their assemblies they conceded to him the place of honour. And when Othman was besieged in his house at Medina he commissioned Ibn Abbas to conduct the pilgrimage to Mekka. According to some writers, Ibn Abbas was instructed in the Koran by Ali himself; certain it is that Ali always lived on the friendliest terms with Ibn Abbas and his brothers; and they repaid his friendship with a steady and zealous devotion to his cause. Ibn Abbas was soldier not less than theologian; and all four brothers were present at 'the Battle of the Camel.' In the long series of encounters on the plain of Siffin, Ibn Abbas commanded the cavalry of Ali; and he was the judge whom Ali would fain have chosen when forced by his troops to submit his claims to the judgment of arbitrators.

After the murder of Ali and the resignation of power by his son Hasan, Ibn Abbas kept up a cold and distant intercourse with Muawia; but when the latter desired to secure the succession to his son Yezid, Ibn Abbas courageously denounced the attempt as a flagrant breach of faith, and a wrong to the undoubted rights of the House of Ali. When Yezid became khalif, Ibn Abbas, together with Hosain, Abdallah Ibn Zobair, and some others, declined to take the oath of allegiance. Entirely devoted to Ali and his sons, Ibn Abbas regarded the Ommayas as usurpers; but he viewed with an equally unfriendly eye the conduct of Abdallah Ibn Zobair. The hypocritical zeal which that crafty pretender affected for the sons of Ali never for a moment blinded Ibn Abbas. He did his utmost to dissuade his nephew Hosain from the perilous journey which ended in the catastrophe of Kerbela, and warned him not to trust to the insidious counsels of Ibn Zobair. The sorrow caused by the death of Hosain is said to have shortened his life. Driven out of Mekka by the menaces of Abdallah ibn Zobair, he died in the village of Taief (A.H. 68) at the age of seventy-one.

Abdallah Ibn Abbas had several children, but only the youngest of these left children behind him. His name was Ali; and his son, Muhammad—the father of the two first Abbaside khalifs—appears to have been the first to conceive the idea of forming a party and aspiring to the khalifate. There was no lack of prognostications setting forth the approaching greatness of his family. I cite one here as illustrative of the superstitions of the time. It must be premised that the rupture between the Abbasides and Ibn Zobair had reconciled the former with the court at Damascus. Ali was an especial favourite with the khalif Abd al Malek. 'We happened,' so it is related as coming from the lips of Hejjaj, 'to be with Abd al Malek ibn Merwan at a country seat of his . . . . . He was conversing with a physiognomist and addressing questions to him when Ali ibn Abdallah came in accompanied by his son Muhammad. On seeing him approach, Abd al Malek ceased from conversation, his colour changed, and he began to mutter some words between his lips. I immediately sprang up with the intention of preventing Ali from advancing, but the khalif made me a sign that I should let him alone. He then drew near and made his salutation, on which Abd al Malek seated him by his side, and while he passed his hands carelessly over his clothes, he signed to Muhammad that he should also be seated. He then commenced discoursing with Ali, the agreeable tone of whose conversation was well known. A repast being brought in, the khalif washed his hands and ordered the tray to be placed near Ali ibn Abdallah, but he said that he was keeping a fast, and, rising up suddenly, he retired. Abd al Malek followed him with his eyes, till he had nearly disappeared from sight, and then turning to the physiognomist, he asked him if he knew who he was. The man replied that he did not, but that he knew one thing respecting him. The khalif desired to know what that was, and the physiognomist said: "If the youth who is with him be his son there will come forth from his loins a number of Pharaohs destined to possess the earth, and slay whoever attempts to resist them!" On hearing these words Abd al Malek turned pale, and said: "A monk at Aileh who once saw him with me, pretended that thirteen kings should come forth from his loins, and he described to me the appearance of each."'

This Ali was hardly less eminent among the Faithful, by reason of his zeal, devotion, and knowledge, than his father Ibn Abbas had been. He possessed, it is said, five hundred olive trees, and he said every day a prayer of two *rakas* at the foot of each. From the number of his prostrations, callosities were formed on his knees like those on the limbs of camels. Whenever he came to Mekka to perform the pilgrimage or to visit the Temple, the Kuraish suspended the assemblies which they held in the Sacred Mosque, and deserted the places where public lessons were usually given, for the purpose of keeping him company, and giving him a mark of the profound respect and veneration they bore him; when he stood up they stood up, and when he walked they all crowded round, and walked with him. Thus they continued to do till he left the Sacred Territory. He resided, as I have said, principally at the Court of Damascus, where his agreeable manners, witty conversation, and wide learning made him an especial favourite of the khalif Abd al Malek; but towards the close of his life he incurred the displeasure of this sovereign and his son and successor, Walid. This was provoked by his taking in marriage, Lubbana, a divorced wife of Abd al Malek. The khalif Walid was more incensed by this even than his father. He caused Ali to be arrested on the ground that he sought to degrade the khalifs by marrying their mothers, and had him flogged, and then paraded through the streets of Damascus, mounted on a camel, with his face towards the tail, whilst a crier proclaimed: 'This is Ali ibn Abdallah, the liar.' Ali died about A.H. 117 or A.H. 118.

The desire to revenge the indignities inflicted upon his father seems to have first suggested to Muhammad, the son of Ali, the idea of overthrowing the dynasty of the Ommayas; and the eagerness with which the provinces of the old Persian monarchy had gathered round Yezid ibn Mouhalleb indicated with sufficient clearness where he could hope to find adherents.

A Muhammadan tradition relates that at the moment of the Prophet's birth the sacred fires in all the temples of Persia were extinguished; the great Nushirwan was visited by a dream in which he beheld the towers of his palace overthrown; and the chief 'mobed,' or high priest of Persia, saw in a vision a multitude of large and strong camels contending with camels from Arabia, weak in body and few in number. Nevertheless, the former were put to flight, and the Arab camels, crossing the Tigris and penetrating into Persia, spread over the whole land. An eminent diviner, profoundly versed in the religion and the aspirations of the Arabs, was consulted on the signification of these portents; and from him they learned that a great prophet was born in Arabia, whose religion would spread over Persia. Fourteen kings were still to sit on the throne of the Sassanides; then their power would come to an end, and the followers of the Prophet would reign in their stead.

This prediction, it is needless to say, was fulfilled to the letter. But no idea of Muhammadan conquest can be more erroneous than the popular one which supposes that the Arabs wiped out, as with a sponge, all traces of the civilisation which preceded them, and on the *tabula rasa* thus obtained erected the pure faith of Islam. The empire of the Sassanides succumbed with such celerity before the blows of the invading Muhammadans from a vice in its constitution common to all Oriental monarchies —the excessive centralisation of authority. The Persian monarchy was the realised ideal of despotism. Masoudi has preserved for us their theory of government. It was an extremely simple one. They regarded the State as a sort of magnified man. They perceived that in man the presence of a single will made all his powers, bodily and spiritual, work harmoniously together towards a predetermined end; and reasoning by analogy, they affirmed that society in like manner must be under the unconditional rule of a single will. The individual man, they said, were he to be subject to a multitude of wills, would be torn in pieces by divers passions impelling him this way and that; and so also in the State, any division or limitation of authority would necessarily introduce conflicting purposes destroying the unity and wrecking the peace of the body politic. The Persians did not shrink from the extremest consequences of this theory. They were the most abject slaves of royalty the world has ever seen. And consequently, with the fall of the last monarch of the Sassanides, the empire collapsed, like a man stabbed to the heart.

But in the provinces, thus easily overrun, there was much that was imperishable. There the mightiest monarchies the world had seen had flourished and decayed; and the people clung with devoted enthusiasm to these remembrances of past greatness and splendour. These lands had been a sort of common seed-field where the thoughts of Greek and Hindoo, Jew and Christian, had mingled together to result in that profound conception of man and the world, as a battle-field for the warring powers of light and darkness. The reverence for intellectual light, as symbolised by fire, had covered the land with magnificent temples, and imposed upon its inhabitants, as the most important of their duties, that of striving constantly against the principle of evil. Darkness, so said some of these old sages, had rushed into the regions of Light; like clouds around the setting sun, the intruder was irradiated with a fitful beauty, and shot through and through with gleams of splendour; but the Light strove in vain to emancipate itself from the embraces of Darkness; like a man sinking in a quagmire, every effort which it made to ascend, only resulted in engulphing it more deeply.

Not unlike this ancient parable was the destiny of ancient Persia in the presence of Islam. She lit it up with a glory not its own, but gradually sank in the darkness which she could beautify, but had not the power to overcome. Nevertheless, to her idea of Light as the final goal of man, of Evil or Darkness as something monstrous and alien to his nature, is to be attributed almost all that there is of spiritual warmth and light in the religious history of Islam; while to the empire of the Sassanides the Muhammadan world owes its administrative machinery. This had been brought to great perfection. An elaborate method for surveying and assessing the cultivated land had been introduced by Nushirwan the Just, and completed by his successors. The provinces of the empire were united to the capital by an admirable system of posts. Great high roads traversed the country; and along these at easy stages were picketed 'the king's horses,' for the use of the royal messengers carrying despatches to and fro between Madain and the various provinces. The cities, large and small, were under a careful supervision. According to the population, there was a fixed number of artificers, merchants, soldiers, and caterers for the public amusement. This number was forbidden to be increased, as the rest of the population was supposed to be employed in agriculture, and any decrease in their number would, it was held, have endangered the food supply. Royal hospitals were in all the large cities, where physicians appointed by the king attended gratuitously to the sick; special buildings were set apart for the women, and here the patients were attended by female physicians; and along the great highways, karavanserais were erected at convenient distances to afford shelter to travellers. The Arabs, barbarous and unskilled, had no choice but to adopt in its entirety the administrative machinery of their predecessors, and to entrust its management to the people they had conquered. Accordingly, until the reign of the khalif Abd al Malek, the *divans*, or official bureaux, in Irak and Syria were not only entirely officered by Persians and Syrians, but in the former province all the records were kept in Persian, and in the latter in Greek. Abd al Malek was the first sovereign who altered this custom, and made Arabic the official language of the Muhammadan empire.

At first sight it may seem that this necessity would do much to reconcile the subject races to their new masters. But more than this is needed to fuse alien races into a harmonious unity. The experience of British rule in India shows that where the subtle and persuasive power of sympathy is wanting, where social equality does not or cannot exist, there the gulf which divides the conqueror from the conquered remains unfilled. Within the boundaries of Hindostan we have established peace, and placed within the reach of her people the intellectual treasures which the happier West has accumulated, but we are farther than ever from winning their affections. Never, perhaps, did the people of India regard the Englishman with a profounder dislike than at the present day. There are hundreds of educated Muhammadans and Hindoos in that country who are as clearly convinced as any European of the falseness of their ancestral beliefs, the incompatibility of their old ways of life with intellectual and social progress. But such convictions do not detach them from the external profession of those beliefs, the diligent observance of those obsolete practices. They cling to them as a kind of protest against the conqueror. They prefer to bury themselves in the darkness, than be led towards the light by guides whom they abhor. And why is this? It is because the presence of the Englishman in India is a wound inflicted on their self-respect, which never heals, which the experience of almost every day causes to bleed afresh. The Englishman does not mean to lacerate their feelings. He cannot help conveying in his speech, his manners, and his actions, that calm, undoubting conviction of immeasurable superiority with which he is inwardly possessed; his exclusiveness is due, partly of course, to his insular rigidity, but far more to the constitution of native society which renders free intercourse between the two races simply impossible. But, on the other hand, it is not strange that the native should be unable to make allowances for difficulties of this kind. He only sees an alien race settled in the land which his ancestors ruled, and conducting themselves as though they were beings made of a finer clay than the people whom they govern. He knows and feels that he cannot enter their presence without being reminded at every instant that he is regarded as an inferior. His inability to resent the tacit insult (for so he regards it), his powerlessness to free himself from the strong hand which holds him in his grasp, tend, of course, to intensify the bitterness of his hate. What we have done for India is to convert it into a gigantic model prison. The discipline we have established is admirable, but the people know they are prisoners, and they hate us as their jailers. And until a prison is found to be an effective school for the inculcation of virtue, and a jailer a successful evangelist, it is folly to expect the regeneration of India. Reports on her material and moral progress will, of course, continue to be written, but if we estimate the effects of British rule, not by trade statistics, but by its results on the spirit of man, we shall find that the races of India have declined in courage and manliness, and all those qualities which produce a vigorous nation, in proportion to the period they have been subjected to the blighting influence of an alien despotism. There is no human power which can avail to arrest the progress of decay in a people bereft of political freedom, except the restitution of that freedom. This sentence of doom glares forth from the records of all past history, like the writing of fire on the wall of Belshazzar's palace. It is an hallucination to suppose that British rule in India is a reversal of the inexorable decree.

The rule of the Arabs in Asia was marked by all the defects of British rule in India, aggravated tenfold, and possessed none of its compensations. The last revelation of Muhammad to the Faithful had been the mandate of universal war. He had consecrated and set apart for Divine uses the ferocity, lust, and greed of a savage and bloodthirsty people. The indulgence of these to the uttermost he had affirmed to be the surest method of forcing an entrance into Paradise. 'Do the Faithful imagine,' he had said, 'that the giving of drink to the pilgrims, and the visiting of the holy places, are actions as meritorious as those performed by him who fighteth for the cause of God? They shall not be held equal with God.' The events which followed immediately on the death of Muhammad seemed to impart a prophetic signification to these words. All Arabia, except the Hejaz, fell away from the new faith; but the divided and undisciplined tribes were everywhere defeated by the trained armies of the Faithful. The revolts were suppressed with terrible severity. The small patches of cultivated land were laid waste; the wealth of the tribes—their camels, their horses, and their flocks were carried off and sent to Medina. At this moment the khalif Abou Bekr proclaimed the war of religion against Syria and Persia. One host assembled at Medina, another at Yemama. It was not an ordinary military invasion, but an emigration. The tribes who had lost all they possessed, and saw famine staring them in the face, perceived that in war and robbery existed the only hope of subsistence for themselves, their wives, and their children. As the tidings of their marvellous victories, of the wealth they had acquired, of the hosts of captive damsels who literally made for the Faithful a Paradise upon earth, were borne back to the deserts they had abandoned, their compatriots who still roamed over those inhospitable wastes were irresistibly impelled to follow in the track of those who had gone before them. Thus the ravages of war were made good, and thus new hosts were continually created to extend further and further the margin of conquest. When, at last, the final limit was reached, it was found that in each subjected province the tribe or tribes which had overrun it, formed a kind of standing army which held the people in subjection. They built military encampments, in which they lived, divided according to their tribes and families. In Irak, for example, these great military stations were Koufa, Basra, and subsequently Wasit; in Syria they were Damascus, Emessa, Kinnesrin, and others; in Khorasan, Merou and Ispahan.

It was the conception of the khalif Omar to form the whole body of the Faithful into a gigantic military community supported at the cost of the races they subdued. With this end in view, the Faithful were prohibited from acquiring any rights of property in the conquered soil. The produce from the various taxes levied on the subject people was paid into the central treasury at Medina; and the tribes received from thence a monthly stipend, their provisions being supplied gratuitously at the cost of the district on which they were quartered. The khalif hoped to achieve a double end by this regulation. By prohibiting the sale of land to the Arabs, he provided against a wholesale emigration of the conquered peoples. And by converting the Faithful into a purely military caste, he trusted to preserve them untainted by the contaminating influences of luxury and heresy. To promote this last object—to foster the natural pride of the Arab, and bring constantly and clearly before his mind the infinite worth of the Faithful, and the degradation of all other races, he also devised a multitude of humiliations for the Fire-worshippers and the polytheists, *i.e.* Persians, Jews, and Christians. The *Zimmis* (*i.e.* unbelievers) were not to ride on horses or mules or valuable asses; and they were on no account to make use of ornamented saddles. They were to mount on such beasts as it was lawful for them to use only in back streets and solitary places. In public places, where the Faithful were collected and liable to be scandalised by the disgraceful spectacle of a mounted Zimmi, they must proceed on foot. The Zimmis were not to collect together in public places for purposes of conversation; they were not to walk along the pathway so as to encumber the free progress of the Faithful; they were not permitted to speak with a loud voice in the presence of the Faithful; neither were they to have servants following them; and still less to have domestics to clear the road before them. They were not to wear fine clothing, but to appear in public in plain and coarse garments; they were always to rise and salute when a Moslem approached them; the dress of their women must be clearly distinguished from the dress of the Moslem women in order to guard against the unspeakable scandal of a Moslem degrading himself by an act of courtesy towards them. The houses of the Zimmis must not rise higher than those of the Moslems, and the exteriors were not to be decorated. Every Zimmi must provide food and shelter for three days and three nights to any Moslem demanding them of him. Free access to their sacred buildings must be given to any Moslem who desired to sojourn in them; and the doors, if necessary, must be enlarged to enable him to do so with ease.

The manner of paying the tribute or head-tax imposed on all unbelievers was elaborately set forth: 'Upon the day fixed the Zimmi shall go in person, and not by the agency of a *vakeel*, to the house of the official charged with the duty of collecting the poll tax; the latter is to be seated on an elevated daïs in fashion like a throne; the Zimmi will come forward, carrying the tax in the palm of his hand, from whence the officer will take it in such a manner that his hand shall be above and that of the Zimmi below. After this the officer will strike the Zimmi a blow with his fist on the nape of his neck; and a man will stand ready near the officer, thereupon to hustle the Zimmi forcibly out of the room; then a second, then a third, presenting themselves in like manner, will be subjected to similar treatment, as well as all who shall follow. All the Faithful shall be admitted to enjoy this spectacle. It shall not be permitted to any of them to employ a deputy for the payment of this tax; it is necessary that they should experience, each in his own person, this mark of humiliation; because, perhaps, they will thereby be brought to believe in God and His prophet.'

Omar's decree prohibiting the Faithful to become landholders in the countries they had overrun was broken through by his successors, but the arrogant, bigoted, and inhuman spirit of his other legislation was too much in harmony with the teaching of the Prophet to fall into desuetude. It has, in effect, been the formative power which to this day moulds and regulates the policy of the entire Muhammadan world. Sunk in an ever-deepening barbarism, a prey to almost every evil, social and political, which can descend upon much enduring humanity, the Muhammadan still conceives himself to be the elect of God. He regards, not with compassion—that word is too humane—but with contempt unspeakable, as 'logs' reserved for 'hell fire,' the votaries of all other creeds. Wherever he has the power, he holds it to be his mission to trample upon and persecute them. If the Faithful, fallen as they are upon evil days, be such as we see them now, conceive what they must have been in the first flush of their early triumphs, 'when the nations lay prone in their porches, and the world was a steed for their rein.' It will not then be hard to understand the intensity of hate with which the Persians regarded their arrogant masters—these Arabs, whom, in the days of their splendour, they had been wont to regard as the least among the nations.[1]

The Arabs cared little to make proselytes to their creed. Indeed, the majority of the Faithful had reduced their creed to the simple intellectual acknowledgment of the unity of God. That, they held, sufficed to ensure the salvation of a Muhammadan. 'How are you prepared,' said Hasan al Basri to the libertine poet, Farazdak, as they walked side by side in a funeral procession—'how are you prepared for a day like this?' 'By the testimony that I have borne for sixty years to the unity of God,' was the calm reply. And that in so saying the profligate poet did not offend against the religious sense of his countrymen is evidenced by the narrative which is generally appended by way of commentary to the above

[1] Makrisi is the only Arabic historian who has preserved for us any details of the internal government of the Arabs at this early period of their history. The information he gives is confined to Egypt, but there is no reason to suppose that this province was more harshly treated than other parts of the dominions of the khalif. Among many other equally significant facts, he tells us that the monks being liable to the capitation tax were ordered to be branded on the hands with an iron ring in which were inscribed their names and the convent to which they belonged. Those who could not exhibit this mark had their hands hacked off, and many were for the same reason beheaded or beaten to death.

saying. A female belonging to the tribe of Tamim declared that Farazdak was seen in a dream, and being asked how the Lord had treated him, he answered: 'He pardoned me.' Being then asked for what reason, he replied: 'For a word which I said in a conversation with Hasan al Basri.' As for the subject races, the Arabs preferred that these should remain in unbelief, as only then were they liable to a capitation tax. The holy Prophet had declared that the Arabs 'were the best folk that had been raised up among mankind;' that they 'enjoined the just and forbade the evil.' The legislation of the khalif Omar brought out this agreeable truth in clear relief. It demonstrated the high value of the Arab; it reduced all other races to the level of dogs and swine. As establishing this great fact, the leaders in Islam were bound to see it exactly and rigorously executed.

But such petty indignities were to the ardent and devout among the Faithful a very unsatisfactory fulfilling of the law. They loved to marshal in long array all the passages from the Koran which set forth the nature of infidelity. They regarded these as so many delineations of the inner state of Jews, Christians, and Fire-worshippers, painted by the hand of God Himself. And what did they affirm? They declared that 'as for the infidels, their wealth and their children would avail them nothing against God. They would be the inmates of the fire, to abide therein eternally.' They warned the true believer not to take infidels for their friends—that 'whoso did this had nothing to hope from God.' The infidels would not fail to corrupt them. They longed for the ruin of the Faithful. Hatred was in their mouths, but more grievous was that which their bosoms concealed. The Moslem who consorted with them would assuredly become like to them, and so furnish God with a 'clear right' to punish him. The purity of the faith could be preserved only by a complete separation from those who disbelieved in God and rejected the mission of His Prophet. To confer offices of public trust in a Muhammadan state on men accursed of God and reserved hereafter for 'the lowest abyss of the fire,' was clearly a breach of the Divine commandment. Such a state of things might be tolerated by the free-thinking khalifs of the House of Ommaya, but with the accession of a devout Muhammadan like the khalif Omar ibn Abd al Aziz to the headship of God's people, it necessarily came to an end. One of Omar's first acts was to publish an order throughout his dominions to expel summarily from their places in the administration all functionaries who did not believe in Allah and His Prophet. 'O believers!' he wrote, 'those who associate other gods with God are unclean. God has ranged them on the side of Satan. He has rendered them, by reason of their actions, the most accursed among men. . . . . . I have been told that formerly when the armies of the Faithful entered a country the polytheists came to meet them, and that the true believers accepted of their assistance in the administration on account of their sound judgment and the knowledge they possessed as secretaries and in the levying of the impost; but there can be neither experience nor judgment among those who provoke the wrath of God and of His Prophet. . . . . . Their suppression is for you a duty not less than the destruction of their faith.

Restore them, then, to the state of disgrace and degradation to which God has assigned them; and let each of you inform me what he has done in his province.'

This sweeping decree was put forth about a year before the revolt of Yezid ibn Mouhalleb, and doubtless contributed much towards that eager sympathy in his success which was awakened amid the provinces of the old Persian monarchy. But it had another, and, for the khalifs of the House of Ommaya, a much more disastrous result. It brought about the nominal conversion of crowds of Persians. These new converts affected an excessive zeal for the rights of the House of Ali. They vehemently affirmed the verity of the mission of Muhammad; but by means of arguments which I have already set forth, they demonstrated the impossibility of reconciling a belief in that mission with an allegiance to the House of Ommaya—that house which had never ceased to persecute and slaughter the family of the blessed Prophet and those who loved it. The blessed Prophet had declared that the martyrs Hasan and Hosain were among the chief of those in Paradise; the khalifs of the House of Ommaya cursed them from all their pulpits. Here, then, was a clear issue; if the Prophet were the elect of Heaven, it was plain that the khalifs who cursed his offspring must be the children of the Evil One. This teaching, enforced as it was by the lax and luxurious lives of the sovereigns assailed, and the constant endurance of wrong, attracted numerous believers; and Muhammad, when he chose Khorasan for the theatre of his operations, came in contact with a people already ripe for revolt.

The Oriental is a passionate gambler, and likes no game so well as that where his own life is staked against a kingdom. From among the nominally converted Persians, Muhammad found no difficulty in collecting a body of followers to aid him in his hazardous enterprise. The one thing still to be done was to give to the movement a religious character. It must not be a revolt against Islam, but an endeavour to restore the faith to its primal purity. Any open endeavour to subvert the Muhammadan faith by means of the subject races would have stilled the noise of domestic feuds among the Arabs, and united them as one man against the aggressors. Muhammad and his friends perceived and bowed to this necessity. They must either preach war in favour of the Imams of the House of Ali, or proclaim Muhammad himself as the veritable Imam. It is impossible to understand these earlier annals of Islam unless we enter into this eager and passionate longing after an Imam, or spiritual head. It was a desire engendered and fed by the ceaseless disorder of the times. Men cried aloud, in the anguish of their souls, that the last and greatest of the prophets could never have intended this heritage of misery to descend upon the Faithful. There must be somewhere upon earth the true interpreter of his will, the divinely-appointed leader and chief of the believers. Hitherto every revolt against the House of Ommaya had been undertaken for the Imams of the House of Ali. The arguments in favour of their title were irrefutable but for one great fact which robbed them of much of their cogency. And this was their uniform ill success. Since Hosain had fallen on the field of Kerbela, chief after chief had proclaimed the cause of his house and taken the field in its name; but all had perished—Suleiman, al Moktar, Yezid ibn Mouhalleb, and many another. Was it possible that those who upheld a divine cause should be thus persistently worsted? Was it not rather a proof that the men for whom they had fought and failed were, in truth, not the veritable Imams of Islam? Who then were so? Assuredly not these accursed khalifs of the House of Ommaya, who had sacked Medina and burned the Kaaba, the very House of God? Such was the dilemma which enabled Muhammad to interpose, and suggest a third solution of the difficulty.

The difficulty, he admitted, was a real one, for, in fact, these unfortunate descendants of the martyrs Hasan and Hosain were not the veritable Imams of Islam. On the murder of Hosain at Kerbela, the Imamate had not been transmitted to his surviving son, but to Muhammad ibn al Hanafiya, another son of the khalif Ali, and so called because his mother was a member of the tribe of Hanifa. He was the divinely-chosen Imam. He had never died, but had been translated from the earth to some unknown valley, where, together with forty of his friends, he received his sustenance from God. On one side of him was a lion, on the other a panther, and near him were two springs running—the one with water and the other with honey. This Muhammad had transmitted the dignity of Imam to his son Abou Hashim, and Abou Hashim, when on his death-bed, attended by a number of his followers, had summoned Muhammad ibn Ali to his presence, and addressed him in these words: 'Up to the present hour we have believed that the Imamate belonged to us, but from this day there is no further doubt on this subject; and we render homage to the truth when we declare that you are the veritable Imam, and that your children will sit on the throne of the khalifs. Hasten, then, to Koufa, where you will find faithful partisans.'

In that credulous age this legend sufficed for the consolation of those whose faith had been staggered by the abortive efforts of al Moktar and others to overthrow the House of Ommaya. To blind those who still clung to the descendants of Hasan and Hosain, the missionaries of Muhammad affirmed that they were working for 'the family of Muhammad.' Under this ambiguous title, the family of Abbas had hitherto co-operated with the children of Ali. The representatives and adherents of that unfortunate house little suspected the treachery that was hidden beneath the well-known expression, and extended their favour and protection over those who were plotting their ruin. But the mainspring of the movement lay in its appeal to the vanquished Persians to rise against their Arab oppressors. The leading missionaries of Muhammad were men of Persian extraction. To their own countrymen they proclaimed, not a creed, at which they themselves scoffed, but an approaching day of deliverance. The Arabs in Khorasan, busy with their feuds, and encased in their haughty exclusiveness, paid little heed to the mine that was being dug under their feet. Now and again an Abbaside missionary would be seized by an angry and alarmed governor and promptly put to death; but, like ourselves in India, the Arabs held themselves too far aloof from the people they ruled, to track the ramifications of a movement like this. Silently, but with extreme swiftness, the province of Khorasan became virtually a province ruled by the House of Abbas. In every city there was formed a party who waited only for the signal to rise in arms. And the triumph of the rising cause was assured by the conversion of the celebrated Abou Moslem the Khorasani, the chief agent in the overthrow of the Ommayas and the triumph of the Abbasides.

The accounts given of the origin and early life of this eastern king-maker are confusing and contradictory, but we find him some time in A.H. 123 or 124 at Mekka in attendance upon some partisans of the House of Abbas who had gone thither to pay their respects to the Imam. In the frequent visits they paid to Muhammad ibn Ali, Abou Moslem accompanied them. The Imam one day enquired of them if the young man was a slave or not. They replied that they did not know; he himself asserted that he was free; but the family whom he served declared that he was a slave. Muhammad replied: 'I know not what he may be; but I see in him a highly intelligent young man, and from many signs I have observed, I predict that he will be one of the most ardent promoters of our dynasty.' 'O Imam!' cried his hearers, 'when will that be, for the power of the Ommayas endures eternally?' Muhammad answered: 'By God! it shall be in our day. I have heard my father say that "*in the year of the ass*" God will cause our power to appear; our work of proselytism will terminate, and the reign of the Ommayas come to an end. The black banner will be raised in Merou and all Khorasan, and the Bani Ommaya will fall by the sword in caves and behind rocks.' They asked of Muhammad the meaning of the expression 'the year of the ass.' 'No dynasty,' he replied, 'has passed the hundredth year of its existence without violent commotions which have brought it to ruin. Remember what is written in the Koran: "Or how he demeaned him who passed by a city which had been laid in ruins." "How," said he, "shall God give life to this city after she hath been dead?" And God caused him to die for an hundred years, and then raised him to life. And God said: "How long hast thou waited?" He said: "I have waited a day or part of a day." He said: "Nay, thou hast waited an hundred years. Look on thy food and thy drink; they are not corrupted; and look on thine ass: we would make thee a sign unto men. And look on the bones of thine ass: how we will raise them, then clothe them with flesh." And when this was shown to him he said: "I acknowledge that God hath power to do all things" (Sura II. v. 261). The time is now at hand. Know that we are in the "year of the ass," the hundredth year of the reign of the Ommayas, and that this young man will defend our cause. Watch him; when he gives the signal, follow his example and give him aid and assistance. As for me, you will see me no more after this year; for I feel that my strength is waning and the time of my departure near at hand. But my son Ibrahim will succeed me, and should misfortune light upon him, there is my other son Abdallah' (subsequently the first of the Abbaside khalifs), 'and should aught occur to him, there is my third son Abdallah Abou Djafar' (afterwards the second of the Abbaside khalifs).[1]

[1] I do not vouch for the authenticity of this singular prophecy. I have inserted it merely as an illustration of the method of interpreting the Koran, which recommends itself to Muhammadan theologians as natural and obvious, at the present day as much as in the old time.

Muhammad died A.H. 124 or 125, and his son Ibrahim was recognised as Imam. Abou Moslem remained in Ibrahim's service, accompanying him in his travels and staying with him wherever he took up his residence. But before a year, or at the most two, had elapsed, the khalif Walid had been murdered, his successor Yezid had followed him to the grave after a brief and tumultuous reign of six months, and the khalif Merwan had ascended the tottering throne of the Ommayas. Then broke forth that whirlwind of pent-up hate and revenge which I attempted to describe in my last chapter. Everywhere the rival Arab tribes abandoned their guard over the subject races to seize each other by the throat and wrestle in a death-struggle. The hour had struck for which the down-trodden populations of Khorasan had waited so long. Their leaders called on Ibrahim to send a man to place himself at the head of the movement. He despatched Abou Moslem. 'I have put him,' he said, 'to the test, and know his interior as well as his exterior; he is the rock of the earth, and will crush all before him.'

CHAPTER V.

THE FALL OF THE OMMAYAS.

A.D. 743–750.

NOWHERE in the Muhammadan empire had the rivalry and the hatred between the Arabs of Yemen and the tribes of Modhar been so keen and bitter as in Khorasan. There the Yemenite Arabs were represented by the tribe of Azd—the brotherhood to which belonged the family of Mouhalleb—and the Arabs of Modhar, by the tribe of Temim—the most numerous and powerful of those included in the Maadique confederation. As Yemenite or Modharite influence preponderated at Damascus, the chiefs in Khorasan of the one party or the other acquired the power to humiliate and oppress their rivals. Thus Kutaiba, the favourite of Hejjaj, had imprisoned or put to death the partisans of the family of Mouhalleb; himself falling a victim to the rage of the Azdites when the death of the khalif Walid elevated Yezid ibn Mouhalleb to the first place in the Muhammadan empire. With the fall of Yezid, the Arabs of Modhar regained the pre-eminence; but during the earlier years of the reign of the khalif Hisham, we find a Yemenite chief at the head of the province—Asad, a brother of that Khalid ibn Abdallah al Kasri whose murder I related in a previous chapter. This

Asad, enraged by the ill success of an expedition he had made beyond the Oxus, summoned to his presence the chiefs of the Arabs of Modhar, and attributing the ill fortune of his arms to their evil counsels, he caused them to be stripped and beaten, their beards to be shaven (the very greatest indignity that can be put upon a Muhammadan), and sent them as prisoners, heavily chained, to his brother in Irak. For these outrageous proceedings he was deprived of his office by the khalif Hisham, and a Modhar chief appointed in his stead. This change naturally had no effect in stilling the spirit of rivalry, and accordingly, a few years after, we find a Yemenite chief in open rebellion against the governor of Khorasan, and holding as his own a large number of the towns of Khorasan.

During the events related in the last chapter Khorasan had been governed by a Modharite Arab, Nasr ibn Seyaur. He had been among those whom Asad ibn Abdallah had shaven and beaten; and he flung himself into the quarrels between the two Arab races with all the ardour of a man smarting under a keen sense of undeserved injury. The Yemenites were expelled from all posts of trust and emolument; the cities of Khorasan were entrusted exclusively to Arabs of the tribes of Modhar; by every means in his power Nasr ibn Seyaur sought to make his enemies feel the bitterness of subjection. The head man of the Yemenites at this time was a man of the tribe of Azd, and a cousin of the great Mouhalleb. His name was Djodai ibn Ali; but he is known in history by the designation of 'the Kermani,' from the circumstance that he was born in the province of Kerman. The Arabs of

Yemen gathered round him, and besought him to wait upon Nasr ibn Seyaur, and endeavour to mitigate the severity with which they were treated. The Kermani undertook the mission; but Nasr ibn Seyaur, who had received intelligence of the great victory gained by the khalif Merwan at Ain Aldjarr, responded to these complaints by throwing the Kermani into prison. This harsh treatment had the effect of hurrying the Yemenites into open rebellion. They succeeded in liberating the Kermani by means of an underground passage; and his fortified house, not far from Merou, the seat of the government of Khorasan, became the rallying point of the rebels.

Nasr perceived too late the impolicy of his actions. The khalif, hemmed in by enemies, was unable to send him relief. He had to guard against a vigilant and active enemy beyond the frontier. He knew his own province to be honeycombed by the ramifications of the Abbaside conspiracy. And now, by his own harsh temper, he had driven the Yemenites to revolt. The party, moreover, which had gathered round the Kermani was continually fed by the relics of the Yemenite armies which Merwan was attacking and scattering with such tremendous vigour in Irak. The rebellion, hewn in pieces by the sword of the Khalif, in the western provinces, was collecting its scattered members, and renewing its vigour in the eastern. Nasr did what he could to dissipate the storm he had conjured up. He sent messenger after messenger to induce the Kermani to relinquish his hostile attitude. But his envoys were repulsed with insults and threats. At last he ventured to attack him. Three bodies of chosen men were sent in succession to assail the fortified house where the

Kermani resided. They were routed with heavy loss. The civil war had now fairly commenced. The inhabitants of Merou barricaded the doors of their houses and closed their shops. The two hostile parties formed entrenched camps outside the city; and for a year a desultory war of skirmishes was kept up.

Abou Moslem had worked in secret till the civil war broke out between the Kermani and the governor of Khorasan. He now perceived that the moment had come to strike. He sent word to his partisans in all the cities of Khorasan to raise the standard of revolt. The cause was proclaimed to be the rights of 'the People of the House' against the usurpation of the Ommayas. A short time previously a grandson of the Imam, Zain-al-Aibadin, had revolted and been killed, and his body was exposed upon a gibbet. This gave Abou Moslem the means to conceal his real purpose and effectually deceive the Yemenites, who were adherents of the House of Ali. He ordered the remains of the Imam to be taken down and buried with every possible mark of honour; and as a symbol at once of their grief and their resolve to be revenged, he directed his followers to clothe themselves in black—which colour remained ever after the distinguishing mark of the House of Abbas. The despatch of these orders revealed the enormous extent to which the missionaries of the Abbasides had spread their doctrines. The black garments of the revolt thronged the streets of every city, and crowded every village. It was the vanquished Persian people rising as one man against their Arab conquerors. The bloody work of reprisals was commenced without delay. The partisans of the House of Ommaya were hunted and killed like vermin. Eighty thousand of them are said to have been massacred; but this is a wild and impossible exaggeration. While these events were occurring in the province, Abou Moslem sent a message to the Kermani, offering to assist him against Nasr ibn Seyaur, and on receiving an affirmative response, joined him with a thousand chosen soldiers.

Nasr beheld with alarm the tempest that had gathered so blackly and with such swiftness. He hurried one missive after another to the khalif Merwan, entreating speedy aid. He warned him that there was a movement commencing in Khorasan which 'would blanch with terror the heads of children.' Merwan did not underrate the peril. He was anxious to proceed in person to Khorasan; but feared, if he did so, he should lose his hold upon Syria. In the end, he could only send Nasr directions to do the best he could with the means at his disposal. Nasr turned in despair to Omar ibn Hobaira, the governor of Irak; but that officer, at death-grips with the Kharegites, could not spare a man to aid his colleague in Khorasan; and Nasr played his last card in an attempt to sow discord between the Kermani and his new ally, Abou Moslem. He wrote to the Kermani, warning him against the treachery of Abou Moslem, and proposing a conference to arrange the terms of a reconciliation between the Arab tribes, and a plan of action against the common enemy. This letter the Kermani showed to Abou Moslem; and it was agreed between them that he should accept the proposal of Nasr ibn Seyaur, and murder him during the interview. Each of the chiefs, it had been agreed, was to appear at the interview, attended by five hundred followers; but the

Kermani was so elated at the cleverness of the contrivance by which he hoped to make away with his old enemy, and drank so many bumpers of wine to his own prosperity, that he arrived at the place of meeting thoroughly intoxicated, and incapable of giving any orders to his followers. Nasr, who had repaired thither with a design precisely the same, found it unexpectedly easy of execution; and one of his attendants transfixed the jovial Kermani with his lance. His treachery brought him no advantage. Abou Moslem no sooner heard of the murder of his ally than he attacked Nasr in his entrenched encampment, and after an obstinate struggle drove him and his troops to take refuge in Merou.

The death of the Kermani was, in truth, a great gain to the cause of the rebellion. It moved out of the way one who might have been a dangerous rival of Abou Moslem, and made the latter the sole and unquestioned head of the movement. He was a man fit for the crisis. 'Low in stature,' writes a contemporary, 'of a tawny complexion, with handsome features and engaging manners, he was never observed to laugh; the gravest events could hardly disturb the serenity of his countenance; he received news of the most important victories without expressing the least symptom of joy; under the greatest reverses of fortune he never betrayed the slightest uneasiness; and when angered he never lost his self-control.' This impassive exterior concealed a heart as hard as flint and pitiless as death. He never spared an enemy or forgave a fault. The inhabitants of Khorasan trembled before him; the taxes were paid with a regularity and promptitude long unknown; and he was prayed for in the mosques as the representative of the family of Muhammad. Nasr abandoned the struggle in despair; and remained inactive in his house in Merou. Abou Moslem summoned four of his principal officers, and directed them to repair to the house of Nasr ibn Seyaur, and inform him that Abou Moslem had communications of importance to make to him, and to assure him of safety if he would repair to his camp. The deputation went and delivered the message, but one of their number, urged by a sudden impulse of compassion, let fall a quotation from the Koran to suggest to Nasr the fate which awaited him if he credited the assurances of Abou Moslem. Nasr understood the hint; he replied to the deputation that he would be at their service in a few moments. Then going into an inner apartment, he let himself down through the window into the garden. The night had fallen; and under cover of the darkness Nasr, mounted on a favourite horse, and accompanied by a single attendant, fled to Nishapore. The deputation, after waiting a long time in expectation of his return, perceived that their intended victim had broken through his toils. Abou Moslem, when he learned the particulars of the interview, at once divined the cause which had awakened the suspicions of Nasr; and the quoter of the Koran lost his head as a penalty for his untimely benevolence. Abou Moslem entered Merou the next day; the house of Nasr ibn Seyaur he caused to be pillaged and burnt; and the officials, high and low, of the late administration were seized and executed. Nasr himself escaped, only to die of dysentery brought on by fatigue and anxiety.

Khorasan was now in the possession of Abou Moslem. Nothing as yet had been divulged of the ultimate purpose of the movement. 'The People of the House,' was the watchword everywhere proclaimed; and that ensured the neutrality of the Shia where it did not incite his active co-operation. The death of Nasr set free Abou Moslem to despatch an army into Irak. One success rapidly followed upon another; and though Omar ibn Hobaira still kept the field at the head of a formidable and unbroken force, the city of Koufa was delivered over by a sort of popular vote to the chief of the insurgent army. The policy of concealment could be maintained no longer. The excitable population of Koufa was wrought up to the highest pitch of impatience and curiosity as Hasan ibn Khataba—the lieutenant of Abou Moslem—filed into the city at the head of his troops. Rumour, of course, was busy with her hundred tongues speculating on the next event of the great drama unfolding before them. Hasan continued to dissimulate to the last moment. Abou Salama Jaffier—the agent or vizier of the House of Ali—waited upon him, and was received with the utmost honour and deference. 'My master,' Hasan said, 'has ordered me to obey you in all things.' A proclamation was issued in the name of Abou Salama and in that of Hasan ibn Kahtaba, inviting the inhabitants to meet next day at the principal mosque. At the appointed hour the mosque was crowded; not a person of respectability stayed away. The object of the assembly had been studiously concealed, and the curiosity of the multitude was intense. It was, however, condemned to remain yet awhile unsatisfied. Abou Salama, after conducting the public prayer as usual, simply dismissed the assembly, requesting all who could mount a horse or put on armour to appear the next day in the same place, arrayed in black, to swear allegiance to the new khalif.

On the next morning at break of day the streets of Koufa appeared all shrouded in black; the people hastened to the mosque in prodigious crowds, in black turbans and vestures, and with black banners floating above them. In due time Abou Salama appeared, also clothed in black. After leading the prayers he addressed the people, and asked of them if they were willing to acquiesce in the act he was about to propose to them. They demanded an explanation. He then proceeded to say that Abou Moslem, the representative of the family of the Prophet, had determined to deliver the world from the tyranny of the House of Ommaya. With this purpose in view, he had sought for a new leader in Islam, but had discovered nowhere a person so eminent for piety and ability as Abdallah, the son of Muhammad, the great grandson of the pious and learned Abbas, of the House of Hashim, and of the family of the Prophet. Him, therefore, he had selected, and he now hoped that his choice would be confirmed by the approbation of the Faithful in Koufa. The fickleness of the people of Koufa had passed into a proverb. From the days of Ali to the present time they had wavered between two opinions—now espousing the cause of his family, and shedding their blood like so much water in its defence; then, with a sudden revulsion of feeling, abandoning them to slaughter, nay, even actively aiding in their destruction. Their loyalty to his descendants had invariably been the love of a Dalilah which lures its victim to his death; and they were now to give the most memorable illustration of this fickle and uncertain temperament. The last word had hardly passed the lips of Abou Salama when the air was rent with the shouts of the applauding multitude; the assembly declared with one voice that the choice must have been the result of a Divine inspiration; and the awful shout of 'God is most powerful!' was caught up and repeated again and again by the enthusiastic crowd. Abdallah was at that moment hidden in Koufa; but to explain how he came there, and why he was thus selected by Abou Moslem to be the first in the long line of Abbaside khalifs, we must go back to the period when Nasr ibn Seyaur escaped from Khorasan.

On reaching a place of safety, Nasr's first care was to inform the khalif Merwan that he had abandoned Khorasan, and that a movement had commenced there which would terminate only with the overthrow of the House of Ommaya. Merwan was at this time encamped in Harran. He had not finished reading the letter, when some of his officers brought before him a courier sent from Khorasan by Abou Moslem to the Imam Ibrahim, to acquaint him of the progress of events in that province. Having perused the intercepted letter, the khalif turned to the bearer of it. 'How much,' he asked, 'has your master paid you for this business?'—'Such and such a sum.' 'Only so much! then he has paid you but badly. See, here are ten thousand dirhems for you. Take that letter to Ibrahim; reveal to him nothing of what has happened here, and bring me his reply.' The man obeyed. Merwan read the reply which Ibrahim had written with his own hand, urging Abou Moslem to redouble his efforts, and giving him a variety of directions. Merwan kept the courier in custody, and at the same time sent orders to the governor of Damascus to arrest Ibrahim, in the small town in which he was lying concealed. This was effected; and Ibrahim was brought, bound, into the presence of the khalif. When charged with complicity in the acts of Abou Moslem, he vehemently denied having any knowledge of the man. 'Villain that you are!' said the khalif, 'is not this your answer to the letter Abou Moslem wrote to you?' Then summoning the captured courier into the chamber, he added: 'Know you this man?' At the sight of the courier, Ibrahim perceived that he was lost, and remained mute. Merwan did not, however, put him to death. He knew that the Imam once dead a new one would be chosen; Ibrahim alive, but a prisoner, was harmless, and the insurrection deprived of a head. Ibrahim accordingly was thrown into a prison at Harran. But aware of the perils with which he was surrounded, he had, previous to his arrest, drawn up a testament making over the Imamate to his brother Abou'l Abbas Abdallah, should anything happen to him. This testament was entrusted to the care of a favourite freedman, who had orders, the instant that the toils closed upon Ibrahim, to hasten off to the residence of Abdallah, and hand over the document to him. This the freedman did. Abdallah enjoined him to keep the purpose of his coming secret. He then communicated the intelligence he had received to his brother Abou Jaafar Abdallah, his uncle Abdallah ibn Ali, and one or two others of his nearest relatives. They knew that Khorasan was now in possession of Abou Moslem, and that a large army had entered Irak in order to force a way to Koufa, where also they knew that the Abbaside missionaries had zealously laboured and won many partisans. They determined accordingly to journey disguised to Koufa, and there, concealed in the houses of their friends, await the coming of the army of Khorasan. On the journey thither they met and were recognised by an uncle of the young Abdallah. He inquired the purpose of this strange and hurried journey. Abdallah took him into their confidence. 'What!' said his uncle, amazed at their audacity; 'you think to possess yourself of Koufa, whilst that Merwan, the sheikh and prince of the Ommayas, in the midst of the populations of Syria and Mesopotamia, holds in awe that of Irak; whilst Ibn Hobaira, the sheikh of the Arabs, is obeyed in all the Arab tents of Irak!' 'Dear uncle,' replied Abdallah, 'he who loves his life must be content to vegetate.' And the uncle was so charmed by the daring spirit of his young nephew that he, too, turned the bridle of his horse, and accompanied him to Koufa. The party entered Koufa in the month of Safar, A.H. 132 (A.D. 749), and remained there in concealment till the entry of Hasan ibn Kahtaba and the army of Khorasan.

As soon as the shouts of the multitude gathered in the great mosque had ratified his proposal, Abou Salama despatched a message to the young khalif. He soon appeared, clothed from head to foot in sable garments and riding upon a she-camel. He ascended the pulpit, and delivered an address setting forth his zeal for Islam and his rights to the Imamate. A few days before he would assuredly have been destroyed as a heretic had he ventured to claim the dignity of Imam in a Koufa mosque; but that time was past and forgotten. The people of Koufa had no thought for the moment but to welcome the new sovereign; and the khalif had no sooner quitted the pulpit than the crowd trampled each other down in their frantic endeavours to get forward and proffer—each man personally—their allegiance and their homage. This scene took place on Friday, 12th of the second Rebi, A.H. 132 (October 28, A.D. 749).

On the intelligence reaching Harran that the people of Koufa had saluted Abdallah as khalif, Merwan caused his prisoner Ibrahim to be put to death by thrusting his head into a sack of quicklime. He then put himself at the head of a numerous army, and marched in the direction of Basra, picking up reinforcements as he went. An army, at the same time, under the command of Abdallah, an uncle of the Abbaside khalif, had left Koufa to meet Merwan, and the two hosts confronted each other on the banks of a small stream—the Zab—which flows a few miles distant from Mosule. The army of Merwan had the river in its rear. The battle lasted two days. At the close of the first day's fighting, the army of Merwan had decidedly the advantage. The courage and military skill of the Ommaya khalif seemed to be sufficient to deliver his throne from the very brink of destruction; when an accident changed the course of Muhammadan history. The second day's battle had joined; there was some wavering and indecision in the army of Merwan; it was partly composed of Yemenite Arabs, and these hesitated to advance against their compatriots in the opposite ranks. Merwan, who was on foot, hastened to fling himself on his horse, and lead on in person the Arabs of Modhar. The horse was one of singular spirit and beauty—surpassing, it is said, all the horses of that time; and just at this crisis it broke away from its groom, and galloped riderless through the ranks of the Syrian army. Believing their leader to be killed, the Syrian soldiers flung away their arms and fled in every direction. Three hundred of them were drowned in the waters of the Zab; and the slaughter in the flight was terrible. The luckless Merwan fled to Mosule; but the inhabitants refused to admit him, and donned the black uniform of the Abbasides. He went on without halting to Harran, where was the palace in which he ordinarily resided. This place had been distinguished by the warmth of its devotion to the House of Ommaya and the bitterness of its hatred to the family and relatives of Ali. But it, too, refused an asylum to the flying prince. Emessa, even Damascus, closed their gates; and he passed with the wreck of his army through Syria and Palestine, until he reached the confines of Egypt. Ten thousand men followed hard upon his traces. He continued his flight, burning and wasting the country behind him as far as Fostât, the ancient capital of Egypt. Fatigue and despair had greatly diminished the numbers of his followers; he continued his flight along the western bank of the Nile, his attendants falling away at every march, until he was left with only a single domestic. He had laid down to take a little rest in a small Christian chapel, when the place was surrounded by his pursuers. Determined to sell his life dearly, the hunted khalif rushed out, sword in hand, and fell transfixed with a lance. Thus perished the last eastern khalif of the House of Ommaya (Dzul Kada, A.H. 132).

The battle on the Zab decided the fate of the Muhammadan empire. No further resistance was made. The march of the Abbasides was a triumphal progress. The cities everywhere flung open their gates, and the inhabitants, clothed in black, received the victorious troops with shouts and acclamations. The Ommayas, terrified and hopeless, sought only to conceal themselves. The young Abbaside khalif entrusted to his uncle Daoud ibn Ali the government of the two holy cities, with orders to search out and put to death all the members of the family of Ommaya. The order was pitilessly executed. Search was made in the remotest spots, in the recesses of ruins, in every cave in the hill sides, and every fugitive found lurking there was put to death. The same instructions were sent to Abdallah, the victor in the battle on the Zab, who had assumed the government of Damascus. He had recourse to artifice to get his victims into his power. He caused proclamation to be made that an amnesty would be granted to all members of the House of Ommaya, and all partisans who would repair to the palace and take the oath of allegiance to the new khalif. The adherents of the fallen dynasty, rejoiced by this unlooked-for clemency, came in great numbers to the palace. There were eighty kinsmen and relatives of the late khalif, besides a crowd of followers and attendants. The treacherous Abdallah mingled in the assembly with a smiling and friendly countenance. But when he seated himself, apparently to receive the homage of the unsuspecting chiefs, his soldiers formed a circle round the Ommayas. At a preconcerted signal they fell upon their victims, beating them to the ground with blows from heavy maces; and, simultaneously with the slaughter within the palace, the servants and followers outside were massacred. When all was over, Abdallah ordered the bodies of the eighty chiefs, many of them still gasping in their last agonies, to be arranged in rows and covered with planks. On this dreadful table a gorgeous banquet was then spread for his officers and chief men, to heighten their rejoicing, so he said, 'with the last gasps of the Ommayas.' But the hatred of the young khalif—*as-Saffah*, or the Bloodshedder, as he was henceforth called—was not yet satisfied. He sent orders to his uncle to break open the tombs of the khalifs, take out their bones, and burn them.[1] Some of his victims were not allowed even the cruel mercy of a swift death. A grandson of the khalif Hisham had one hand and one foot cut off;

[1] Masoudi has inserted the following relation in that chapter of his 'Meadows of Gold' which treats of the reign of Hisham ibn Abd al Malek:—'Al-Haitham ibn Adi states that Omar ibn Hani related to him as follows: "I went forth with Abdallah ibn Ali, the uncle of as-Saffah and Al-Mansur. When we came to the tomb of the Omayide khalif Hisham ibn Abd al Malek, we dug out the body. It was in good preservation, and nothing was missing but the cartilage of the nose. Abd Allah gave it eighty strokes of a whip and then had it burnt. He then went to the territory of Dâbik (near Aleppo) and opened the grave of Sulaiman ibn Abd al Malek. There we found nothing more than the backbone, the skull, and the ribs. These we burned, and did the same with the other bodies of the Ommayas who were interred at Kinnesrin. We then went to Damascus and opened the grave of Walid ibn Abd al Malek, but found in it no remains, either great or small. We dug open the grave of Abd al Malek, and found only some bones of the skull. Having then opened the grave of Yezid ibn Muawia, we found in it only one bone, and remarked in the place where the body had been deposited a dark line of a matter like ashes, which extended from one end of the cavity to the other. We then visited successively the other tombs, situated in different countries, and burned whatever remains we found in them."'

thus mutilated, he was mounted on an ass, and paraded through all the towns and villages of Syria, accompanied by a herald, who exhibited him to the people. 'Behold!' he cried, 'Abou, the son of Muawia; him whom they called the most accomplished cavalier of the House of Ommaya!' This punishment endured until death put an end to it.

One enemy remained still unsubdued. When the army of Khorasan had invaded Irak, Yezid ibn Hobaira, the representative of Merwan, had striven gallantly to impede its advance. But worsted in more than one battle, he had thrown himself into Wasit, a fortified town built midway between Koufa and Basra, by Hejjaj, in order to overawe those two turbulent cities. This he had further strengthened, and amply stored with provisions, so that to the rude methods of attack known to the Arabs in those early days, the place was virtually impregnable. Yezid himself was a man of mighty influence among the Arabs of Modhar; and all those who clung to the memory of the fallen family, who had nothing to hope from the clemency, and everything to dread from the savage vindictiveness of the 'Bloodshedder,' crowded into Wasit as their last hope and place of safety. A single decisive battle is sufficient to crush even an established Oriental throne; it could not fail to be fatal to a monarch who had only just planted an unsteady step on the ruins of the power which preceded him. So long therefore as Yezid retained possession of Wasit, the destiny of the Muhammadan empire remained uncertain.

The khalif as-Saffah had despatched his brother Abou Jaafar to take command of the army which lay before

Wasit under the leadership of Hasan ibn Kahtaba. Frequent messages passed between him and Ibn Hobaira. Ultimately the latter agreed to surrender if a full pardon were granted to him and his army. A paper to that effect was drawn up and sent to him. He passed forty days in consulting the doctors of the law on its validity before he consented to accept it. Abou Jaafar, to whom it was then brought, sent it to as-Saffah, who ordered him to ratify it. Abou Jaafar's intention was to fulfil all the conditions granted, but as-Saffah never took a decision without the approbation of Abou Moslem, who had a spy to keep him informed by letter of all as-Saffah's proceedings. Abou Moslem, as soon as he heard of the terms conceded to Ibn Hobaira, wrote these words to as-Saffah: 'The best of roads is a bad one if there be stones on it, and, by Allah! no road is good in which one meets with Ibn Hobaira.' These words decided as-Saffah to put Yezid to death.

In the meantime, on the faith of the amnesty, Yezid had placed Abou Jaafar in possession of Wasit, and was an almost daily visitor at his residence. So much had the frank and manly manners of the Arab chief won the heart of the khalif's brother that when he received the mandate to put him to death he flatly refused to do so. He declared that such an act of tyranny would be the ruin of the empire. The khalif, however, would not forego his purpose. He was a younger man than his brother Abou Jaafar, but his heart was less open to the impulses of humanity; and it was for his hard and merciless character, that the Imam Ibrahim, in nominating a successor, had passed over an elder brother to fix his choice on the 'Bloodshedder.' He now forced Abou Jaafar with threats to execute his mandate, adding: 'By Allah! you must kill him, or else I shall send a person who will take him out of your enclosure and put him to death.' This menace decided Abou Jaafar. He caused all the rooms of the public treasury in Wasit to be sealed up, and sent for the principal officers in Ibn Hobaira's service. When they came, his doorkeeper stepped forward and called out the names of two eminent chiefs. They stood up and went in, and were immediately deprived of their swords, and handcuffed by three officers whom Abou Jaafar had posted within the tent, with one hundred men. Then two other chiefs were introduced, and treated in the same manner. Two others were then let in, and underwent a similar treatment. This was done also with the rest. They were then put to death, and their signet rings taken off. They numbered forty-two men in all.

This butchery finished, the three officers and the hundred men went off to Ibn Hobaira's residence. They sent a message to him, demanding where he had deposited his treasures. He told his door-keeper to go with them, and point out where they were deposited. They then placed guards at each of the doors, and began to search every corner of the house. Ibn Hobaira had with him his son, his secretary, his door-keeper, and several of his freedmen, and in his arms he was holding an infant son. Alarmed at the sight of these people, he exclaimed: 'I declare, by Allah! that the looks of these men portend nothing good.' They went up to him; but the door-keeper placed himself before them, and said: 'Stand off!' on which one of the officers gave him a sabre cut on his shoulder and brought him to the ground. The adult son then attacked the murderers, but was speedily cut down and killed. The freedmen also were slaughtered. On this Ibn Hobaira laid down the child, exclaiming: 'Take care of the boy!' and prostrated himself in prayer. He was slain whilst in that position; and the head cut off and taken to Abou Jaafar. But the officers engaged in this cowardly business resented the work on which they had been employed. 'Look at the enormous size of the head,' said Abou Jaafar to the officer who had brought it to him. 'The safeguard granted to him was a greater enormity than his head,' was the cutting retort.

With the murder of Yezid ibn Hobaira, the ruin of the Ommayas was complete.

The khalif as-Saffah was remarkable for the un-Oriental practice of remaining content with a single wife. Regarding this lady, Masoudi, in his 'Meadows of Gold,' has a pleasantly-told story, which may be inserted here, as a relief to the story of carnage and treachery which has been my theme for so many pages:—The lady's name was Omm Salama, and she had been twice married before she espoused the khalif. "She knew so well," says Masoudi, "to make herself beloved that he (the khalif) swore never to espouse another wife, and never to abandon her. She bore him a son and a daughter. Her ascendency over her husband was so great that he decided nothing without her advice, or even her sanction. Become khalif, he knew no other woman, either free or slave, but held stedfastly to the promise he had made to give her no rival. One day, during his khalifate, he found himself *tête-à-tête* with Khaled ibn Safwan. 'Prince of Believers,' said the latter to him, 'there is a certain matter that I have reflected upon often; you, a powerful monarch, the master of a vast empire, content yourself with a single wife; you limit your desires to her. If she falls sick, you fall sick; if she goes, you go. You voluntarily renounce the pleasure to have new slaves, to learn all their little histories, to indulge, in their society, all your caprices. And yet, Sire, there is the damsel tall and pliant, the maiden with the white skin, the full-grown woman with the ruddy complexion, the piquante brunette, the berberines with the rounded outlines! Ah! Prince, if you had only

LIST OF AUTHORITIES

PART I.— ISLAM.

Chapters I., II., III.—Tareek-i-Tabari
'Histoire des Arabes.'

The life of Muhammad has been the subject
and such thoroughly competent writers, that there
left for controversy in regard to the leading incidents
been content to take my narrative from the Persian version
Tabari, comparing it as I went along with the standard biogra
Prophet by Sprenger, Weil, and Muir. The citations from t
these chapters and throughout the book are made from M
translation.

Chapter IV. ALI AND HIS SONS.—Tareek-i-Tabari;
'Meadows of Gold' (Meynard); Ibn Khallikan's Biographica
(Slane).

Chapter V. THE STRUGGLE FOR EMPIRE.—Tareek-i-T
soudi's 'Meadows of Gold;' Ibn Khallikan's Biographical
Shahrestani's 'Muhammadan Sects;' (Dr. Haarbrucker).

PART II.—THE FATIMIDES.

Chapter I. THE SHIA.—Masoudi's 'Meadows of Gold;
tani's 'Muhammadan Sects;' Ibn Khallikan's Biographical
Sacy's 'Histoire des Druses;' Ibn Khaldun's Prolegomen
Ala Eddin Djouveiny 'Jour. Asiatique,' 5me serie, tom. V

Chapter II. THE ARAB AND THE BERBER.—Ibn Nowairi
of Afrikia and Magreb' (Slane); Shahrestani's 'Muhamma
Ibn Khaldun's 'Afrikia sous les Aghlabites' (A. Noel de
Abu'l Fœda's Geography (Reinaud); El. Bekri, 'Northern

39 Paternoster Row, E.C.
London, *March* 1876.

GENERAL LIST OF WORKS

PUBLISHED BY

Messrs. Longmans, Green, and Co.

HISTORY, POLITICS, HISTORICAL MEMOIRS, &c.

The History of England from the Accession of James II.

By the Right Hon. Lord Macaulay.

Student's Edition, 2 *vols. cr.* 8*vo.* 12*s.*
People's Edition, 4 *vols. cr.* 8*vo.* 16*s.*
Cabinet Edition, 8 *vols. post* 8*vo.* 48*s.*
Library Edition, 5 *vols.* 8*vo.* £4.

Critical and Historical Essays contributed to the Edinburgh Review.

By the Right Hon. Lord Macaulay.

Cheap Edition, *crown* 8*vo.* 3*s.* 6*d.*
Student's Edition, *crown* 8*vo.* 6*s.*
People's Edition, 2 *vols. crown* 8*vo.* 8*s.*
Cabinet Edition, 4 *vols.* 24*s.*
Library Edition, 3 *vols.* 8*vo.* 36*s.*

Lord Macaulay's Works. Complete and uniform Library Edition. Edited by his Sister, Lady Trevelyan.

8 *vols.* 8*vo. with Portrait*, £5. 5*s.*

The History of England from the Fall of Wolsey to the Defeat of the Spanish Armada. By J. A. Froude, M.A.

CABINET EDITION, 12 *vols. cr.* 8*vo.* £3. 12*s.*
LIBRARY EDITION, 12 *vols.* 8*vo.* £8. 18*s.*

The English in Ireland in the Eighteenth Century. By J. A. Froude, M.A.

3 *vols.* 8*vo.* £2. 8*s.*

Journal of the Reigns of King George the Fourth and King William the Fourth. By the late Charles Cavendish Fulke Greville, Esq. Edited by H. Reeve, Esq.

Fifth Edition. 3 *vols.* 8*vo. price* 36*s.*

The Life of Napoleon III. derived from State Records, Unpublished Family Correspondence, and Personal Testimony. By Blanchard Jerrold.

In Four Volumes 8*vo. with numerous Portraits and Facsimiles.* VOLS. I. *and* II. *price* 18*s. each.*

*** *The Third Volume is now in the press.*

Recollections and Suggestions, 1813–1873. By John Earl Russell, K.G.

New Edition, revised and enlarged. 8*vo.* 16*s.*

Introductory Lectures on Modern History delivered in Lent Term 1842; *with the Inaugural Lecture delivered in December* 1841. By the late Rev. Thomas Arnold, D.D.

8*vo. price* 7*s.* 6*d.*

On Parliamentary Government in England: its Origin, Development, and Practical Operation. By Alpheus Todd.

2 *vols.* 8*vo.* £1. 17*s.*

The Constitutional History of England since the Accession of George III. 1760–1870. By Sir Thomas Erskine May, K.C.B. D.C.L.

Fifth Edition. 3 *vols. crown* 8*vo.* 18*s.*

Democracy in Europe; a History. By Sir Thomas Erskine May, K.C.B. D.C.L.

2 *vols.* 8*vo.* [*In the press.*

Lectures on the History of England from the Earliest Times to the Death of King Edward II. By W. Longman, F.S.A.

Maps and Illustrations. 8*vo.* 15*s.*

The History of the Life and Times of Edward III. By W. Longman, F.S.A.

With 9 *Maps*, 8 *Plates, and* 16 *Woodcuts,* 2 *vols.* 8*vo.* 28*s.*

History of England under the Duke of Buckingham and Charles the First, 1624–1628.
By S. Rawson Gardiner, late Student of Ch. Ch.
2 vols. 8vo. with two Maps, 24*s.*

Popular History of France, from the Earliest Times to the Death of Louis XIV.
By Elizabeth M. Sewell, Author of 'Amy Herbert' &c.
Crown 8vo. [*Nearly ready.*

The History of Prussia, from the Earliest Times to the Present Day; tracing the Origin and Development of her Military Organisation.
By Captain W. J. Wyatt.
Vols. I. & II. A.D. 700 *to* A.D. 1525. *8vo.* 36*s.*

History of Civilisation in England and France, Spain and Scotland.
By Henry Thomas Buckle.
3 *vols. crown 8vo.* 24*s.*

A Student's Manual of the History of India from the Earliest Period to the Present.
By Col. Meadows Taylor, M.R.A.S.
Second Thousand. Cr. 8vo. Maps, 7*s.* 6*d.*

Studies from Genoese History.
By Colonel G. B. Malleson, C.S.I. Guardian to His Highness the Mahárájá of Mysore.
Crown 8vo. 10*s.* 6*d.*

The Native States of India in Subsidiary Alliance with the British Government; an Historical Sketch.
By Colonel G. B. Malleson, C.S.I. Guardian to the Mahárájá of Mysore.
With 6 *Coloured Maps, 8vo. price* 15*s.*

The History of India from the Earliest Period to the close of Lord Dalhousie's Administration.
By John Clark Marshman.
3 *vols. crown 8vo.* 22*s.* 6*d.*

Indian Polity; a View of the System of Administration in India.
By Lieut.-Colonel George Chesney.
Second Edition, revised, with Map. 8vo. 21*s.*

Waterloo Lectures; a Study of the Campaign of 1815.
By Colonel Charles C. Chesney, R.E.
Third Edition. 8vo. with Map, 10*s.* 6*d.*

Essays in Modern Military Biography.
By Colonel Charles C. Chesney, R.E.
8vo. 12s. 6d.

The British Army in 1875; with Suggestions on its Administration and Organisation.
By John Holms, M.P.
New and Enlarged Edition. Crown 8vo. with Diagrams, 4s. 6d.

The Oxford Reformers—John Colet, Erasmus, and Thomas More; being a History of their Fellow-Work.
By Frederic Seebohm.
Second Edition. 8vo. 14s.

The New Reformation, a Narrative of the Old Catholic Movement, from 1870 to the Present Time; with an Historical Introduction.
By Theodorus.
8vo. price 12s.

The Mythology of the Aryan Nations.
By Geo. W. Cox, M.A. late Scholar of Trinity College, Oxford.
2 vols. 8vo. 28s.

A History of Greece.
By the Rev. Geo. W. Cox, M.A. late Scholar of Trinity College, Oxford.
Vols. I. and II. 8vo. Maps, 36s.

The History of the Peloponnesian War, by Thucydides.
Translated by Richd. Crawley, Fellow of Worcester College, Oxford.
8vo. 10s. 6d.

The Tale of the Great Persian War, from the Histories of Herodotus.
By Rev. G. W. Cox, M.A.
Fcp. 8vo. 3s. 6d.

General History of Greece to the Death of Alexander the Great; with a Sketch of the Subsequent History to the Present Time.
By the Rev. George W. Cox, M.A. Author of 'The Aryan Mythology' &c.
Crown 8vo. with Maps, 7s. 6d.

General History of Rome from the Foundation of the City to the Fall of Augustulus, B.C. 753—A.D. 476.
By the Very Rev. C. Merivale, D.D. Dean of Ely.
With 5 Maps, crown 8vo. 7s. 6d.

History of the Romans under the Empire.
By Dean Merivale, D.D.
8 vols. post 8vo. 48s.

The Fall of the Roman Republic; a Short History of the Last Century of the Commonwealth.
By Dean Merivale, D.D.
12mo. 7s. 6d.

The Sixth Oriental Monarchy; or the Geography, History, and Antiquities of Parthia. Collected and Illustrated from Ancient and Modern sources.
By Geo. Rawlinson, M.A.
With Maps and Illustrations. 8vo. 16s.

The Seventh Great Oriental Monarchy; or, a History of the Sassanians: with Notices Geographical and Antiquarian.
By Geo. Rawlinson, M.A.
With Map and 95 Illustrations. 8vo. 28s.

Encyclopædia of Chronology, Historical and Biographical; comprising the Dates of all the Great Events of History, including Treaties, Alliances, Wars, Battles, &c. Incidents in the Lives of Eminent Men, Scientific and Geographical Discoveries, Mechanical Inventions, and Social, Domestic, and Economical Improvements.
By B. B. Woodward, B.A. and W. L. R. Cates.
8vo. 42s.

The History of Rome.
By Wilhelm Ihne.
Vols. I. and II. 8vo. 30s. Vols. III. and IV. in preparation.

History of European Morals from Augustus to Charlemagne.
By W. E. H. Lecky, M.A.
2 vols. 8vo. 28s.

History of the Rise and Influence of the Spirit of Rationalism in Europe.
By W. E. H. Lecky, M.A.
Cabinet Edition, 2 vols. crown 8vo. 16s.

Introduction to the Science of Religion: Four Lectures delivered at the Royal Institution; with two Essays on False Analogies and the Philosophy of Mythology.
By F. Max Müller, M.A.
Crown 8vo. 10s. 6d.

The Stoics, Epicureans, and Sceptics.
Translated from the German of Dr. E. Zeller, by Oswald J. Reichel, M.A.
Crown 8vo. 14s.

Socrates and the Socratic Schools.
Translated from the German of Dr. E. Zeller, by the Rev. O. J. Reichel, M.A.
Crown 8vo. 8s. 6d.

Plato and the Older Academy.

Translated, with the Author's sanction, from the German of Dr. E. Zeller by S. Frances Alleyne and Alfred Goodwin, B.A. Fellow of Balliol College, Oxford.

Post 8vo. [*Nearly ready.*

Sketch of the History of the Church of England to the Revolution of 1688.

By T. V. Short, D.D. sometime Bishop of St. Asaph.

New Edition. Crown 8vo. 7s. 6d.

The Historical Geography of Europe.

By E. A. Freeman, D.C.L.

8vo. Maps. [*In the press.*

The Student's Manual of Ancient History: containing the Political History, Geographical Position, and Social State of the Principal Nations of Antiquity.

By W. Cooke Taylor, LL.D.

Crown 8vo. 7s. 6d.

The Student's Manual of Modern History: containing the Rise and Progress of the Principal European Nations, their Political History, and the Changes in their Social Condition.

By W. Cooke Taylor, LL.D.

Crown 8vo. 7s. 6d.

The History of Philosophy, from Thales to Comte.

By George Henry Lewes.

Fourth Edition, 2 vols. 8vo. 32s.

The Crusades.

By the Rev. G. W. Cox, M.A.

Fcp. 8vo. with Map, 2s. 6d.

The Era of the Protestant Revolution.

By F. Seebohm, Author of 'The Oxford Reformers.'

With 4 Maps and 12 Diagrams. Fcp. 8vo. 2s. 6d.

The Thirty Years' War, 1618–1648.

By Samuel Rawson Gardiner.

Fcp. 8vo. with Maps, 2s. 6d.

The Houses of Lancaster and York; with the Conquest and Loss of France.

By James Gairdner.

Fcp. 8vo. with Map, 2s. 6d.

Edward the Third.

By the Rev. W. Warburton, M.A.

Fcp. 8vo. with Maps, 2s. 6d.

The Age of Elizabeth.

By the Rev. M. Creighton, M.A., late Fellow and Tutor of Merton College, Oxford.

Fcp. 8vo. with Maps, 2s. 6d.

BIOGRAPHICAL WORKS.

The Life and Letters of Lord Macaulay.
By his Nephew, G. Otto Trevelyan, M.P.
2 vols. 8vo. with Portrait, price 36s.

The Life of Sir William Fairbairn, Bart. F.R.S. Corresponding Member of the National Institute of France, &c.
Partly written by himself; edited and completed by William Pole, F.R.S. Member of Council of the Institution of Civil Engineers.
[In the press.

Arthur Schopenhauer, his Life and his Philosophy.
By Helen Zimmern.
Post 8vo. with Portrait, 7s. 6d.

The Life, Works, and Opinions of Heinrich Heine.
By William Stigand.
2 vols. 8vo. with Portrait of Heine, price 28s.

Memoirs of Baron Stockmar.
By his Son, Baron E. Von Stockmar. Translated from the German by G. A. M. Edited by F. Max Müller, M.A.
2 vols. crown 8vo. 21s.

Admiral Sir Edward Codrington, a Memoir of his Life; with Selections from his Correspondence.
Abridged from the larger work, and edited by his Daughter, Lady Bourchier.
With Portrait, Maps, &c. Crown 8vo. price 7s. 6d.

Life and Letters of Gilbert Elliot, First Earl of Minto, from 1751 to 1806, when his Public Life in Europe was closed by his Appointment to the Vice-Royalty of India.
Edited by the Countess of Minto.
3 vols. post 8vo. 31s. 6d.

Autobiography.
By John Stuart Mill.
8vo. 7s. 6d.

Isaac Casaubon, 1559-1614.
By Mark Pattison, Rector of Lincoln College, Oxford.
8vo. price 18s.

Biographical and Critical Essays, reprinted from Reviews, with Additions and Corrections.
By A. Hayward, Q.C.
Second Series, 2 vols. 8vo. 28s. Third Series, 1 vol. 8vo. 14s.

The Memoirs of Sir John Reresby, of Thrybergh, Bart. M.P. for York, &c. 1634–1689. Written by Himself. Edited from the Original Manuscript by James J. Cartwright, M.A.

8vo. *price* 21s.

Lord George Bentinck; a Political Biography. By the Right Hon. B. Disraeli, M.P.

New Edition. Crown 8vo. 6s.

Essays in Ecclesiastical Biography. By the Right Hon. Sir J. Stephen, LL.D.

Cabinet Edition. Crown 8vo. 7s. 6d.

Leaders of Public Opinion in Ireland; Swift, Flood, Grattan, O'Connell. By W. E. H. Lecky, M.A.

Crown 8vo. 7s. 6d.

Dictionary of General Biography; containing Concise Memoirs and Notices of the most Eminent Persons of all Ages and Countries. By W. L. R. Cates.

New Edition, 8vo. 25s. *Supplement,* 4s. 6d.

Life of the Duke of Wellington. By the Rev. G. R. Gleig, M.A.

Crown 8vo. *with Portrait,* 5s.

The Rise of Great Families; other Essays and Stories. By Sir Bernard Burke, C.B. LL.D.

Crown 8vo. 12s. 6d.

Memoirs of Sir Henry Havelock, K.C.B. By John Clark Marshman.

Crown 8vo. 3s. 6d.

Vicissitudes of Families. By Sir Bernard Burke, C.B.

2 *vols. crown* 8vo. 21s.

MENTAL and POLITICAL PHILOSOPHY.

Comte's System of Positive Polity, or Treatise upon Sociology. Translated from the Paris Edition of 1851–1854, and furnished with Analytical Tables of Contents. In Four Volumes, each forming in some degree an independent Treatise:—

Vol. I. General View of Positivism and Introductory Principles. Translated by J. H. Bridges, M.B. *formerly Fellow of Oriel College, Oxford.* 8vo. *price* 21s.

Vol. II. The Social Statics, or the Abstract Laws of Human Order. Translated by Frederic Harrison, M.A. 8vo. *price* 14s.

Vol. III. The Social Dynamics, or the General Laws of Human Progress (the Philosophy of History). Translated by E. S. Beesly, M.A. *Professor of History in University College, London.* 8vo. [*Nearly ready.*

Vol. IV. The Synthesis of the Future of Mankind. Translated by Richard Congreve, M.D., *and an Appendix, containing the Author's Minor Treatises, translated by* H. D. Hutton, M.A. *Barrister-at-Law.* 8vo. [*In the press.*

Order and Progress: Part I. Thoughts on Government; Part II. Studies of Political Crises.
By Frederic Harrison, M.A. of Lincoln's Inn.
8vo. 14s.

'We find from this book—a large part, and by far the more valuable part, of which is new—that Mr. HARRISON has devoted careful attention to what we shall call the constructive problems of political science. Whoever has mistaken him for a commonplace Radical, either of the Chartist or the Trades Unionist type, has been wrong.... The best political thinkers for a quarter of a century or upwards have more or less vaguely felt that one grand problem they had to solve was how our governing apparatus may be made to yield good government; but we are not aware that any writer has looked it more fully in the face, or more carefully scanned it with a view to a solution, than Mr. HARRISON.'
LITERARY WORLD.

Essays, Political, Social, and Religious.
By Richd. Congreve, M.A.
8vo. 18s.

Essays, Critical and Biographical, contributed to the Edinburgh Review.
By Henry Rogers.
New Edition. 2 vols. crown 8vo. 12s.

Essays on some Theological Controversies of the Time, contributed chiefly to the Edinburgh Review.
By Henry Rogers.
New Edition. Crown 8vo. 6s.

Democracy in America.
By Alexis de Tocqueville. Translated by Henry Reeve, Esq.
New Edition. 2 vols. crown 8vo. 16s.

On Representative Government.
By John Stuart Mill.
Fourth Edition, crown 8vo. 2s.

On Liberty.
By John Stuart Mill.
Post 8vo. 7s. 6d. crown 8vo. 1s. 4d.

Principles of Political Economy.
By John Stuart Mill.
2 vols. 8vo. 30s. or 1 vol. crown 8vo. 5s.

Essays on some Unsettled Questions of Political Economy.
By John Stuart Mill.
Second Edition. 8vo. 6s. 6d.

Utilitarianism.
By John Stuart Mill.
Fourth Edition. 8vo. 5s.

A System of Logic, Ratiocinative and Inductive.
By John Stuart Mill.
Eighth Edition. 2 vols. 8vo. 25s.

Examination of Sir William Hamilton's Philosophy, and of the principal Philosophical Questions discussed in his Writings.
By John Stuart Mill.
Fourth Edition. 8vo. 16s.

Dissertations and Discussions.
By John Stuart Mill.
4 vols. 8vo. price £2. 6s. 6d.

Analysis of the Phenomena of the Human Mind. By James Mill. New Edition, with Notes, Illustrative and Critical.

2 vols. 8vo. 28s.

The Law of Nations considered as Independent Political Communities; the Rights and Duties of Nations in Time of War. By Sir Travers Twiss, D.C.L. F.R.S.

New Edition, revised; with an Introductory Juridical Review of the Results of Recent Wars, and an Appendix of Treaties and other Documents. 8vo. price 21s.

Church and State; their relations Historically Developed.

By T. Heinrich Geffcken, Professor of International Law at the University of Strasburg. Translated from the German by E. Fairfax Taylor. [In the press.

A Systematic View of the Science of Jurisprudence.

By Sheldon Amos, M.A.

8vo. 18s.

A Primer of the English Constitution and Government.

By Sheldon Amos, M.A.

Second Edition. Crown 8vo. 6s.

Outlines of Civil Procedure. Being a General View of the Supreme Court of Judicature and of the whole Practice in the Common Law and Chancery Divisions under all the Statutes now in force. With Introductory Essay, References, Time Table, and Index. Designed as a Systematic and Readable Manual for Students, and as a Handbook of General Practice.

By Edward Stanley Roscoe, Barrister-at-Law.

12mo. price 3s. 6d.

Principles of Economical Philosophy.

By H. D. Macleod, M.A. Barrister-at-Law.

Second Edition, in 2 vols. Vol. I. 8vo. 15s. Vol. II. Part I. price 12s.

The Institutes of Justinian; with English Introduction, Translation, and Notes.

By T. C. Sandars, M.A.

Fifth Edition. 8vo. 18s.

Lord Bacon's Works,

Collected and Edited by R. L. Ellis, M.A. J. Spedding, M.A. and D. D. Heath.

New and Cheaper Edition. 7 vols. 8vo. £3. 13s. 6d.

Letters and Life of Francis Bacon, including all his Occasional Works. Collected and edited, with a Commentary, by J. Spedding.

7 vols. 8vo. £4. 4s.

The Nicomachean Ethics of Aristotle. Newly translated into English.

By R. Williams, B.A.

8vo. 12s.

The Politics of Aristotle; Greek Text, with English Notes.

By Richard Congreve, M.A.

New Edition, revised. 8vo. 18s.

The Ethics of Aristotle; with Essays and Notes.

By Sir A. Grant, Bart. M.A. LL.D.

Third Edition. 2 vols. 8vo. price 32s.

Bacon's Essays, with Annotations.

By R. Whately, D.D.

New Edition. 8vo. 10s. 6d.

Picture Logic; an Attempt to Popularise the Science of Reasoning by the combination of Humorous Pictures with Examples of Reasoning taken from Daily Life.

By A. Swinbourne, B.A.

Second Edition; with Woodcut Illustrations from Drawings by the Author. Fcp. 8vo. price 5s.

Elements of Logic.

By R. Whately, D.D.

New Edition. 8vo. 10s. 6d. cr. 8vo. 4s. 6d.

Elements of Rhetoric.

By R. Whately, D.D.

New Edition. 8vo. 10s. 6d. cr. 8vo. 4s. 6d.

An Outline of the Necessary Laws of Thought: a Treatise on Pure and Applied Logic.

By the Most Rev. W. Thomson, D.D. Archbishop of York.

Twelfth Thousand. Crown 8vo. 6s.

An Introduction to Mental Philosophy, on the Inductive Method.

By J. D. Morell, LL.D.

8vo. 12s.

Philosophy without Assumptions.

By the Rev. T. P. Kirkman, F.R.S. Rector of Croft, near Warrington.

8vo. price 10s. 6d.

Ueberweg's System of Logic, and History of Logical Doctrines.

Translated, with Notes and Appendices, by T. M. Lindsay, M.A. F.R.S.E.

8vo. 16s.

The Senses and the Intellect.
By A. Bain, LL.D.
Third Edition, 8vo. 15s.

The Emotions and the Will.
By Alexander Bain, LL.D. Professor of Logic in the University of Aberdeen.
Third Edition, thoroughly revised, and in great part re-written. 8vo. *price* 15s.

Mental and Moral Science; a Compendium of Psychology and Ethics.
By A. Bain, LL.D.
Third Edition. Crown 8vo. 10s. 6d. *Or separately: Part I. Mental Science*, 6s. 6d. *Part II. Moral Science*, 4s. 6d.

On the Influence of Authority in Matters of Opinion.
By the late Sir George Cornewall Lewis, Bart.
New Edition, 8vo. 14s.

Hume's Treatise on Human Nature.
Edited, with Notes, &c. by T. H. Green, M.A. and the Rev. T. H. Grose, M.A.
2 *vols.* 8vo. 28s.

Hume's Essays Moral, Political, and Literary.
By the same Editors.
2 *vols.* 8vo. 28s.

*** *The above form a complete and uniform Edition of* HUME'S *Philosophical Works.*

MISCELLANEOUS & CRITICAL WORKS.

Miscellaneous and Posthumous Works of the late Henry Thomas Buckle.
Edited, with a Biographical Notice, by Helen Taylor.
3 *vols.* 8vo. £2. 12s. 6d.

Short Studies on Great Subjects.
By J. A. Froude, M.A.
CABINET EDITION, 2 *vols. crown* 8vo. 12s.
LIBRARY EDITION, 2 *vols. demy* 8vo. 24s.

Manual of English Literature, Historical and Critical.
By Thomas Arnold, M.A.
New Edition. Crown 8vo. 7s. 6d.

Lord Macaulay's Miscellaneous Writings.
LIBRARY EDITION, 2 *vols.* 8vo. *Portrait*, 21s.
PEOPLE'S EDITION, 1 *vol. cr.* 8vo. 4s. 6d.

Lord Macaulay's Miscellaneous Writings and Speeches.
Students' Edition. Crown 8vo. 6s.

Speeches of the Right Hon. Lord Macaulay, corrected by Himself.
People's Edition. Crown 8vo. 3s. 6d.

The Rev. Sydney Smith's Essays contributed to the Edinburgh Review.
Authorised Edition, complete in One Volume. Crown 8vo. 2s. 6d. *sewed, or* 3s. 6d. *cloth.*

The Wit and Wisdom of the Rev. Sydney Smith.
Crown 8vo. 3*s.* 6*d.*

German Home Life; a Series of Essays on the Domestic Life of Germany.
Reprinted, with Revision and Additions, from FRASER'S MAGAZINE. 1 *vol. crown 8vo.* [*Nearly ready.*

The Miscellaneous Works of Thomas Arnold, D.D. Late Head Master of Rugby School and Regius Professor of Modern History in the Univ. of Oxford.
8vo. 7*s.* 6*d.*

Realities of Irish Life. By W. Steuart Trench.
Cr. 8vo. 2*s.* 6*d. sewed, or* 3*s.* 6*d. cloth.*

Lectures on the Science of Language. By F. Max Müller, M.A. &c.
Eighth Edition. 2 *vols. crown 8vo.* 16*s.*

Chips from a German Workshop; being Essays on the Science of Religion, and on Mythology, Traditions, and Customs. By F. Max Müller, M.A.
4 *vols. 8vo.* £2. 18*s.*

Southey's Doctor, complete in One Volume. Edited by Rev. J. W. Warter, B.D.
Square crown 8vo. 12*s.* 6*d.*

Lectures delivered in America in 1874. By Charles Kingsley, late Rector of Eversley.
Crown 8vo. 5*s.*

Families of Speech. Four Lectures delivered at the Royal Institution. By F. W. Farrar, D.D.
New Edition. Crown 8vo. 3*s.* 6*d.*

Chapters on Language. By F. W. Farrar, D.D.
New Edition. Crown 8vo. 5*s.*

A Budget of Paradoxes. By Augustus De Morgan.
Reprinted, with Author's Additions, from the Athenæum. *8vo.* 15*s.*

Apparitions; a Narrative of Facts. By the Rev. B. W. Savile, M.A. Author of 'The Truth of the Bible' &c.
Crown 8vo. price 4*s.* 6*d.*

The Oration of Demosthenes on the Crown. Translated by the Right Hon. Sir R. P. Collier.
Crown 8vo. 5*s.*

Miscellaneous Writings of John Conington, M.A. Edited by J. A. Symonds, M.A. With a Memoir by H. J. S. Smith, M.A.
2 *vols. 8vo.* 28*s.*

Recreations of a Country Parson.
By A. K. H. B.
Two Series, 3s. 6d. each.

Landscapes, Churches, and Moralities.
By A. K. H. B.
Crown 8vo. 3s. 6d.

Seaside Musings on Sundays and Weekdays.
By A. K. H. B.
Crown 8vo. 3s. 6d.

Changed Aspects of Unchanged Truths.
By A. K. H. B.
Crown 8vo. 3s. 6d.

Counsel and Comfort from a City Pulpit.
By A. K. H. B.
Crown 8vo. 3s. 6d.

Lessons of Middle Age.
By A. K. H. B.
Crown 8vo. 3s. 6d.

Leisure Hours in Town.
By A. K. H. B.
Crown 8vo. 3s. 6d.

The Autumn Holidays of a Country Parson.
By A. K. H. B.
Crown 8vo. 3s. 6d.

Sunday Afternoons at the Parish Church of a Scottish University City.
By A. K. H. B.
Crown 8vo. 3s. 6d.

The Commonplace Philosopher in Town and Country.
By A. K. H. B.
Crown 8vo. 3s. 6d.

Present-Day Thoughts.
By A. K. H. B.
Crown 8vo. 3s. 6d.

Critical Essays of a Country Parson.
By A. K. H. B.
Crown 8vo. 3s. 6d.

The Graver Thoughts of a Country Parson.
By A. K. H. B.
Three Series, 3s. 6d. each.

DICTIONARIES and OTHER BOOKS of REFERENCE.

A Dictionary of the English Language.

By R. G. Latham, M.A. M.D. Founded on the Dictionary of Dr. S. Johnson, as edited by the Rev. H. J. Todd, with numerous Emendations and Additions.

4 *vols.* 4*to.* £7.

Thesaurus of English Words and Phrases, classified and arranged so as to facilitate the expression of Ideas, and assist in Literary Composition.

By P. M. Roget, M.D.

Crown 8*vo.* 10*s.* 6*d.*

English Synonymes.

By E. J. Whately. Edited by Archbishop Whately.

Fifth Edition. Fcp. 8*vo.* 3*s.*

Handbook of the English Language. For the use of Students of the Universities and the Higher Classes in Schools.

By R. G. Latham, M.A. M.D. &c. late Fellow of King's College, Cambridge; late Professor of English in Univ. Coll. Lond.

The Ninth Edition. Crown 8*vo.* 6*s.*

A Practical Dictionary of the French and English Languages.

By Léon Contanseau, many years French Examiner for Military and Civil Appointments, &c.

Post 8*vo.* 7*s.* 6*d.*

Contanseau's Pocket Dictionary, French and English, abridged from the Practical Dictionary, by the Author.

Square 18*mo.* 3*s.* 6*d.*

A New Pocket Dictionary of the German and English Languages.

By F. W. Longman, Balliol College, Oxford. Founded on Blackley and Friedländer's Practical Dictionary of the German and English Languages.

Square 18*mo. price* 5*s.*

A Dictionary of Roman and Greek Antiquities. With 2,000 *Woodcuts from Ancient Originals, illustrative of the Arts and Life of the Greeks and Romans.*

By Anthony Rich, B.A.

Third Edition. Crown 8*vo.* 7*s.* 6*d.*

New Practical Dictionary of the German Language; German-English and English-German.
By Rev. W. L. Blackley, M.A. and Dr. C. M. Friedländer.
Post 8*vo.* 7*s.* 6*d.*

The Mastery of Languages; or, the Art of Speaking Foreign Tongues Idiomatically.
By Thomas Prendergast.
Second Edition. 8*vo.* 6*s.*

A Greek-English Lexicon.
By H. G. Liddell, D.D. Dean of Christchurch, and R. Scott, D.D. Dean of Rochester.
Sixth Edition. Crown 4*to.* 36*s.*

A Lexicon, Greek and English, abridged for Schools from Liddell and Scott's Greek-English Lexicon.
Fourteenth Edition. Square 12*mo.* 7*s.* 6*d.*

An English-Greek Lexicon, containing all the Greek Words used by Writers of good authority.
By C. D. Yonge, M.A.
New Edition. 4*to.* 21*s.*

Mr. C. D. Yonge's New Lexicon, English and Greek, abridged from his larger Lexicon.
Square 12*mo.* 8*s.* 6*d.*

A Latin-English Dictionary.
By John T. White, D.D. Oxon. and J. E. Riddle, M.A. Oxon.
Fifth Edition, revised. 1 *vol.* 4*to.* 28*s.*

White's College Latin-English Dictionary; abridged from the Parent Work for the use of University Students.
Third Edition, Medium 8*vo.* 15*s.*

A Latin-English Dictionary adapted for the use of Middle-Class Schools,
By John T. White, D.D. Oxon.
Square fcp. 8*vo.* 3*s.*

White's Junior Student's Complete Latin-English and English-Latin Dictionary.
Square 12*mo.* 12*s.*

Separately { ENGLISH-LATIN, 5*s.* 6*d.*; LATIN-ENGLISH, 7*s.* 6*d.* }

M'Culloch's Dictionary, Practical, Theoretical, and Historical, of Commerce and Commercial Navigation.
Edited by H. G. Reid.
8*vo.* 63*s.*
Supplement, price 5*s.*

A General Dictionary of Geography, Descriptive, Physical, Statistical, and Historical; forming a complete Gazetteer of the World.
By A. Keith Johnston.
New Edition, thoroughly revised. [In the press.

The Public Schools Manual of Modern Geography. Forming a Companion to 'The Public Schools Atlas of Modern Geography'
By Rev. G. Butler, M.A.
[In the press.

The Public Schools Atlas of Modern Geography. In 31 Maps, exhibiting clearly the more important Physical Features of the Countries delineated.
Edited, with Introduction, by Rev. G. Butler, M.A.
Imperial 8vo. price 5s. cloth; or in imperial 4to. 3s. 6d. sewed & 5s. cloth.

The Public Schools Atlas of Ancient Geography.
Edited, with an Introduction on the Study of Ancient Geography, by the Rev. G. Butler, M.A.
Imperial Quarto. [In the press.

ASTRONOMY and METEOROLOGY.

The Universe and the Coming Transits; Researches into and New Views respecting the Constitution of the Heavens.
By R. A. Proctor, B.A.
With 22 Charts and 22 Diagrams. 8vo. 16s.

Saturn and its System.
By R. A. Proctor, B.A.
8vo. with 14 Plates, 14s.

The Transits of Venus; A Popular Account of Past and Coming Transits, from the first observed by Horrocks A.D. 1639 to the Transit of A.D. 2012.
By R. A. Proctor, B.A.
Second Edition, revised and enlarged, with 20 Plates (12 Coloured) and 27 Woodcuts. Crown 8vo. 8s. 6d.

Essays on Astronomy: A Series of Papers on Planets and Meteors, the Sun and Sun-surrounding Space, Stars and Star Cloudlets.
By R. A. Proctor, B.A.
With 10 Plates and 24 Woodcuts. 8vo. 12s.

The Moon; her Motions, Aspect, Scenery, and Physical Condition.
By R. A. Proctor, B.A.
With Plates, Charts, Woodcuts, and Lunar Photographs. Crown 8vo. 15s.

The Sun; Ruler, Light, Fire, and Life of the Planetary System.
By R. A. Proctor, B.A.
Second Edition. Plates and Woodcuts. Cr. 8vo. 14s.

The Orbs Around Us; a Series of Familiar Essays on the Moon and Planets, Meteors and Comets, the Sun and Coloured Pairs of Suns.

By R. A. Proctor, B.A.

Second Edition, with Chart and 4 Diagrams. Crown 8vo. 7*s.* 6*d.*

Other Worlds than Ours; The Plurality of Worlds Studied under the Light of Recent Scientific Researches.

By R. A. Proctor, B.A.

Third Edition, with 14 *Illustrations. Cr. 8vo.* 10*s.* 6*d.*

Brinkley's Astronomy. Revised and partly re-written, with Additional Chapters, and an Appendix of Questions for Examination.

By John W. Stubbs, D.D. and F. Brunnow, Ph.D.

With 49 *Diagrams. Crown 8vo.* 6*s.*

Outlines of Astronomy. By Sir J. F. W. Herschel, Bart. M.A.

Latest Edition, with Plates and Diagrams. Square crown 8vo. 12*s.*

The Moon, and the Condition and Configurations of its Surface.

By Edmund Neison, Fellow of the Royal Astronomical Society &c.

Illustrated by Maps and Plates. [*Nearly ready.*

Celestial Objects for Common Telescopes.

By T. W. Webb, M.A. F.R.A.S.

New Edition, with Map of the Moon and Woodcuts. Crown 8vo. 7*s.* 6*d.*

'By universal consent of observers in this country, Mr. WEBB's *Celestial Objects* has taken the place of a standard text-book. With a book so well known and so highly appreciated, we have little more to do than to mention the appearance of a new edition, which we know has been wanted for some time, and which those who survey the glories of the heavens will be anxious to obtain.'

The STUDENT.

A New Star Atlas, for the Library, the School, and the Observatory, in 12 *Circular Maps (with* 2 *Index Plates).*

By R. A. Proctor, B.A.

Crown 8vo. 5*s.*

Larger Star Atlas, for the Library, in Twelve Circular Maps, photolithographed by A. Brothers, F.R.A.S. With 2 *Index Plates and a Letterpress Introduction.*

By R. A. Proctor, BA.

Second Edition. Small folio, 25*s.*

Dove's Law of Storms, considered in connexion with the ordinary Movements of the Atmosphere.

Translated by R. H. Scott, M.A.

8vo. 10*s.* 6*d.*

Air and Rain; the Beginnings of a Chemical Climatology.

By R. A. Smith, F.R.S.

8vo. 24s.

Air and its Relations to Life, 1774–1874; a Course of Lectures delivered at the Royal Institution of Great Britain in 1874, with some Additions.

By Walter Noel Hartley, F.C.S. Demonstrator of Chemistry at King's College, London.

Small 8vo. with Illustrations, 6s.

Nautical Surveying, an Introduction to the Practical and Theoretical Study of.

By J. K. Laughton, M.A.

Small 8vo. 6s.

Schellen's Spectrum Analysis, in its Application to Terrestrial Substances and the Physical Constitution of the Heavenly Bodies.

Translated by Jane and C. Lassell; edited, with Notes, by W. Huggins, LL.D. F.R.S.

With 13 Plates and 223 Woodcuts. 8vo. 28s.

NATURAL HISTORY and PHYSICAL SCIENCE.

Professor Helmholtz' Popular Lectures on Scientific Subjects.

Translated by E. Atkinson, F.C.S.

With many Illustrative Wood Engravings. 8vo. 12s. 6d.

Ganot's Natural Philosophy for General Readers and Young Persons; a Course of Physics divested of Mathematical Formulæ and expressed in the language of daily life.

Translated by E. Atkinson, F.C.S.

Second Edition, with 2 Plates and 429 Woodcuts. Crown 8vo. 7s. 6d.

The Correlation of Physical Forces.

By the Hon. Sir W. R. Grove, F.R.S. &c.

Sixth Edition, with other Contributions to Science. 8vo. 15s.

Weinhold's Introduction to Experimental Physics, Theoretical and Practical; including Directions for Constructing Physical Apparatus and for Making Experiments.

Translated by B. Loewy, F.R.A.S. With a Preface by G. C. Foster, F.R.S.

With 3 Coloured Plates and 404 Woodcuts. 8vo. price 31s. 6d.

Ganot's Elementary Treatise on Physics, Experimental and Applied, for the use of Colleges and Schools.

Translated and edited by E. Atkinson, F.C.S.

Seventh Edition, with 4 Coloured Plates & 758 Woodcuts. Post 8vo. 15*s.*

*** *Problems and Examples in Physics, an Appendix to the Seventh and other Editions of Ganot's Elementary Treatise. 8vo. price* 1*s.*

Text-Books of Science, Mechanical and Physical, adapted for the use of Artisans and of Students in Public and Science Schools.

Small 8vo. Woodcuts.

The following Text-Books in this Series may now be had:—

Anderson's *Strength of Materials*, 3*s.* 6*d.*
Armstrong's *Organic Chemistry*, 3*s.* 6*d.*
Barry's *Railway Appliances*, 3*s.* 6*d.*
Bloxam's *Metals*, 3*s.* 6*d.*
Goodeve's *Mechanics*, 3*s.* 6*d.*
——— *Mechanism*, 3*s.* 6*d.*
Griffin's *Algebra & Trigonometry*, 3*s.* 6*d.*
Notes on the same, with Solutions, 3*s.* 6*d.*
Jenkin's *Electricity & Magnetism*, 3*s.* 6*d.*
Maxwell's *Theory of Heat*, 3*s.* 6*d.*
Merrifield's *Technical Arithmetic*, 3*s.* 6*d.*
Key, 3*s.* 6*d.*
Miller's *Inorganic Chemistry*, 3*s.* 6*d.*
Preece and Sivewright's *Telegraphy*, 3*s.* 6*d.*
Shelley's *Workshop Appliances*, 3*s.* 6*d.*
Thorpe's *Quantitative Analysis*, 4*s.* 6*d.*
Thorpe *and* Muir's *Qualitative Analysis*, 3*s.* 6*d.*
Watson's *Plane & Solid Geometry*, 3*s.* 6*d.*

*** *Other Text-Books, in extension of this Series, in active preparation.*

Principles of Animal Mechanics.

By the Rev. S. Haughton, F.R.S.

Second Edition. 8vo. 21*s.*

Fragments of Science.

By John Tyndall, F.R.S.

New Edition, crown 8vo. 10*s.* 6*d.*

Heat a Mode of Motion.

By John Tyndall, F.R.S.

Fifth Edition, Plate and Woodcuts. Crown 8vo. 10*s.* 6*d.*

Sound.

By John Tyndall, F.R.S.

Third Edition, including Recent Researches on Fog-Signalling; Portrait and Woodcuts. Crown 8vo. 10*s.* 6*d.*

Researches on Diamagnetism and Magne-Crystallic Action; including Diamagnetic Polarity.

By John Tyndall, F.R.S.

With 6 Plates and many Woodcuts. 8vo. 14*s.*

Contributions to Molecular Physics in the domain of Radiant Heat.

By John Tyndall, F.R.S.

With 2 Plates and 31 Woodcuts. 8vo. 16*s.*

Six Lectures on Light, delivered in America in 1872 and 1873.

By John Tyndall, F.R.S.

Second Edition, with Portrait, Plate, and 59 Diagrams. Crown 8vo. 7*s.* 6*d.*

Notes of a Course of Nine Lectures on Light, delivered at the Royal Institution.
By John Tyndall, F.R.S.
Crown 8vo. 1s. sewed, or 1s. 6d. cloth.

Notes of a Course of Seven Lectures on Electrical Phenomena and Theories, delivered at the Royal Institution.
By John Tyndall, F.R.S.
Crown 8vo. 1s. sewed, or 1s. 6d. cloth.

A Treatise on Magnetism, General and Terrestrial.
By H. Lloyd, D.D. D.C.L.
8vo. price 10s. 6d.

Elementary Treatise on the Wave-Theory of Light.
By H. Lloyd, D.D. D.C.L.
Third Edition. 8vo. 10s. 6d.

The Comparative Anatomy and Physiology of the Vertebrate Animals.
By Richard Owen, F.R.S.
With 1,472 Woodcuts. 3 vols. 8vo. £3. 13s. 6d.

Sir H. Holland's Fragmentary Papers on Science and other subjects.
Edited by the Rev. J. Holland.
8vo. price 14s.

Kirby and Spence's Introduction to Entomology, or Elements of the Natural History of Insects.
Crown 8vo. 5s.

Light Science for Leisure Hours; Familiar Essays on Scientific Subjects, Natural Phenomena, &c.
By R. A. Proctor, B.A.
First and Second Series. 2 vols. crown 8vo. 7s. 6d. each.

Homes without Hands; a Description of the Habitations of Animals, classed according to their Principle of Construction.
By Rev. J. G. Wood, M.A.
With about 140 Vignettes on Wood. 8vo. 14s.

Strange Dwellings; a Description of the Habitations of Animals, abridged from 'Homes without Hands.'
By Rev. J. G. Wood, M.A.
With Frontispiece and 60 Woodcuts. Crown 8vo. 7s. 6d.

Insects at Home; a Popular Account of British Insects, their Structure Habits, and Transformations.
By Rev. J. G. Wood, M.A.
With upwards of 700 Woodcuts. 8vo. 21s.

Insects Abroad; being a Popular Account of Foreign Insects, their Structure, Habits, and Transformations.
By Rev. J. G. Wood, M.A.
With upwards of 700 Woodcuts. 8vo. 21s

Out of Doors; a Selection of Original Articles on Practical Natural History.
By Rev. J. G. Wood, M.A.
With 6 Illustrations from Original Designs engraved on Wood. Crown 8vo. 7s. 6d.

Bible Animals; a Description of every Living Creature mentioned in the Scriptures, from the Ape to the Coral.
By Rev. J. G. Wood, M.A.
With about 112 Vignettes on Wood. 8vo. 14s.

The Polar World: a Popular Description of Man and Nature in the Arctic and Antarctic Regions of the Globe.
By Dr. G. Hartwig.
With Chromoxylographs, Maps, and Woodcuts. 8vo. 10s. 6d.

The Sea and its Living Wonders.
By Dr. G. Hartwig.
Fourth Edition, enlarged. 8vo. with many Illustrations, 10s. 6d.

The Tropical World.
By Dr. G. Hartwig.
With about 200 Illustrations. 8vo. 10s. 6d.

The Subterranean World.
By Dr. G. Hartwig.
With Maps and Woodcuts. 8vo. 10s. 6d.

The Aerial World; a Popular Account of the Phenomena and Life of the Atmosphere.
By Dr. George Hartwig.
With Map, 8 Chromoxylographs, and 60 Woodcuts. 8vo. price 21s.

Game Preservers and Bird Preservers, or 'Which are our Friends?'
By George Francis Morant, late Captain 12th Royal Lancers & Major Cape Mounted Riflemen.
Crown 8vo. price 5s.

A Familiar History of Birds.
By E. Stanley, D.D. late Ld. Bishop of Norwich.
Fcp. 8vo. with Woodcuts, 3s. 6d.

Rocks Classified and Described.
By B. Von Cotta.
English Edition, by P. H. LAWRENCE *(with English, German, and French Synonymes), revised by the Author. Post 8vo. 14s.*

Excavations at the Kesslerloch near Thayngen, Switzerland, a Cave of the Reindeer Period.
By Conrad Merk. Translated by John Edward Lee, F.S.A. F.G.S. Author of 'Isca Silurum' &c.
With Sixteen Plates. Royal 8vo. 7s. 6d.

The Origin of Civilisation, and the Primitive Condition of Man; Mental and Social Condition of Savages.
By Sir J. Lubbock, Bart. M.P. F.R.S.
Third Edition, with 25 Woodcuts. 8vo. 18s.

The Native Races of the Pacific States of North America.
By Hubert Howe Bancroft.

Vol. I. Wild Tribes, their Manners and Customs; with 6 Maps. 8vo. 25s.
Vol. II. Native Races of the Pacific States. 8vo. 25s.
Vol. III. Myths and Languages. 8vo. price 25s.
Vol. IV. Antiquities and Architectural Remains, with Map. 8vo. 25s.
Vol. V. Aboriginal History and Migrations; Index to the Entire Work. With 2 Maps, 8vo. 25s.
*** *This work may now be had complete in 5 volumes, price £6. 5s.*

The Ancient Stone Implements, Weapons, and Ornaments of Great Britain.
By John Evans, F.R.S.
With 2 Plates and 476 Woodcuts. 8vo. 28s.

The Elements of Botany for Families and Schools.
Eleventh Edition, revised by Thomas Moore, F.L.S.
Fcp. 8vo. *with 154 Woodcuts,* 2s. 6d.

The Rose Amateur's Guide.
By Thomas Rivers.
Tenth Edition. Fcp. 8vo. 4s.

On the Sensations of Tone, as a Physiological Basis for the Theory of Music.
By H. Helmholtz, Professor of Physiology in the University of Berlin.
Translated by A. J. Ellis, F.R.S.
8vo. 36s.

A Dictionary of Science, Literature, and Art.
Re-edited by the late W. T. Brande (the Author) and Rev. G. W. Cox, M.A.
New Edition, revised. 3 *vols. medium* 8vo. 63s.

The History of Modern Music, a Course of Lectures delivered at the Royal Institution of Great Britain.
By John Hullah.
New Edition. Demy 8vo. 8s. 6d.

The Transition Period of Musical History; a Second Course of Lectures on the History of Music from the Beginning of the Seventeenth to the Middle of the Eighteenth Century, delivered at the Royal Institution.
By John Hullah.
New Edition, 1 *vol. demy* 8vo.
[*In the Spring.*

The Treasury of Botany, or Popular Dictionary of the Vegetable Kingdom; with which is incorporated a Glossary of Botanical Terms.
Edited by J. Lindley, F.R.S. and T. Moore, F.L.S.
With 274 Woodcuts and 20 Steel Plates. Two Parts, fcp. 8vo. 12s.

A General System of Descriptive and Analytical Botany.

Translated from the French of Le Maout and Decaisne, by Mrs. Hooker. Edited and arranged according to the English Botanical System, by J. D. Hooker, M.D. &c. Director of the Royal Botanic Gardens, Kew.

With 5,500 *Woodcuts. Imperial* 8*vo.* 31*s.* 6*d.*

Loudon's Encyclopædia of Plants; comprising the Specific Character, Description, Culture, History, &c. of all the Plants found in Great Britain.

With upwards of 12,000 *Woodcuts.* 8*vo.* 42*s.*

Handbook of Hardy Trees, Shrubs, and Herbaceous Plants; containing Descriptions &c. of the Best Species in Cultivation; with Cultural Details, Comparative Hardiness, suitability for particular positions, &c. Based on the French Work of Decaisne and Naudin, and including the 720 Original Woodcut Illustrations. By W. B. Hemsley.

Medium 8*vo.* 21*s.*

Forest Trees and Woodland Scenery, as described in Ancient and Modern Poets.

By William Menzies, Deputy Surveyor of Windsor Forest and Parks, &c.

With Twenty Chromolithographic Plates. Folio, price £5. 5*s.*

CHEMISTRY and PHYSIOLOGY.

Miller's Elements of Chemistry, Theoretical and Practical.

Re-edited, with Additions, by H. Macleod, F.C.S.

3 *vols.* 8*vo.*

PART I. CHEMICAL PHYSICS, 15*s.*
PART II. INORGANIC CHEMISTRY, 21*s.*
PART III. ORGANIC CHEMISTRY, *New Edition in the press.*

Health in the House, Twenty-five Lectures on Elementary Physiology in its Application to the Daily Wants of Man and Animals.

By Mrs. C. M. Buckton.

New Edition. Crown 8*vo. Woodcuts,* 2*s.*

Outlines of Physiology, Human and Comparative. By J. Marshall, F.R.C.S. Surgeon to the University College Hospital.

2 *vols. cr.* 8*vo. with* 122 *Woodcuts,* 32*s.*

Select Methods in Chemical Analysis, chiefly Inorganic.
By Wm. Crookes, F.R.S.

With 22 *Woodcuts. Crown* 8*vo.* 12*s.* 6*d.*

A Dictionary of Chemistry and the Allied Branches of other Sciences. By Henry Watts, F.C.S. assisted by eminent Scientific and Practical Chemists.

6 *vols. medium* 8*vo.* £8. 14*s.* 6*d.*

Supplement completing the Record of Discovery to the year 1873.

8*vo. price* 42*s.*

The FINE ARTS and ILLUSTRATED EDITIONS.

Poems.
By William B. Scott.

I. Ballads and Tales. II. Studies from Nature. III. Sonnets &c.

Illustrated by Seventeen Etchings by L. Alma Tadema *and* William B. Scott. *Crown* 8*vo.* 15*s.*

Half-hour Lectures on the History and Practice of the Fine and Ornamental Arts.
By W.B. Scott.

Third Edition, with 50 *Woodcuts. Crown* 8*vo.* 8*s.* 6*d.*

A Dictionary of Artists of the English School: Painters, Sculptors, Architects, Engravers, and Ornamentists; with Notices of their Lives and Works.
By Samuel Redgrave.

8*vo.* 16*s.*

In Fairyland; Pictures from the Elf-World. By Richard Doyle. With a Poem by W. Allingham.

With 16 *coloured Plates, containing* 36 *Designs. Second Edition, folio,* 15*s.*

The New Testament, illustrated with Wood Engravings after the Early Masters, chiefly of the Italian School.

Crown 4*to.* 63*s.*

Lord Macaulay's Lays of Ancient Rome. With 90 *Illustrations on Wood from Drawings by G. Scharf.*

Fcp. 4*to.* 21*s.*

Miniature Edition, with Scharf's 90 *Illustrations reduced in Lithography.*

Imp. 16*mo.* 10*s.* 6*d.*

Moore's Irish Melodies, Maclise's Edition, with 161 *Steel Plates.*

Super royal 8*vo.* 31*s.* 6*d.*

Sacred and Legendary Art.
By Mrs. Jameson.

6 *vols. square crown* 8*vo. price* £5. 15*s.* 6*d. as follows:—*

Legends of the Saints and Martyrs.

New Edition, with 19 *Etchings and* 187 *Woodcuts.* 2 *vols.* 31*s.* 6*d.*

Legends of the Monastic Orders.

New Edition, with 11 *Etchings and* 88 *Woodcuts.* 1 *vol.* 21*s.*

Legends of the Madonna.

New Edition, with 27 *Etchings and* 165 *Woodcuts.* 1 *vol.* 21*s.*

The History of Our Lord, with that of his Types and Precursors.
Completed by Lady Eastlake.

Revised Edition, with 13 *Etchings and* 281 *Woodcuts.* 2 *vols.* 42*s.*

The USEFUL ARTS, MANUFACTURES, &c.

Industrial Chemistry; a Manual for Manufacturers and for Colleges or Technical Schools. Being a Translation of Professors Stohmann and Engler's German Edition of Payen's 'Précis de Chimie Industrielle,' by Dr. J. D. Barry.
Edited, and supplemented with Chapters on the Chemistry of the Metals, by B. H. Paul, Ph.D.

8*vo. with Plates and Woodcuts.*
[*In the press.*

Gwilt's Encyclopædia of Architecture, with above 1,600 *Woodcuts.*
New Edition (1876), *with Alterations and Additions, by Wyatt Papworth.*

8*vo.* 52*s.* 6*d.*

The Three Cathedrals dedicated to St. Paul in London; their History from the Foundation of the First Building in the Sixth Century to the Proposals for the Adornment of the Present Cathedral.
By W. Longman, F.S.A.

With numerous Illustrations. Square crown 8*vo.* 21*s.*

Lathes and Turning, Simple, Mechanical, and Ornamental.
By W. Henry Northcott.

With 240 *Illustrations.* 8*vo.* 18*s.*

Hints on Household Taste in Furniture, Upholstery, and other Details.
By Charles L. Eastlake, Architect.

New Edition, with about 90 *Illustrations. Square crown* 8*vo.* 14*s.*

Handbook of Practical Telegraphy.

By R. S. Culley, Memb. Inst. C.E. Engineer-in-Chief of Telegraphs to the Post-Office.

Sixth Edition, Plates & Woodcuts. 8vo. 16*s.*

A Treatise on the Steam Engine, in its various applications to Mines, Mills, Steam Navigation, Railways and Agriculture.

By J. Bourne, C.E.

With Portrait, 37 *Plates, and* 546 *Woodcuts. 4to.* 42*s.*

Catechism of the Steam Engine, in its various Applications.

By John Bourne, C.E.

New Edition, with 89 *Woodcuts. Fcp. 8vo.* 6*s.*

Handbook of the Steam Engine.

By J. Bourne, C.E. forming a KEY *to the Author's Catechism of the Steam Engine.*

With 67 *Woodcuts. Fcp. 8vo.* 9*s.*

Recent Improvements in the Steam Engine.

By J. Bourne, C.E.

With 124 *Woodcuts. Fcp. 8vo.* 6*s.*

Encyclopædia of Civil Engineering, Historical, Theoretical, and Practical. By E. Cresy, C.E.

With above 3,000 *Woodcuts. 8vo.* 42*s.*

Ure's Dictionary of Arts, Manufactures, and Mines. Seventh Edition, re-written and greatly enlarged by R. Hunt, F.R.S. assisted by numerous Contributors.

With 2,100 *Woodcuts.* 3 *vols. medium 8vo. price* £5. 5*s.*

Practical Treatise on Metallurgy,

Adapted from the last German Edition of Professor Kerl's Metallurgy by W. Crookes, F.R.S. &c. and E. Röhrig, Ph.D.

3 *vols. 8vo. with* 625 *Woodcuts.* £4. 19*s.*

Treatise on Mills and Millwork.

By Sir W. Fairbairn, Bt.

With 18 *Plates and* 322 *Woodcuts.* 2 *vols. 8vo.* 32*s.*

Useful Information for Engineers.

By Sir W. Fairbairn, Bt.

With many Plates and Woodcuts. 3 *vols. crown 8vo.* 31*s.* 6*d.*

The Application of Cast and Wrought Iron to Building Purposes.

By Sir W. Fairbairn, Bt.

With 6 *Plates and* 118 *Woodcuts. 8vo.* 16*s.*

The Theory of Strains in Girders and similar Structures, with Observations on the application of Theory to Practice, and Tables of the Strength and other Properties of Materials.
By Bindon B. Stoney, M.A. M. Inst. C.E.
New Edition, royal 8vo. with 5 Plates and 123 Woodcuts, 36s.

Practical Handbook of Dyeing and Calico-Printing.
By W. Crookes, F.R.S. &c.
With numerous Illustrations and Specimens of Dyed Textile Fabrics. 8vo. 42s.

Occasional Papers on Subjects connected with Civil Engineering, Gunnery, and Naval Architecture.
By Michael Scott, Memb. Inst. C.E. & of Inst. N.A.
2 vols. 8vo. with Plates, 42s.

Mitchell's Manual of Practical Assaying.
Fourth Edition, revised, with the Recent Discoveries incorporated, by W. Crookes, F.R.S.
crown 8vo. Woodcuts, 31s. 6d.

Naval Powers and their Policy: with Tabular Statements of British and Foreign Ironclad Navies; giving Dimensions, Armour, Details of Armament, Engines, Speed, and other Particulars.
By John C. Paget.
8vo. price 10s. 6d. cloth.

Loudon's Encyclopædia of Gardening; comprising the Theory and Practice of Horticulture, Floriculture, Arboriculture, and Landscape Gardening.
With 1,000 Woodcuts. 8vo. 21s.

Loudon's Encyclopædia of Agriculture; comprising the Laying-out, Improvement, and Management of Landed Property, and the Cultivation and Economy of the Productions of Agriculture.
With 1,100 Woodcuts. 8vo. 21s.

Reminiscences of Fen and Mere.
By J. M. Heathcote.
With 27 Illustrations and 3 Maps. Square 8vo. price 28s.

RELIGIOUS and MORAL WORKS.

An Exposition of the 39 Articles, Historical and Doctrinal.
By E. H. Browne, D.D. Bishop of Winchester.
New Edition. 8vo. 16s.

Historical Lectures on the Life of Our Lord Jesus Christ.
By C. J. Ellicott, D.D.
Fifth Edition. 8vo. 12s.

An Introduction to the Theology of the Church of England, in an Exposition of the 39 Articles. By Rev. T. P. Boultbee, LL.D.
Fcp. 8vo. 6s.

Three Essays on Religion: Nature; the Utility of Religion; Theism.
By John Stuart Mill.
Second Edition. 8vo. *price* 10s. 6d.

Sermons Chiefly on the Interpretation of Scripture.
By the late Rev. Thomas Arnold, D.D.
8vo. *price* 7s. 6d.

Sermons preached in the Chapel of Rugby School; with an Address before Confirmation.
By the late Rev. Thomas Arnold, D.D.
Fcp. 8vo. *price* 3s. 6d.

Christian Life, its Course, its Hindrances, and its Helps; Sermons preached mostly in the Chapel of Rugby School.
By the late Rev. Thomas Arnold, D.D.
8vo. 7s. 6d.

Christian Life, its Hopes, its Fears, and its Close; Sermons preached mostly in the Chapel of Rugby School.
By the late Rev. Thomas Arnold, D.D.
8vo. 7s. 6d.

Religion and Science, their Relations to Each Other at the Present Day; Three Essays on the Grounds of Religious Beliefs.
By Stanley T. Gibson, B.D. Rector of Sandon, in Essex; and late Fellow of Queen's College, Cambridge.
8vo. *price* 10s. 6d.

Notes on the Earlier Hebrew Scriptures.
By Sir G. B. Airy, K.C.B.
8vo. *price* 6s.

Synonyms of the Old Testament, their Bearing on Christian Faith and Practice.
By Rev. R. B. Girdlestone.
8vo. 15s.

The Primitive and Catholic Faith in Relation to the Church of England.
By the Rev. B. W. Savile, M.A. Rector of Shillingford, Exeter.
8vo. price 7s.

The Eclipse of Faith; or a Visit to a Religious Sceptic.
By Henry Rogers.
Latest Edition. Fcp. 8vo. 5s.

Defence of the Eclipse of Faith.
By Henry Rogers.
Latest Edition. Fcp. 8vo. 3s. 6d.

A Critical and Grammatical Commentary on St. Paul's Epistles.
By C. J. Ellicott, D.D.
8vo. Galatians, 8*s.* 6*d.* Ephesians, 8*s.* 6*d.* Pastoral Epistles, 10*s.* 6*d.* Philippians, Colossians, & Philemon, 10*s.* 6*d.* Thessalonians, 7*s.* 6*d.*

The Life and Epistles of St. Paul.
By Rev. W. J. Conybeare, M.A. and Very Rev. J. S. Howson, D.D.

LIBRARY EDITION, *with all the Original Illustrations, Maps, Landscapes on Steel, Woodcuts, &c. 2 vols. 4to. 42s.*

INTERMEDIATE EDITION, *with a Selection of Maps, Plates, and Woodcuts. 2 vols. square crown 8vo. 21s.*

STUDENT'S EDITION, *revised and condensed, with 46 Illustrations and Maps. 1 vol. crown 8vo. 9s.*

An Examination into the Doctrine and Practice of Confession.
By the Rev. W. E. Jelf, B.D.
8vo. price 3s. 6d.

Evidence of the Truth of the Christian Religion derived from the Literal Fulfilment of Prophecy.
By Alexander Keith, D.D.
40th Edition, with numerous Plates. Square 8vo. 12s. 6d. or in post 8vo. with 5 Plates, 6s.

Historical and Critical Commentary on the Old Testament; with a New Translation.
By M. M. Kalisch, Ph.D.
Vol. I. Genesis, *8vo. 18s. or adapted for the General Reader, 12s. Vol. II.* Exodus, *15s. or adapted for the General Reader, 12s. Vol. III.* Leviticus, *Part I. 15s. or adapted for the General Reader, 8s. Vol. IV.* Leviticus, *Part II. 15s. or adapted for the General Reader, 8s.*

The History and Literature of the Israelites, according to the Old Testament and the Apocrypha.
By C. De Rothschild and A. De Rothschild.
Second Edition. 2 vols. crown 8vo. 12s. 6d. Abridged Edition, in 1 vol. fcp. 8vo. 3s. 6d.

Ewald's History of Israel.
Translated from the German by J. E. Carpenter, M.A. with Preface by R. Martineau, M.A.
5 vols. 8vo. 63s.

Ewald's Antiquities of Israel.
Translated from the German by Henry Shaen Solly, M.A.
8vo. 12s. 6d.

The Types of Genesis, briefly considered as revealing the Development of Human Nature.
By Andrew Jukes.
Third Edition. Crown 8vo. 7s. 6d.

The Second Death and the Restitution of all Things; with some Preliminary Remarks on the Nature and Inspiration of Holy Scripture.
By Andrew Jukes.
Fourth Edition. Crown 8vo. 3s. 6d.

History of the Reformation in Europe in the time of Calvin.
By the Rev. J. H. Merle D'Aubigné, D.D. Translated by W. L. R. Cates, Editor of the Dictionary of General Biography.
6 *vols. 8vo. price £4. 10s.*

*** VOLS. VII. & VIII. *completing the Work, are preparing for publication.*

Commentaries, by the Rev. W. A. O'Conor, B.A. Rector of St. Simon and St. Jude, Manchester.
Crown 8vo.
Epistle to the Romans, price 3s. 6d.
Epistle to the Hebrews, 4s. 6d.
St. John's Gospel, 10s. 6d.

Some Questions of the Day.
By Elizabeth M. Sewell, Author of 'Amy Herbert,' 'Passing Thoughts on Religion,' &c.
Crown 8vo. 2s. 6d.

An Introduction to the Study of the New Testament, Critical, Exegetical, and Theological.
By the Rev. S. Davidson, D.D. LL.D.
2 *vols. 8vo. price 30s.*

Thoughts for the Age.
By Elizabeth M. Sewell.
New Edition. Fcp. 8vo. 3s. 6d.

Preparation for the Holy Communion; the Devotions chiefly from the works of Jeremy Taylor.
By Elizabeth M. Sewell.
32mo. 3s.

Bishop Jeremy Taylor's Entire Works; with Life by Bishop Heber.
Revised and corrected by the Rev. C. P. Eden.
10 *vols. £5. 5s.*

Hymns of Praise and Prayer.
Collected and edited by Rev. J. Martineau, LL.D.
Crown 8vo. 4s. 6d. 32mo. 1s. 6d.

Spiritual Songs for the Sundays and Holidays throughout the Year. By J. S. B. Monsell, LL.D.

9th Thousand. Fcp. 8vo. 5s 18mo. 2s.

Lyra Germanica; Hymns translated from the German by Miss C. Winkworth.

Fcp. 8vo. 5s.

Lectures on the Pentateuch & the Moabite Stone; with Appendices. By J. W. Colenso, D.D. Bishop of Natal.

8vo. 12s.

Endeavours after the Christian Life; Discourses. By Rev. J. Martineau, LL.D.

Fifth Edition. Crown 8vo. 7s. 6d.

Supernatural Religion; an Inquiry into the Reality of Divine Revelation.

Sixth Edition carefully revised, with 80 pages of New Preface. 2 vols. 8vo. 24s.

The Pentateuch and Book of Joshua Critically Examined. By J. W. Colenso, D.D. Bishop of Natal.

Crown 8vo. 6s.

TRAVELS, VOYAGES, &c.

The Indian Alps, and How we Crossed them: being a Narrative of Two Years' Residence in the Eastern Himalayas, and Two Months' Tour into the Interior, towards Kinchinjunga and Mount Everest. By a Lady Pioneer.

With Illustrations from Original Drawings made on the spot by the Authoress. Imperial 8vo. 42s.

Tyrol and the Tyrolese; being an Account of the People and the Land, in their Social, Sporting, and Mountaineering Aspects. By W. A. Baillie Grohman.

With numerous Illustrations from Sketches by the Author. Crown 8vo. 14s.

'The Frosty Caucasus;' an Account of a Walk through Part of the Range, and of an Ascent of Elbruz in the Summer of 1874. By F. C. Grove.

With Eight Illustrations engraved on Wood by E. Whymper, from Photographs taken during the Journey, and a Map. Crown 8vo. price 15s.

A Journey of 1,000 Miles through Egypt and Nubia to the Second Cataract of the Nile. Being a Personal Narrative of Four and a Half Months' Life in a Dahabeeyah on the Nile. By Amelia B. Edwards.

With numerous Illustrations from Drawings by the Authoress, Map, Plans, Facsimiles, &c. Imperial 8vo.

[In the Autumn.

Over the Sea and Far Away; being a Narrative of a Ramble round the World.

By Thos. Woodbine Hinchliff, M.A. F.R.G.S. President of the Alpine Club, Author of 'Summer Months among the Alps,' &c.

1 vol. medium 8vo. with numerous Illustrations. [Nearly ready.

Discoveries at Ephesus. Including the Site and Remains of the Great Temple of Diana.

By J. T. Wood, F.S.A.

1 vol. imperial 8vo. copiously illustrated. [In the press.

Through Bosnia and the Herzegovina on Foot during the Insurrection, August and September 1875; with a Glimpse at the Slavonic Borderlands of Turkey.

By Arthur J. Evans, B.A. F.S.A.

Post 8vo. with Map and numerous Illustrations. [In the press.

Italian Alps; Sketches in the Mountains of Ticino, Lombardy, the Trentino, and Venetia.

By Douglas W. Freshfield, Editor of 'The Alpine Journal.'

Square crown 8vo. Illustrations. 15s.

Memorials of the Discovery and Early Settlement of the Bermudas or Somers Islands, from 1615 to 1685. Compiled from the Colonial Records and other original sources.

By Major-General J. H. Lefroy, R.A. C.B. F.R.S. Hon. Member New York Historical Society, &c. Governor of the Bermudas.

8vo. with Map. [In the press.

Here and There in the Alps.

By the Hon. Frederica Plunket.

With Vignette-title. Post 8vo. 6s. 6d.

The Valleys of Tirol; their Traditions and Customs, and How to Visit them.

By Miss R. H. Busk.

With Frontispiece and 3 Maps. Crown 8vo. 12s. 6d.

Two Years in Fiji, a Descriptive Narrative of a Residence in the Fijian Group of Islands; with some Account of the Fortunes of Foreign Settlers and Colonists up to the time of British Annexation.

By Litton Forbes, M.D.

Crown 8vo. 8s. 6d.

Eight Years in Ceylon. By Sir Samuel W. Baker, M.A. F.R.G.S.

New Edition, with Illustrations engraved on Wood by G. Pearson. Crown 8vo. Price 7s. 6d.

The Rifle and the Hound in Ceylon. By Sir Samuel W. Baker, M.A. F.R.G.S.

New Edition, with Illustrations engraved on Wood by G. Pearson. Crown 8vo. Price 7s. 6d.

Meeting the Sun; a Journey all round the World through Egypt, China, Japan, and California. By William Simpson, F.R.G.S.

With Heliotypes and Woodcuts. 8vo. 24s.

The Dolomite Mountains. Excursions through Tyrol, Carinthia, Carniola, and Friuli. By J. Gilbert and G. C. Churchill, F.R.G.S.

With Illustrations. Sq. cr. 8vo. 21s.

The Alpine Club Map of the Chain of Mont Blanc, from an actual Survey in 1863–1864. By A. Adams-Reilly, F.R.G.S. M.A.C.

In Chromolithography, on extra stout drawing paper 10s. or mounted on canvas in a folding case, 12s. 6d.

The Alpine Club Map of the Valpelline, the Val Tournanche, and the Southern Valleys of the Chain of Monte Rosa, from actual Survey. By A. Adams-Reilly, F.R.G.S. M.A.C.

Price 6s. on extra Stout Drawing Paper, or 7s. 6d. mounted in a Folding Case.

Untrodden Peaks and Unfrequented Valleys; a Midsummer Ramble among the Dolomites. By Amelia B. Edwards.

With numerous Illustrations. 8vo. 21s.

The Alpine Club Map of Switzerland, with parts of the Neighbouring Countries, on the scale of Four Miles to an Inch. Edited by R. C. Nichols, F.S.A. F.R.G.S.

In Four Sheets, in Portfolio, price 42s. coloured, or 34s. uncoloured.

The Alpine Guide. By John Ball, M.R.I.A. late President of the Alpine Club.

Post 8vo. with Maps and other Illustrations.

Eastern Alps.

Price 10s. 6d.

Central Alps, including all the Oberland District.

Price 7s. 6d.

Western Alps, including Mont Blanc, Monte Rosa, Zermatt, &c.

Price 6*s.* 6*d.*

Introduction on Alpine Travelling in general, and on the Geology of the Alps.

Price 1*s.* *Either of the Three Volumes or Parts of the 'Alpine Guide' may be had with this Introduction prefixed,* 1*s. extra. The 'Alpine Guide' may also be had in* Ten *separate* Parts, *or districts, price* 2*s.* 6*d. each.*

Guide to the Pyrenees, for the use of Mountaineers.

By Charles Packe.

Second Edition, with Maps &c. and Appendix. Crown 8*vo.* 7*s.* 6*d.*

How to See Norway; embodying the Experience of Six Summer Tours in that Country.

By J. R. Campbell.

With Map and 5 *Woodcuts, fcp.* 8*vo.* 5*s.*

WORKS of FICTION.

Higgledy-Piggledy; or, Stories for Everybody and Everybody's Children.

By the Right Hon. E. H. Knatchbull - Hugessen, M.P. Author of 'Whispers from Fairyland' &c.

With 9 *Illustrations from Original Designs by R. Doyle, engraved on Wood by G. Pearson. Crown* 8*vo. price* 6*s.*

Whispers from Fairyland.

By the Rt. Hon. E. H. Knatchbull - Hugessen, M.P. Author of 'Higgledy-Piggledy' &c.

With 9 *Illustrations from Original Designs engraved on Wood by G. Pearson. Crown* 8*vo. price* 6*s.*

'A series of stories which are certain of a ready welcome by all boys and girls who take delight in dreamland, and love to linger over the pranks and frolics of fairies. The book is dedicated to the mothers of England, and more wholesome food for the growing mind it would be unreasonable to desire, and impossible to procure. . . . . This welcome volume abounds in vivacity and fun, and bears pleasant testimony to a kindly-hearted Author with fancy, feeling, and humour.' MORNING POST.

The Folk-Lore of Rome, collected by Word of Mouth from the People.

By Miss R. H. Busk.

Crown 8*vo.* 12*s.* 6*d.*

Becker's Gallus; or Roman Scenes of the Time of Augustus.

Post 8*vo.* 7*s.* 6*d.*

Becker's Charicles: Illustrative of Private Life of the Ancient Greeks.

Post 8*vo.* 7*s.* 6*d.*

Novels and Tales.

By the Right Hon. Benjamin Disraeli, M.P.

Cabinet Editions, complete in Ten Volumes, crown 8*vo.* 6*s. each, as follows :—*

Lothair, 6*s.*	*Venetia*, 6*s.*
Coningsby, 6*s.*	*Alroy, Ixion, &c.* 6*s.*
Sybil, 6*s.*	*Young Duke, &c.* 6*s.*
Tancred, 6*s.*	*Vivian Grey*, 6*s.*

Henrietta Temple, 6*s.*

Contarini Fleming, &c. 6*s.*

The Modern Novelist's Library.

Atherstone Priory, 2s. boards; 2s. 6d. cloth.
Mlle. Mori, 2s. boards; 2s. 6d. cloth.
The Burgomaster's Family, 2s. and 2s. 6d.
MELVILLE'S *Digby Grand*, 2s. and 2s. 6d.
——— *Gladiators*, 2s. and 2s. 6d.
——— *Good for Nothing*, 2s. & 2s. 6d.
——— *Holmby House*, 2s. and 2s. 6d.
——— *Interpreter*, 2s. and 2s. 6d.
——— *Kate Coventry*, 2s. and 2s. 6d.
——— *Queens Maries*, 2s. and 2s. 6d.
——— *General Bounce*, 2s. and 2s. 6d.
TROLLOPE'S *Warden*, 1s. 6d. and 2s.
——— *Barchester Towers*, 2s. & 2s. 6d.
BRAMLEY-MOORE'S *Six Sisters of the Valleys*, 2s. boards; 2s. 6d. cloth.
Elsa: a Tale of the Tyrolean Alps. Translated from the German of Mme. Von Hillern by Lady Wallace. Price 2s. boards; 2s. 6d. cloth.

Tales of Ancient Greece.

By the Rev. G. W. Cox, M.A.

Crown 8vo. 6s. 6d.

Stories and Tales.

By Elizabeth M. Sewell. Cabinet Edition, in Ten Volumes:—

Amy Herbert, 2s. 6d.
Gertrude, 2s. 6d.
Earl's Daughter, 2s. 6d.
Experience of Life, 2s. 6a.
Cleve Hall, 2s. 6d.
Ivors, 2s. 6d.
Katharine Ashton, 2s. 6d.
Margaret Percival, 3s. 6d.
Laneton Parsonage, 3s. 6d.
Ursula, 3s. 6d.

POETRY and THE DRAMA.

Ballads and Lyrics of Old France; with other Poems.

By A. Lang, M.A.

Square fcp. 8vo. 5s.

The London Series of French Classics.

Edited by Ch. Cassal, LL.D. T. Karcher, LL.B. and Léonce Stièvenard.

The following Plays, in the Division of the Drama in this Series, are now ready:—

CORNEILLE'S *Le Cid*, 1s. 6d.
VOLTAIRE'S *Zaire*, 1s. 6d.
LAMARTINE'S *Toussaint Louverture*, double volume, 2s. 6d.

Milton's Lycidas and Epitaphium Damonis.

Edited, with Notes and Introduction, by C. S. Jerram, M.A.

Crown 8vo. 2s. 6d.

Lays of Ancient Rome; with Ivry and the Armada.

By the Right Hon. Lord Macaulay.

16*mo.* 3s. 6d.

Lord Macaulay's Lays of Ancient Rome. With 90 Illustrations on Wood from Drawings by G. Scharf.

Fcp. 4*to.* 21s.

Miniature Edition of Lord Macaulay's Lays of Ancient Rome, with Scharf's 90 Illustrations reduced in Lithography.

Imp. 16*mo.* 10s. 6d.

Horatii Opera, Library Edition, with English Notes, Marginal References and various Readings. Edited by Rev. J. E. Yonge, M.A.

8vo. 21s.

Southey's Poetical Works with the Author's last Corrections and Additions.

Medium 8vo. *with Portrait*, 14s.

Bowdler's Family Shakspeare, cheaper Genuine Edition.

Complete in 1 *vol. medium* 8vo. *large type, with* 36 *Woodcut Illustrations*, 14s. *or in* 6 *vols. fcp.* 8vo. *price* 21s.

Poems by Jean Ingelow.

2 *vols. Fcp.* 8vo. 10s.

FIRST SERIES, *containing 'Divided,' 'The Star's Monument,' &c.* 16*th Thousand. Fcp.* 8vo. 5s.

SECOND SERIES, *'A Story of Doom,' 'Gladys and her Island,' &c.* 5*th Thousand. Fcp.* 8vo. 5s.

Poems by Jean Ingelow. First Series, with nearly 100 *Woodcut Illustrations.*

Fcp. 4to. 21s.

The Æneid of Virgil Translated into English Verse. By J. Conington, M.A.

Crown 8vo. 9s.

RURAL SPORTS, HORSE and CATTLE MANAGEMENT, &c.

Annals of the Road, being a History of Coaching from the Earliest Times to the Present. By Captain Malet. With Practical Hints on Driving and all Coaching matters, by Nimrod.

Reprinted from the SPORTING MAGAZINE *by permission of the Proprietors.* 1 *vol. medium* 8vo. *with Coloured Plates, uniform with Mr. Birch Reynardson's 'Down the Road.'* [*On May* 1.

Down the Road; or, Reminiscences of a Gentleman Coachman. By C. T. S. Birch Reynardson.

Second Edition, with 12 *Coloured Illustrations from Paintings by H. Alken. Medium* 8vo. *price* 21s.

Blaine's Encyclopædia of Rural Sports; Complete Accounts, Historical, Practical, and Descriptive, of Hunting, Shooting, Fishing, Racing, &c.

With above 600 *Woodcuts* (20 *from Designs by* JOHN LEECH). 8vo. 21s.

A Book on Angling: a Treatise on the Art of Angling in every branch, including full Illustrated Lists of Salmon Flies. By Francis Francis.

Post 8vo. *Portrait and Plates*, 15s.

Wilcocks's Sea-Fisherman: comprising the Chief Methods of Hook and Line Fishing, a glance at Nets, and remarks on Boats and Boating.

New Edition, with 80 Woodcuts. Post 8vo. 12s. 6d.

The Ox, his Diseases and their Treatment; with an Essay on Parturition in the Cow.

By J. R. Dobson, Memb. R.C.V.S.

Crown 8vo. with Illustrations 7s. 6d.

Youatt on the Horse.

Revised and enlarged by W. Watson, M.R.C.V.S.

8vo. Woodcuts, 12s. 6d.

Youatt's Work on the Dog, revised and enlarged.

8vo. Woodcuts, 6s.

Horses and Stables.

By Colonel F. Fitzwygram, XV. the King's Hussars.

With 24 Plates of Illustrations. 8vo. 10s. 6d.

The Dog in Health and Disease.

By Stonehenge.

With 73 Wood Engravings. Square crown 8vo. 7s. 6d.

The Greyhound.

By Stonehenge.

Revised Edition, with 25 Portraits of Greyhounds, &c. Square crown 8vo. 15s.

Stables and Stable Fittings.

By W. Miles, Esq.

Imp. 8vo. with 13 Plates, 15s.

The Horse's Foot, and how to keep it Sound.

By W. Miles, Esq.

Ninth Edition. Imp. 8vo. Woodcuts, 12s. 6d.

A Plain Treatise on Horse-shoeing.

By W. Miles, Esq.

Sixth Edition. Post 8vo. Woodcuts, 2s. 6d.

Remarks on Horses' Teeth, addressed to Purchasers.

By W. Miles, Esq.

Post 8vo. 1s. 6d.

The Fly-Fisher's Entomology.

By Alfred Ronalds.

With 20 coloured Plates. 8vo. 14s.

WORKS of UTILITY and GENERAL INFORMATION.

Maunder's Treasury of Knowledge and Library of Reference; comprising an English Dictionary and Grammar, Universal Gazetteer, Classical Dictionary, Chronology, Law Dictionary, Synopsis of the Peerage, Useful Tables, &c.
Fcp. 8*vo.* 6*s.*

Maunder's Biographical Treasury.
Latest Edition, reconstructed and partly rewritten, with about 1,000 *additional Memoirs, by W. L. R. Cates.*
Fcp. 8*vo.* 6*s.*

Maunder's Scientific and Literary Treasury; a Popular Encyclopædia of Science, Literature, and Art.
New Edition, in part rewritten, with above 1,000 *new articles, by J. Y. Johnson.*
Fcp. 8*vo.* 6*s.*

Maunder's Treasury of Geography, Physical, Historical, Descriptive, and Political.
Edited by W. Hughes, F.R.G.S.
With 7 *Maps and* 16 *Plates. Fcp.* 8*vo.* 6*s.*

Maunder's Historical Treasury; General Introductory Outlines of Universal History, and a Series of Separate Histories.
Revised by the Rev. G. W. Cox, M.A.
Fcp. 8*vo.* 6*s.*

Maunder's Treasury of Natural History; or Popular Dictionary of Zoology.
Revised and corrected Edition. Fcp. 8*vo. with* 900 *Woodcuts,* 6*s.*

The Treasury of Bible Knowledge; being a Dictionary of the Books, Persons, Places, Events, and other Matters of which mention is made in Holy Scripture.
By Rev. J. Ayre, M.A.
With Maps, 15 *Plates, and numerous Woodcuts. Fcp.* 8*vo.* 6*s.*

The Theory and Practice of Banking.
By H. D. Macleod, M.A.
Third Edition, revised throughout. 8*vo price* 12*s.*

The Elements of Banking.
By Henry Dunning Macleod, Esq. M.A.
Crown 8*vo.* 7*s.* 6*d.*

Modern Cookery for Private Families, reduced to a System of Easy Practice in a Series of carefully-tested Receipts.
By Eliza Acton.
With 8 *Plates &* 150 *Woodcuts. Fcp.* 8*vo.* 6*s.*

A Practical Treatise on Brewing; with Formulæ for Public Brewers, and Instructions for Private Families.
By W. Black.
Fifth Edition. 8*vo.* 10*s.* 6*d.*

English Chess Problems.
Edited by J. Pierce, M.A. and W. T. Pierce.
With 608 *Diagrams. Crown* 8*vo.* 12*s.* 6*d.*

The Theory of the Modern Scientific Game of Whist.
By W. Pole, F.R.S.
Seventh Edition. Fcp. 8*vo.* 2*s.* 6*d.*

The Correct Card; or, How to Play at Whist: a Whist Catechism.
By Captain A. Campbell-Walker.
Fcp. 8*vo.* [*Nearly ready.*

The Cabinet Lawyer; a Popular Digest of the Laws of England, Civil, Criminal, and Constitutional.
Twenty-fourth Edition, corrected and extended. Fcp. 8*vo.* 9*s.*

Pewtner's Comprehensive Specifier; a Guide to the Practical Specification of every kind of Building-Artificer's Work.
Edited by W. Young.
Crown 8*vo.* 6*s.*

Chess Openings.
By F. W. Longman, Balliol College, Oxford.
Second Edition, revised. Fcp. 8*vo.* 2*s.* 6*d.*

Hints to Mothers on the Management of their Health during the Period of Pregnancy and in the Lying-in Room.
By Thomas Bull, M.D.
Fcp. 8*vo.* 5*s.*

The Maternal Management of Children in Health and Disease.
By Thomas Bull, M.D.
Fcp. 8*vo.* 5*s.*

INDEX.

Published by

Facsimile Publisher
Ashok Vihar, Delhi-110052 (India)
Website: www.facsimilepublisher.com

Distributed by

Gyan Books Pvt. Ltd.
5, Ansari Road, Daryaganj, New Delhi-110002 (India)
E-mail: books@gyanbooks.com, Website: www.gyanbooks.com

2 222000 013790